D1222239

Edited by ERVIN STAUB
University of Massachusetts, Amherst

PERSONALITY
Basic Aspects and Current Research

PRENTICE-HALL, INC.
Englewood Cliffs, New Jersey 07632

Library of Congress Cataloging in Publication Data

Main entry under title:

Personality.

Includes bibliographies and index.
1. Personality. I. Staub, Ervin.
BT698.P373 155.2 79-19169
ISBN 0-13-657932-9

Printed in the United States of America

10 9 8 7 6 5 4 3 2

Prentice-Hall International, Inc., *London*
Prentice-Hall of Australia Pty. Limited, *Sydney*
Prentice-Hall of Canada, Ltd., *Toronto*
Prentice-Hall of India Private Limited, *New Delhi*
Prentice-Hall of Japan, Inc., *Tokyo*
Prentice-Hall of Southeast Asia Pte. Ltd., *Singapore*
Whitehall Books Limited, *Wellington, New Zealand*

contents

About the Book

This book is intended both as a scholarly contribution to the field of personality psychology, and as an alternative to traditional textbooks that primarily review the many existing theories of personality. In the course of teaching personality psychology, over the years I increasingly wanted my students to read about and study certain topic areas that I considered basic to human functioning—thereby acquiring more direct understanding of the phenomena and dimensions of personality—and to learn about theories in relation to these topics. I found no book with this approach: the present book is intended, in part, to fill that gap.

Many aspects of the personality theories that have accumulated over time, while of historical significance, are of limited usefulness to our understanding of personality today. Other aspects are still highly influential in providing guidance for research and in our understanding of human beings. Thus, a systematic review of traditional theories seems to me less meaningful than their examination in relation to current research on important aspects of personality, which is the approach of this book. New theoretical approaches are also examined in relation to these topics. There is also a brief discussion of theories in general in Chapter 1, and extensive discussion of the role of theory and theorizing in personality psychology in Maddi's chapter.

What we psychologists regard as important about personality varies greatly (see Chapter 1 for further discussion of this point). What one regards as basic and important about human beings is a matter of judgment, taste, one's own theoretical orientation and assumptions about the nature of human beings, as well as the current beliefs within one's culture, both within the discipline of psychology itself and in the larger society of which one is a part. We might slowly progress, I believe, hopefully through increasing knowledge, toward greater agreement about the importance of specific phenomena—such as the child's interest in exploring the world (see Chapter 2) and the self-concept (Chapter 3). I hope the reader will share some of my views on the importance of the topics selected for this book or that he will at least come to judge their selection as reasonable as he reads the discussion of the topics at the end of Chapter 1, and the chapters in this volume.

As stated above, the topics were selected based on my judgment of what is important in understanding human personality, but they were also selected so that they stand in meaningful relationship to each other and represent interrelated themes. Rather than including more topics, I opted for examining fewer topics in greater depth. While there are some disagreements among the authors of these chapters on specific points, there are important communalities in orientation. These communalities and the interrelatedness of the topics will hopefully help the reader to integrate the material in these chapters and to begin to envision the possibility of the development of a relatively coherent conception of human personality.

In planning the book, I assumed that there need not be a contradiction in a book representing both a scholarly contribution to the field and serving as a textbook. The authors who agreed to contribute to this book are outstanding researchers and scholars who have done extensive research and writing on the topics of their chapters. An attempt was made to organize the chapters in relatively parallel form: the authors first review theory and research on their topics, then integrate existing knowledge and/or present new or extended theoretical conceptions. We also attempted to present the material, through examples and in other ways, so that it would be of interest to students. The relevance of the topics to our experiences in our lives is clear enough for readers to relate what they read to themselves.

The introductory chapter is the only one, I believe, with a split personality: Its major aim is to introduce students to the study of personality, but it has substantive content as well. It defines personality as a field of psychology, presents a few basic concepts, discusses methodology in research, and comments on the nature of theories. However, some topics in this chapter are discussed at greater length—for example, the role of heredity and socialization in personality development and certain long-standing assumptions about human nature—not only to prepare readers to consider the relevant material and issues in later chapters, but also to communicate information.

I hope that teachers of personality courses who want the kind of alternative that I wanted will find this book useful, and that others will appreciate the authors' scholarly efforts.

Acknowledgements

I would like to express my appreciation to the contributors of this book, who were patient with the revisions required and the cooperation demanded by a collaborative effort, to Terry Shumann who helped with the preparation of my chapters, and to my family, Sylvia, Adrian and Daniel, for their continued patience with me, while I worked on this project.

The use of the third person pronoun poses a continued problem for me, as for many writers today. I have encountered many ingenious suggestions for dealing with the problem, but continue to find them sometimes cumbersome, sometimes funny, and sometimes horrifyingly convoluted. In my chapters, I opted for the traditional form, *he,* in the interests of simplicity of style, fully recognizing that it does represent a bias. It is, however, a bias embedded in our language, not reflecting my own. I want to suggest, here also, my favorite solution, that we write in Hungarian, which has only a single third person pronoun for he, she and it.

Contributors

James R. Averill is Professor of Psychology and Director of the Graduate Program at the University of Massachusetts, Amherst. A 1966 Ph.D. from UCLA, he also studied at the University of Bonn and Düsseldorf Medical Academy, West Germany, while on a Fulbright fellowship. Before coming to the University of Massachusetts in 1971, he worked as a research psychologist at the University of California, Berkeley.

Dr. Averill has published approximately 40 articles on the general topic of stress and emotion, and had edited a book, *Patterns of psychological thought,* on the historical and philosophical foundations of psychology. He has also served as consulting editor for the *Journal for the Theory of Social Behavior, Personality and Social Psychology Bulletin,* and *Psychophysiology.*

Edward L. Deci is a Professor in the Department of Psychology at the University of Rochester. His Ph.D. in social psychology is from Carnegie-Mellon University (1970). He has also studied at the University of London, the University of Pennsylvania, and Hamilton College. In 1973-74 he was on leave from the University of Rochester as an interdisciplinary postdoctoral fellow at Stanford University.

Dr. Deci has done research on many aspects of human motivation and has authored or edited six books including: *Intrinsic motivation* (1975), *Management and motivation* (with Victor Vroom, 1970), *Interpersonal influence* (with Ladd Wheeler, et al., 1978), and the forthcoming *Psychology of self-determination.*

He has published in numerous professional journals and is an editorial consultant for many journals and publishing houses. Deci is a Fellow of the American Psychological Association, and a member of several other professional organizations. He has consulted for Universities, boards of education, businesses and other organizations throughout the United States, Canada, and Japan; and he has a private practice as a psychotherapist.

Seymour Epstein is Professor of Psychology and Chairman of the Personality Program at the Amherst campus of the University of Massachusetts. He received his Ph.D. degree from the University of Wisconsin in 1953. He is a diplomate in clinical psychology and a Fellow of the American Psychological Association. He has served on several editorial boards for professional journals and has been an editorial consultant for many others. He has served on study sections for the National Institute of Mental Health, and has consulted with or referred research proposals for the National Science Foundation, the Canada Research Council, the National Institute of Dental Research, and the Veterans Administration.

Dr. Epstein's research interests are equally divided between field studies and laboratory research. He has been particularly interested in finding real situations that provide natural laboratories for the study of selected issues in a highly controlled manner. In this respect, he is probably best known for studies with Professor Fenz on anxiety in sport-parachuting. His research publications cover the following topics: classical conditioning, conflict, schizophrenia, projective testing, anxiety, anger and aggression, and, most recently, the self-concept, and the stability of behavior. The above research has received 23 years of consecutive support from the National Institute of Mental Health, and more recently, from the National Science Foundation.

Herbert M. Lefcourt was born in New York, educated at Antioch College, and received his Ph.D. from Ohio State University in 1963. Since then he has been at the University of Waterloo in Ontario, where he is a full Professor.

Dr. Lefcourt has authored many journal articles and book chapters and has written a book entitled *Locus of control.* He is currently in the process of writing and editing a second book focusing upon innovations in locus of control research.

Salvatore R. Maddi, Ph.D. Harvard, took a position at the University of Chicago in 1950, where he has since 1968 been Professor of Psychology and Social Sciences in the Department of Behavioral Sciences and the College. He has been visiting professor at Harvard and at the Educational Testing Service.

In 1961, his book with Donald W. Fiske, *Functions of varied experience,* appeared. Much of Dr. Maddi's early theorizing and research concerned the beneficial effects of variety on development and adult functioning. Starting in 1967 and continuing until the present, he has done significant conceptual and empirical work on a rigorous version of existential personality theory. In the last half of the 1960s, he also conducted a longitudinal study of personality in persons training to enter the Catholic religious vocation.

His influential textbook, *Personality theories: A comparative analysis* first appeared in 1968 and is now going into its fourth edition. He edited a reader for this book, *Perspectives on personality: A comparative approach,* in 1971.

With Paul T. Costa, Jr., Dr. Maddi wrote another book, *Humanism in personology*, which appeared in 1972.

At present, Dr. Maddi is embarked, with Suzanne C. Kobasa, on a large-scale research project concerning identification of the personality characteristics that decrease the likelihood that stressful life events will eventuate in illness symptoms.

Donald Meichenbaum received his bachelor's degree from City College of New York in 1962 and his Ph.D. in clinical psychology from the University of Illinois, Champaign, Illinois in 1966. He has been at the University of Waterloo, Waterloo, Ontario, since 1966 and is presently Professor of Psychology and Director of the clinical training program in Waterloo. He has consulted at the Clarke Institute of Psychiatry in Toronto and for Ontario Department of Reform Institutions and the Oxford Regional Center for Retardation.

Dr. Meichenbaum's research interests include cognitive development and cognitive factors in behavior modification. He has written a book on *Cognitive behavior modification: An integrative approach* and has lectured widely and published extensively on this topic. He is associate editor of the journal *Cognitive Therapy and Research* and serves on the editorial board of several journals.

Ervin Staub was born in Hungary, studied in Budapest, Vienna, and Minneapolis, and received his Ph.D. from Stanford University in 1965. He taught clinical psychology and personality at Harvard University until 1971, and since then has taught at the University of Massachusetts, Amherst, where he is Professor of Psychology. He has been a visiting professor at Stanford and at the University of Hawaii.

His primary research and writing are in personality psychology, and in personality and social development, with special focus on positive behavior such as sharing, helping, and responsiveness to others' needs. He conducted research on varied determinants of such behavior and their development in children. In addition to many research papers and book chapters, he has published two books in this area, *Positive social behavior and morality.* (Vol. 1), *Personal and social influences,* 1978; (Vol. 2), *Socialization and development,* 1979. He also has written on aggression and conducted research and published articles on the relationship of self-control and information to fear and avoidance behavior.

Dr. Staub is a Fellow of the American Psychological Association and a member of the Society for Research in Child Development. He has served on the editorial board of *Child Development* and the *Journal of Personality,* and has been an editorial consultant to many other journals, including the *Journal of Personality* and *Social Psychology.*

ERVIN STAUB

The Nature and Study of Human Personality

DEFINING PERSONALITY

Personality as the Study of Universal Principles and Individual Differences

A major aim of psychologists has always been to identify the characteristics which are universal to all human beings and to discover the universal principles that underlie human functioning. However, people are certainly not only alike, but are also different in all conceivable ways. Even in physical functioning, such as walking and talking, they differ in their customary speed, style, and manner. They certainly differ in what they say. They differ in their thoughts, in their emotional reactions to events, and frequently in their behavior under identical circumstances. Personality psychology is concerned both with universal characteristics of human beings and differences among them.

Concern with individual differences lies at the heart of personality psychology. Such differences are everpresent. For example, in Nazi Germany the population was exposed to tremendous indoctrination against non-Aryan peoples, especially Jews, but also Slavs, Orientals, blacks and many others. In addition, terror inflicted by the Nazis showed that resistance and giving aid to the "enemy"–such as Jews–was highly dangerous. While some part of the population actively participated in Nazi atrocities and in the extermination of Jews, and others passively stood by, a small number of individuals risked their lives in helping Jews escape (London, 1970). The Nazi practices that lead to collaboration or passivity by most did not work with these people. What personality characteristics did these "rescuers" possess? How did they differ from the majority? What psychological experiences–what thoughts and affects–led to their behavior? These are among the questions that personality psychologists ask. (In

Chapter 6, in the context of how social behavior is determined, the determinants of the behavior of this particular group of individuals will be discussed.)

While personality psychology is concerned with how persons with varied characteristics function, many theories of personality attempt to provide a conception of human beings in general. Psychoanalytic theory, certain cognitive theories, social learning theory, all of which have been regarded as theories of personality, aim at universal descriptions of human beings. However, these theories also point to which individual differences are important, and enable us to study these individual differences. For example, one cognitive theory, Kelly's (1955) theory of personal "constructs," suggests that a fundamentally important determinant of how people function is the nature of the constructs they employ, that is, their characteristic ways of ordering and explaining events.

Human beings have a need to know and to control their world. They go about exploring and testing their world like scientists, and they develop and choose among ways of construing, looking at and interpreting the world. One person may look at and think about his relationships to other people in terms of the loyalty of the other person in the relationship, while another may construe his relationships in terms of how much he can give to another person. Their constructs also affect the way people anticipate and react to events. Kelly's theory points to the tremendous significance of what constructs particular people employ. It suggests, further, that in order to bring about personality change–an important domain of personality psychology (see Chapter 7)–which is often necessary to help a person improve the quality of his life, one has to change his construct system.

One controversy about how we should study human beings has revolved around the issue of using nomothetic versus idiographic approaches. The nomothetic approach is the study of groups, or of people in general, which presumably leads to the knowledge of universal characteristics and general laws. The idiographic approach focuses on the intensive study of individuals. Allport (1937, 1961), the best known advocate of the idiographic approach, persistently argued that every human being is unique. People have certain characteristics in common with other people, but other characteristics are unique to them. In order to properly study human beings, we have to focus on the full uniqueness of each individual. (The usual method of doing this has been an in-depth case study, using varied procedures to get full information about every aspect of a person's characteristics and functioning.)

One could argue that if we *focus* on the uniqueness of every human being, we cannot generalize from one person to another. Since the aim of science is to discover laws or principles–applicable at least to some, if not to all people–what we will learn will not contribute to a science of psychology. While we may want to understand each person's complexity and uniqueness, we certainly want to know in what ways people are similar to some others and in what ways they are similar to all other people.

Concise Definitions and Aspects of Personality

Because of its wide-ranging domain, brief definitions of the concept of "personality" are, of necessity, abstractions that cannot give a feel for the richness of its phenomena, for its broad content area, and for its varied aspects. Nonetheless, many writers have attempted to give concise definitions of personality. The following is a sample. Personality is–

–the culmination of all relatively enduring dimensions of individual differences on which he (an individual) can be measured (Byrne, 1974, p. 26);

–the distinctive patterns of behavior (including thoughts and emotions) that characterize each individual's adaptation to the situations of his or her life (Mischel, 1976, p. 2);

–a relatively enduring pattern of interpersonal situations that characterize a human life (Sullivan, 1953, p. 111);

–the dynamic organization within the individual of those psychophysical systems that determine his characteristic behavior and thought (Allport, 1961, p. 28);

–a person's unique pattern of traits (Guilford, 1959, p. 5);

–the most adequate conceptualization of a person's behavior in all its detail (McClelland, 1951, p. 69).

All these definitions except the last one imply or clearly state that the distinctiveness of a person's characteristics and/or their combination defines personality. That is, the emphasis is on individual differences. Mischel's definition focuses on how individuals *adapt* to the circumstances of their lives. Sullivan's definition makes interpersonal situations the major defining aspect of personality. Allport's definition stresses that it is not only the personal characteristics that a person possesses that is important, but also their *organization.* It also indicates that the organization of characteristics is not unchanging, but dynamic and variable. Most of the definitions also imply a *constancy* in individual characteristics–the words *enduring* and *characteristic* are repeatedly used. Jointly, these definitions help provide a picture of what personality psychologists regard as central to the conception of personality.

Aspects of Personality. We can attempt to circumscribe personality by identifying important aspects of it. The words *person* and *personality* originate from the word *persona,* the name for the masks used by Greek actors. Each mask indicated to the audience what characteristics, what behaviors and attitudes, they could expect from the wearer. Over time the word came to also imply a dichotomy between surface appearance and underlying characteristics, and further, between superficial and fundamental characteristics (Allport, 1937, pp. 25-26). Monte notes a further implication, that "below the surface of public behavior there is a private, and perhaps different, person concealed from view" (1977, p. 18). Some psychologists, such as Maslow and Rogers, imply that the inner person is more real or genuine than the surface phenomena. It seems appropriate to distinguish between self-presentation, and thoughts, behaviors, desires, and other characteristics that underlie self-presentation, but to consider both real and important. Personality psychologists must be concerned with both, as well as with the relationship between the two.

Another useful distinction can be drawn between how human beings relate to themselves and to the world around them. Consider an article in the *New York Times Magazine* describing one of our most famous actors. This extremely successful man has gained fame, received recognition for his outstanding performances, and has acquired wealth. According to the article, others in his profession like him and admire him. Women are attracted to him. It would seem that his way of relating to the world is highly competent, effective, and successful in most realms. However, he is described in this article as discontent and given to rage and violence–towards objects, rather than people–in response to his dissatisfaction with himself. His success in relating to himself and to the world around him seems unequal. A person's internal world, including his self-evaluation, feelings, and thoughts, and his sense of happiness or unhappiness, are important aspects of his personality.

The Difficulty of Defining Personality

It may be evident by now that the term *personality* is difficult to define in a precise manner. One reason is that the term customarily refers to the study of all aspects of individuals and of their functioning. Personality psychology is intertwined with most other branches of psychology: some say it is at the crossroads of other branches (Liebert & Spiegler, 1978). Interpersonal relationships, attitudes, social norms, and group functioning are all traditionally part of social psychology. But personality psychologists are also vitally interested in both general principles and individual differences in these areas of knowledge. Since persons differ, their attitudes will differ, they will participate in different ways in interpersonal relationships, and act differently in groups. Some people accept social norms as their own, others do not, or hold personal norms that deviate from social norms.

Developmental psychologists are concerned with how human beings mature, grow, develop, or change from birth on. Early differences among children–many already present in infancy–modify how socialization and experience affect children. Personal characteristics and differences in social behavior are, moreover, important outcomes of development. Aberrations in socialization and in children's experiences, sometimes in conjunction with aberrant genetic makeup, result in personal characteristics that gain expression in malfunctioning, mental illness, and profound unhappiness–the phenomena of clinical psychology. It is by application of principles of personality change that psychotherapists of all varieties try to help people who are mentally ill, maladjusted, or unhappy. By tradition, personality psychology does not focus on human *capacities* such as physical abilities and intelligence. But wherever personal capacities gain expression–in sports, at school, in work–motivation, attitudes, and other personal characteristics modify the influence of capacities.

Personality psychology is also difficult to define because different personality psychologists focus their attention on different aspects of human functioning, depending on the assumptions they make about what is important. Some of the differences will be discussed in subsequent sections of this chapter. However, what appears unimportant to one group of theorists may seem crucial to another. While behaviorists such as Skinner consider subjective experience–how a person feels, what a person thinks–unimportant for understanding human beings and predicting their behavior, phenomenologists like Rogers believe that inner, subjective experience is the most important aspect of human functioning and the best predictor of behavior (see chapters by Epstein and Maddi in this volume). Theories are not simply descriptions of people, but are attempts to make sense of what we know, providing guidance for where we must look to learn more. They sum up, integrate, and generalize about existing knowledge. Thus, differences in their assumptions gain expression in many ways.

The analogy of the elephant and the blind man is an apt one for conveying the nature of personality psychology. Unable to see the whole elephant, a blind man's description of it will depend on whether he is touching the elephant's trunk, or foot, or tail, or tusk, or some other part. Similarly, different theories of personality approach the study of human beings from different perspectives. Hopefully, however, new theories will progressively be based on a broader range of the phenomena of personality, and represent progressively higher integrations. Behavior, perception, emotion, interest in the world, the self-concept, unconceptualized (unconscious) experience, and motivation (see below) are all important aspects of functioning. Progressively, we must find ways to relate them to each other and to integrate them into a comprehensive picture. The orientation of this book is, I believe, integrative even when dealing with relatively specific phenomena such as intrinsic motivation (see Deci's chapter). The authors acknowledge, and attempt in their conceptualizations to deal with, varied human characteristics and psychological functions.

The interests of personality psychologists can be further identified by three questions which they frequently ask. First, what are people like? This question asks for descriptions of people. Second, what are the relationships among varied personal characteristics? One aspect of this question is what determines how thoughts, feelings, and other characteristics of people relate to (and perhaps determine) their behavior? Third, how do people come to be the way they are? That is, how does personality develop? The following sections are elaborations of the meaning of these questions.

THE DESCRIPTIONS OF PERSONS

What are the various ways in which people perceive, think, and feel. What are their various desires and behaviors? What are important dimensions along which these characteristics vary? People differ in the way they perceive, evaluate, and think about the world around them, but also in the way they perceive and evaluate themselves.

As one considers the question, "What are human beings like?" it becomes important to differentiate between description and interpretation. We rarely remain at the level of pure description. Description easily, and necessarily, leads to interpretation. I might say that yesterday Joe punched Peter in the nose, today he shouted at Judy and threatened her, and last week I saw him pick a fight with his brother. If someone asks me what Joe is like, I remain at the strictly descriptive level only if, in response, I describe these and/or other examples of Joe's behavior. If I say "Joe is an aggressive person," I go beyond description–I generalize. I communicate a concept of Joe. The kind of concepts we tend to use in psychology can be closer to description, or further removed. Such concepts may summarize in some form what is described, give the events meaning, and/or imply future events: they are elements of theories. Theoretical concepts embody assumptions about people and about how they function that go beyond description. They provide understanding and a basis for predicting future reactions and actions of people.

An Example: Some Dimensions of Perception

The way a person perceives his environment has many aspects and can be described in many ways. Perception of the environment can be considered in terms of persistent individual *styles,* which are usually referred to as cognitive styles, indicating that perception and thinking are regarded as intimately interrelated. For example, some people tend to differentiate aspects of their environment, separate them out from each other, and see different aspects individually (an "analytic" style). Other people see things more in relation to each other (a "relational" style). The difference may be as simple and basic as one person reporting on a test that he or she sees a man, a pipe, and smoke in a picture, another person describing it as a man smoking a pipe.

People can also be described by the content and meaning of what they perceive. For some people, others' appearance, their beauty or ugliness, is a salient characteristic. What people find ugly or beautiful also varies. People differ in the kind of motives and intentions they attribute to others on the basis of their actions. Some are more likely to attribute hostility and anger, others less so. Some may see one who was kind to them as a good and helpful person. Others may see that person as one who did something kind hoping to gain from it, perhaps anticipating reciprocation. Any single act can be motivated by varied purposes, intentions, and desires, and different people may assume different reasons for the act.

An important aspect of differences in people's perception of reality has been called "defensive styles." Freud assumed that people avoid perceiving and processing information that is highly threatening. They defend themselves against anxiety by not seeing, not recognizing, or by distorting things in the world and/or in themselves. For example, they may not perceive other people as angry or as feeling hostile toward themselves; or they may not perceive their own feelings or needs, such as anger or sexual desire. Repression, closing things out of one's conscious awareness and keeping them out of awareness, is one important type of defense. But what is repressed continues to exert an influence. People frequently act for "unconscious" reasons and/or to satisfy unconscious motives or impulses. Most of us recognize that at least occasionally we do things for reasons we do not understand, and are guided by causes we cannot state.

While there are important differences in what people notice and how they see things, such variations are usually not pathological. We may call them defenses, but many psychologists regard them as simply differences in perceptual-cognitive modes or styles.

Some Descriptive Concepts

Defenses and perceptual styles are not observable: they are theoretical concepts inferred from observation. There are many descriptive, theoretical concepts that have been used by different theorists. A concept mentioned earlier, Kelly's (1955) "personal construct," is a further example. One of the best known descriptive concepts is that of "trait" (Allport, 1937). Traits are distinguishable and relatively enduring ways in which one individual differs from another. Traits are inferred on the basis of the recurrent quality of observable acts of behavior, which can include recurrent expressions of moods, feelings, or thoughts (e.g., cheerful, optimistic, aggressive, or generous). In psychological research, traits are frequently inferred from self-reports, which is certainly a less objective basis of inferring traits than is actual observation. Self-report is likely to represent a person's self-concept, how a person views himself, which may or may not be a valid indicator of a person's actual behavior or other characteristics.

Motive is another important concept. The concept of motive, and the more general one of motivation, attempt to deal with the question, "Why do people act, and why do people act in particular ways?" Some writers, such as Kelly, do not believe that we need to explain why people act: it is the nature of the human organism, in Kelly's view, to be active. Others proposed that organisms have basic biological needs, related to maintaining a necessary internal (homeostatic) state of the body, such as the need for food and water. Such needs and the psychological states corresponding to them, hunger and thirst, drive organisms to take action. The nature of the action depends on past learning about how the need can be reduced, about what actions lead to food or water. This kind of theorizing, called drive theory, associated with Stimulus-Response learning theory, conceived of motivation as mechanistic (see Deci's chapter). Motives, when they are active, exert a push on the organism. Social motives, in this view, develop out of the biologically based ones through principles of conditioning. For example, attachment to human beings would develop in infants as a result of association between the satisfaction of the biological needs and the presence of human caretakers. Through more complicated chains of association other motives, such as achievement, also develop out of basic biological needs in this view.

It is also possible to think of motives as learned goals. In the course of their socialization and experience people develop varied desires, and come to value corresponding outcomes or end states. The anticipation of these outcomes gives rise to a motivated state. In this conception motivated behavior is purposeful, its aim being not to reduce some bodily deficiency, but to reach some desired purpose (see Deci and Staub in this volume).

A motivated state can be thought of as having two primary components: an increased degree of activation, shown by physiological arousal or some form of activity; and the activity having some direction (directionality). However, people can desire or value outcomes without actually attempting to reach them. Motivation does not always gain expression in goal-directed behavior.

Obviously, people vary greatly in what outcomes they value. For example, achievement in school, in work, and success in the world may be of great importance to some people. For others, association with other people—sometimes called "affiliation"—may be of primary importance. Each person's motives can be conceptualized as hierarchically ordered according to their importance to that person.

RELATIONSHIPS AMONG PERSONAL CHARACTERISTICS

People can be described by their characteristic ways of perceiving, thinking, feeling, and acting, or by the use of theoretical concepts that refer to individual characteristics such as perceptual styles, traits, motives, or goals. How do personal characteristics combine? For example, what is the relationship between the way a person perceives, thinks, feels, and acts in response to events? Many different combinations are possible. Consider, as one example, people who habitually perceive others as hostile. One such person may react to the hostility he perceives with anger, and proceed to act angry and aggressive himself; another may respond to the perceived hostility with fear of being attacked, and act upon this fear by withdrawing from the situation and/or avoiding the hostile person. Still others may respond to perceived hostility with either anger or fear, but exercise self-control and not express their emotions in behavior. Not only may different characteristics combine in different ways in different people, but even within the same person the combination of characteristics is flexible, not static. Personality is dynamic. The necessity to talk to a hostile superior and the opportunity to talk to a friend can lead to the mobilization of some of the same and some different personal characteristics, in different combinations.

Many theorists use seemingly descriptive concepts, such as that of "trait," or "motive," to imply certain interrelationships among characteristics. For example, in Allport's (1937) view, people who possess a particular trait would both act and perceive the relevance of events in terms of that trait: "Traits have the capacity to render many stimuli functionally equivalent, and to initiate and guide consistent (equivalent) forms of adaptive and expressive behavior." A generous person may see opportunities for generosity where another person would not; a greedy person may see opportunities for gain in many places and act to achieve that gain.

Earlier, we discussed the controversy over studying human beings by the nomothetic approach (studying people in groups) or the idiographic approach (the in-depth study of each person). The emphasis on idiography may have originated in dissatisfaction with the lack of depth and complexity in assessing and studying human beings, which frequently characterizes the nomothetic approach. Although psychologists who learned about their patients in the course of therapy, such as Freud or Rogers, usually considered how characteristics of individuals are related to each other, research psychologists have not sufficiently done so. We need to consider combinations of characteristics if we are to gain meaningful understanding of personality. A balance is necessary. If we attempt to categorize people on the basis of the combination of *all* their characteristics, we will end up with each individual in a different category, and we will be studying the uniqueness of each person. But groups of people can certainly be found who have similar constellations of a number of characteristics. Exploring the nature of interrelationships among characteristics and the behavioral consequences (correlates) of varied constellations would be extremely important. Carlson, commenting on the state of personality research, wrote in 1971, "Not a single published study attempted an even minimal inquiry into the organization of personality variables within the individual" (p. 209). Lack of a theory that would guide such research work, lack of proper methodology, and the amount of effort that is demanded may all have contributed to this state of affairs. Two of the chapters in this book (Epstein and Staub) present theory and research that deals with the organization of personality characteristics and their relationship to behavior.

PERSONALITY DEVELOPMENT

What influences shape personality and social behavior? The authors in this book discuss particular developmental processes as they relate to aspects of personality they are writing about. In order to provide a general framework for understanding development, as well as to communicate a few substantive points, I will attempt to provide here a brief description of what appears to be major classes of influences on the development of children's personality (see also Staub, 1979).

The Influence of Heredity

Genetic makeup is one source of personality characteristics. While the genetic makeup of humans is shared to a substantial degree–resulting in characteristics shared by our species–our genetic makeup also greatly varies. To what extent are individual differences the result of differences in genetic makeup? This is an ancient question. Psychologists once thought about the influence of heredity and environment in terms of percentages–what percentage of the characteristics of organisms is the result of heredity, what percentage is the result of environment. In contrast, heredity and environment are now seen as interacting influences. Hereditary potential cannot develop, cannot be actualized, without the opportunity to express and exercise this potential. This opportunity is a function of the environment.

How can one best conceive of the influence of heredity on personality? Wiggins and his associates (1971) suggest two principles by which differences in heredity may exert influence. One of them is the principle of *differential susceptibility*. This principle suggests that individual differences in heredity exist which make people susceptible to the influence of certain environments. Given certain experiences, individuals with varied hereditary potentials would develop in different ways. For example, people who come from a family with a history of tuberculosis are apparently genetically predisposed to it, and are more likely to develop tuberculosis than those without such a history–but only if they are exposed to contagion; that is, only in an environment in which contamination is possible. There is evidence of hereditary influence in the development of schizophrenia. According to the above principle, people who have a hereditary susceptibility to schizophrenia would be likely to develop the disease if they grow up in certain environments. The frequent experiences of stress is one likely element of such environments.

Another principle that Wiggins proposed is that of *differential exposure* to experiences. Physical characteristics of individuals, such as body build and facial structure (and thus physical attractiveness), are largely due to heredity. People who differ in these characteristics are likely to be the objects or recipients of different reactions from other people. Other people's reactions, in turn, shape their personality. There is evidence, for example, that people perceive and judge differently the actions of physically more attractive and less attractive children (Dion, 1972). The same wrongdoing by a more attractive child is judged as less serious than by a less attractive child. The findings that "mesomorphs" (people with a muscular body build) are more frequent among adolescent juvenile delinquents than adolescents with other body builds, may also be explained as the result of differential exposure to experience (Lindzey, 1965). In subcultures where juvenile delinquency is relatively frequent, peers may turn to such individuals for leadership in dangerous and/or physically demanding activities, or at least may "select" them and induce them to participate in such activities. Their success in such activities may also be greater, so that they are more frequently reinforced for participation.

Heredity also exerts influence by placing limitations on various capacities. Consider intellectual or athletic performance. Regardless of the opportunities for learning or the amount of effort and diligence invested in these areas, truly outstanding intellectual achievement or athletic performance cannot be reached by everyone, because of the upper limit set by heredity. Differences in these capacities must affect the child's experience in the world, and thereby the development of his or her personality, by affecting the degree of success he achieves and the experiences he has along the way. Differences in capacities would affect the self-concept—the awareness of what one can and cannot do—and affect motivation, the desire for what one wants to do. However, they might not necessarily affect self-*esteem,* the child's evaluation of himself. Their effect on self-esteem probably strongly depends on how parents and other socializers relate to and guide the child (Coopersmith, 1967).

Many personality psychologists currently believe that there are important hereditary influences on personality. We do not as yet know a great deal about the extent and nature of these influences. Their extent certainly varies from variable to variable. We know that individual differences exist among infants: in the frequency and intensity of crying; in their capacity to soothe themselves (by sucking their thumbs while waiting for food rather than crying); in the manner in which they handle stimulation and excitation (some infants respond with their whole bodies, in an active and intense manner, while others watch and observe but respond little with their bodies; Escalona, 1968); and in other dimensions. Many differences are already apparent during the first four days of life (Korner, 1971). There is also reason to believe, on the basis of research with twins (in which identical and fraternal twins were compared with very sophisticated methodology), that some of the early individual differences are hereditarily based, rather than the result of prenatal factors (that is, of the influence of nutritional and hormonal factors in the uterus). Identical twins were found more similar to each other in varied ways, such as motor development and sociability, than fraternal twins (Freedman, 1965).

We do not know as yet, however, in what manner and to what extent early individual differences exert continuing influence and result in later differences in personality. Some research programs claimed that early differences exist in infants' ease or difficulty in dealing with new stimuli, in the intensity of their reactions to events, in the regularity of their sleeping and eating, and in other characteristics that are sometimes called temperamental (Thomas, Chess, Birch, Hertiz & Korn, 1963). Moreover, these differences were found to persist. However, methodological issues, including the start of the research not at birth but after six weeks of age, makes it difficult to assume that these differences had a hereditary origin. There is increasing evidence from research studies that parents' influence on children is not unidirectional; that children, even infants, also exert influence on parents. The development of a transactional relationship, a system of relating, may in part explain stability in the above characteristics.

Watson, the father of behaviorism, argued that man is like a "tabula rasa," an empty sheet on which anything can be written. He believed that the training and experience to which a person is exposed completely determines what he will become. Most contemporary psychologists would probably agree that this is substantially overstated. Nonetheless, the range of possibilities for most of us is probably wide: heredity sets rather broad limits, particularly in the domain of personality.

Forms of Socialization

Socialization is usually defined as that process whereby the rules, standards of conduct, expectations, and knowledge of the adult culture are transmitted to children throughout the period of their maturation and development. Since in reality socialization also attempts to transmit culturally valued and appropriate emotional reactions, desirable motivations, and the definitions of the meaning of many aspects of life, it obviously concerns itself with all aspects of the development of the child's personality and social behavior.

Several classes of socializing influences can be differentiated. Traditionally, attention was directed nearly exclusively at *parental child-rearing,* since socialization by parents has been regarded as the dominant influence on children's personality. The influence of parents (and other adults) is multifaceted. Children may learn directly from them, through rewards and punishments that they receive for various actions, and through verbal communication or tuition that they are exposed to. Children may learn indirectly, through modeling, or through identification which leads to the imitation and/or adoption of adult beliefs, values and behavior. The affective relationships between parents and children, the existence of affection and caring in contrast to hostility or other negative emotions, is important in its own right and affects what children learn from parental instruction and child-rearing techniques. Different constellations of practices by parents are likely to lead to different characteristics of children. For example, parental affection and nurturance, firm but reasonable control over the child, and reasoning with the child—explaining why certain behaviors are desirable, others prohibited—are likely to contribute to positive characteristics of children, such as high self-esteem and positive behavior toward others (Baumrind, 1975; Staub, 1979). However, highly forceful means of control by parents, particularly frequent physical punishment, engender aggression and hostility in children.

I recently proposed another form of socialization, which I called *natural socialization* (Staub, 1979). Children learn not only from the direct influence of parents and other adults, or from what they observe, but also from their own participation in activities. For example, by engaging in helpful behavior, children may come to see themselves as helpful persons and to value others' welfare more. By working on tasks, children may come to see themselves as interested in such activities, and if successful, as good at them (see also Deci's chapter on intrinsic motivation). The children's learning results directly from participation in the activities. Adults, of course, exert guidance and influence what children do. Moreover, the environment surrounding them can affect how children experience their participation. In addition, using threat and other forceful means to induce children to work on tasks will make it unlikely that they perceive their activity as due to their own interest, or that they come to value and enjoy the task. (However, such force may be reduced over time, with a corresponding change in what children might learn from the activity; see Staub, 1979). Adults can also guide children's interpretation of their experience, and can influence how they perceive its meaning.

A third type of socialization is *peer socialization.* Theory and research about the long-term influence of peers on each other has been minimal. Considering the amount of time that children spend in each others' company from an early age on, and considering children's immediate influence on each others' behavior (Hartup, 1970), this is an important omission.

There is evidence of reciprocity in peers' interactions (Staub, 1979): frequently, positive behavior begets positive behavior, and negative behavior begets negative behavior. If, over the long run, some children get "locked" into a negative pattern of interaction with other children, they will certainly have a different experience of the world and of people than children who experience a predominantly positive pattern. The ways of relating to both the self and the world outside must be affected by such differences in social experience with peers. As Meichenbaum (in Chapter 7 of this book) notes, children who are unpopular or isolated in their childhood have a greater likelihood of psychiatric problems later in life than do more popular children.

The structure of the child's *environment* is also extremely important in the development of the child's personality. The environment can be divided into several levels or domains. Schools can teach children democratically, allowing them reasonable freedom of choice, or autocratically. Peer groups can be completely uncontrolled by adults, so that aggression and negative interactions among children are uncontrolled; or firm limits can exist that still allow considerable freedom. Different subcultures and cultures set different rules for how to behave, and ascribe to different ideals. How these larger environments affect the child directly, and indirectly through the family, are just beginning to receive attention (Bronfenbrenner, 1977; Staub, 1979).

METHODS OF STUDYING PERSONALITY

The impressionistic knowledge of individuals that we all gain from experiences in everyday life is, in important ways, different from the kind of knowledge about people that we need to gain in order to develop valid theories about personality. How do we, in fact, acquire our "knowledge" of the people with whom we interact in our everyday life? Mainly, through three sources: from the impressions and judgments that we form by observing people's behavior, such as their interactions with ourselves and others; from verbal self-presentation, either implicit or explicit, that people provide (for example, we have all met people who, early in a relationship, verbally communicate to us that they are helpless, intelligent, or possess some other quality); and from information we gain from third parties.

However, we differ in many important ways as "data collectors" in our everyday contacts with people. For one thing, we develop different "constructs" about people, so that two people will perceive and interpret the same behaviors in different ways. In other words, we have low "inter-observer reliability." Agreement among observers about what they see is a prerequisite in psychological research. Secondly, our own personality affects the way others relate to us. We also differ in the kind of "data" on which we base our influences–for example, in the extent to which we accept as valid others' verbal self-presentation.

Data Collection Methods

How much more reliable are the methods of data collection used by personality psychologists? The scientific method of the contemporary social sciences requires that we collect information, or "data," in certain ways. However, "scientific method" is not unchanging and absolute; it is rather a matter of agreement among members of the scientific community at any one time as to what is acceptable. Moreover, sometimes it is recognized that although the rules or criteria by which the scientific method operates have not been adequately applied in certain instances, important information has nonetheless been gained.

Clinical Interviews. Information that is gained about patients in psychotherapy has been the basis of several influential theories of personality, such as Rogers' phenomenological theory and Freud's psychoanalytic theory. The verbal interview and verbal exchanges characterize psychotherapeutic interaction. Many social scientists do not believe that such methods are scientifically valid for *con-*

firming hypotheses. Consider, for example, Freud's method of free association, in which the patient or interviewee is directed to communicate all the contents of his or her consciousness, no matter how seemingly irrelevant or unimportant, on the assumption that the flow of a person's consciousness will provide clues to his unconscious. Using free association, or information collected in psychotherapy in general, the interviewer is usually the only person present. Because the perception or memory of what the client actually says cannot be checked or validated by another observer, and because the therapist construes what the patient says according to his theory, there is no inter-observer reliability. Most importantly, therapists in the course of interacting with patients often lead them, albeit unintentionally and unconsciously, to provide information that fits the therapists' preconceptions or theories (Frank, 1974). Nonetheless, extensive interviews and verbal exchanges in psychotherapy over an extended period of time can and do provide important information, insights, and understandings, which serve as a basis for theoretical ideas and hypotheses for later research that is more stringently guided by the "scientific method." This kind of information is difficult to gain by other means.

Self-Reports in Research. Interviews can also serve the single purpose of assessing personality, unrelated to therapy. Interviews can be unstructured, allowing free exchange between interviewer and interviewee, with the possibility that the latter will provide more extensive and important information, but with the danger that the nature of the interaction between interviewer and interviewee will determine what the latter says. In contrast, interviews can be highly structured, with the sequence of questions carefully predetermined. Questionnaires can also be relatively unstructured, asking for free responses according to what the respondents judge important; or they can ask for highly specific information, allowing only yes or no responses, or ratings on some scale. People can, of course, be asked about any aspect of their perception of themselves and the world, ranging from their self-evaluation to how they think they might act under specific conditions, or to what they think about human nature.

Sometimes people are presented with incomplete stories and are asked to complete them, or are asked to invent stories about pictures with ambiguous meanings. Such techniques of personality assessment or measurement are called "projective" techniques. It is assumed that people will "project" their own thoughts, feelings, or even ways of behaving into their responses, and reveal certain aspects of their personality in a way and to an extent that they would be unwilling or unable to do if they were asked directly.

Assessing Behavior. There are many ways of assessing or measuring human behavior. We can ask people who are familiar with a subject to rate his or her behavior; for example, teachers can be asked to rate their pupils on a particular dimension. We can observe, and in varied ways code or rate behavior in real-life settings. Both in field settings and in psychological laboratories, we can provide people with some kind of stimuli and observe their reactions to them. By doing this under relatively identical circumstances, we can compare the reactions of different people, and/or compare people who had different preceding experiences.

In all our assessments of personality, we have to be concerned with both reliability and validity. Reliability has been repeatedly referred to. For example, in coding behavior in life settings, we must be certain that different observers code the same behavior in identical ways. A child's pushing of another child can represent play, or aggression, or—depending on its form—even expression of affection. Unless different observers usually code the same behavior in identical ways, our observations will have little value. Validity refers to the notion that information that we have collected has some value, that we can establish that it really says something about a person. If a person describes himself or herself as extremely well liked, such a self-description is valid if in observing this person we see others show interest, express liking, and behave in a friendly way toward this person. If others show dislike and disinterest, it is still possible that the self-description has a kind of validity. Perhaps it correlates with other self-descriptions, and other information which shows that people who say that they are extremely well liked have a high need for approval by others. Since this response contributes to defining the theoretical construct "need approval," this kind of validity is called construct validity. There are varied types of validity that information about someone's personality might have; but without some type of validity, our data have little value.

Research Methods

How is the collected data used in research? In other words, what is the overall research plan, or strategy, into which this data is fitted in order to answer certain questions, or to confirm certain hypotheses? Three primary research strategies will be briefly described here, the experimental, correlational, and semi-experimental methods. The choice of method depends on several factors: the nature of the question being studied, the existence of certain traditions in the study of particular domains of psychology, certain ethical and practical considerations, and, last but not least, the personal preference and scientific inclination of the researcher.

The Experimental Method. In an "experiment" a number of "subjects"—individuals either randomly selected or chosen for certain characteristics such as age, social class, or intelligence—are exposed together or one by one to some experience or "treatment." Other groups of persons, selected in the same manner, may be exposed to other experiences. These treatments, which vary along some particular dimension, are called the *independent variable.* Then the presumed effects of these experiences are measured. Usually one group of subjects, referred to as the control group, is exposed to some kind of neutral experience (or to no particular experience), and their reactions are compared to those in the experimental treatments. This enables researchers to evaluate the extent to which the reactions of experimental subjects may be due to incidental influences, including the influence of the testing situation.

Imagine, as an example of such an experiment, that different groups of children are exposed to different degrees and kinds of aggression (the independent variable) in films presented to them on closed-circuit television. Many experiments used some variant of this procedure, following the classic experiments of Bandura and his associates (e.g., Bandura, Ross, & Ross, 1961, 1963). In a control group, children are exposed to a film with neutral, nonaggressive content, for the same length of time. The behavior of the children is subsequently observed, in interaction with other people and objects (such as dolls), and the amounts and kinds of aggression they display is rated (the dependent variables). Since the experimental conditions differed only in the presence, degree, and type of aggression seen by children on TV, the researcher can conclude that subsequent differences in aggression between groups of children exposed to different programs were caused by what they saw on TV. The experimental method tells us about average or typical differences among individuals that are the result of particular experiences.

The Correlational Method. In contrast to examining reactions caused by some events or experiences, as the experimental method does, the correlational method of research examines the relationships between events. To what extent and in what way do two or more events "correlate," or vary together? Correlational methods can be used with naturally occurring events. In contrast to experimental strategies, people do not have to be deliberately exposed to some experience or another. For example, physical punishment by parents of their children's wrongdoing and the frequency of aggression by the children can be measured. Thus, two items of information are collected about each child. The extent to which they are related can be expressed by a "correlation coefficient," a statistic which represents the "strength" of the relationship.

The correlation may be positive, suggesting that more physical punishment goes together with greater frequency of aggression by children. The larger the size of the correlation, which ranges from 0 to 1, the greater the degree of association. The correlation may also be negative, so that the more frequent the physical punishment, the *less* frequent is the aggression shown by the children. In reality, this relationship was found to be positive (see Staub, 1979). It is usually explained by one or both of two hypotheses: (1) that children model the aggressive behavior of their parents, which is directed at them; and (2) that physical punishment generates anger and hostility in children.

Note, however, that while this explanation assumes that physical punishment causes aggression, in correlational research causation cannot be established. For one thing, the direction of causation might go either way. In the above example, frequent aggression by children may elicit more physical punishment from parents, rather than the other way around. Or a third variable may account for the relationship. For instance, the values of a particular subculture, or general life circumstances such as poverty and deprivation, can generate anger and aggression and/or diminish impulse control in both parents and children. According to this explanation, the two correlated variables have no causal influence on each other, but are both "caused" by a third factor. The more knowledge and information we have, the more we can entertain hypotheses about causality, which we can then test in experimental research. For example, we might expose children to punishment that varies in degree of severity and then measure how much aggression they subsequently show. Will more severe punishment cause more aggression?

Here, the important issue of ethical considerations in the choice of research methods enters. Obviously, researchers should not impose severe punishment on children. In fact, one reason that correlational techniques are important in psychological research is that they enable us to study questions that we could or would not study experimentally. Another advantage of correlational techniques is that we can study what constellations of characteristics and events occur together. In addition to studying the nature of parental punishment and child aggression, we can assess a family's economic circumstances and parental values, and examine the relationship among all four variables. Correlational research is an important tool in the study of personality. To state the obvious, we cannot create personality characteristics by experimental treatments. But we can measure them and, using correlational techniques, study the relationships among them and their relationship to other characteristics and events.

Semi-Experimental Procedures. The experimental method, since it looks at how people in general behave, helps to establish general laws or principles. However, findings in experimental studies can be misleading, because people usually react differently to experience as a function of their own characteristics. For example, let's assume that two different kinds of children were used as subjects in the experimental study I described before. One group of children, on the basis of previous observations, was judged as aggressive in their interactions with other children. The other group of children was judged to be relatively nonaggressive. If this were done, one might find that while exposure to mild aggression on TV increased subsequent aggressive behavior by both groups, exposure to severe aggression on television resulted in the greatest increase in aggression by aggressive children, but a decrease in aggression by the nonaggressive children. The inhibitions about aggression that children in the latter group acquired may have been activated by the high-intensity aggressive behavior they saw on TV. A procedure in which people are exposed to experimental treatments, but are also divided on personality characteristics that might modify or change the influence of the experimental treatments on them—a semi-experimental procedure—is a highly desirable strategy for studying many questions about personality, particularly that of the joint (interactive) influence of personality and situations. The semi-experimental procedure combines experimental and correlational procedures. The findings imply differences in the *relationship* between personal characteristics (e.g., the tendency to behave aggressively) and a dependent measure (specific aggressive acts) under different conditions (following exposure to varying aggression by filmed models).

All of the above techniques of information gathering and research will be discussed in this book, with the discussion embedded in the presentation of theory and research findings in particular domains that the individual chapters deal with.

"TRADITIONAL" THEORIES OF PERSONALITY

Many theories of personality have been developed in psychology's short history. Several of the best-known traditional theories attempt to be comprehensive; they try to encompass varied aspects of human psychological functioning. However, in these theories, both the focus of interest and the methodology for assessing personality varies. Some theories, such as psychoanalytic theory, focus on unconscious motivation and on intrapsychic conflicts; others, like Rogerian theory, focus on the nature of human consciousness and subjective awareness. Behaviorism, and social-learning theory in its early phase, focused on overt behavior and on principles guiding the acquisition of particular responses. These theories tend to be comprehensive in that, having assumed that the aspects of human functioning they focus on are central, they try to derive all other aspects of human functioning from these central phenomena. These large-scale theories have by now become part of psychology's tradition. They are often presented in textbooks and in personality courses in their totality. Some aspects of these theories seem, however, to have limited contemporary value, while other aspects have been further developed by extensions of the original theories or adopted by new theoretical and research approaches.

Cognitive processes have acquired a central role in current versions of social-learning theory (Bandura, 1977; Mischel, 1973, 1977). Carl Rogers' theoretical conceptions are represented in current "self" theories (see Epstein's chapter). Freud's concepts of the child's "identification" with socializing agents, primarily parents, and the "internalization" of beliefs, values, and behavior that results from identification with parents, have substantially contributed to much of the theory and research in child development (Staub, 1979). Many experiments were conducted by social-learning oriented psychologists who explored hypotheses derived from psychoanalysis or other theories. Consider the research about the influence of models on children's behavior, which explored whether variation in the amount of a model's nurturance toward children affects their imitation of the model's behavior. This research question is a direct derivative of the Freudian conception that parental love, and anxiety about loss of love, are important origins of children's identification with parents.

Some of the concepts of traditional theories appear to have been disconfirmed by research findings. One such example, which I will consider further below, is the notion that organisms seek the reduction of stimulation. The hypotheses that age of weaning of infants and severity of toilet training strongly affect later personality, derived from Freudian theory, have also not received confirmation by research (Ferguson, 1970). (Severity of parental treatment of children in general, but not severity of toilet training in particular, seems important.) Other ideas seem outdated. Modes of thinking change due to new research findings, new theoretical ideas, and the influence that changes in society exert on psychologists. Hopefully, these changes usually represent a broader and deeper understanding of human beings. While some theoretical conceptions may never gain influence or may lose it over time, the influence of other ideas increases. The Lewinian (1948) conception about the necessity to jointly consider personality and the life space that surrounds people in order to understand psychological functioning and behavior, which for a long time exerted limited influence, is currently considered an important notion (Bronfenbrenner, 1977; Hornstein, 1976; see Maddi's and Staub's chapters in this volume).

Thus, while some aspects of these theories remain influential, frequently in some transformation, other aspects seem outdated. One reason for the diminished influence of certain aspects of traditional theories may be that they were based on inadequate or inappropriate data sources, and consequently the theories appear inadequate. For example, Freud developed a theory of stages of development during childhood (see Deci's chapter). However, he developed this theory primarily in his analytical work with adults, by talking to them about their childhood memories or recovering such childhood memories through dreams and other means. He had only one child patient; and even in this case, he obtained his information from the child's parents.

Many purportedly comprehensive theories focused their attention on a restricted range of phenomena, assuming that they were centrally important, and used limited methods of data collection, which necessarily provided a limited data base and further restricted the theory. Behaviorists focused on stimuli and responses; psychoanalysts on unconscious motivation and conflict and signs that indicated their presence; phenomenologists on the role of subjective awareness. The former two theories assumed that subjective awareness—for example, how people perceive and evaluate interpersonal relations—is not important in its own right. For psychoanalytic theorists, subjective awareness is important primarily to the extent that it provides clues to unconscious motivation and conflict. For behaviorists, subjective awareness was an epiphenomenon—a by-product, something that has no real significance, exerts no influence—and was, besides, not really observable and therefore not testable. Given these assumptions, data that might have expanded the original theories—for example, by showing significant relationships between behavior (or unconscious motivation) and subjective awareness (or the cognitive system of the individual that affects the nature of subjective awareness) was not collected.

Ideally, varied phenomena should be studied with varied methodologies, which are able to highlight different aspects of functioning. Personality psychology as a discipline needs to have in its repertoire a large range of techniques applicable for use in the study of human interactive behavior, thought and imagination, moods and emotions, and varied manifestations of all of these. Interviews, paper-and-pencil tests, observations of behavior in naturalistic and laboratory settings, experimental influences, all can provide information about different aspects of human functioning; all are important to employ.

Differences in assumptions about what is important to study, and in the explanation and integration of findings—that is, in theories—will continue to exist. Conflicts and contrasts among different theories can give rise to higher levels of integration of what we know. They can also stimulate the development of new methodologies that enable us to study important questions in increasingly effective ways. New methodologies, in turn, give rise to new conceptions. For example, new techniques used to study the reactions and behavior of extremely young infants enable us to specify what individual differences exist at an early age. Relatively new techniques for measuring infants' eye movements enable researchers to study infants' expectations about events. They can explore infants' expectations about the reappearance of an object that disappears from view, and thereby demonstrate the existence of "object constancy," the emerging knowledge that objects that disappear continue to exist. Observational techniques make it possible to explore the transactional nature of infant-parent interactions, the mutual influence they exert on each other. The evidence of mutual influence, in turn, supports new conceptions about personality development.

In the chapters of this book, various aspects of traditional theories are presented, as well as some "mini-theories" which, while related to broader theoretical orientations, are primarily theories about particular aspects of functioning. The theories about locus of control and related phenomena (Lefcourt's chapter) and about intrinsic motivation (Deci's chapter) may be regarded as examples of such mini-theories. Several of the chapters also attempt integration of insights from several theories, and/or propose new theories.

ASSUMPTIONS ABOUT HUMAN NATURE: IS MAN BASICALLY "GOOD" OR "BAD"?

It is commonly assumed that all human beings share certain characteristics, presumably due to their common biological makeup. What are these characteristics? Philosophers have long made assumptions about human nature. Psychological theories also embody varied assumptions. An example of one type of such assumptions is the belief in either the basic "goodness" or "badness" of human nature. Selecting this assumption reflects this writer's strong interest in human kindness and positive behavior. Since the assumptions that psychologists make about the "goodness" or "badness" of human beings are similar to those that philosophers made long ago, the discussion will also show the historical continuity of certain ideas.

Human Beings are Basically Good. Some philosophers have believed that man is basically good. Socrates, for example, believed that man is potentially perfectable and that through self-examination he can gain virtue. Socrates believed that knowledge is the path to virtue, in the sense that coming to know ourselves through critical examination will lead to virtuous action. In contrast, Rousseau believed that man is basically virtuous to begin with: he is good by nature and will continue to be good if he is not corrupted by the institutions of society. People who live outside society (i.e., "noble savages") and therefore are not corrupted by society, will be good. "Good" for Rousseau meant unselfish, concerned not only with one's own interests, but with the welfare of others. For Socrates, it primarily meant living the examined, wise life.

Maslow and Rogers are the best known psychologists who make similar assumptions about man. According to Maslow (1965) in the course of "self-actualization" man reaches the point where he fulfills his deficiency needs (his biological needs and needs for security) and can devote himself to the fulfillment of higher needs such as love and creativity. Maslow strongly condemned the view that man's nature is evil. Man does have an inner core that he brings with himself at birth, which (as far as we know) is definitely not evil, but is either what we call in our culture "good" or else it is neutral. Maslow (1965) believed that a proof of man's goodness is that "uncovering" therapy decreases aggression, hostility, greed, and other negative characteristics and increases love, kindness, and creativity. He concluded that the latter are deeper, more natural, and more basic characteristics than the former. The views of Rogers and the early views of Fromm (1941) coincide with those of Maslow in believing that man is basically good.

Unfortunately, it is difficult if not impossible to test this basic assumption about human nature. Rogers (1959), for example, reasoned that difficulties in functioning are caused by lack of unconditional acceptance by others, starting in childhood. Unconditional acceptance would lead to unimpaired growth and the development of positive characteristics. One can, of course, provide children with different environments, and this leads, as we know, to different personality characteristics, including a more positive or negative orientation to other human beings, as well as to the self (Staub, 1978, 1979). Can one argue, however, that one of these orientations is more an expression of basic human nature than the other, that one environment more fully allows our "basic" human nature to unfold while another has a corrupting influence? It seems at least as valid to say that human beings have the potential for kindness as well as selfishness and cruelty, and that they will develop different characteristics as a function of their environment and experience. A basic question is, in fact, what limitations are set by the biological makeup of human beings in general, and of individual human beings in particular, and how do biological-genetic makeup and experiences that the environment provides interact in shaping personal characteristics?

Human Beings are Basically Selfish. Some philosophers and psychologists assumed that man is basically selfish. Hobbes (1851) believed that man is only concerned with his own interests, and will pursue his interests even if other people are thereby harmed. He believed that a strong government was necessary to ensure that people would not harm and make life intolerable for each other in the pursuit of their own selfish interests.

Freud also believed that human beings are basically selfish. Infants are concerned only with the satisfaction of their own needs, and would grow up into selfish human beings were they not guided by their environment to learn to consider the interests of others. According to Freud, in the course of socialization children learn that people around them will not tolerate certain kinds of behavior, and learn values and standards of conduct. They internalize these values and standards, which come to guide their behavior towards other people. In contrast to Hobbes, who advocated external controls (the government), Freud believed that people must acquire internal controls in the course of socialization. Obviously, just as it is very difficult to establish that human beings are good by nature, so it is also difficult to establish that they are basically selfish. Certainly, many examples can be seen and have been cited in the literature which show acts of kindness as well as aggression by children at a very early age (Staub, 1979).

Human Beings are Capable of Enlightened Self-Interest. A third approach, represented in philosophy by Hume, is that while man may be basically self-seeking, he is capable of learning to live according to his "enlighted self-interest." In order to be treated in a positive fashion by others, to protect himself, man can learn to behave positively toward others.

Social exchange theory (Homans, 1961; Chadwick-Jones, 1976; Staub, 1972, 1978), which explains human interactive behavior in terms of gains and losses, and the concepts of equity and reciprocity that are incorporated into this theory, represent this view on the current psychological scene. There is extensive evidence, in fact, that people engage in give-and-take, that they reciprocate others' kindness and consider others' merits and what others deserve (Staub, 1978).

How does one resolve these different approaches and assumptions? The world is full of aggression and violence and selfishness, as well as kindness and self-sacrifice. It is reasonable to believe that human beings have varied potentialities. Which of these potentialities develop and evolve depends, to a large extent, on the kind of environment that people grow up in and live in, that is, on the nature of their experiences.

Specific Theories and How to Evaluate Them

The discussion in this chapter suggests that the reader may find it useful to ask several questions in reading about personality theories in general, and as they are discussed in the context of particular topics in subsequent chapters.

Two of the most important questions might be, first, What are the major concepts of the theory? and second, What are the major assumptions of the theory about human nature? These two issues are frequently intertwined, because, as discussed above, theoretical concepts frequently embody assumptions about human nature. However, how explicit or implicit such assumptions are can vary greatly. Psychoanalytic theory and drive-reduction theory explicitly assume that human beings seek to reduce internal stimulation or arousal. Freud assumed, for example, that we have two basic biologically based (id) impulses or instincts. Sometimes he regarded them as sexual and aggressive, sometimes as life and death instincts. One of the characteristics of these impulses is that they have a bodily source; this is an energy source and a form of tension or irritation. Another characteristic is that they have an aim, which is energy or tension reduction (i.e., the reduction of internal stimulation; Freud, 1957). Thus, the assumption that organisms seek reduction in internal stimulation was explicit. An opposite assumption, based on much empirical evidence, is that human beings *seek* stimulation (see Deci's chapter). Assumptions can also be implicit, usually implied by explicit ones. This is the case in psychoanalytic theory with the assumption that human beings are self-seeking, a result of assumptions about the nature of id impulses, which continually seek gratification.

The third and fourth questions are: What are the techniques or approaches to the assessment of personality that the theory employs? and What are the major research strategies? By what strategies are data collected and how are they processed or used to answer questions and test hypotheses.

Theories have varied formal properties, and they can be evaluated by varied criteria. Epstein, who considers the self-concept a self-theory, describes in his chapter criteria for evaluating theories such as extensivity, parsimony, empirical validity, internal consistency, testability, and usefulness. As part of preparation for the rest of the book, reading this section of Epstein's chapter might be useful.

THE CONTENTS OF THIS BOOK

The following chapters discuss what are, in my view, some profoundly significant aspects of human personality and functioning. The phenomena and principles of human functioning that these chapters deal with are the basis for the development and/or understanding of characteristics involved in many aspects of human functioning other than those specifically dealt with in the chapters.

The following discussion is not intended as a review of the chapters. While my comments reflect the contents of the chapters, they primarily intend to show how I saw these topics, their significance and the interrelationships among them, and intend thereby to give meaning to their selection for the book.

Intrinsic Motivation and Personality (*Edward Deci,* Chapter 2). The topic of Chapter 2 is a concept which refers to the interest in the world that human beings show from birth on. From infancy, humans appear motivated to relate to the world, to examine and explore it, to experience it and learn from it, to manipulate it and make it vary. While everyday observations of children, as well as research with children and adults, testify to the existence of these interrelated phenomena, explanations of these phenomena vary. Some researchers and theorists view them as manifestations of a primary and basic motive, as part of a basic human tendency to explore, look, see, feel, master, and seek stimulation. Other theorists—for example Freud, as well as "drive" (homeostatic) theorists—assume that human beings want above all to eliminate the experience of internal excitement and to avoid stimulation. They believe that we engage in stimulus seeking and exploration and show interest in the world in order to learn ways to reduce our needs or drives and to satisfy, and thereby reduce, our basic needs or impulses. They thus view our interest in the world as secondary, in the service of other—"primary"—motives.

The motivation to look, see, manipulate, explore, and seek excitement came to be called "intrinsic," reflecting the assumption of many contemporary psychologists that organisms engage in these activities for their own sake. Such activities have important functions for our development as human beings. They lead to the accumulation of knowledge about the world; they help the child, through interaction with the world, to develop a sense of self; in particular, they contribute to the development of a sense of efficacy or control over the environment. Intrinsic motivation also contributes to the development of varied social motives, not only that of achievement—to which its connection is fairly obvious, but of others as well. When the environment supports intrinsically motivated activities, when parents reward them and promote them, such activities can become a source of pleasure and satisfaction, and are intentionally sought out. They can be a source of positive self-concept and self-esteem, and can contribute to a perception of one's ability to influence events—topics that, respectively, Epstein and Lefcourt discuss. Intrinsic motivation can be diminished and enhanced, and its direction and form can be shaped by the socializers in the child's environment and by the child's experiences. Deci examines these varied aspects of intrinsic motivation and discusses further issues such as conceptions of motivation and of development. He also reviews research on individual differences in intrinsic motivation.

The Self-Concept (*Seymour Epstein,* Chapter 3). Very early, children begin to discriminate between themselves and the world, the "me" and the "not me." In the course of exploring the world, they also explore and learn about themselves, as well as about their relationship to the world. It is inevitable that children develop a self-concept, but many variations can exist in its content or nature. A child may learn, for example, that he is good or bad, competent or incompetent, from his or her experience–an important part of which is adults' reactions to the child, both emotional reactions that are not verbally expressed and verbal communications and actions toward the child. Learning about the world and about the self must be intertwined: learning that people are kind or unkind, that one's needs will or will not be satisfied, must also affect the self-concept. Depending on the nature of his or her experience, the child may have vague or undifferentiated conceptions of his or her self, or may develop clear, differentiated ways of seeing the self (I am kind, competent, stupid, know how to make friends, etc.). The extent to which experience or knowledge about the self will be consciously held or be unconscious–beyond clear perception, or not admitted to awareness–may also vary.

The nature of a person's self-concept, once developed, will importantly affect how the person sees and experiences the world, how the person relates to himself or herself (thinks and feels), and how a person acts. Epstein extensively reviews theories of the self. Several are phenomenological theories stressing the significance of a person's subjective experience, of his or her perception and construction of events.

Epstein conceives of the self-concept as a theory of one's self that each person holds. Like any other theory, self-theory has specific functions or roles, extremely important ones for the adaptive functioning of human beings. Epstein discusses these functions and examines the implications of his theory of the self for psychopathology, adjustment, and psychotherapy, and he shows how his theory can serve to integrate insight from other theories. He stresses the stability of the self-concept and the resulting consistency in behavior.

The Emotions (*James Averill,* Chapter 4). To varying degrees, ranging from barley perceptible to extremely intense, we experience affect, or emotion, most of the time. Our thoughts often have emotional consequences; they generate and/or are accompanied by affect. Our feelings, in turn, are likely to further influence what and how we think. Consider, for example, that even a seemingly trivial positive experience–receiving a free advertising sample in a suburban mall–affects subsequent thought or judgments (Isen et al., 1978). Presumably because it led to a momentary positive affect or mood, it resulted in people evaluating the quality of their car and television set significantly more positively, in comparison to people who did not receive such a gift. Seemingly, our current mood or emotion can affect our general optimism or pessimism. Our desires–the outcomes that we value and want to reach, or that we dislike and want to avoid—are maintained in part by the emotions that we experience on reaching them. Even the likelihood that people will pursue desired outcomes depends on feelings that accompany the work or activities involved in reaching those outcomes. Thus, self-regulation depends on accompanying thoughts and feelings (Masters & Mokros, 1974; Staub, 1979). The nature of the self-concept we hold is likely to strongly influence our emotional responses to ourselves and to situations that we face and have to deal with. This is especially clear with regard to one of the most important components of the self-concept, namely, self-esteem. The esteem or value that we place on ourselves is highly emotional in nature and generates strong feelings in us.

How do emotions arise? What determines whether people experience emotions, or the kind of emotions they experience? How do emotions affect behavior? What individual differences exist in the realm of emotional experience? Averill examines these and other questions. He describes past theories and research about emotions, and then develops an original conception of how emotions in general and different types of emotions in particular arise. He conceives of emotions not as passively experienced states, but as the result of active processes by the organism. (His theory suggests, in fact, more active processes by persons in generating emotions, and even greater interconnectedness between affect and thought, than implied by my own preceeding comments.) As part of his theory, Averill differentiates among impulsive emotions (e.g., grief), which become our second nature in the course of socialization; conflictive emotions such as romantic love and anger, which help resolve conflicting demands placed on individuals; and transcendental emotional stresses such as mystical experiences and anxiety, which involve a breakdown in cognitive structures. Averill explores different conceptions of individual differences in emotional reactivity and relevant research. The chapter raises challenging questions such as, To what extent do we use emotions as justifications for behavior that social rules or etiquette frowns on, but that we want to engage in?

Locus of Control and Coping with Life's Events (*Herbert Lefcourt,* Chapter 5). An extremely important aspect of the self-concept, which has received attention in its own right, is a person's belief about or feeling of his efficacy. The belief that one can control, shape, or influence events by one's actions, has profoundly important consequences. Such a belief can affect the quality of one's life and even survival, as Lefcourt's chapter indicates. A belief or feeling of helplessness, powerlessness, or inability to influence important events or aspects of one's life can generate strong negative emotions—anxiety or fear, hopelessness and depression—and can make it unlikely that a person will even attempt to control, shape, and influence events. Without a feeling of personal efficacy, if someone in authority treats you cruelly or unfairly, you may simply live with it, however miserably, even if the relationship could be changed. If you like someone and would like to develop a friendship with that person, your belief that you can successfully approach other people and initiate relationships, in contrast to a belief that you cannot do so, will affect the fate of this potential relationship.

While the belief that events in your life and in your environment depend not on you but on "fate," higher powers, or other people may frequently have negative consequences, its effects are a function of the exact belief that a person holds. For example, powers outside you can be seen as either malevolent or benevolent. Moreover, the belief in one's capacity to influence events, and/or a feeling that one usually needs to exert control in order to be safe or to gain benefits, can also have negative consequences. Being constantly on the alert would be stressful.

Lefcourt's chapter examines in depth the phenomena sketched here. He explores reactions to the possibility of control over particular events, or lack of control; personality differences in the belief that one can exercise control, and its emotional and behavioral correlates; and the development of personality differences in locus of control, and in related characteristics and motives. He extensively describes his own and others' research in these realms, and discusses related theories.

Social Behavior and Prosocial Behavior (*Ervin Staub,* Chapter 6). The earlier chapters examined basic characteristics of human beings, and individual differences in these characteristics which strongly affect how people function in the world. An important aspect of human functioning is social, interpersonal behavior. Social behavior has always been of primary interest to psychologists; Sullivan, as noted in an earlier section, even defined personality in terms of interpersonal behavior.

Chapter 6 examines an issue which is currently the subject of much attention and controversey—the meaning and extent of consistency in personality and in social behavior. A basic assumption of personality psychology has been that people are consistent; that is, that an individual will show similar characteristics across varying circumstances and on repeated occasions. After all, how can we talk about differences among individuals if people are different from moment to moment? How can we talk about personality characteristics if people continuously vary? Are people consistent; and if so, in what dimensions? In ways of perceiving, thinking, and feeling? To what extent would such consistencies gain expression in behavior? To what extent will people act in the same way on different occasions, and to what extent will they act differently, showing responsiveness and adaptability to their circumstances? Can we understand what determines how people behave on specific occasions? On the basis of our understanding, can we predict their behavior?

How people behave must depend on both their personality and the circumstances that surround them—on the interaction of the two. A primary characteristic of well-functioning human beings is the ability to respond to circumstances in an adaptive fashion. However, different people have different views of what is adaptive–what is socially appropriate and personally desirable for them–and the same person is likely to regard different behavior as adaptive under different circumstances.

What personality characteristics are important in affecting what people find appropriate and desirable to do on specific occasions? Personal motives seem profoundly important. For one person, doing well in school may be of prime importance; while another person wants to meet, be with, and develop close relationships with people; and a third thinks that nothing is more enjoyable and personally satisfying than sports. Competencies, perception of one's ability to exercise control, and other characteristics also seem of substantial importance in determining how people behave. The chapter examines the relationship between consistency and predictability in behavior. While focusing on behavior in one particular domain–positive behavior toward other people, kindness and helpfulness, with emphasis on reactions to others' physical and psychological distress–it presents a model of the determinants of social behavior and specifies the personality and situational influences that are important influences on such behavior. Research relevant to the model is reviewed, and ways of testing the model are discussed.

Stability of Personality, Change and Psychotherapy ***(Donald Meichenbaum,*** **Chapter 7).** In addition to the interest in consistency in personality, the extent to which characteristics of individuals, once formed, are stable over extended periods of time has also been of interest. What is the extent of stability? To what extent do people change, and on what dimensions of personality? People face changing circumstances in their lives as they move from childhood to adolescence and to adulthood with the changing demands of a career, of marriage, and of parenthood–and of changing cultural mores and societal conditions. They have to change if they are to adapt to their changing life circumstances in ways satisfactory to others and to themselves. Thus, stability and change must coexist. Meichenbaum examines the evidence for stability in personality, and the nature of stability. The same characteristics can gain different expression in behavior at different times; dependency in an adult must be expressed in different ways than in a child. While specific behavior may not be stable, basic needs or personal inclinations may remain.

Whatever stabilities exist, we can expect continuous learning, development, and change. Change becomes essential when a person's personality and life circumstances lead to adaptations that are unsatisfactory–when the person is unable to function effectively in the world, or in ways that others can tolerate, or is unhappy or dissatisfied with himself or herself. Under such circumstances, intervention that provides opportunities for learning and change becomes desirable. Having discussed stability and change, Meichenbaum discusses psychotherapeutic intervention. What kinds of changes will ideally result from such intervention? What brings about change, and by what principles do changes come about?

Meichenbaum extensively describes three factors involved in psychotherapeutic change: (1) the client's behavior and the reactions it elicits from the environment, (2) the client's internal dialogue, or what he says to himself before, during, and following his behavior, and (3) the client's cognitive structures, which give rise to the internal dialogue. Changes in these—for example, in the way the client talks to himself—are essential if therapy is to be effective. The means by which changes can be brought about are described. Meichenbaum demonstrates how change comes about, by discussing the treatment of problems with expressing anger. While change is brought about by different means in different types of psychotherapy, the processes of change that Meichenbaum presents seem to be processes through which change occurs in all therapies.

The Uses of Theorizing in Personality (*Salvatore Maddi,* Chapter 8). In this final chapter, Maddi presents a wide-ranging commentary on the field of personality psychology, with special emphasis on the significance of theorizing in the field. The chapter includes a critique of various theoretical approaches, and identifies certain communalities among them. It suggests that important progress in personality psychology might result from identifying the major issues that separate theories. It discusses issues of measurement, the nature of measurement operations, and the relationship between observation and theory. It touches on the controversy about the effectiveness of psychotherapy, and suggests that to provide a basis for evaluating the effectiveness of therapy, we must theorize about what constitutes the good life. Maddi stresses the importance of learning from the history of personality psychology in order to avoid unnecessary repetition of that history, and the importance of attending to and learning from other branches of psychology and other sciences, with examples of what might be learned.

An intriguing aspect of Maddi's chapter is that some of his views conflict with some of the implicit or explicit views expressed in other chapters. Thus, the reader has the opportunity to weigh somewhat conflicting views. For example, Maddi considers the "rediscovery" of the interactionist approach to personality as the result of our having ignored history, since he feels that personality psychology has included interactionist views for several decades. In contrast, I consider this rediscovery of genuine significance, since it gave impetus to important empirical work and theorizing (see Chapter 6). The work of psychologists who in varied ways contributed to the recent interest in interactionist approaches (Bowers, 1973; Endler & Magnusson, 1976; Jones & Nisbett, 1971; Mischel, 1968, 1973; and others) seems correspondingly important.

Some Final Comments

While there are differences among the views of some of the writers, mainly on specific issues, more important are a number of communalities in the approach of most of the contributors to this book. First, there is the assumption that human beings are active organisms, actively seeking interaction with the world around them. The assumption of active involvement and self-guidance applies even to the generation of our emotions (Averill's chapter). Further, the importance of consciousness and cognition–the manner in which we perceive, see, and interpret events–is emphasized by most of these writers. However, also recognized are the existence of unconscious processes, the importance of attending to and measuring behavior, the existence of varied levels at which human beings function, and their interrelatedness. Although the chapters differ in how broad or narrow are the aspects of functioning which are considered, implicit in all of them is an awareness of the wholeness of the human being.

REFERENCES

Allport, G. W. *Personality: A psychological interpretation.* New York: Holt, Rinehart & Winston, 1937.

____. *Pattern and growth in personality.* New York: Holt, Rinehart, & Winston, 1961.

Bandura, A. *Social learning theory.* Englewood Cliffs, N.J.: Prentice-Hall, 1977.

____. **Ross, D., & Ross, S. A.** Transmission of aggression through imitation of aggressive models. *Journal of Abnormal Social Psychology,* 1961, *63,* 575-582.

____. Imitation of film-mediated aggressive models. *Journal of Abnormal Social Psychology,* 1963, *66,* 3-11.

Baumrind, D. *Early socialization and the discipline controversy.* Morristown, N.J.: General Learning Press, 1975.

Bowers, K. S. Situationism in psychology. An analysis and a critique. *Psychological Review,* 1973, *80,* 307-336.

Bronfenbrenner, U. Toward an experimental ecology of human development. *American Psychologist,* 1977, *32,* 513-531.

Byrne, D. *An introduction to personality.* Englewood Cliffs, N.J.: Prentice-Hall, 1974.

Carlson, R. Where is the person in personality research? *Psychological Bulletin,* 1971, *75,* 203-219.

Chadwick-Jones, J. K. *Social exchange theory: Its structure and influence in social psychology.* New York: Academic Press, 1976.

Coopersmith, S. *Antecedents of self-esteem.* San Francisco, Calif.: Fremont & Company, 1967.

Dion, K. K. Physical attractiveness and evaluation of children's transgressions. *Journal of Personality & Social Psychology,* 1972, *24,* 207-213.

Endler, N. S., & Magnusson, D. Toward an interactional psychology of personality. *Psychological Bulletin,* 1976, *83,* 956-974.

Escalona, S. K. *The roots of individuality.* Chicago: Aldine, 1968.

Ferguson, L. R. *Personality development.* Belmont, Calif.: Brooks/Cole Publishing Company, 1970.

Frank, J. *Persuasion and healing.* New York: Shocken Books, 1974.

Freedman, D. G. Hereditary control of early social behavior. In B. M. Foss (Ed.), *Determinants of infant behavior, III.* New York: Wiley, 1965.

Freud, S. (1915a) Instincts and their vicissitudes. In James Strachey (Ed.), *Standard edition of the complete psychological works of Sigmund Freud,* Vol. XIV. London: Hogarth Press, 1957.

Fromm, E. *Escape from freedom.* New York: Holt, Rinehart & Winston, 1941.

Guilford, J. P. *Personality.* New York: McGraw-Hill, 1959.

Hartup, W. W. Peer interaction and social organization. In P. H. Mussen (Ed.), *Carmichael's manual of child psychology.* New York: Wiley, 1970.

Hobbes, T. *Leviathan.* New York: The Bobbs-Merrill Company, 1851.

Homans, G. C. *Social behavior: Its elementary form.* New York: Harcourt, Brace & World, 1961.

Hornstein, H. A. *Cruelty and kindness. A new look at aggression and altruism.* Englewood Cliffs, N.J.: Prentice-Hall, Inc., 1976.

Isen, A. M., Shalker, T. E., Clark, M., & Karp, L. Affect, accessibility of material in memory, and behavior: A cognitive loop? *Journal of Personality and Social Psychology,* 1978, *36,* 1-13.

Jones, E. E., & Nisbett, R. E. *The actor and the observer: Divergent perceptions of the causes of behavior.* New York: General Learning Press, 1971.

Kelly, G. A. *The psychology of personal constructs.* Vols. 1 & 2. New York: Norton, 1955.

Korner, A. F. Individual differences at birth: Implications for early experience and later development. *American Journal of Orthopsychiatry,* 1971, *41.*

Lewin, K. *Resolving social conflicts.* New York: Harper, 1948.

Liebert, R. M., & Spiegler, M. D. *Personality: Strategies & issues* (3rd ed.). Homewood, IL: The Dorsey Press, 1978.

Lindzey, G. Morphology and behavior. In G. Lindzey & C. S. Hall (Eds.), *Theories of personality: Primary sources and research.* New York: John Wiley & Sons, 1965.

London, P. The rescuers: Motivational hypotheses about Christians who saved Jews from the Nazis. In J. Macaulay & L. Berkowitz (Eds.), *Altruism and helping behavior.* New York: Academic Press, 1970.

Maslow, A. H. Some basic propositions of a growth and self-actualization psychology. In G. Lindzey & C. S. Hall (Eds.), *Theories of personality: Primary sources and research.* New York: John Wiley & Sons, 1965. (Originally published in Perceiving, Behaving, Becoming: A New Focus for Education.

1962 Yearbook of Association for Supervision and Curriculum Development, Washington, D.C.).

Masters, J. C., & Mokros, J. R. Self-reinforcement processes in children. In *Advances in child development and behavior,* Vol. 9. New York: Academic Press, 1974.

McClelland, D. C. *Personality.* New York: Holt, Rinehart & Winston, 1951.

Mischel, W. *Personality and assessment.* New York: Wiley, 1968.

____. Towards a cognitive social learning reconceptualization of personality. *Psychological Review,* 1973, *80,* 252-283.

____. *Introduction to personality* (2nd ed.). New York: Holt, Rinehart & Winston, 1976.

____. On the future of personality measurement. *American Psychologist,* 1977, *32,* 246-254.

Monte, C. F. *Beneath the mask: An introduction to theories of personality.* New York: Praeger, 1977.

Rogers, C. R. A theory of therapy, personality, and interpersonal relationships, as developed in the client-centered framework. In S. Koch (Ed.), *Psychology: A study of a science,* Vol. 3. New York: McGraw-Hill, 1959.

Staub, E. Instigation to goodness: the role of social norms and interpersonal influence. *Journal of Social Issues,* 1972, *28,* 131-151.

____. *Positive social behavior and morality, Vol. 1: Personal and social influences.* New York: Academic Press, 1978.

____. *Positive social behavior and morality, Vol. 2: Socialization and development.* New York: Academic Press, 1979.

Sullivan, H. S. *The interpersonal theory of psychiatry.* New York: Norton, 1953.

Thomas, A., Chess, S., Birch, H. G., Hertzig, M. E., & Korn, S. *Behavioral individuality in early childhood.* New York: New York University Press, 1963.

Wiggins, J. S., Renner, K. E., Clore, G. L., & Rose, R. J. *The psychology of personality.* Massachusetts: Addison-Wesley Publishing Company, 1971.

EDWARD L. DECI

Intrinsic Motivation and Personality

2

One of the most extraordinary aspects of human beings is their capacity to be aware of what they need and to find ways of satisfying those needs. The study of human motivation is the study of peoples' needs and the way they behave to satisfy them.

Traditionally, motivation theory has viewed people mechanistically, assuming that they are passive agents of various internal and external forces. Environmental forces were said to attain their potence because of their relationship to people's internal drives—hunger, sex, the avoidance of pain, and so on. These traditional approaches have proved inadequate. People are not passive. They are, by their very nature, active organisms who operate on their surroundings to achieve desired outcomes. Thus, an organismic approach to motivation, one which views people as active beings, seems to hold much greater potential for providing an understanding of the intricacies and complexities of human behavior. An organismic view of motivation focuses on internal processes in its explication of human behavior. Cognitive and affective processes (i.e., thoughts and feelings) are recognized as integrally related to motivation, and external stimuli are studied in terms of their meaning for the people who encounter them.

An organismic theory has two central elements which differ from the earlier passive-mechanistic theories. The first is that it assumes that people have the capacity to decide what to do. These decisions result from people's interpreting and processing information which is available to them from the environment, from their memory, and from their internal organs and tissues. In deciding what to do, people are attempting to satisfy their various needs: they might decide to eat to satisfy their hunger; or to do what their supervisor requests to satisfy their need for approval from significant others; or to make love to satisfy their sexual need. The second important element to an organismic view is that it

Preparation of this chapter was facilitated by research grant MH 28600-01 from the National Institute of Mental Health to the author.

assumes that people engage in many behaviors in order to feel competent and self-determining; to feel like causal agents who are effective in their interactions with the environment. This second point may seem obvious; yet traditional theories of motivation have recognized only the physiological drives (hunger, sex, etc.) as motivators of behavior. It is now clear that, in addition to being motivated by drives, people are intrinsically motivated to grow, to do what interests them. Intrinsic motivation is central to the development of personality and cognitive structures.

This chapter is about intrinsic motivation and about the ways in which it relates to other motives, to personality, and to development. The earlier parts of the chapter will focus more on trends in motivation theory, whereas the latter part relates more directly to personality and development.

EVOLUTION OF MOTIVATION THEORY

Until recently, the two dominant thrusts in motivation theory were Hullian drive theory (Hull, 1943) and Freudian instinct theory (Rapaport, 1960). Both theories were mechanistic in that behavior was said to be caused by associations that existed between stimuli and responses. People were essentially viewed as machines being pushed around by the associations which were activated by stimuli. In drive theory, the stimuli are generally external to the organism—things like the smell of food or the sight of a particular object—whereas in instinct theory, the stimuli are internal to the organism—things like unconscious sexual urges. Both theories considered only physiological drives to be the basis of motivation; Freud considered sex and aggression to be most important, while Hull focused on hunger, thirst, and pain.

The central commonalities of the theories are two: first, they view people mechanistically, and second, they focus only on drives as motivators. There are, of course, enormous differences between the theories, some of which will be discussed below; however, I am pointing to these two similarities because the newer approaches to motivation stand in sharp contrast to Freudian and Hullian theories on these two dimensions.

Freudian Theory

Psychoanalytic theory as developed by Freud (e.g., 1949) was at once a theory of personality and personality development, a theory of motivation, a theory of psychopathology, and an approach to psychotherapy. As such, it is extraordinarily complex and comprehensive. In this chapter I shall be concerned only with the aspects related to motivation and to personality development, and even these will be treated very cursorily. Here I shall deal with motivational aspect of the theory; later I shall discuss personality development.

In Freud's system, motives are internal forces of two types: instinctual drives (or instincts), and derivatives of instinctual drives. Thus, instincts represent the basis of all motivation. Instincts are psychical representations of bodily needs which provide energy and place demands upon the organism to work toward discharge of that energy. Instincts are forces which give direction to behavior and press to be discharged through behaving in relation to appropriate objects or persons.

There are two classes of instincts: the death instincts and the life instincts. The most notable of the death instincts is aggression, which provides the energy for a considerable amount of behavior–fighting, verbally aggressing, self-flagellation, and so on. The life instincts relate to survival both of the person and the species. The life instinct which is most central to Freud's theory is the sexual instinct, the energy of which is called *libido.* As we will see later, libidinal forces are centrally important in Freud's theory of personality development.

The aim of instinctual energy is release–in other words, the satisfaction of the bodily need out of which the instinct emerged. Instinctual energy causes people to develop attachments to or appetites for objects or people through which the energy may be discharged. These attachments are called *cathexes.* People behave toward cathected objects unless some inner force, termed *anti-cathexis,* prevents them from doing so.

The determinants of cathexis are a complex interaction of innate characteristics of the person, the stage of development of the person, and the interaction of the person with the environment. For example, as children progress through the various stages of psychosexual development (to be discussed later), the cathexes which they form depend on the stage of development they are at, the objects available in the environment, the strength of their instincts at that time, and so on.

The notions of instinctual drives and cathexes represent the heart of Freud's theory of motivation. A motive is an internal force which seeks gratification through a cathected object. For example, the sexual instinct may seek gratification through sexual intercourse, masturbation, or a variety of other means. The chosen means of gratification will depend on what alternatives are available at that time, and upon which alternative seems most attractive. Which alternative is most attractive depends on the development of cathexes in one's early experience. Motives have a number of limiting characteristics (Rapaport, 1960). They are peremptory; that is, there is a mandatory quality to them, in that they will persist until satisfied. Further, behavior is flexible toward the cathected object; the organism will use a variety of means to reach the desired object. In the event that the cathected object is unreachable (either for some reason out of the control of the person or because of an anti-cathexis within the person), the motive will be displaced onto some substitute object. These three characteristics–called peremptoriness, selectiveness, and displaceability–operate mechanistically. The inner stimulation, which is associated with certain behaviors, is absolutely unyielding in its press for discharge, and becomes displaced automatically when forced by the situation to do so.

The fourth characteristic of motives, according to psychoanalytic theory, is that they are cyclical in nature. The strength of the motive rises until there is a consummatory response, and then the strength decreases markedly, ready again to begin its climb. This is the aspect of the theory which ties all motives to the primary drives.

Actually, Freudian theory does posit the psychic process of *sublimation,* which explains behaviors that "appear" to be non-drive-based. Through sublimation, libidinal energy is transformed to create cathexes for activities such as reading and writing. Nonetheless, although the theory pays some attention to such behaviors, it does so in a derivative fashion, thereby failing to accord this aspect of motivation appropriate centrality.

We have briefly considered the psychoanalytic approach to motivation, noting two significant aspects: its mechanistic nature and its insistence on drives as the only basis of motivated behavior. We turn now to a similarly brief look at Hullian theory.

Hullian Theory

Whereas psychoanalytic instinct theory developed out of Freud's work with patients in his psychiatric consultation office, drive theory developed out of Hull's work with rats in his experimental laboratory. Its evolution was intertwined with the evolution of a theory of learning. Hull asserted that behavior is caused by internal associative links which develop between stimuli and responses. He was concerned both with how these associations develop (a question of learning) and how these associations are activated at any given time (a question of motivation). The concepts of drive and drive-reduction lie at the heart of the answers to both these questions. Drives are motivational forces which are representations of physiological needs such as hunger. Hull asserted that organisms seek to maintain a balance or equilibrium in their physiological needs. When a disequilibrium occurs, a drive results, the aim of which is to restore the balance.

Associative links between stimuli and responses develop when a response is reinforced in the presence of a stimulus. These stimuli can be one of three kinds: internal drive stimuli, external stimuli, or proprioceptive stimuli in the musculature of the organism. *Reinforcement,* which is a process of strengthening associations, occurs when a drive is reduced (i.e., when a tissue balance is restored). Thus, we see that the essence of the answer to the learning question is that learning is the strengthening of bonds between stimuli and responses which occurs when a response is reinforced (i.e., when it leads to the restoration of a tissue balance).

Hull proposed that when a disequilibrium exists, it creates what is called a drive stimulus, which instigates behaviors that have been bonded to that stimulus through prior reinforcement. Presumably, of course, those behaviors will return the organism to a state of equilibrium, since that return is what previously created or strengthened the bonding. Hull's theory is a homeostatic one, which operates in a mechanistic fashion in accord with past experiences that have removed tissue deficits. The core of the answer to the motivational question is that drives are forces which cause the organism to behave in certain ways because those behaviors had become linked to the corresponding stimuli by reinforcement processes. It is clear, of course, even from this brief discussion, that Hull's theory, like Freud's, is both mechanistic and based only in biological drives. As noted, these two characteristics are the central commonalities between the two theories, and they are the characteristics which have been refuted by the newer theories.

Like Freudian theory, Hullian theory also has a mechanism to explain behaviors which appear to be non-drive-based. This mechanism is secondary reinforcement. If a stimulus is present when a drive is reduced, that stimulus will take on secondary reinforcing properties as a result of this pairing with primary reinforcement. Thus, for example, if exploration is paired with hunger reduction, exploration will become reinforcing.

The relegation of these motivational processes to a secondary status seems inadequate to me. Berlyne (1966), in criticizing the secondary reinforcement account, pointed out that avid exploration occurs so soon after birth that it is difficult to image how it could be due to secondary reinforcement. Further, according to Hullian theory, secondary reinforcers must occasionally be re-paired with primary reinforcers in order to maintain their secondary reinforcing properties; however, experiments (Butler, 1953) have shown that activities such as exploration continue to be reinforcing even when they are not paired with the so-called primary reinforcers.

The Inadequacy of Drive Theories

Just as the two theories of motivation evolved in wholly different settings—the consultation room versus the experimental laboratory—they have been criticized, found inadequate, and elaborated in both these realms. Students of Freud have realized that a theory of motivation based in the instincts for sex and aggression is an inappropriately limited conceptualization and one which, while it seems to contain considerable truth, is inadequate as a means of understanding motivation and development. These "neo-Freudians" were more concerned with personality and development than with motivation theory, yet one can infer from their discussions of personality and development that Freud's motivation theory was also judged to be incomplete.

Many of the neo-Freudians reinterpreted psychoanalytic theory in interpersonal terms (e.g., Horney, 1939; Sullivan, 1953). Rather than concentrating on libidinal energy as it develops and interacts with the surroundings, the neo-

Freudians talk more about the stages of development and sources of growth in terms of the interpersonal interactions between child and parents. Parents, whose job it is to socialize the child (i.e., to establish appropriate anti-cathexes) will necessarily conflict with what the child wants (i.e., the child's unbridled desires for satisfaction of the instinctual drives). Whereas Freud theorized about these conflicts as they relate to the libidinal drive, the neo-Freudians abandoned the instinctual focus and theorized more broadly about parent-child interactions. The important point for our purposes is that they were implying that a narrow, drive-based model of motivation represents only part of the picture of human motivation.

Other students of psychoanalytic theory have deviated from orthodoxy more drastically than those who employ the interpersonal model. Notable among this latter group are Reich (1960) and Perls (1947, 1973). Perls began deviating in a fairly modest way by emphasizing the hunger instinct, both as an important motivator and as an influence in personality development. Later, he challenged the theory more fully by rejecting the mechanistic assumptions of psychoanalytic theory. Whereas Freud asserted that one's personality is largely determined during the first six years and can be modified only through the analytic procedure of reliving those early phases of psychosexual development, Perls asserted that one need only concentrate on the present if one wishes to bring about meaningful growth and change. Thus, although he did not really discuss motivation theory, Perls was abandoning both the deterministic nature of Freud's theory and its focus on the instinctual drives of sex and aggression as the basis of all motivation.

Just as Freudian theory evolved from Freud's interactions with patients rather than from experimental data, the critics of his theory have based their points of view largely on experience with patients or clients. Therefore, these theories have been accepted or rejected largely on the basis of whether they fit with people's experience of themselves and their patients or clients and whether they meet standards such as elegance, comprehensiveness, and parsimony.

In the experimental laboratories, the pillars of Hull's drive-based motivation theory were also being shaken. Many investigators were beginning to find that animals would explore avidly in a way which seemed not to be related to any of the recognized drives. These findings were initially handled by postulating a host of new drives: for exploration (Montgomery, 1954), to avoid boredom (Myers & Miller, 1954), for manipulation (Harlow, 1953), for sensory stimulation (Isaac, 1962), for visual exploration (Butler, 1953), and so forth. This approach to dealing with the behaviors which were not readily explainable with drive theory was quite inadequate. First, the list of so-called drives seemed to be expanding, while understanding of the phenomena was at a standstill; and further, these so-called drives did not fit the definition of drives. To accept these as drives would have required a new conceptualization of drive. The definition of drives stated that they (a) exist in tissue needs, (b) demand consummatory responses, and

(c) strengthen responses through drive-reduction. For example, the basis of hunger (a) is in tissue factors such as one's blood sugar level, (b) is a strong and persistent force until satisfied, and (c) strengthens behaviors which lead to its satisfaction. These three characteristics do not seem to apply to something called an "exploratory drive," since there is no evidence of its being based in non-nervous-system tissues, and it does not operate in the cyclical fashion characteristic of the primary drive. Other attempts to deal with the exploratory and manipulatory phenomena using drive theory asserted that they were instances of secondary reinforcement or anxiety reduction; yet these attempts also proved unsatisfactory. As we saw earlier in the chapter, the secondary-reinforcement explanation was inadequate because the phenomena appear so soon after birth and because they do not require pairing with primary reinforcers. As for the anxiety-reduction explanation, when there is an uncertain and frightening situation ahead, one would predict, using a theory which focuses on the need to reduce anxiety, that people or animals would withdraw from the frightening stimulus; yet, they tend to explore rather than retreat, thereby disconfirming the anxiety prediction (White, 1959).

To summarize, we have seen that the drive theories of Freud and Hull were found inadequate when scrutinized closely by scholars and practitioners. Their contributions have been enormous; but we have come to the point where the form of the theories seems to impair rather than facilitate further development of motivation theory. I shall now consider the beginnings and elaboration of the two significant elements in motivation theory which have moved us toward a more meaningful organismic understanding of human motivation.

Choice and Cognition

During the reign of drive theories as the dominant force in motivation, personality, and learning, a number of other theorists were doing research which began to establish the study of cognition as a central consideration for psychology. We shall be concerned primarily with its impact on motivation.

As Hull was structuring his theory, Tolman (1932), another prominent learning theorist, was criticizing the associationistic nature of Hull's theory and insisting that cognitions–or thought processes–play a significant role in the determination of behavior. Learning was not a mechanistic process of cementing stimuli to responses, but rather a process of elaborating cognitive structures. Motivation was not an automatic process of initiating behaviors bonded to stimuli, but rather a process of setting goals to satisfy what Tolman called drive-stimulations. These are internal conditions which (1) can be distinguished among by the organism, (2) energize behavior and (3) have value-giving properties (Tolman, 1959). The value-giving properties are the basis for goal selection which precedes the subsequent behavior.

Tolman's work represented an important first step in the break from mechanistic drive theories; yet he was not so much presenting a theory of motivation as of learning, and he was still rather mechanistic in his approach. This is seen most clearly in the way that goal selection is said to transpire. Tolman proposed that drive stimulations have value-giving properties which lend positive or negative value to "terminal stimuli" or potential goals. This all seems to operate without the help of information processing; it seems to be automatic and machine-like. As such, it does not allow enough room for consideration of the person as an active organism. A hunger drive-stimulation might well give positive value to a dish of apple pie ã la mode; yet, in spite of one's love for the food, one sometimes chooses not to eat it, perhaps because of a diet or a sugar disorder. The point is that goal selection and subsequent behaviors may depend on a variety of types of information other than just the value giving properties of drive stimulations. So, Tolman took a step toward the introduction of a cognitive, non-mechanistic orientation to motivation theory. Yet further development was necessary.

Lewin (1936, 1938, 1951a), working with social and developmental problems in the mode of Gestalt psychology, made important strides in the theory of motivation. Lewin emphasized that an understanding of psychological phenomena requires that the investigator be cognizant of the person's perceptions or phenomenology. In other words, people do not respond to objective external stimuli; they respond to stimuli *as they perceive them.* This is an extraordinarily important point, and one which is still not recognized by some psychologists. Stimuli have different meanings to different people, and people behave in accordance with the meaning which the stimuli hold for them. Lewin, like Tolman, proposed that the motivation process has an energy source–which he referred to as tensions. These tensions lead to the establishment of goals through the process of giving valence to goal objects. In turn, people engage in behaviors which lead to the valued goals and reduce the tension.

Lewin (1951b) addressed the question of will, and asserted that when people *will,* it creates a tension in them which pushes to be discharged just as other tensions do.

Based on this early work of Tolman and Lewin, a number of investigators have worked toward the elaboration and specification of this approach to the study of human motivation (Atkinson, 1964; Atkinson & Raynor, 1974; Irwin, 1971; Peak, 1955; Vroom, 1964). Later in this chapter I shall present an organismic view of motivation which has evolved in part out of the work of these various researchers.

Intrinsic Motivation

A most interesting and important phenomenon which emerged from the animal learning studies was that rats and monkeys (and later, people) were recognized as avid explorers and manipulators. Dashiell (1925) and Nissen (1930) reported that the rats in their studies were active explorers, and that they would even endure the pain of crossing an electrified grid in order to have the opportunity to explore novel spaces. Berlyne (1950), utilizing rats, and Welker (1956), utilizing chimpanzees, found that the animals persistently explored and manipulated novel stimuli, and that once they had fully explored the objects, they appeared to lose interest in them. In a similar vein, Harlow (1953) reported that monkeys seemed to enjoy puzzle solving.

These experimental findings posed a problem for drive theories. Behaviors which were clearly purposeful, persistent, and non-random seemed to have no understandable relationship to the known drives; and various attempts to account for these behaviors using drive theory proved inadequate.

Following the period of drive-naming as a strategy for dealing with these behaviors, there have been three general approaches to explaining the phenomena. The first (Hebb, 1955; Leuba, 1955) focused at the level of physiological functioning, positing that organisms need an optimal level of physiological arousal in the reticular formation of the central nervous system, and that behaviors such as exploration and manipulation provided this stimulation. Since our concern here is with psychological rather than physiological functioning, I shall concentrate on the other two approaches.

The second approach is also a theory involving an optimal level. Here, the hypothesis is that organisms need an optimal level of psychological incongruity (Dember & Earl, 1957; Hunt, 1965). Incongruity refers to a discrepancy between some internal standard or mental structure and a stimulus in the present environment. When you go to a new city, there is considerable incongruity; most of the stimuli are new and uncertain. Hunt has proposed that people need the stimulation caused by an optimal level of this incongruity, and that they function most effectively when they are interacting with situations which provide this optimal incongruity.

I agree with the assertion that organisms seek out situations which provide optimal stimulation; however, I believe that seeking optimal incongruity is part of an ongoing process of seeking incongruity and then reducing the incongruity. The optimal incongruity is not an end, but rather is part of a life process. The reduction of the incongruity which represents the second half of the ongoing process is akin to what Festinger (1957) has called cognitive dissonance reduction. People, he said, need to reduce discrepancies between various related thoughts. Indeed they do; however, the fascinating thing about it is that when they do not have discrepancies to reduce, they seek them out and then set about reducing those new-found discrepancies.

The third general approach to explaining exploratory and manipulatory phenomena was introduced by White (1959), who suggested that people have a basic need to utilize their potentials competently and to be effective in dealing with their environments. He suggested the term *effectance motivation* as a name for the type of motivation which energizes exploration, manipulation, and other activities which are intended to produce an effect on the environment. This type of motivation is generally referred to as *intrinsic motivation,* and seems to be an ongoing source of energy to motivate behaviors when one of the homeostatic drives is not demanding the person's attention.

Intrinsic motivation—which, unlike the traditional drives, seems to have no appreciable basis in the non-nervous-system tissues of the organism—is now generally seen to be an important aspect of motivation. DeCharms (1968), holding a view similar to White's, stated that people's primary motivational propensity is to be the causal agent in their interactions with the environment; they strive to be "origins" of behavior rather than "pawns" to impinging forces.

For drive-based behaviors, rewards are mediated externally; they are things like food or praise. Yet with effectance motivation the reward is internal to the person. White has stated that the rewards for intrinsically motivated behaviors are the feelings of efficacy which result from one's dealing competently with one's surroundings. For deCharms, the reward is said to be the feelings of personal causation.

More recently I suggested that intrinsically motivated behaviors are based in people's need to be competent and self-determining (Deci, 1975). This position is in agreement with both White and deCharms, and the terminology emphasizes the two important and inextricable aspects to this form of motivation. People strive to be competent and effective in dealing with their environments, and an essential ingredient to this is that they be personally causative—that they be willful or self-determining. One might become proficient at playing a tune on the piano when "forced" by external constraints to do so; yet this has little to do with intrinsic motivation. One is intrinsically motivated when the cause of the behavior is one's desire for efficacy. When people are intrinsically motivated, there is likely to be a deeper involvement and fascination with the activity; the activity seems to beckon and absorb them.

At first glance, this approach to intrinsic motivation may simply seem like one more attempt at the type of drive-naming to which I previously objected. It is in fact a naming of a motivational force, though it differs from drive naming in several key respects. First, the definition of drive involves a tissue imbalance as the source of the motivation; intrinsic motivation does not. Second, the named drives tend to be narrow in scope and are therefore relevant for a small class of behaviors; the idea of an intrinsic motive for competence and self-determination is much broader in scope and provides the basis for the development of a more comprehensive theory of intrinsically motivated behavior. Finally, the concept of drive has existed in a tradition that views the human being as a passive agent to mechanistic forces; intrinsic motivation emphasizes the opposite.

People's need to be competent and self-determining leads them to an active engagement with the environment in which they *seek out and attempt to conquer challenges which are optimal for their abilities.* People feel competent and self-determining when they have met these challenges, many of which require considerable ingenuity and resourcefulness. Here we can see the relationship between the competence and self-determination approach on the one hand and the optimal incongruity approach on the other. Incongruities represent challenges. Thus, my assertion that people seek and conquer challenges can be thought of in terms of seeking out and reducing incongruities.

An interesting point about the conceptualization of intrinsic motivation as being based in the need for competence and self-determination is that it implies that people have choice about how to behave; otherwise, they could never satisfy their need for competence and self-determination. Thus, acceptance of intrinsic motivation requires the other major change which has evolved in motivation theory, namely that people have the capacity to choose what behaviors to engage in. *The need for competence and self-determination leads people to be active in their behaving rather than being passively acted upon.*

AN ORGANISMIC VIEW OF MOTIVATION

A theory of motivation must do a number of things. It must describe how behavior is initiated, energized, directed, and terminated. I think that the key to this resides in the concept of needs. To function effectively, people must satisfy their needs—for food, for love, for status, and so on. Some are more urgent and critical than others; some are innate while others are learned; some are basic to the organism while others evolve as substitute needs when more basic needs cannot be satisfied. Still, whatever the need, people direct their behaviors in an attempt to satisfy these needs. A complete theory of motivation will, I think, always end up by isolating needs and understanding where the needs have come from. The two prevailing theories of motivation have been based in needs, their problem being that their conceptualization of needs was narrowly restricted to drives. Tolman and Lewin also dealt with the concept of needs, referring to them as drive stimulations and tensions.

Having said that a theory of motivation must deal with needs, let me point out that needs are aspects of the human organism which we infer because it is useful in integrating our observations. These inferences can in part be verified through biological and chemical investigations, though their primary verification is their utility in accounting for and predicting behavior.

A theory of motivation must also deal with human emotion. Emotions are integrally related to the motivational process. People behave out of anger, love, excitement, and aesthetic pleasure. Further, a theory of motivation must deal with the fact that people have thoughts and make decisions which lead them to behave in certain ways.

Much of the work in the area of motivation has concentrated on one or another aspect of motivation. Maslow (1943) focused on needs; Vroom (1964) on decision making; Locke (1968) on the relation between goals and performance; Brehm (1962) on the motivating properties of cognitive dissonance. It is becoming increasingly necessary to conceptualize the motivational process in a more complete way and in a way which is meaningful in relation to these mini-theories.

The heart of what I propose as an organismic theory of motivation is that people act in the service of their needs, and that this is done in accord with their interpretation of the information available to them. Mandler (1975) asserted that humans have a cognitive-interpretive system which organizes information into units and gives meaning to those units, based on the person's individual experience. I agree with this point of view and suggest that the cognitive-interpretive system working in the service of human needs provides the foundation for my understanding of human motivation.

DeCharms (1976) has made a similar point. He stated that personal experience and interpretation mediate between antecedent events and consequent behaviors. Personal experience is central to interpreting incoming information, and it often leads different people to perceive stimuli very differently. It attaches meaning to the perceptions in terms of what satisfaction is obtainable for the person. And it influences the selection of behavior since different people have learned different ways of achieving desired outcomes.

The importance of this personal experience and interpretation cannot be overemphasized in our discussion of motivation. Lewin called attention to this by claiming that a person's "life space" or internal representational space is the appropriate reference point for the analysis of behavior. Many psychologists have, however, failed to give the concept of "personal experience and interpretation" its just consideration.

I shall now elaborate my theoretical framework of motivation.

Inputs

As complex information processors, humans receive information from three sources. Some comes from the external environment and is received through the senses. Other inputs come from within the human organism and are similarly detected by sensory apparatus and transmitted to the central nervous system. This category of inputs includes things like the detection of adrenalin in the body or the detection of changes in muscle tonicity. The third source of inputs is one's memory. Past experiences influence people and remain a part of them by being stored in memory. Inputs may come from memory when stimulated by a person, object, or event, or they may come into awareness without an external stimulus—which happens, for instance, in daydreaming.

These informational inputs are processed and interpreted so they have meaning to people in terms of their own cognitive structures. Stimuli may be interpreted differently by different people because people have different cognitive structures which they utilize in giving meaning to informational inputs. Cognitive structures are internal representations of information. To say that someone knows something is to say that the something exists as part of the person's cognitive structure. Thus, the process of learning is a process of elaborating one's cognitive structures (Piaget, 1952). As people encounter information, they will be partially *assimilating* the information (i.e., modifying the information to fit their structure) and partially *accommodating to* the information (i.e., adjusting their cognitive structure to reflect the new information). These processes of accommodating and assimilating are brought to each new situation along with a person's existing cognitive structures, and they are the basis of the person's unique interpretation of a situation.

From a motivational perspective, people's memory and physiology represent what are generally referred to as needs. Hunger exists in people's memory and physiology; so does the need for being competent and self-determining. I shall therefore refer to the combination of memory and physiology as one's *motive structure.* All needs exist here, and provide information to the central nervous system when an imbalance occurs in the tissues, when an external stimulus triggers a memory, or when for some other reason they enter awareness.

Motives

The informational inputs are assembled in such a way that people become aware of some potential satisfaction which is available to them; in other words, people become aware of what they need at that time. These awarenesses are *motives;* they are transitory, cognitive representations of some future state which would be satisfying for the person, given the person's current state. Seeing an ice-cream cone might lead to the establishment of a motive which could be satisfied by eating ice cream, but this will depend on the state of one's organism at that moment. One who has just finished a huge meal is less likely to have that motive than one who has not eaten for days. Thus motives–these transitory awarenesses–come into existence from an interplay of (1) environmental stimulation; (2) one's motive structure, and (3) one's organismic state at that moment (i.e., satiation, level of arousal, etc.).

Intrinsic motivation, the need for being competent and self-determining, is an ongoing motivation which is ever present as an awareness of potential satisfaction, in the absence of more salient awarenesses. The aim of an intrinsic motive is the feeling of competence and self-determination. Thus, intrinsically motivated behaviors begin when stimulus inputs lead to the awareness of potential satisfaction from undertaking some optimal challenge, and they terminate either when the person achieves the feeling of competence and self-determination or when for some reason the sequence is interrupted.

Traditionally, behavior was said to be motived by drives. Within the present organismic theory, drive-motivated behavior begins when informational inputs lead to an awareness of potential satisfaction–getting warmer, ingesting food, relieving pain, and so forth. When the awareness occurs (i.e., when the motive emerges), it provides the energy for behavior, and it will persist until the satisfaction has been achieved or until something more urgent interrupts. Finally, emotions also serve to motivate behavior (Young, 1961). Emotions, like needs, are based in one's physiology and memory. When one becomes aware of an emotion, it becomes a motive, with the aim being to achieve a more positive (or less negative) state. Traditionally, this has been referred to as hedonism, and has been an important element in various theories of motivation (McClelland, Atkinson, Clark, & Lowell, 1953; Young, 1961). Drive theories have ignored the importance of emotions, while affective-arousal theories have claimed that it is the basis of all motivation. The two, drives and emotions, must both be included in a theory of motivation, along with intrinsic motivation, if we are to achieve a fuller understanding of human motivation.

In outlining this framework for the study of motivation, I have implied that *all* behavior is motivated in this conscious, non-mechanistic way. In fact, people do sometimes behave mechanistically. You may have heard people say, "I had to do it; I felt like I had no control of the situation," or "I did it without even realizing it." I shall not, however, deal with those mechanistic aspects of behavior in this chapter, since my aim here is to elaborate the organismic aspect of functioning. Anyone interested in interplay of organismic and mechanistic functioning is referred to my recent discussion of the matter (Deci, 1978).

An important characteristic of information-processing approaches to behavior is that they utilize feedback loops as a mechanism to govern behavior (Miller, Galanter, & Pribram, 1960). A feedback loop is a process in which information about one's current state is continually compared with one's desired state as a way of keeping one on track. Thus, a feedback loop begins with some internal standard of comparison—which might, for example, be a physiological condition such as an optimal blood sugar level, or a thought such as what a finished painting should look like, or a pleasant feeling of being efficacious. People aim to achieve the standard, so they continually compare where they are to where they want to be. If there is incongruence, they continue to behave; if there is congruence, they terminate that set of behaviors. Miller and his associates (1960) conceptualized this process as a TOTE unit, which stands for the sequence of *Testing* one's state against the standard, *Operating* if there is a discrepancy, again *Testing,* and finally *Exiting* when there is a match between the standard and one's state of being.

In the organismic model of motivation, the motive becomes a standard for the operation of a TOTE feedback loop. Once a person becomes aware of some potential satisfaction, he or she will engage in behaviors aimed at achieving the satisfaction. Upon reaching the satisfaction, the state of the organism will match the standard (i.e., the motive) and the sequence will end.

Behavioral Choice

Once people have motives, they decide how to achieve the desired satisfaction. A hungry person decides whether to prepare and eat a meal, drink a nutriment, or go to an ice-cream parlor. An intrinsically motivated person decides whether to play the piano, write a story, or build a bird house. In making that choice, people attempt to achieve the desired satisfaction, given their capacities, resources, and limitations. In some instances, people will be able to choose behaviors which will allow for the satisfaction of several motives at the same time. For example, deciding to prepare and eat a gourmet meal with your best friend may satisfy motives related to hunger, competence, and affection all through the same set of behaviors.

The process of selecting behaviors to satisfy motives has been specified by various theorists, such as Lewin (1938) and Shapira (1976). Atkinson (1964) focused on intrinsic, achievement-related aspects of decision making in one formulation of motivation, and Vroom (1964) focused on extrinsic aspects of decision making in another. The commonality between their theories is that both proposed that the two critical elements which go into making the decision are the valence or psychological value of each behavioral outcome and the probability of being able to attain that outcome. In other words, people choose behaviors which they expect to lead to outcomes that will produce the desired satisfaction. Their motivation to behave is a function of the value of an outcome, times the probability that the behavior will in fact lead to the outcome. The decision-making phase may include two aspects, behavior and extrinsic rewards. At times when the motives are extrinsic, the decision involves selecting what extrinsic rewards to strive for and what behaviors to undertake in quest of the rewards. When the motives are intrinsic, the decisions simply involve behavioral selection.

This phase of the motivational sequence is often referred to as goal setting. Such a formulation is quite accurate when we think of goals as the receipt of an external reward, the completion of a set of behaviors, or a combination of the two. Goals should not, however, be confused with motives. The object of a goal is the completion of a set of behaviors or the receipt of an extrinsic reward, while the object of a motive is the internal experience of satisfaction. Of course, one hopes and expects that completing a goal will result in satisfaction of the motive or motives, since that was the basis for selecting the goal. However, one's expectations are not always accurate, since one often makes decisions which involve substantial uncertainty. If one's expectations were correct, satisfaction of the motive will follow from goal attainment; if one's expectations were incorrect, the person will need to set a new goal based on the new information.

Setting a goal, or deciding what behaviors to undertake, constitutes a standard for the second feedback loop in a complete sequence of motivated behavior. The first standard was the motive, and the operation of TOTE guides one to the desired satisfaction. Within this feedback loop is another. The standard for the second loop (which is a subroutine of the first) is the goal, and the operation of TOTE guides one to the completion of the set of behaviors which represents the goal. Since people set goals which they expect to lead to the desired satisfaction, the satisfaction will follow the goal completion if they planned accurately. If so, then both the inner and outer TOTE unit will terminate following the set of behaviors. If, however, the person erred in planning, the satisfaction will not follow the goal completion. In this instance, the person will not have terminated the outer feedback loop, and will have to "Operate" again. That means setting a new goal, which the person expects to lead to the desired satisfaction, then completing that goal in hopes of achieving the satisfaction, and finally terminating the outer feedback loop if the satisfaction is achieved.

Consider this example. A man becomes aware of being hungry. That creates a motive. It is an awareness which might have derived from internal information about blood-sugar level and gastric mobility and/or from realizing that he had not eaten in five hours. The motive is the awareness of the internal experience he would have by satisfying his hunger need. The motive, or "awareness of potential satisfaction," is the standard which guides the outer TOTE unit. Having established the motive of wanting to satisfy his hunger, he decides how to do that. Let's say he decides to prepare and ingest a cheese-and-mushroom omelette. That is his goal, and it represents the standard for the inner feedback loop. He then sets about achieving the goal. Once he has consumed his magnificent omelette he has achieved the goal and terminated the inner TOTE. The remaining question is whether he has achieved the satisfaction of his motive. If his planning were accurate he should now be satisfied, and thus the outer TOTE unit will also be terminated. If not, he will need to set a new goal. He may decide to go to the local "sweet shoppe" for a banana split. That is a new goal which when completed should leave him satisfied and thereby terminate the outer TOTE unit.

Goal-Directed Behavior

Once a person has chosen behavioral goals, the completion of which is expected to lead to the desired satisfaction, the person begins behaving to achieve the goals—in other words, doing the chosen behavior. Many people have done research on this phase of the sequence. Locke (1968) has discovered that people who have set difficult goals perform better than people with less difficult goals. Also, people who have specific goals, (for example, "writing 12 pages per day"), accomplish more than people who have set non-specific goals (for example, "writing as much as possible each day").

McGraw (1978) has reviewed many studies which have demonstrated that rewarding people impairs their performance on problem solving or learning activities, and improves their performance on more routine, well-learned activities. Apparently, the introduction of rewards diverts part of people's attentions away from the activity to the reward. Thus, if they know how to do the activity, they can work a little harder to get the reward; but if it is an activity like problem solving which requires creativity, resourcefulness, and attention, the diverted attention caused by the reward impairs the performance.

Satisfaction

Some behaviors are chosen because people expect them to lead to desired extrinsic rewards—money, praise, status, or promotions. Others are chosen simply because the behaviors produce satisfaction directly—they leave the people feeling competent and self-determining. In the former case, the satisfaction which was the aim of the motive is mediated by an external reward; in the latter case, the satisfaction is mediated only by the successful completion of the goal behaviors. Thus, the final phase of a sequence of motivated behavior is achievement of the satisfaction which was the standard of the outer TOTE feedback loop. In some cases, there will be a mediating external reward; in others there will not. The sequence of motivated behavior is represented schematically in Figure 2-1.

In the figure, the sequence begins with stimulus inputs which lead to the creation of a motive, namely an awareness of potential inner satisfaction. People then set goals, the completion of which they expect to satisfy the motive. Having set a goal, they behave in an attempt to achieve the goal. This behavior is governed by a TOTE unit, with the goal as the standard. Once they have achieved the goal (i.e., successfully completed the behaviors, and in some cases received an extrinsic reward), they will, if they planned correctly, experience internal satisfaction of the motive. The experience of satisfaction will lead to termination of the sequence if it matches the motive, which is the standard for the outer TOTE unit. If it does not match, the person sets a new goal aimed at the desired satisfaction. The two feedback channels which appear in the figure will be explained in the next section.

EXTRINSIC REWARDS AND INTRINSIC MOTIVATION

In the last few years there has been considerable research into the question of how extrinsic rewards affect intrinsic motivation. What, for example, happens to children's intrinsic motivation for painting when the children are rewarded with candy or praise for painting "nice pictures"? Or what happens to people's intrinsic curiosity when they are made to learn certain things and are given grades for doing so? To answer these questions, various researchers have created analogous situations in the experimental laboratory.

My colleagues and I have conducted a series of inquiries into this question. In the first study we investigated whether monetary rewards would affect people's intrinsic motivation for an interesting activity. To test this, we used college students as subjects. They reported individually to the laboratory and were told that they would be doing two things in the course of the session: first, working on some puzzle problems, and second, answering some questions about how they worked on the problems. Each subject was alone in the experimental room, with the experimenter observing through a one-way window. The puzzle, which was on a table in front of the subject, consisted of differently shaped, three-dimen-

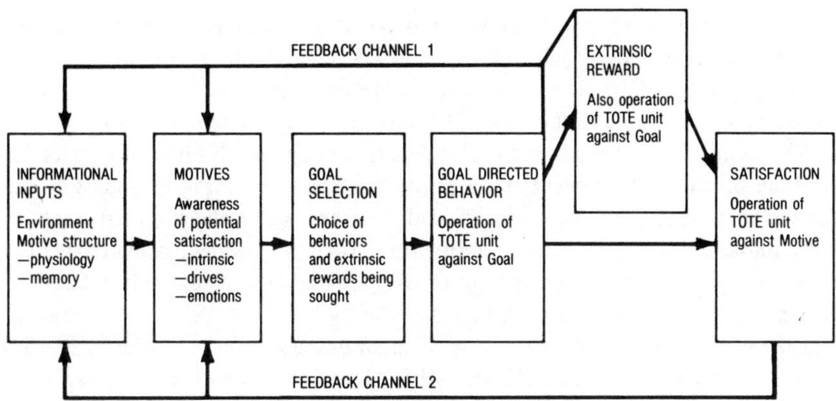

Figure 2-1. A schematic representation of an organismic theory of motivated behavior.

sional pieces which could be arranged to form various figures. Subjects were asked to use the pieces to construct figures which had been drawn on paper for them. College students found the activity quite involving and interesting.

The subjects were given four puzzles and allowed 10 minutes to solve each. Half the subjects were told that they would be given one dollar for each puzzle which they were able to solve in the allotted time. For the other half there was no mention of money. This constituted the experimental manipulation, and the purpose of the experiment was to compare these two groups on the dependent measure of intrinsic motivation following the experimental session. To assess the intrinsic motivation of the subjects following the puzzle solving, the subjects were left alone in the room for eight minutes while the experimenter was out of the laboratory. The subjects could work on additional puzzle configurations, read magazines which were available for them, or do whatever they chose. We reasoned that people could be considered intrinsically motivated to do an activity if they spent time working on the puzzles when there were other things available to them, when there was no reward attached to the activity, and when they thought no one was observing them. Thus, the measure of intrinsic motivation was the number of seconds, out of 480, which they spent working on the puzzle during this free-choice period. The rationale given by the experimenter for the free-choice period was:

> As I mentioned earlier, I'd like you to answer some questions about how you worked on the puzzles. We have many different questions and I am going to allow the computer to select the questions most appropriate for you. In order to do that, I'll need to leave for a few minutes to go to the computer so I can feed in the results of your problem solving. While I'm gone you may do anything you like, but please stay in the room.

To summarize the experimental paradigm, subjects all worked on four puzzle configurations. Half were rewarded (in this particular study the reward was one dollar per puzzle solved) and half were not. Then they were given an eight minute free-choice period during which a second experimenter surreptitiously observed them. The amount of time they spent working on the puzzle during the free-choice period was used as the dependent measure of intrinsic motivation.

The results of this experiment revealed that subjects who had been paid for working on the puzzles spent significantly less free-choice time attending to the puzzles than those who had not been paid. In other words, the payments seem to have undermined their intrinsic motivation for the puzzles. Apparently, the experience of being rewarded for the activity created an instrumentality between the activity and the reward such that the activity became a means to the reward, and therefore was less likely to be performed in the absence of a reward contingency. Following the work of Heider (1958) and DeCharms (1968), I referred to this process of instrumentality development as a change in perceived locus of causality (Deci, 1975). Whereas for intrinsically motivated activities the perceived locus of causality is internal to the person (since the reward is simply internal satisfaction), for extrinsically motivated activities the perceived locus of causality is external to the person (since the reward is mediated outside the person). When intrinsically motivated behaviors are rewarded, people's perceived locus of causality appears to change from internal to external as an instrumentality develops between the activity and the extrinsic reward. We also checked performance of the paid and unpaid subjects to be sure that the apparent decrease in intrinsic motivation was not just a satiation effect. If the paid subjects had worked harder, then we could not have been sure that the subsequent decrease was really an undermining of intrinsic motivation. The performance scores of the two groups were not different, so this supported our interpretation.

If the change in perceived-locus-of-causality process operates as suggested, one would expect other rewards to have similar effects. To test that, subjects were rewarded with the avoidance of a noxious sound for each puzzle which they were able to solve in the allotted time (Deci & Cascio, 1972). Otherwise the paradigm was the same as the one described above. The results were also the same. Subjects who solved interesting puzzles and avoided an unpleasant stimulus by doing so spent less free-choice time working on the puzzles than control subjects who were not trying to avoid the sound. Here too, subjects seem to have been perceiving the activity as a means to the avoidance of unpleasant occurrences, rather than as an interesting activity which they engaged in for the simple intrinsic satisfaction of feeling competent and self-determining.

Lepper, Greene, and Nisbett (1973) provided a further test of this change in perceived-locus-of-causality process. Their paradigm was similar to that described above, though they used preschool children as subjects and used drawing as the intrinsically motivated activity. Children were either told that they would receive a desired "good player award" for drawing, or told nothing about a reward. Several days later they were observed while they were in a free-play situation. There were several activities available to them, including the drawing materials. The researchers found that those children who had been promised and given rewards spent less free-play time working with the drawing materials than did non-rewarded children. Lepper and associates had a third condition in this experiment. One group of children was given unexpected rewards after the experimental drawing, though there had been no mention of it before the drawing. These children did not show the decrease in intrinsic motivation evidenced in the expected reward condition. This finding, of course, makes good sense. Since the children were not drawing in order to get rewards, the instrumentality did not develop between the activity and reward. They did not begin to perceive the activity as a means to the reward, because when they engaged in the activity, it was not a means to get the reward. Perhaps with several such occurrences of being unexpectedly rewarded for a given activity, the perceived locus of causality would begin to change. However, with just one occurrence there was no evidence of the change.

Sense of Competence and Self-Determination

In another experiment, we investigated the effects of positive feedback on the intrinsic motivation of male college students. We used only males because of a restricted subject pool. For the experimental group we made statements such as, "That's good, you did that very quickly," each time they solved a puzzle. The control subjects got no feedback. Unlike the other rewards, praise increased the intrinsic motivation of these male subjects; they spent more free-choice time working on the puzzle than did the control subjects. Praising males for working on puzzles does not seem to establish instrumentalities between the activity and reward; instead, it apparently strengthened their sense of competence and self-determination which is the basis of their intrinsic motivation. This suggests that there is a second process through which intrinsic motivation may be affected. Intrinsic motivation will change when information produces a change in one's sense of competence and self-determination.

Although many rewards (i.e., money, good-player awards, and the avoidance of punishment) have been shown to decrease intrinsic motivation, and I have asserted that this is caused by a change in perceived locus of causality, it is interesting to note that rewards can also convey positive information about one's competence and self-determination. Thus, one might expect that rewards could either decrease intrinsic motivation by changing the perceived locus of causality, or they could increase intrinsic motivation by strengthening one's sense of competence and self-determination. This raises the question of when one might expect each of the processes to be operating.

Two Aspects to Rewards

In dealing with this question, I suggested (Deci, 1975) that every reward has two aspects: an *informational* aspect which conveys information about one's efficacy, and a *control* aspect which brings the behavior under the control of the reward. Therefore, whichever aspect is more salient will determine the effects of the reward on intrinsic motivation. If the controlling aspect is more salient, a change in perceived locus of causality will follow, resulting in decreased intrinsic motivation; whereas if the positive informational aspect is more salient, a change in feelings of competence and self-determination will follow, resulting in increased intrinsic motivation.

There are several factors which might result in one aspect of a reward being more salient than the other. First, the reward itself sometimes has acquired meaning through general usage. Money, for example, has always had widespread use in getting people to do things they would not otherwise do—"Pay him enough and he'll do anything!" Therefore, one would expect money to have a very salient controlling aspect which would generally undermine intrinsic motivation. And indeed the experiments have shown this to be so. If, on the other hand, the informational aspect were somehow made very salient, the money ought not undermine intrinsic motivation. Joe Porac and I tested this notion in an unpublished experiment with two payment conditions: in one condition, subjects were simply paid 50¢ for each correct puzzle solution; in the other, they were told that if they did better than 80% of the subjects they would get 50¢; if they were better than 50% they would get 25¢; otherwise, no payments. We did this so as to emphasize the informational aspect of the money. Each time the subjects solved a puzzle, in either condition, they would receive 50¢. The results showed that the payment/information group had significantly more intrinsic motivation than the non-informational payment group. When the different aspects of the reward were made differentially salient, the reward had different effects on intrinsic motivation.

A second factor which could affect the relative salience of the two aspects is characteristics of the people receiving the rewards. Because of our past experiences, rewards take on different meaning to different people. Some children are given candy or money as a way of getting them to do things when they have said, "No, I don't want to do that." This would enhance the controlling nature of those rewards. In some homes, approval and acceptance are meagerly dispensed and made contingent upon being good children; for these people, approval would be a very controlling reward.

In one experiment (Deci, Cascio, & Krusell, 1975), we used both a male and a female experimenter to administer praise to male and female subjects who worked on the puzzles. Recall that our earlier study with praise (or positive feedback) had utilized only males. In this experiment we found, as previously, that the praise enhanced the intrinsic motivation of males; this was so when the experimenter was either male or female. However, we also discovered that the praise decreased the intrinsic motivation of females, both with the male and with the female experimenter. Praise seems to have different meaning to males and females. For the males, it seems that the informational aspect was more salient, thereby enhancing their sense of competence and self-determination; for the females, it seems that the controlling aspect was more salient, thereby co-opting some of their intrinsic motivation by changing the perceived locus of causality. This seems to be an instance in which socialization processes have given praise different meanings for males and females. Boys have traditionally been socialized to be strong, independent achievers who "stand on their own and pay no attention to what others think of them." Girls, on the other hand, have traditionally been socialized to be more dependent on others' opinions. They give and receive compliments more often, and traditionally have been taught that they will get married and be dependent on their husbands for support. These traditional learnings have had an impact on many of us. They have, on the average, made the meaning of praise different for males and females. If these differences are due to socialization, as I have suggested, then of course different socialization processes would lead to differences in dependence, achievement, and responses to praise. With the increased awareness to matters of sex roles, it may well be that socialization of sex roles will be considerably different in future generations than they have been in the past.

Negative Feedback

So far, we have considered the change in feelings of competence and self-determination only in relation to *positive* feedback. If, however, the information about one's competence and self-determination is negative, one might expect the information to decrease intrinsic motivation. We tested this in two ways (Deci, 1975). First, we gave negative verbal feedback to one group of subjects, and compared them to control subjects who did the same puzzles without getting feedback. The experiment made statements such as, "Although you did solve that you did it more slowly than most other people," following each correct solution, and statements such as "Most people have been able to solve that one," following subjects' failures to solve a puzzle. As expected, the subjects who received negative feedback spent less free-choice time working with the puzzles than did control subjects. In another study, the experimental subjects were given more difficult puzzles than the control groups, so that their failure rate would be considerably higher. Thus, the failure subjects would be getting "self-administered" negative feedback by failing at most of the puzzles. Again, the results indicated that subjects in the negative-feedback group were significantly less intrinsically motivated than subjects in the control group. Thus, negative feedback apparently diminishes people's sense of competence and self-determination, thereby decreasing their intrinsic motivation.

Cognitive Evaluation Theory

We have been considering the effects of extrinsic rewards on intrinsic motivation. We have also discussed the two processes through which rewards can affect intrinsic motivation, and we noted that there are two aspects to every reward and that the relative salience of these aspects determines which of the two processes will be initiated. I have referred to this set of postulates about the way in which rewards affect intrinsic motivation as cognitive evaluation theory (Deci, 1975). Let us now examine how the processes of cognitive evaluation theory are involved in the organismic theory of motivation outlined earlier in this chapter.

The perceived-locus-of-causality process suggests that instrumentalities develop between behaviors and rewards which subsequently affect one's intrinsic motivation; that is, they affect people's motive structure and motives. Thus, we can see that this process is simply a channel of feedback which starts in the link between behavior and extrinsic rewards and feeds back to the motive and motive-structure phase. In Figure 2-1 this process is labeled Feedback Channel 1.

The competence and self-determination process suggests that the information which people gain about their efficacy can either strengthen or weaken their intrinsic motivation. This represents a second channel of feedback, which begins with the satisfaction or lack of satisfaction of one's intrinsic need and feeds back to the motive structure and motive phases of the sequence. This is shown as Feedback Channel 2. Therefore, the two processes of cognitive evaluation theory are represented by the two feedback channels in the organismic theory of motivation.

When we say that one's intrinsic motivation is changed, what does this actually mean? The answer to this question remains speculative. However, according to the organismic theory, motivation begins as needs which make up one's motive structure and which exist in people's memory and physiology. Thus, a change in intrinsic motivation means a change in people's memory and physiology. People develop cognitive structures to store these new learnings. In addition, theorists such as Reich (1960) have suggested that people also hold some learnings in their musculature, in the form of what he has called "character armor." People interfere with aspects of their own natural functioning through muscular tightenings or blockages. While this speculation awaits additional verification, there are many new psychotherapies (Lowen, 1966) which work directly on the musculature and report marked changes in affect, intrinsic motivation, and behavior.

THE DEVELOPMENT OF INTRINSIC MOTIVATION

Intrinsic motivation and the development of a person have a great deal to do with each other. In this section we will consider one aspect of that relationship; namely, the way in which intrinsic motivation develops and evolves in a person as the person grows and matures. In a later section we will see that intrinsic motivation energizes development. In this regard we will focus on the Piagetian approach to development. Finally, we will consider the relation of intrinsic motivation to personality development by focusing on Freud's stages of psychosexual development.

The very idea of intrinsic motivation implies innateness. I assume that all people are born with the intrinsic need for feeling competent and self-determining. It is not something that is learned or programmed into a person; it is an integral part of being human. Still, intrinsic motivation does evolve and change with time and experiences. We saw in the preceding section, for example, that intrinsic motivation is strengthened and weakened by experiences of efficacy and inefficacy and by experiences with extrinsic rewards. We will now see that not only does the strength of one's intrinsic motivation change, but also its form; some people are intrinsically motivated to perform music, others to succeed at business ventures.

Early Development of Intrinsic Motivation

Hunt (1965) has described the forms of intrinsic motivation during the first year of a child's life. There are three discernible stages. During the first three to five months of life a child is responsive to stimulation and to patterns in that stimulation. When there are changes in the pattern of sensory stimulation, the child responds. This response to stimulus changes is the earliest form of intrinsically motivated behavior. Intrinsic motivation keeps the child attending to the environment, and thereby facilitates development. The key elements in these earliest months are attention and response. The behavior operates like the orienting reflex (Sokolov, 1963); when a stimulus input is different from the child's adaptation level (Helson, 1964), the child responds. Gradually, the adaptation levels adjust to the stimulus, and the orienting reflex ceases until the next stimulus change.

In the second stage of the development of intrinsically motivated behavior, the child is not just responding to stimulus changes, but rather displays the rudiments of purposive behavior. In this stage, which extends from about the fourth to the ninth month, the child is concerned with maintaining pleasurable stimulation. Thus, when children are enjoying some stimulation which stops, they will not only display the orienting response, but they will engage in some behavior apparently intended to restore the stimulation. The behaviors might be, for example, shaking their hands or feet. They are not truly purposive, in that they have no real relationship to the desired stimulation. The children have not yet developed the cognitive structures necessary to understand the cause-effect relationship in behavior. Still, the intent of their behaving is clearly that of restoring the stimulation, even though the behaviors themselves cannot do that.

In the third stage, which begins at about the ninth month, children begin to seek out novelty. Their intrinsically motivated behaviors are more clearly purposive, and they seek new experiences. The form of their intrinsic motivation is much like that of adults. They are acting on the environment, expressing their own willfulness, attempting to master new situations; in short, they are beginning to seek out and conquer situations which provide optimal challenge for their capacities, and which are intended to bring about the intrinsic reward of experiencing themselves as competent and self-determining.

Differentiation of Needs

As the child grows older, the basic intrinsic need becomes channelled into specific intrinsic needs—for cognizance, mastery, achievement, and so on. These needs may be linked to different interests; a person might, for example, work toward mastery of music, pottery, or mechanics. This process of the differentiation of intrinsic motivation into these specific needs is influenced by two primary factors: innate capacities and environmental experiences. People have what Woodworth (1918) called different "native equipment"; these are biologically based predispositions. For example, the capacity for differentiating pitch and responding to rhythm are significantly influenced by one's heredity.

By the same token, the environment in which one is raised, and the specific reward contingencies, will also have a large impact on these various skills and abilities as well as on one's motivation to engage in the corresponding behaviors. A child who is raised by parents who are artists will be exposed to various forms of art in ways that a farm child is likely not to be. Thus, the availability of these activities, and the awareness that the loved and significant people in one's life are deeply involved in them, will influence the child's desires for expressing his or her creative capacities through these art forms.

It is important to recognize that although the environment influences a child's behaviors and appetities, the process through which this occurs is not a simple matter of conditioning, as the reinforcement theorists would have us believe. Rather, a child's intrinsic motivation—the curiosity, creativity, and interest in the novel—become directed toward certain kinds of activities as a result of a complex interplay of environment and genes.

Kagan (1972) has explained how this differentiation process works in relation to what he calls the need to reduce uncertainty. Kagan posited that children learn strategies for reducing uncertainty, and these strategies underlie the establishment of particular needs. For example, if children find that when they are experiencing uncertainty their parents will always comfort them and reduce the uncertainty, the children are likely to develop a strong dependency need. Other children learn to withdraw, to seek approval, or to bully younger children as effective strategies for reducing uncertainty. Concomitant with these learned strategies comes the development of specific needs. Thus, we see how a need may differentiate or become channeled into specific directions as a result of effective and ineffective interactions with the environment.

The intrinsic need which has received the most attention is the need for achievement (McClelland et al., 1953, McClelland, 1961). Defined as the tendency to strive for success against some standard of excellence, this need motivates various behaviors which are aimed at the internal satisfaction and pride which accompany successful achievement.

The need to achieve has been most often discussed with regard to entrepreneurial behavior, though there are also several studies relating it to academic performance. Within the context of the differentiation hypothesis, the need for achievement is one specific need which derives out of the more general intrinsic need for effective interactions with the environment. As a result of one's history of interactions with the environment, one develops some level of need to achieve. McClelland (1961) has asserted that an important determinant of the level of one's need for achievement is the type of child-rearing practices to which one was exposed. Several studies have provided evidence of a relationship between early experiences and one's level of achievement motivation.

Rosen and D'Andrade (1959) went into the homes of 20 boys (aged 9-11) who were very high need-achievers and 20 who were very low need-achievers. They observed the parent-child interactions while the children were working on an achievement task, and they noted rather marked differences between the parental interactions of the two groups. The parents of boys who displayed high need for achievement communicated higher expectations for their sons than parents of low need-achievers. In addition, the parents of the high group were warmer and more supportive toward their sons than were parents of the low group; and the mothers of the high group tended to be more dominant and demanding than the mothers of the low group. This study is important in that it gives us clues about what kinds of elements are important in determining the way in which the basic intrinsic need for competence and self-determination differentiates into specific needs. Here we see that parental expectations, parental warmth and supportiveness, and certain characteristics of the mother affect boys' needs for achievement. Studies from our laboratory, which were reported earlier in the chapter, further suggest that the types of rewards, and whether one succeeds or fails on certain types of activities, will affect whether one will be intrinsically motivated to do those activities. The conclusion from this is that children's interactions with the environment–particularly their record of successes and failures at various types of activities, and the nature of their interactions with their parents–determine the form and level of their intrinsic motivation, through a process in which the general need for being competent and self-determining differentiates into specific needs.

INDIVIDUAL DIFFERENCES IN INTRINSIC MOTIVATION

As with all human traits, individuals differ in the strength and form of their intrinsic motivation. Since different people have had different patterns of being rewarded, their intrinsic motivations will have been differentially affected. Since they have had different histories of success and failure, their intrinsic motivations will also have been differentially affected by those experiences. The process of differentiation of motives also affects people differently because they have different innate capacities and they have had different childhood experiences. From this we can infer that there are differences among people in their intrinsic motivation, and we have a meaningful theoretical account of these differences. Traditionally in psychology, however, the study of individual differences involves the use of some psychometric device which purports to measure the extent to which people possess some trait or traits of interest.

Utilizing the measurement perspective as the basis for the study of individual differences, there have been several programs of research which have investigated some aspect of intrinsic motivation. The concept of intrinsic motivation is of course much too broad to be assessed accurately by any single measure. However, different measures have been used successfully to investigate questions related to some aspect of intrinsic motivation. We shall consider a few of these measures, beginning with Zuckerman's (1974) sensation seeking research.

Sensation Seeking

When the original exploration studies began to indicate that a drive-based motivation theory was inadequate, there were various approaches used to explain what has come to be called intrinsic motivation. As I mentioned earlier, one of the more prominent approaches dealt with the concept of optimal stimulation. Some researchers focused on the psychological level, positing that organisms need an optimal level of psychological incongruity or stimulation (Hunt, 1965; McClelland *et al.*, 1953; Dember & Earl, 1957; Berlyne, 1969); whereas others focused on the physiological level, asserting that organisms need an optimal level of physiological arousal in the reticular activating system of the brain (Hebb, 1955; Leuba, 1955; Fiske & Maddi, 1961).

Hunt proposed that organisms need to be stimulated by situations in which there is some optimal level of discrepancy between their own inner structure and the stimulus. Thus, people seek information which is optimally discrepant from what they know, so they can set about learning it. If it is too discrepant from what they know, it will not be interesting because they do not have the competence to deal with it; if it is too close to what they know it will be boring. Hunt proposed that people are drawn toward situations with this optimal discrepancy because of their intrinsic need to maintain an optimal level of psychological incongruity. As I mentioned earlier, people do seek situations of optimal incongruity; rather, they need to find challenging situations and then conquer the challenges. In other words, they need to find optimal incongruity and then achieve congruity.

Nonetheless, the idea that people seek stimulation because of a need for incongruity has considerable merit, and Zuckerman's work on individual differences is based on the optimal-stimulation definition of intrinsic motivation. Zuckerman (1974) has proposed that people have a "restless drive . . . to seek out the novel, to explore the limits of mind, muscle, and senses, to take great risks in spite of fear . . . " (p. 80). People are indeed intrinsically motivated to seek novelty and take risks, though the term *restless drive* may be somewhat misleading. I would simply term it an intrinsic need, since one of the important learnings from the research into intrinsic motivation is that the drive conception of human motivation is inadequate. Clearly this need does not fit the traditional definition of drive since it is not based in tissue imbalances; so referring to it in this way conveys a flavor of mechanism–it implies that the human organism is being pushed by this ever-nagging inner urge. As I stated earlier, I find it more useful to view humans as active organisms interacting with the environment in an attempt to be competent and self-determining. Still, the active organism, with its need to be competent and self-determining, will need to seek out stimulation; in other words, situations which provide some optimal degree of challenge. Thus, research into sensation seeking is in fact quite germane to our investigations of intrinsic motivation.

Zuckerman has proposed that each person has an optimal level of psychological stimulation and an optimal level of physiological arousal which are characteristic for him or her. People differ in the levels which are characteristic for them, and therefore Zuckerman constructed a measure, called the Sensation Seeking Scale, to assess individuals' needs for seeking stimulation. In the measure, respondents are given several pairs of statements, and must choose which of two statements in each pair is most characteristic of them. For instance, they must choose between: (a) I like "wild" uninhibited parties, and (b) I prefer quiet parties with good conversation. Choosing statements such as preferring wild parties indicates high sensation seeking.

Factor analyses have shown that the scale contains four subscales which constitute aspects of the general need for sensation: (1) Thrill and Adventure Seeking, as in wild parties and dangerous activities, (2) Experience Seeking, as in sensory experiences or fantasy, (3) Disinhibition, as in finding release through alcohol and sexual variety, and (4) Boredom Susceptibility, which appears more clearly in males than females, and is the dislike of routine and repetition.

The bulk of the research using the sensation seeking scale has attempted to determine if the scale is useful as a means of predicting whether people will like or dislike and do or not do various behaviors. The scale has been shown to relate (a) to other traits such as impulsive extroversion, to the desire for varied experiences with sex, food, and perception; (b) to the willingness to participate in unusual experimental sessions; (c) to certain types of nonconformity; and (d) to some behaviors labeled delinquent and schizoid. Thus, the scale or its subscales have categorized people on the basis of preferences and have predicted various types of behaviors (Zuckerman, 1974).

Sales (1971) utilized a kinesthetic procedure, rather than a paper-and-pencil scale to measure need for stimulation. Blindfolded subjects who underestimated the size of stimulus materials which they had previously handled were assumed to need a high level of stimulation, while those who subsequently overestimated the size of the stimulus materials were assumed to have a low need for stimulation. Sales argued that although this appears to be a peculiar measure of stimulus seeking, it does have considerable construct validity and seems to be quite useful for integrating various research results.

The measure has been useful in distinguishing people who enjoy high-stimulation contact sports (Ryan & Foster 1967), teenagers who become juvenile delinquents perhaps in search of thrills (Petrie, McCullock, & Kazdin, 1962), and the measure has been related to extroversion (Eysenck, 1955). Sales (1971) reported that people high in need for stimulation as measured by this procedure show positive responses to interesting stimuli, attend closely to complex verbal messages, and are quite active in stimulus-deprived situations and group discussions.

To summarize, one area of research on individual differences which relates to intrinsic motivation has focused on sensation seeking, which has been measured with both a questionnaire and a kinesthetic-estimation procedure. Both methods have been successful in predicting traits and behaviors which relate to the trait of sensation seeking.

Sensation seeking relates to intrinsic motivation through the conceptualization of intrinsic motivation as a need for maintaining an optimal level of stimulation. I find it more useful to conceptualize intrinsic motivation as the need for effective, self-determined interactions with the environment. Thus, out of the need for effectance, people seek stimulation as part of the process of seeking and conquering challenges. These cycles may be short, as when people try different puzzles, or they may take much longer, as when people gather materials for problem solving and then allow solutions to emerge from an array of materials. Some of the gathering or seeking behaviors may be temporally quite antecedent to the conquering phase of the cycle; yet it is still more usefully considered as part of the effectance cycle than simply as seeking stimulation. There are some aspects of sensation seeking, such as having wild parties, which may not be directly related to intrinsic motivation. Further, people may choose to challenge their capacities by doing some very quiet, apparently nonactive behaviors, such as Zen meditation. Thus, it is important to maintain the perspective that sensation seeking is related to, but not identical to, intrinsic motivation.

Projective Measures

McClelland and his associates have, over the last quarter century, established a research tradition in which they use projective measures to investigate various aspects of human motivation. They have been particularly interested in the operation of specific motives, such as the need for achievement (McClelland *et al.*, 1953; McClelland, 1961; Atkinson & Raynor, 1974), the need for power (Winter, 1973; McClelland, 1975), the motive to avoid success (Horner, 1974), and the origin-pawn variable (deCharms, 1976).

As I pointed out previously, these specific needs are assumed to derive from the basic undifferentiated intrinsic need to relate effectively with the environment. I have conceptualized the need for achievement as one of the specific needs which differentiates into various strengths and forms as a result of childhood interactions with one's parents and other elements of the environment. The need for power is also based partially in effectance motivation, though there surely are other components to its development. The motive to avoid success is, of course, not based directly in intrinsic motivation, but rather develops when people learn that there are salient negative consequences associated with component and self-determining interactions with the environment. The origin-pawn variable as discussed by deCharms (1968, 1976) is perhaps the closest of any of the measured concepts to the general notion of intrinsic motivation. An origin is a person who is internally motivated, who is not pushed around by others, who seeks his or her own goals and originates his or her own behavior. An origin is active; an origin feels commitment and seeks to be competent. On the other hand, a pawn is a person who is pushed around by external forces, who is used by others to further their ends. If motivated at all, a pawn is motivated primarily by extrinsic controls. An origin therefore is highly intrinsically motivated and will seek to feel competent and self-determining by seeking out and attempting to conquer challenges which are optimal for his or her capacities. In so doing, these encounters will provide the origin with a level of stimulation which is optimal for effective functioning.

These various concepts related to intrinsic motivation have been reliably measured through content analyses of thought samples. In this procedure you might be asked to look at a picture and to write a brief story about what you see. The type of story which you write is assumed to reflect your various motivational propensities. Imagine a picture which shows a man sitting at a desk staring into space. What type of story would you make up to describe the picture? If the theme of your story had the man thinking about how to do his job better, to get a promotion, and develop a successful career in his organization, you would be scored high in achievement motivation. Similarly, other types of motivation could be assessed by looking for themes and concepts which relate to the type of motivation being considered.

Sometimes the cues for stories are provided by statements rather than pictures. For example, in a study on the fear of success, one might use a cue such as "At the end of her first semester of medical school, Mary is at the top of her class." Stories which indicated that the writer experiences conflict—because she believes it is inconsistent to be a successful student and to be liked as a woman—suggest motivation to avoid success. For example, people high in this motivation might tell a story about how Mary does not have a very active social life and is worried about finding a husband with whom she will be happy.

DeCharms (1976) has used thought samples in a similar fashion to assess the origin-pawn variable in elementary and junior-high-school children. As deCharms pointed out, the origin-pawn concept is not a specific need like the need for achievement, since there is not a specific class of goals which are the aim of the behaviors. Instead, it is a more general motivational propensity. Therefore, in measuring the concept, the investigators rate stories on the following points: whether there is (1) internal goal setting, (2) behavior which the person himself or herself decided to do, (3) realistic consideration of aspects in the person and the environment which are relevant to the behavior, (4) assumption of personal responsibility as evidenced by determination to carry through the behavior and concern for the effects of the behavior on others, (5) self-confidence and an expectation of succeeding, and (6) internal control of behavior.

Utilizing this conceptualization of intrinsic motivation and its corresponding measurement procedure, deCharms has conducted a large research project in inner-city schools, in which he worked with teachers to develop methods for enhancing the intrinsic motivation and origin-like behavior of children. The project showed clear improvement in the motivation and academic achievement of children who were in classes which had been trained in goal setting, self-initiation, personal responsibility, and so on.

In sum, the use of content analyses of responses to written or pictorial cues has been widely used in the study of human motivation. Described in detail in Atkinson (1958), this procedure has been used in a variety of research projects, some of which are reported in Atkinson and Raynor (1974), deCharms (1976), McClelland (1961; 1975), and Winter (1973).

Locus of Control

Earlier I suggested, in line with Heider (1958) and deCharms (1968), that when a behavior is intrinsically motivated, the perceived locus of causality of the behavior is internal, whereas when the behavior is extrinsically motivated, the perceived locus of causality is external. A concept which is related to, often confused with, and not the same as locus of causality, is locus of control (Rotter, 1966). Developing out of Rotter's (1954) work in social-learning theory, the concept deals with whether the control of reinforcements is internal to the person or external in the environment. People who believe that reinforcements are contingent upon their own behaviors or personal characteristics are considered *internals,* while people who believe that reinforcements are largely controlled by luck or fate are considered *externals.*

The locus-of-control concepts (Rotter, 1966) have analogues in locus-of-causality terminology (Heider, 1958). Personal causality refers to intentional behavior whether the intention derives from intrinsic needs or extrinsic needs; therefore, personal causality involves a belief in a relationship between behavior and responses in the environment. Hence, I am suggesting that personal causality and internal control are analogous concepts. Since an internal locus of causality and an external locus of causality both are instances of personal causality, we can see that internal-control people may be operating, at any given time, with either an internal or an external locus of causality. On the other hand, impersonal causality refers to behavior which is caused by forces in the environment and does not involve personal intentions. Thus, impersonal causality is analogous to external control. Behavior is caused by forces in the environment, and the person believing that there is no relationship between behaviors and responses from the environment would not be forming intentions.

Rotter (1966) has developed a scale for measuring locus of control. This individual-difference variable is one of the most frequently discussed and researched variables in the personality literature. I shall not review that work here, however, since another chapter in this book (Lefcourt, Chapter 5) deals with it in considerable detail. My aim here was simply to clarify its relationship to intrinsic motivation and locus-of-causality concepts, and to point out that it is another personality variable which has some relationship to intrinsic motivation and which has been widely researched.

THE INTRINSIC MOTIVATION OF DEVELOPMENT

Growth and maturation of the human organism has been studied from a variety of perspectives. In this section we shall look briefly at two aspects of the large and complex picture of human development. First, we will be concerned with cognitive development utilizing a Piagetian-type analysis. Second, we will consider personality development employing a Freudian-type perspective. I have chosen to deal with these two aspects of the picture because they are particularly illustrative of the way in which intrinsic motivation plays a role in human development.

Cognitive Development

Piaget pioneered an approach to the study of human development which has had a major impact on modern developmental psychology. Piaget views the child as an active organism interacting with the environment. His focus has been to map out the processes through which people's cognitive structures are developed and elaborated. These structures are the variants in Piaget's system; development is the change in these structures, which are referred to as schemata.

Cognitive structures provide the means for organizing and interpreting information, and they direct or govern behavior. Growth in cognitive structures occurs as people accommodate to and assimilate the environment. These two processes, or functions, through which structures become modified are the invariants in the system. In other words, accommodating and assimilating are ever-present processes in people's interactions with their surroundings.

Accommodation is a process through which the organism changes its existing structures to include some new aspect of the environment. Informational inputs often modify some aspect of a cognitive structure so as to represent more closely the environment as it exists. This is accommodation. If you did not previously know about the process of accommodation, I hope that you have now accommodated to this paragraph so that the cognitive structures which you utilize in interpreting human development are modified to include a Piagetian perspective.

Assimilation is a process in which the organism modifies the environment to fit with pre-existing cognitive structures. In other words, as information comes into the system, not only does the system change to accommodate to the information, but the inputs are changed by the system. So, for example, when we perceive an object in the world, there is not a perfect match between the stimulus and the perception; in part, we modify what we perceive so as to make it more consistent with our existing cognitive structures; we partially assimilate the material.

Development involves the continual operation of the processes of assimilation and accommodation. Ideally, the two processes will be in balance such that neither is predominant. Organisms accommodate and assimilate through the operation of the assimilation schema. This schema governs the ongoing process of seeking moderately discrepant inputs and then reducing the discrepancy through accommodating to and assimilating the inputs.

Implicit in Piaget's theory (Piaget, 1952; Mischel, 1971) is the notion that people are intrinsically motivated to develop more elaborated and complex cognitive structures. This is another way of saying that people are intrinsically motivated to encounter moderately assimilable stimuli since cognitive structures develop as people encounter moderately assimilable stimuli and then accommodate to and assimilate those stimuli.

Let us recapitulate. Development involves the elaboration of cognitive structures. This occurs through the processes of assimilation and accommodation. People are intrinsically motivated to seek inputs which are moderately discrepant from existing structures and then to accommodate to and assimilate the inputs. An input which is nearly identical to a structure will be fully assimilable and is therefore uninteresting; an input which is widely discrepant will also be avoided, since the person does not have the necessary structures for handling the input.

This perspective is entirely consistent with the point of view that people are intrinsically motivated to be competent and self-determining. Competence and self-determination involves the development of capacities or structures for dealing effectively with the environment. These capacities continue to develop as people encounter and overcome optimal challenges. Thus, the intrinsic motivation to be competent and self-determining leads people to engage in optimally challenging situations, which results in more elaborate cognitive structures and leaves people feeling competent and self-determining.

Growth Cycles. Elkind (1971), in discussing cognitive growth cycles, has discussed the motivational basis of cognitive development. He suggested that growth in cognitive structures, with the corresponding increment in one's capacities for behaving, can be usefully characterized in terms of growth cycles. These cycles involve seeking out some novelty which represents the *nutriments* for one's growth. The child utilizes these nutriment inputs in various ways which result in mastery of the situation. In detailing these cycles, Elkind has provided an account of what we have been referring to as the cyclical process of seeking and conquering optimal challenges.

Seeking stimulus nutriments is an active process in that it occurs even in the absence of any eliciting elements in the situation. Out of intrinsic motivation, people seek novelty; they do not simply respond to environmental forces. People can nourish their cognitive growth by a wide variety of stimulus inputs. The ones which they utilize will affect the way their intrinsic motivation becomes channeled in subsequent interactions with the environment. Elkind has said that they will be developing long-term preferences. Within the framework of the differentiation hypothesis presented earlier in this chapter, I would say that the nutriments which a child utilizes influence the way the general intrinsic need for competence and self-determination becomes differentiated into specific intrinsic needs.

As a child's attention is focused on some nutriment, the child must block out irrelevant stimuli and allow into awareness only the stimulus elements which have utility at that time. As children accommodate to the new inputs, they generally engage in what Elkind called intellectual play to utilize their new capacities and demonstrate mastery. In so doing they will be experiencing the intrinsic rewards of feeling competent and self-determining. Of course, after some amount of repetition in this play process, they will begin to be bored and will then initiate a new search for stimulus nutriment, and a new cycle will be underway.

Behavior Manifestations. Earlier in the chapter we noted that intrinsic motivation has three rather distinct categories during a child's first year of life (Hunt, 1965). The final stage, beginning around the ninth month, represents the emergence of the desire to encounter novel, stimulating, or challenging situations.

This seeking out the novel remains as a central aspect of intrinsic motivation throughout the remainder of one's life. However, as Harter (1978) has pointed out, the type of behaviors for which one is intrinsically motivated will be different at different ages. She found, for instance, that 10-year-olds who worked on an interesting task seemed very concerned about achieving the correct solution, whereas 4-year-olds were quite concerned with various sensori-motor effects, such as making the lights go on and off. When such fundings are considered in light of developmental theories such as that of Piaget, they are quite understandable.

Piaget's theory (Baldwin, 1967; Flavell, 1963) suggests that there are four important stages in the development of adult cognitive capacities. The first stage, called sensori-motor, encompasses the first two years of life. During this period a child is able to respond adaptively to sensory information. However, the child does not yet have a conceptual representation of the stimuli or the behavior. During this first stage the child's primary accomplishments are the coordination of information from various sensory modalities (e.g., knowing that the toe which one touches is the same as the toe which one sees), the ability to behave as if the world were permanent (e.g., to recognize that an item which disappeared behind a door still exists and can be found), and finally to behave in ways which appear to be goal directed and which follow from the child's intentions.

The second stage of development in Piaget's theory lasts from about the end of the second to the seventh year and is called the preoperational period. The child, during this period, develops the capacity for an internal representation of external events. These representations are, of course, the basis for the formal, logical thought processes which emerge later. This period is one of some unsettledness for the child, since it is the transition period from operating at a sensori-motor level to operating at a conceptual level. In fact, this preoperational period is sometimes considered a substage of the concrete operational period.

From the age of 7 to 11 the child operates with more formal and stable cognitive processes. This concrete operational period utilizes a rudimentary sense of logic in which the child understands the conservation or invariance of space and number. For instance, a child realizes that the quantity of water poured from one shaped container to a differently shaped container remains constant. Still the child is unable to reason deductively and to engage in more complicated conceptual processes.

The final stage in the developmental sequence, which begins around age 11, is referred to as the formal operational period. As the name suggests, this is the time when a person begins formal, conceptual thought processes, in which abstract processes represent a typical mode of operating.

I have presented these four stages in only the sketchiest form. The point in doing so was to illustrate how a person's capacities and concerns are different at different stages of development. Thus, as Harter has suggested, the types of behavior which are intrinsically motivating will depend on which stage is central for a person at that time. A sensori-motor child might, for instance, be challenged by investigating the action-outcome relationship involved in throwing objects or hitting others. These understandings are, of course, important for competent and self-determining interactions with the environment, and are therefore of central concern for the infant who has not mastered them. A preoperational child will have different concerns and different capacities, so it is only reasonable to expect the behaviors which will interest and delight this child to be concomitant with those capacities. Such a child might, as Harter proposed, engage in imitative role-playing to master new challenges through play. In fact, children's play is the arena through which they engage in what interests them while attempting to learn or master some new activity or concept (Bruner, Jolly, & Sylva, 1976).

In the concrete operational period, Harter pointed out, children will be concerned with classifying, organizing, and categorizing a wide range of objects and behaviors. They will be exploring concrete elements in their lives and the relationship among these concrete elements. Finally, in the formal operational period, people are often intrinsically motivated to solve logical problems or to work out new schemes for mastering some challenge which may be quite complicated and involve many conditional elements.

Personality Development

There have been two general approaches to personality development which have been particularly influential and which parallel the two motivation theories discussed earlier. The first utilizes a learning-theory approach in the Hullian tradition (e.g., Dollard & Miller, 1950) and focuses on the process of socialization in which behavior patterns are acquired through reinforcement processes. This approach makes relatively few assumptions about internal processes, and considers personality to be a complex of learned behaviors which are elicited by stimulus events.

In contrast to the learning-theory approach, the Freudian approach (Freud, 1933, 1938, 1949), as we noted earlier, is dynamic in nature and postulates about deep personality processes. We shall focus on the Freudian approach in this discussion of personality development, by considering the rudimentary outline of his theory of personality development. In so doing, we will be relating the theory to intrinsic motivation as discussed by White (1960).

Freud suggested that the adult personality is to a large extent determined during the first few years of a child's life. During these years the child passes through the first three stages of what is termed psychosexual development. Personality is said to be greatly influenced by what happens to a child during those three stages and by the way each stage is resolved in passing on to the next stage.

We have seen that in Freudian theory the motivational energy which most significantly influences personality and emotional development is libidinal (or sexual) energy. Freud postulated that the central locality of the libido changes with age during the early years of life. In the first year, the mouth is the locus of libidinal energy. During the first few months, the predominant behavior is sucking; during the later part of the year, the child is more concerned with the emergence of teeth and with biting. The first year is the oral phase in the child's psychosexual development. Later we will see how personality develops during the oral phase.

During the second and third years, the anal region is the locus of libidinal energy, and therefore matters of anality have primary influence on personality during these years. The third stage of psychosexual development is the phallic stage. Here, the central concern for boys is with their penis and for girls with the lack thereof. During this period, children are attracted to parents of the opposite sex, and secretly long to replace the same-sex parent as the partner of the desired parent.

Following the phallic stage, the child, according to Freudian theory, spends a few years in a period of sexual latency before emergence at puberty of the final phase, which is the adult genital stage.

The child's desire is to gratify his or her libidinal impulses. Libidinal energy is an aspect of the id, and the sole aim of the id is gratification. As children interact with the environment (which largely means parents) they begin first to develop ego processes which mediate between the id and the external world. Then superego forces, which are internalized parental injunctions, begin to develop, and the combination of ego and superego forces work to keep the id in check. This interaction of id forces with the environment is, according to Freudian theory, the basis of personality development. Since the libidinal id forces are focused in different bodily zones at different ages, the nature of the conflicts which are associated with the desire for libidinal gratification, versus the environmental inhibiting forces, are different at the different ages. Failure to achieve satisfactory resolution of these conflicts is, in the theory, the basis of psychopathology (or mental illness). We shall now consider each of the stages of psychosexual development in terms of the nature of the conflicts involved in each stage, the aspects of personality development most associated with each stage, and the relation of each stage to intrinsic motivation. Just as with the motivational aspects of Freudian theory, we will see that the personality-development aspects are also excessively narrow in their conceptualization, and that they could usefully be supplemented with an intrinsic-motivation component.

Oral Stage. During the first year of life, the child's attention is said to be focused on feeding. Mother's breast and then mother are the first things to be discriminated by a child, and the dependability of the interaction with mother around matters of feeding has a profound impact on the child's development of trust (Erikson, 1950). Similarly, the development of a sense of boundary between self and other is said to be importantly influenced by mother-child interactions around feeding. Attitudes toward receiving in general, whether of gifts, affection, or whatever, are also said to be rooted in the feeding process.

There is little doubt that feeding is of paramount importance to an infant and that sucking provides primary gratification. However, as White (1960) has pointed out, there is also much persistence in the child's play which is not readily consistent with the notion that oral gratification is the only significant matter in the first year. Children begin to play with their food, to try to feed themselves, and to manipulate the instruments of feeding in a way which interferes with ingestion of food. It seems that there is a very important need, namely the need for competence and self-determination, which is evident, especially in the later half of the first year, and which motivates this play, exploration, and manipulation. For children this play is very serious business, and satisfactory experiences with early play seem to be quite necessary for the maintenance of intrinsic motivation and the development of an attitude toward oneself as an efficacious and worthy human being.

Anal Stage. Around the first anniversary of the child's birth, the primary region for erotic delight shifts from the oral to the anal. Children in this stage seek to gratify their libidinal urges primarily through defecation. The monumental conflict is, of course, that society (in the guise of parents) seek to regulate the child's elimination, thereby interfering with the id's business of libidinal gratification.

In the less orthodox psychoanalytic writings of Thompson (1950), Erikson (1950), and others who are referred to as neo-Freudians, the conflict over libidinal discharge takes a back seat to the interpersonal interactions between mother and child, though the matter of toilet training is still the focus of this interpersonal analysis. Clearly, toilet training is a critical event in the life of a two-year-old. It is perhaps the first major clash with the world, in which the world seeks to prevent the child from doing what he or she wants. And there does seem to be clinical support for the hypothesis that children who are severely trained are more tight, rigid, and compulsive whereas more laxly treated children are more expressive, freer, and less restrictive.

In spite of the centrality of toilet training during the second and third years, White postulated that focusing the conflict on the potty is too narrow. He stated that observations alone suggest convincingly that the degree of pleasure which children derive from elimination and retention during their second and third years is not nearly as great as the degree of pleasure they derive from sucking and other oral activities during their first. Thus, although the conflict between the self-determined, willful behavior of the children versus the parental/societal dictation of behavior is undisputably the central concern of two-and three-year olds, positioning this conflict on the toilet seems to do a disservice to the richness of the struggle.

Children in this period go through enormous changes. They begin to walk and talk; they develop considerable coordination. Their intrinsic need for competence and self-determination seems to lead them to try everything new, and to do it their own way. This necessarily tries the patience of even the most understanding of parents and often leads to recurring tests of will between children and parents. Parents, since they are stronger, frequently prevail, and even when they do not, they often punish the child for having won a power struggle. Thus, these tests of will, or more generally, the parent-child interactions around the child's willfulness, are certain to have a genuinely profound impact on the child's sense of competence and self-determination–indeed, on the child's general sense of well-being.

Surely, the matters of elimination and control thereof are important issues around which we see clashes of will. And the extent to which the gastrointestinal tract is the home of psychosomatic malfunction attests to the importance of elimination in the arena of willfulness. Yet it seems equally clear that toilet training is but one aspect of the parent-child clash of wills, and might therefore be more usefully viewed as an instance of the child's struggle to feel competent and self-determining, rather than as the essence of the struggle.

Phallic Stage. The third, and probably most important stage in psychosexual development is the phallic stage. The theory asserts that following a child's third year, the genital region becomes the primary locus of libidinal excitation. At this time, children begin to have sexual and loving desires which are analogous to those of adults. Children long for sexual union with the opposite-sex parent, and therefore find themselves in the midst of an Oedipal conflict. The child covets the opposite-sex parent, yet must resist acting on those urges because of fear of the same-sex parent. This fear is the basis of later identification with the same-sex parent, and thereby a factor in achieving one's own sexual identity.

Children identify with the "imagined" aggressor (namely the same-sex parent) as a way of reducing their fear. Presumably if you "become one" with another person there is no need to fear the other. The identification with the same-sex parent represents the resolution of the Oedipal struggle, and is thereby the path through which a child moves out of the phallic stage.

By the end of the phallic stage, Freud asserted, one's personality is largely determined. What happens in later life will be a function of these first six years, and psychopathology is said to be a function of the poor resolution of these early conflicts. The Oedipal struggle is afforded the greatest import by the theory. This stage is the critical period for development of the superego; one's conscience, ego-ideal, shame, and self-respect are deeply affected by the conflicts of the Oedipal period.

The competence model suggests that this period is one in which enormous progress occurs in language, locomotion, and imagination; the young person graduates from baby to child. But being a child is a mixed blessing. While the child has the satisfaction of enormous advancement, he or she is plagued by recognition of inferiorities in size, strength, cognitive capacities, and so on. Not only are one's genitals the object of inferiority concerns, one's everything comes under such self-scrutiny. Thus, for the competence model, the conflicts of adequacy and respect are played out, not only in mommy and daddy's bedroom, but in every room of the house.

Latency and Genital Stages. A basic tenet of psychoanalytic theory is that one's personality is largely determined by the end of the phallic stage. Thus, the fourth and fifth stages of development take back seats to the first three in the realm of personality development. A competence model, while not denying that the early years are critical ones, suggests that personality is more plastic than the psychoanalytic model allows for, and that in the years following the sixth, one's personality continues to develop.

The latency period, which extends from around the seventh year to puberty, is an important one from the competence perspective. Children of this age venture out of the home to seek friendships, go to school, and become involved in various activities. Their attention shifts somewhat away from parents and toward peers and other adults. It is a time in which one is subject to rejection and ridicule, a time to learn to interact with other people rather than with fantasized others.

The latency period is a crucial time for learning about one's adequacies and competencies. It is a time when one's fears and doubts will be either confirmed or disconfirmed. The early learnings are tested in the real world. In short, White (1960), in line with Sullivan (1953), asserted that it is a critical period for the development of a realistic sense of ego-strength, competence, and self.

The final period of development, the adult period, or genital stage, is a time when questions of competence and self-determination are related to selection and pursuit of life's work and life's relationships.

The Freudian model focuses on the heterosexual, genital union of adults. With puberty comes a sharp increase in the strength of libidinal energy. Thus, the adolescent is required to bring increased ego control to the management of such impulses and to the reconciliation of the impulses with the external pressures to which he or she is subjected.

At the same time, the adolescent will be acquiring interpersonal skills and will be laying the ground work for a career. These matters are of substantial import for teenagers. And, while the upsurge of libido is most certainly a major factor in these adolescent years, the exclusive focus on libido seems to miss the boat when one attempts to explain the development of patterns of working and relating. The use of intrinsic motivation—the need for being competent and self-determining in dealing with one's life and one's surroundings—seems to offer substantial explanatory utility when dealing with these questions as well as with those which arise during the early stages of both personality and cognitive development.

SUMMARY

In this chapter I have discussed the concept of intrinsic motivation—the innate, human need for competence and self-determination—as it relates to motivation in general, to personality, and to development. I asserted that previous theories of motivation, namely Freudian and Hullian theories, were inadequate in their focus on drives as the basis of all motivated behavior and in their mechanistic conception of the human being. Although drives are important motivational forces which greatly influence behavior, I have suggested that people are active in their engagement with the environment, and that they can decide how to behave, based on an awareness of their inner needs, feelings, and thoughts.

I proposed a general approach to the study of human motivation which involves the processing of information from three sources: the environment, one's memory, and one's physiology. I suggested that this information processing leads people to an awareness of motives, which are desired future states of satisfaction, and that people choose behavioral goals based on these motives. They tend to persist until the goals are achieved, and if their expectations about the relation of the goals to the desired satisfaction were correct, the goal attainment will result in need satisfaction and a termination of the motivated sequence.

The goals may involve intrinsic behaviors for which there are no extrinsic rewards, or they may include extrinsic rewards. In either case, the experience of doing well or poorly at the activity and/or the experience of receiving a reward may have an effect on people's motivation. In this regard, I reviewed several studies which investigated the effects of extrinsic rewards on intrinsic motivation, and presented a cognitive-evaluation theory to explain the results of these studies.

The relationship between intrinsic motivation and human development was also discussed. I suggested that although the intrinsic need for competence and self-determination is innate, its form changes with one's experiences; various adult needs, such as the need for achievement, differentiate out of this basic motivational propensity. We then turned to the intrinsic motivation of cognitive development, focusing on Piaget's theory. And finally we considered personality development by presenting Freud's theory of psychosexual development, with White's elaboration of the theory to include the concept of intrinsic, effectance motivation.

REFERENCES

Atkinson, J. W. (Ed.). *Motives in fantasy, action and society.* Princeton, N.J.: Van Nostrand, 1958.

Atkinson, J. W. *An introduction to motivation.* Princeton, N.J.: Van Nostrand, 1964.

———, & **Raynor, J. O.** (Eds.). *Motivation and achievement.* Washington: V. H. Winston & Sons, 1974.

Baldwin, A. L. *Theories of child development.* New York: Wiley, 1967.

Berlyne, D. E. Novelty and curiosity as determinants of exploratory behavior. *British Journal of Psychology,* 1950, *41,* 68-80.

———. Exploration and curiosity. *Science,* 1966, *153,* 25-33.

———. The reward value of different stimulation. In J. T. Tapp (Ed.), *Reinforcement and behavior.* New York: Academic Press, 1969.

Brehm, J. W. Motivational effects of cognitive dissonance. *Nebraska Symposium on Motivation,* 1962, *10,* 51-77.

Bruner, J. S., Jolly, A., & Sylva, K. (Eds.). *Play: Its role in development and evolution.* New York: Basic, 1976.

Butler, R. A. Discrimination learning by rhesus monkeys to visual exploration motivation. *Journal of Comparative and Physiological Psychology,* 1953, *46,* 95-98.

Dashiell, J. F. A quantitative demonstration of animal drive. *Journal of Comparative Psychology,* 1925, *5,* 205-208.

deCharms, R. *Personal causation: The internal affective determinants of behavior.* New York: Academic Press, 1968.

———. *Enhancing motivation: Change in the classroom.* New York: Irvington, 1976.

Deci, E. L. *Intrinsic motivation.* New York: Plenum, 1975.

———. Motivation, will, and well-being. Unpublished manuscript, University of Rochester, 1978.

———, & **Cascio, W. F.** Changes in intrinsic motivation as a function of negative feedback and threats. Eastern Psychological Association Convention, Boston, Mass., 1972.

———, & **Krusell, J.** Cognitive evaluation theory and some comments on the Calder, Staw Critique. *Journal of Personality and Social Psychology,* 1975, *31,* 81-85.

Dember, W. N., & Earl, R. W. Analysis of exploratory, manipulatory, and curiosity behaviors. *Psychological Review,* 1957, *64,* 91-96.

Dollard, J., & Miller, N. E. *Personality and psychotherapy.* New York: McGraw-Hill, 1950.

Elkind, D. Cognitive growth cycles in mental development. *Nebraska Symposium on Motivation,* 1971, *19,* 1-31.

Erikson, E. *Childhood and society.* New York: Norton, 1950.

Eysenck, H. J. Cortical inhibition, figural aftereffect, and theory of personality. *Journal of Abnormal and Social Psychology,* 1955, *51,* 94-106.

Festinger, L. *A theory of cognitive dissonance.* Stanford, Calif.: Stanford University Press, 1957.

Fiske, D. W., & Maddi, S. R. *Functions of varied experience.* Homewood, Ill.: Dorsey, 1961.

Flavel, J. H. *The developmental psychology of Jean Piaget.* Princeton, N.J.: Van Nostrand, 1963.

Freud, S. *New introductory lectures on psychoanalysis.* New York: Norton, 1933.

____. Three contributions to the theory of sex. In *The Basic Writings of Sigmund Freud.* New York: Random House, 1938.

____. *An outline of psychoanalysis.* New York: Norton, 1949.

Harlow, H. F. Motivation as a factor in the acquisition of new responses. *Nebraska Symposium on Motivation,* 1953, *1,* 24-49.

Harter, S. Effectance motivation reconsidered: Toward a developmental model. *Human Development,* 1978, *21,* 34-64.

Hebb, D. O. Drives and the C.N.S. (conceptual nervous system). *Psychological Review,* 1955, *62,* 243-254.

Heider, F. *The psychology of interpersonal relations.* New York: Wiley, 1958.

Helson, H. *Adaptation-level theory.* New York: Harper & Row, 1964.

Horner, M. S. The measurement and behavioral implications of fear of success in women. In J. W. Atkinson & J. O. Raynor (Eds.) *Motivation and achievement.* Washington, D. C.: Winston, 1974.

Horney, K. *New ways in psychoanalysis.* New York: Norton, 1939.

Hull, C. L. *Principles of behavior.* New York: Appleton-Century-Crofts, 1943.

Hunt, J. McV. Intrinsic motivation and its role in psychological development. *Nebraska Symposium on Motivation,* 1965, *13,* 189-282.

Irwin, F. W. *Intentional behavior and motivation.* Philadelphia: Lippincott, 1971.

Isaac, W. Evidence for a sensory drive in monkeys. *Psychological Reports,* 1962, *11,* 175-181.

Kagan, J. Motives and development. *Journal of Personality and Social Psychology,* 1972, *22,* 51-66.

Lepper, M. R., Greene, D., & Nisbett, R. E. Undermining children's intrinsic interest with extrinsic rewards: A test of the "overjustification" hypothesis. *Journal of Personality and Social Psychology,* 1973, *28,* 129-137.

Leuba, C. Toward some integration of learning theories: The concept of optimal stimulation. *Psychological Reports,* 1955, *1,* 27-33.

Lewin, K. *Principles of topological psychology.* New York: McGraw-Hill, 1936.

____. *The conceptual representation and measurement of psychological forces.* Durham, N. C.: Duke University Press, 1938.

____. *Field theory in social science.* Edited by D. Cartwright. New York: Harper & Row, 1951. (a)

———. Intention, will and need. In D. Rappaport (Ed.), *Organization and pathology of thought.* New York: Columbia University Press, 1951, pp. 95-153. (b)

Locke, E. A. Toward a theory of task motivation and incentives. *Organizational Behavior and Human Performance,* 1968, *3,* 157-189.

Lowen, A. *Betrayal of the body.* New York: MacMillan, 1966.

Mandler, G. *Mind and emotion.* New York: Wiley, 1975.

Maslow, A. H. A theory of human motivation. *Psychological Review,* 1943, *50,* 370-396.

McClelland, D. C. *The achieving society.* Princeton, N.J.: Van Nostrand, 1961.

———. *Power: The inner experience.* New York: Irvington, 1975.

———, **Atkinson, J. W., Clark, R. W., & Lowell, E. L.** *The achievement motive.* New York: Appleton-Century-Crofts, 1953.

McGraw, K. The detrimental effects of reward on performance. In M. Lepper & D. Greene (Eds.), *The hidden costs of reward.* Hillsdale, N.J.: Lawrence Erlbaum, 1978.

Miller, G. A., Galanter, E., & Pribram, K. A. *Plans and the structure of behavior.* New York: Holt, 1960.

Mischel, T. Piaget: Cognitive conflict and the motivation of thought. In T. Mischel (Ed.), *Cognitive development and epistomology.* New York: Academic Press, 1971, pp. 311-355.

Montgomery, K. C. The role of exploratory drive in learning. *Journal of Comparative and Physiological Psychology,* 1954, *47,* 60-64.

Myers, A. K. & Miller, N. E. Failure to find a learned drive based on hunger: Evidence for learning motivated by "exploration." *Journal of Comparative and Physiological Psychology,* 1954, *47,* 428-436.

Nissen, H. W. A study of exploratory behavior in the white rat by means of the obstruction method. *Journal of Genetic Psychology,* 1930, *37,* 361-376.

Peak, H. Attitude and motivation. *Nebraska Symposium on Motivation,* 1955, *3,* 149-189.

Perls, F. *Ego, hunger, and aggression.* London: Allen & Unwin, 1947 (Reprinted by Random House, 1969)

———. *The gestalt approach & eye witness to therapy.* Ben Lomand, Calif.: Science and Behavior Books, 1973.

Petri, A., McCulloch, R. & Kazdin, P. The perceptual characteristics of juvenile delinquents. *Journal of Nervous and Mental Disease,* 1962, *134,* 415-421.

Piaget, J. *The origins of intelligence in children.* New York: International Universities Press, 1952.

Rapaport, D. On the psychoanalytic theory of motivation. In M. R. Jones (Ed.) *Nebraska Symposium on Motivation,* 1960, *8,* 173-247.

Reich, W. *Selected writings: An introduction to orgonomy.* New York: Farrar, Strauss, & Giroux, 1960.

Rosen, B. C. & D'Andrade, R. The psychosocial origins of achievement motivation. *Sociometry,* 1959, *22,* 185-218.

Rotter, J. B. *Social learning and clinical psychology.* Englewood Cliffs, N.J.: Prentice-Hall, 1954.

____. Generalized expectancies for internal versus external control of reinforcement. *Psychological Monographs,* 1966, *80*(1), Whole no. 609, pp. 1-28.

Ryan, E. D. & Foster, R. Athletic participation and perceptual augmentation and reduction. *Journal of Personality and Social Psychology,* 1967, *6,* 472-476.

Sales, S. M. Need for stimulation as a factor in social behavior. *Journal of Personality and Social Psychology,* 1971, *19,* 124-134.

Shapira, Z. Expectancy determinants of intrinsically motivated behavior. *Journal of Personality and Social Psychology,* 1976, *34,* 1235-1244.

Sokolov, E. N. Higher nervous functions: The orienting reflex. *Annual Review of Physiology,* 1963, *25,* 545-580.

Sullivan, H. S. *The interpersonal theory of psychiatry.* New York: Norton, 1953.

Thompson, C. *Psychoanalysis: Evolution and development.* New York: Hermitage, 1950.

Tolman, E. C. *Purposive behavior in animals and men.* New York: Century, 1932.

____. Principles of purposive behavior. In S. Koch (Ed.) *Psychology: A study of a science. Vol. II.* New York: McGraw-Hill, 1959, pp. 92-157.

Vroom, V. H. *Work and motivation.* New York: Wiley, 1964.

Welker, W. L. Some determinants of play and exploration in chimpanzees. *Journal of Comparative and Physiological Psychology,* 1956, *49,* 84-89.

White, R. W. Motivation reconsidered: The concept of competence. *Psychological Review,* 1959, *66,* 297-333.

____. Competence and the psychosexual stages of development. *Nebraska Symposium on Motivation,* 1960, *8,* 97-141.

Winter, D. G. *The power motive.* New York: Free Press, 1973.

Woodworth, R. S. *Dynamic psychology.* New York: Columbia University Press, 1918.

Young, P. T. *Motivation and emotion.* New York: Wiley, 1961.

Zuckerman, M. The sensation seeking motive. In B. Maher (Ed.), *Progress in experimental personality theory,* Vol. 7. New York: Academic Press, 1974, pp. 79-148.

SEYMOUR EPSTEIN

The Self-Concept: A Review and the Proposal of an Integrated Theory of Personality

3

Many students in introductory psychology courses are disappointed by what they are taught. They had hoped to be exposed to information that would help them understand themselves and others. Instead, they are told that psychology, as a science, must first uncover fundamental truths about simple behavior before it can hope to make contributions to the understanding of significant human behavior. The emphasis on examining simple behavior that can be objectively studied in the laboratory falls within the behavioristic tradition. Behavioristic psychology is modeled after the physical sciences. After all, chemistry and physics have had remarkable success by studying isolated, simple effects in well-controlled laboratory experiments; and it would seem, at first glance, that the same approach should work for psychology.

Behaviorism has emphasized outwardly observable behavior and paid little attention to people's inner processes, such as their fantasies, thoughts, and feelings, as these cannot be directly measured. Traditional behaviorists have failed to recognize that although such inner reactions cannot be studied by direct observation, they are nevertheless an important aspect of human functioning that deserves to be studied in some manner. If psychologists were to ignore all that is subjective, they would have to ignore a great deal of behavior that is uniquely human. That an extreme behavioristic position is unreasonable becomes apparent if one considers going to a "scientifically" oriented physician with a complaint that one has a headache, only to be told that it is of no consequence because it is nothing more than a feeling.

Among the psychologists who disagree most strongly with a radical behaviorist position are those who emphasize the importance of a self-concept. Behaviorists view the self-concept with suspicion; they regard it as vague and of no more scientific value than the concept of a soul. The psychologists who endorse a self-concept consider it a necessary concept for elucidating what is distinctly

This paper and the research reported in it were supported by research grant MH 20193 from the National Institute of Mental Health, USPHS.

human. They argue that special procedures have to be devised for psychology that do not simply mimic those of the physical sciences.

The self-theorists who differ most from the radical behaviorists are the phenomenologists. Phenomenologists believe that behavior can only be understood from the viewpoint of the person doing the behaving. They believe that, as each individual responds to his or her own personal reality, it is pointless to define stimuli from an objective viewpoint. To illustrate their point, consider the following example. As a person walks by a group of people, they suddenly burst into laughter. The passerby believes they are laughing at him, and feels awkward and embarrassed. Whether, from an external viewpoint, they really were laughing at him is immaterial so far as his reaction is concerned. His embarrassment can only be understood by recognizing that the stimulus that he was reacting to was the subjective perception that they were laughing at him. The chemist has no such problem with his chemicals. When he mixes zinc with hydrochloric acid he knows how they will react. He need not be concerned that the zinc will think the hydrochloric acid is something else and will therefore not produce its customary reaction with it. From the viewpoint of the phenomenologists, psychologists can only develop a meaningful science of human behavior if they base their science on the individual's subjective perception of stimuli.

Unfortunately, the phenomenological approach presents some very real problems for the development of psychology as a science. How is one to objectively classify stimuli in order to examine their effects, if the meaning of each stimulus differs for each individual? How is one to compare people on common dimensions if the dimensions themselves differ among people? Although some intriguing procedures have been proposed, they considerably complicate experimental procedures, and it is therefore not surprising that, to date, phenomenological procedures have had only a limited influence on psychological research.

In summary, behaviorism has the virtue of being objective and highly compatible with scientific procedures as traditionally practiced in other sciences. Offsetting this advantage is the disadvantage that behaviorism is able to be highly objective only at the expense of ignoring certain significant, distinctly human aspects of experience. The advantages and disadvantages of phenomenology are the reverse of these. This raises the question of whether it is possible to combine the advantages of both within a single theory. The present paper attempts to do just that by proposing a theory that recognizes the subjective nature of human perception, yet does so within the framework of an essentially objective psychology. The theory begins with the assumption that all individuals are guided in their behavior by an implicit theory of reality, which has subsections consisting of a self-theory and a world-theory. Such a personal theory is no more mystical than a theory in science. Individuals develop the theory because they need it to exist and would experience chaos without it. Before proceeding further in developing the theory, it will be helpful to present a summary of the views of others on the nature of the self-concept.

VIEWS ON THE NATURE OF THE SELF-CONCEPT

Among those who consider the self-concept important, there are differences of opinion about what the self-concept is. There are those who believe the self-concept should include an executive self that directs behavior, or the self as a "knower," while others argue that the self-concept should be restricted to the views an individual holds about himself or herself, or the self as an object of knowledge. Included among the former are the phenomenologists, who believe that behavior can only be understood from the viewpoint of the individual, and the cognitive psychologists, who emphasize the mediating concepts that individuals use to interpret the objective world around them. The cognitive psychologist's position can be viewed as an attempt to integrate the position of the objectively oriented behaviorist and the subjectively oriented phenomenologist by focusing on the processes by which the individual, through his cognitions, transforms the objective world into a subjective one.

A summary of the positions of different views on the self-concept will be presented under the following headings: (a) the development of a self-concept, (b) the self as an object of knowledge, (c) the self as an integrative structure from a phenomenological perspective, and (d) the self as an integrative structure from a cognitive perspective.

The Development of a Self-Concept

It is obvious that we are able to think about ourselves in the same ways we think about others. We observe that we have brown or green eyes, that we are tall or short, that we run fast or slowly. So long as our views about ourselves are reasonably accurate, it is not surprising that we acquire them; to a large extent, they are a direct consequence of observation. Yet, other views that we have about ourselves are highly inaccurate. People who are highly competent sometimes feel deeply inadequate; people who are inferior feel superior; people with an ordinary appearance feel beautiful; and people who are attractive feel ugly. More impressive yet, some people who have lived exemplary lives are torn with severe guilt to the point they no longer wish to live, while others who have committed horrendous crimes suffer not a twinge of conscience. It is thus apparent that some of our attitudes about ourselves have developed for reasons that have little to do with objective reality; and, once formed, they must be resistant to change, or else they would have been disconfirmed long ago. If some of our views about ourselves do not come directly from our own observations, where do they come from? It will be seen below that Cooley and Mead suggest that society plays a key role in influencing our views about ourselves, while Sullivan emphasizes the role of "significant others" in our childhood.

Cooley. Cooley (1902) defined the self as everything that an individual designates as his own and to which the individual refers with the personal pronouns

"I," "me," and "myself." He noted that whatever is regarded as belonging to the self has the potential for evoking strong emotional responses. He proposed the concept of "the looking-glass self," according to which, we learn to react to ourselves by anticipating how others will react to us. That is, we view ourselves through the eyes of others. Cooley expounded on the looking-glass self as follows:

> In a very large and interesting class of cases the social reference takes the form of a somewhat definite imagination of how one's self . . . appears in a particular mind, and the kind of self-feeling one has is determined by the attitude toward this attributed to that other mind. A social self of this sort might be called the reflected or looking-glass self:
>
> *Each to each a looking-glass*
> *Reflects the other that doth pass*
>
> As we see our face, figure, and dress in the glass, and are interested in them because they are ours, and pleased or otherwise with them according as they do or do not answer to what we should like them to be; so in imagination we perceive in another's mind some thought of our appearance, manners, aims, deeds, character, friends, and so on, and are variously affected by it.
>
> A self-idea of this sort seems to have three principal elements: the imagination of our appearance to the other person; the imagination of his judgment of that appearance; and some sort of self-feeling such as pride or mortification. The comparison with a looking-glass hardly suggests the second element, the imagined judgment, which is quite essential. The thing that moves us to pride or shame is not the mere mechanical reflection of ourselves, but an imputed sentiment, the imagined effect of this reflection upon another's mind. This is evident from the fact that the character and weight of the other, in whose mind we see ourselves, makes all the difference with our feelings. We are ashamed to seem evasive in the presence of a straightforward man, cowardly in the presence of a brave one, gross in the eyes of a refined one, and so on. We always imagine, and in imagining share, the judgments of the other mind. A man will boast to one person of an action—say some sharp transaction in trade—which he would be ashamed to own to another (1902, pp. 152-153).

Cooley makes us aware of how much our views about ourselves, which we like to think of as a direct consequence of our own independent judgments, are influenced by our concern over how others regard us.

Mead. Mead's (1934) views are in many ways similar to those of Cooley. Mead believed that a self-concept can only develop in a social group, "for selves exist only in relation to other selves." Unlike an ant or a bee, that relies on biologically built-in, or instinctive, reactions to guide its social behavior, human beings learn to anticipate the actions of others by imagining how they themselves would respond if they were the other. As a consequence, they learn to attend to their own inner reactions, and this, in turn, makes them aware of a sense of self. This process is actually the opposite of the process described by Cooley, as the individual attempts to anticipate another's behavior by seeing the other's behavior as a reflection of his own tendencies. As a result, the individual "becomes a self" in his experience to the extent that his own attitudes reflect more general social attitudes. For Mead, the development of self-awareness is facilitiated by attempting to become aware of one's own reactions in order to predict how others will behave in similar circumstances. In agreement with Cooley, Mead noted that we also learn to think about ourselves as objects by imagining how others view us. Mead proposed that we form a concept of a "generalized other" to represent in our imagination how certain classes of people react to our behavior. In the process of imagining how the generalized other responds to us, we learn to view ourselves as social objects, or selves. We thus have as many selves as we have views of the roles of different groups of people.

Sullivan. Cultures obviously cannot directly influence individuals; only people can. That is, individuals must act as the transmitters of the values of a culture. Yet each transmitter exerts his or her unique influence as well. According to Sullivan (1953), a few "significant others" exert a particularly strong influence on the development of the self in early childhood. By far the most significant other is "the mothering one," who is usually the child's own mother, but could be a mother substitute. It is evident that the child is dependent on the mothering one not only for pleasure and for relief from pain, but for life itself. Because the mother's good will is necessary for the child's existence, the child develops intense anxiety whenever he or she senses disapproval and withdrawal of the mother's love. The self-system develops out of the desire of the child to gain approval and avoid disapproval. By internalizing the values of the mother, the child is able to correct his or her own tendencies or impulses before behaving in a manner that would incur the mother's disapproval. The child is thereby able to avoid anxiety associated with the anticipation of disapproval and withdrawal of love by the mother. Let us consider a concrete example of this process. At first, when Johnny reaches for the forbidden cookie jar before dinner, his mother says, "Bad Johnny," and slaps his hand. Later, when Johnny finds himself tempted to reach for the cookie jar, he slaps his own hand and says to himself, "Bad Johnny," which helps him refrain from reaching for the cookie jar. By controlling his own behavior in this manner, he avoids the disapproval of his mother that he would have had to contend with if he had not exerted control. Through this process, Johnny develops a conscience, supported by guilt and anxiety if he fails to follow its dictates. His conscience becomes as effective in controlling his behavior as the fear of loss of his mother's love used to be. Instead of being controlled by fear of his mother's disapproval, from this point on he will be controlled by fear of his own disapproval. Because the learning of a conscience is motivated by the desire to avoid anxiety, the attitudes that it reinforces tend to be intense and resistant to change. This accounts for the automatic and persistant nature of conscience, as distinct from other self-evaluative reactions.

Three particularly important components of the self-system for Sullivan are the "good-me," the "bad-me," and the "not-me." The good-me is organized around experiences with the mother that were rewarding. It consists of impulses and thoughts that were approved of by the mother. It follows that a child who is treated with love and approval by the significant people in his or her life will internalize positive feelings toward the self, or, in other words, will have high self-esteem.

The bad-me is organized around experiences in which the mother had expressed moderate levels of disapproval toward the child. The bad-me is associated with anxiety, but anxiety that is not so extreme that the child is unable to cope with it. The bad-me, like the good-me, is a well-differentiated organization that is useful to the individual in everyday life, as it helps the individual to avoid undesirable behavior. Just as the good-me produces positive feelings toward the self, the bad-me produces negative ones. Such feelings are necessary for a conscience, which the individual requires as an automatic deterrent to engaging in antisocial behavior.

The "not-me" serves no such constructive function. Rather, it is associated with psychopathology. It arises from experiences in which the "mothering one" had expressed disapproval so intense that the child was completely overwhelmed with anxiety. Because the organization of the not-me is associated with such strong anxiety, it becomes dissociated from the remainder of the self-system, and is thus inaccessible to, and uncontrollable by, the individual. When experiences occur later in life that are reminders of the not-me, the individual experiences overwhelming anxiety and disruption of his thought. Because it is dissociated from the rest of the self, and exists only in the unconscious mind, material in the not-me remains forever at an infantile level. The not-me is used by Sullivan to account for many of the strange reactions exhibited in psychosis.

Corresponding to concepts of a good-me and a bad-me, the child has concepts of a good-mother and a bad-mother. It is distressing for a child to think of his or her mother as bad, and, consequently, when the mother makes the child feel bad, the child frequently decides that he or she, not the mother, is bad. Nevertheless, there is a tendency to see the mother who makes life miserable as bad. Since it is too frightening for the child to acknowledge that his or her mother is bad, the concept of the bad mother tends to be shut away in the unconscious. Individuals may then emphasize their own badness as a way of denying that they view their mothers as bad. Expressed otherwise, if individuals believe that they are good, then they must believe that a mother who treated them badly is bad. If they wish to believe the mother is good, then they must conclude that the reason the mother treated them badly, is, in fact, that they are bad. Such reactions can account for some of the unrealistic negative self-evaluations and self-destructive behavior that individuals exhibit. They can also explain why some children go through periods in which they are either hostile to their mothers and accept themselves, or are hostile to themselves and accept their mothers. The generalization of such feelings to other figures can account for why some people seem motivated to maintain negative evaluations of themselves, and why others are unable to accept themselves and a loved one at the same time.

The Self as an Object of Knowledge

If I say, "I have green eyes, brown hair, am average in intelligence, and tend to be introverted," I am describing myself as an object of knowledge, much as I might describe someone else. But who is it that is making the judgments and statements about myself? It is I, myself, who makes such judgments about me, myself. The "I" who makes the judgments and the "me" who is being judged both refer to myself. However, in the first case, "myself" is treated as a knower; in the second case, as an object of knowledge.

Psychologists are in agreement on the importance of the concept of the self as an object of knowledge. It is obviously important to know how people regard themselves, including their abilities, personality attributes, and overall assessment of self, as these have widespread influences on feelings and behavior. However, psychologists are not in agreement about the value of the concept of an executive self, or the self as a knower; it suggests to some that there is a little person residing in the head of the larger person, telling him or her what to do. It is then no easier to account for the behavior of the little person than to account for the behavior of the big one. Thus, according to these psychologists, nothing is gained by assuming the existence of an executive self. Later, we will examine the position of those who argue for an executive self. First, let us consider the less controversial views of those who regard the self as an object of knowledge.

William James. James (1907) noted that the boundaries of the self are not defined by our physical bodies, but include an "extended self." The extended self refers to all that we call our own, and all with whom and with which we share a bond of identity, such as our family, possessions, and country. When any aspect of the self is diminished, we feel sadness. The more the self is involved, the greater the emotional reaction. We suffer with people and share their joys to the extent that we identify with them, and we have little concern for people whom we consider alien to ourselves. James described the relationship of the self to the emotions as follows:

> We feel and act about certain things that are ours very much as we feel and act about ourselves. Our fame, our children, the work of our hands, may be as dear to us as our bodies are, and arouse the same feelings and the same acts of reprisal if attacked. And our bodies themselves, are they

> simply ours, or are they *us*? Certainly men have been ready to disown their very bodies and to regard them as mere vestures, or even as prisons of clay from which they should some day be glad to escape . . . . *In its widest possible sense,* however, *a man's Me is the sum total of all that he can call his,* not only his body, and his psychic powers, but his clothes and his house, his wife and children, his ancestors and friends, his reputation and works, his lands and horses, and yacht and bank account. All these things give him the same emotions. If they wax and prosper, he feels triumphant; if they dwindle and die away, he feels cast down—not necessarily in the same degree for each thing, but in much the same way for all (James, 1907, p. 177).

James considered the self to be both differentiated and integrated. Divisions of the self consist of the material me, the social me, and the spiritual me. The material me refers to a person's body, his or her physical needs, clothing, immediate family, and physical possessions, including the home. These are all objects about which the individual has a feeling of possession. Because the person views them as "his" or "hers," he or she will defend such possessions as his or her own body, and sometimes even more. The material me receives its rewards in the form of physical experiences and a feeling of pride of possession.

The social me consists largely of the roles an individual plays. As people have a need to be recognized and admired by others, they acquire social roles that gain them acceptance and approval. A man plays a role as a father, a husband, and a businessman. His actions in all these roles are influenced by how he believes others will respond to the role.

For example, when a man plays the role of a father in the prescribed way, he assumes that his children will, and should, play their role in the prescribed way, such as by respecting, appreciating, and obeying him. Roles are prescribed ways of behaving that have a high likelihood of gaining acceptance in particular settings and of allowing one to predict the reaction of others to one's own behavior. Like Mead, James believed that a person has as many social selves as there are groups of people whose acceptance matters to him or her. The social me receives its rewards in the form of recognition from others. Acceptance, admiration, and honor are obtained if the individual plays his social roles properly; shame and rejection may result if he does not.

The spiritual me refers to the individual's inner self, including his or her feelings, thoughts, fantasies, and impulses. All individuals have a sense of inner identity that is different from their physical selves. They feel they would be essentially themselves even if they lost a part of their body, such as a finger. It is this sense of a stable, nonmaterial aspect of self that people often consider the inner core of their being, similar to a soul, that James wished to call attention to by positing a spiritual me.

A particularly important aspect of the self-system is the individual's overall evaluation of himself or herself. There is a unity in the functioning of self-esteem, such that when any of the empirical selves is enhanced or diminished, a corresponding increase or decrease in the overall assessment of the self occurs. We have a generally good feeling about ourselves when we are pleased with our bodies, with the way we conduct ourselves socially, or with our inner thoughts and motives. In like manner, we feel bad about ourselves, *in general,* when we believe our bodies look unattractive, when we are disappointed in our social behavior, or when we are displeased with our thoughts or impulses. In sum, when we assess any aspect of ourselves favorably, we experience an overall rise in self-esteem, and consequent good feelings; when we assess any aspect of ourselves unfavorably, we experience an overall drop in self-esteem, and consequent bad feelings.

Changes in self-esteem are influenced not by absolute success and failure but by the ratio of an individual's achievement to his or her aspirations. Expressed otherwise, our happiness is as much dependent on our level of aspiration as on our actual achievement.

> So we have the paradox of a man shamed to death because he is only the second pugilist or the second oarsman in the world. That he is able to beat the whole population of the above minus one is nothing; he has "pitted" himself to beat that one; and as long as he doesn't do that nothing else counts. . . . Yonder puny fellow, however, whom every one can beat, suffers no chagrin about it, for he has long ago abandoned the attempt to "carry that line," as the merchants say, of self at all. With no attempt there can be no failure; with no failure, no humiliation (James, 1907, pp. 186-187).

Gordon Allport. Allport (1955) originally accepted the idea of an executive self, but later (1961) agreed with James that the executive self should be banished to the realm of philosophy. For this reason we have grouped him with those who consider the self as an object of knowledge. Nevertheless, Allport uses several concepts that are consistent with a belief in an executive self.

Allport decided that the word *self* has so many confusing meanings that it would be best to start all over with a different word. For this purpose, he suggested that *proprium* be used. The proprium consists of all that is central in the personality and which the individual regards as intimately his own. The proprium has the following attributes: (a) bodily sense, (b) self-identity, or continuity over time, (c) ego-enhancement, (d) ego-extension, (f) rational process, (g) self-image, and (h) propriate striving.

Bodily sense, the most basic attribute, refers to awareness of sensations from the body. Self-identity refers to an individual's awareness that he is a distinct being, similar to, yet different from, others. We tend to take the idea of self-identity for granted. Yet, such awareness does not always exist. It requires an act of conscious effort, and is a product of learning. The infant cannot differentiate its own body from objects that are not part of itself, and has no sense of personal identity. In adults, the self-identity is not entirely stable, but can be lost in drug states and in psychosis. Ego-enhancement refers to the individual's striving for self-esteem. Allport believed that ego-enhancement is a fundamental need of all humans, and is tied to the need for survival. Ego-extension is equivalent to James's idea of an extended self. Rational process refers to the cognitive processes that an individual employs to make sense out of the world and to synthesize inner needs with outer reality. Thus, rational process constitutes the thought processes with which the individual adapts to reality. Self-image refers to the individual's concepts about his abilities, status, roles, and aspirations. Allport noted that the discrepancy between where one is at and where one would like to be need not be a negative state but can serve as a powerful source of motivation for growth. Propriate striving refers to long-term goals, to a tendency for motives to persist in the face of obstacles, thereby contributing to unity in the personality and to maintaining an orientation toward the future. Allport's position on such motives is opposite to the view of behaviorists, who regard motives as states of tension that subside when the motive is satisfied. Allport, like Jung, believed that a person's behavior is as much pulled by his or her conception of the future as it is pushed by memories of the past.

The Self as an Integrative Structure from a Phenomenological Perspective

According to the phenomenological psychologists, to understand someone it is necessary to understand that person's conceptual system regarding the self, which is the nucleus of a more general conceptual system. The self-system from this viewpoint is not an object of knowledge, but is a cognitive organization, which actively influences the experiences an individual seeks out and which determines how the individual interprets experience. From the viewpoint of the phenomenologists, once one knows how a person perceives and interprets the world, one can predict that person's behavior, for behavior always follows directly from an individual's perceptions. While people may behave strangely from another's viewpoint, the behavior is always reasonable from the viewpoint of the people doing the behaving, at least at the moment they are carrying out the behavior.

Lecky. According to Lecky (1969), each person is born into a world that would be experienced as chaotic, if not for the order that the individual imposes on it. The individual's thoughts about himself or herself and the world are organized into a unified system, much like a scientist's views are organized into a single theory. Thus, the achievement of orderliness requires active mental work. The organized conceptual system of an individual is the individual's personality. Lecky defined personality as "the organization of experience into an integrated whole," and, alternatively, as "a unified scheme of experience, an organization of values that are consistent with one another." If the individual's system for organizing experience were to disappear, he or she would be as incapable of functioning as a scientist without a theory. As a result, individuals will go to great lengths to protect the integrity of their conceptual systems. According to Lecky, the one overriding need of the individual is to preserve the unity of his or her conceptual system.

An individual's conceptual system is in a state of continuous flux, assimilating some and rejecting other information. At any one moment in time, only certain information can be assimilated without threatening the stability of the organization of the individual's system. Assimilation is accompanied by pleasant emotions; inability to assimilate, by anxiety. Accordingly, the individual is motivated to seek out experiences that contribute to the unity of his or her conceptual system, and to avoid experiences that threaten its unity. In order to do this, the individual must learn to anticipate events.

There are two basic problems that every individual must solve; namely, maintaining internal consistency in the conceptual system and adapting realistically to the outer world. Adjustment exists to the extent that the individual accomplishes both simultaneously, and maladjustment to the extent that neither is achieved or that one is achieved at the expense of the other.

Lecky attributes a great deal of importance to the evaluative process. He considers the most important evaluation of all to be the individual's overall evaluation of himself or herself, as this evaluation influences all other evaluations. Experiences that the individual regards as consistent with his or her evaluation of self are readily assimilated, while those that are regarded as inconsistent produce anxiety and are therefore usually rejected. Should an incongruent experience occur that is not rejected and that influences an individual's overall self-evaluation his or her entire conceptual system, or personality, would be altered. Expressed otherwise, self-esteem is of such central importance to the organization of the personality that, should it change, widespread changes in the entire personality would ensue.

Emotions can only be understood from a perspective that recognizes the individual's need to maintain the unity of his or her conceptual system. Pleasure occurs when new material is assimilated. The more difficult the assimilation, the greater the pleasure. Love is experienced when a person or object is assimilated that confirms the value of the self. Grief is experienced when there is a loss of someone or something that supported the self, requiring the individual to reorganize his or her personality in order to maintain its unity. Hatred and anger occur when a person is confronted with unassimilable information that threatens the unity of the individual's personality, and that the individual would therefore like to have removed or destroyed. The emotion of horror, or of being overwhelmed with fear, occurs when a threatening situation arises so rapidly that there is not sufficient time for it to be assimilated. Fear is experienced when threat to the organization of the personality is anticipated in the absence of a solution for dealing with the threat. It is noteworthy that, according to Lecky, fear and anger have similar causes, both being instigated by threats to the unity of the self-system. They differ only in that with anger there is an active desire to destroy or remove the source of the threat, while with fear there is uncertainty about how to deal with the threat.

There are two major implications of Lecky's theory for behavior change. First, if one wishes to help another, it is necessary to see the world through that person's eyes. Lecky considered it self-defeating to impose one's own standards on another, as this is apt to cause the other person to feel misunderstood and therefore to resist being influenced. Second, it can be helpful to make an individual aware of his or her own inconsistencies in thinking. Because people strive for consistency, awareness of inconsistencies can motivate an individual to re-examine his or her self-system, which can lead to significant changes in personality.

Snygg and Combs. The views of Snygg and Combs (1949) are similar in many respects to those of Lecky. However, they are presented from the viewpoint of Gestalt Psychology.

Snygg and Combs assume that every individual exists in a "phenomenal field" that defines reality as the individual perceives it. Each person has his own phenomenal field. To understand an individual, it is necessary to infer his phenomenal field, which can only be done by someone who has an overlapping phenomenal field. To some extent, all human beings have overlapping phenomenal fields, as they all are similarly constructed biologically and have all lived in a world of experience that has certain common features. However, while all human beings have the potential for understanding all other human beings, people who come from similar backgrounds are in the best position to understand each other, as they are apt to have the most similar phenomenal fields.

The phenomenal field is both differentiated and integrated. It has a figure and a background that vary from moment to moment. The part of the field that is in the background is unclear, and can be regarded as unconscious. The part of the field that is figure is clearly differentiated, and corresponds to consciousness. Because the phenomenal field is fluid, it is necessary to sample behavior from moment to moment if one wishes to accurately predict another's behavior. By knowing how a person perceives a situation at a moment in time, it is possible to predict his or her behavior, for behavior always follows directly from perception. The problem in prediction is how to obtain a sufficiently thorough picture of how an individual perceives different situations in order to know how he or she will perceive the particular situations in which one wishes to predict. It is important to recognize that, since the phenomenal field of a person is always organized, events in a person's experience can never be judged in isolation, but must always be judged in the context of surrounding events.

Part of the phenomenal field is differentiated into a "phenomenal self." The phenomenal self is an extended self which includes everything that the individual refers to with the words, *I, me,* and *mine.* Snygg and Combs consider the defense of the phenomenal self to be the individual's one most basic need. They state the matter as follows:

> From birth to death the defense of the phenomenal self is the most pressing, most crucial, if not the only task of existence. Moreover, since human beings are conscious of the future, their needs extend into the future as well, and they strive to preserve not only the self as it exists but to build it up and to strengthen it against the future of which they are aware. We might combine these two aspects into a formal definition of the basic human needs as: "the preservation and enhancement of the phenomenal self" (p. 58).

The phenomenal self is the nucleus of the phenomenal field. The phenomenal self organizes the individual's goals and needs, and these in turn influence the person's perceptions and therefore his or her entire phenomenal field. How a person perceives himself or herself influences what experiences are sought out, what experiences are avoided, and how experiences are interpreted. In order to protect the phenomenal self the individual resorts to the kinds of defensive operations discussed by psychoanalysts. Psychopathology arises from the exaggerated use of defense mechanisms. Although preserving and enhancing might well qualify as two needs, Snygg and Combs treat them as essentially one, for they believe that the purpose of enhancing is to protect the phenomenal self from future threats to its stability.

Snygg and Combs stress the importance of creating an atmosphere of acceptance in psychotherapy. Such an atmosphere, they believe, encourages individuals to explore new ways of experiencing the self and the world, and to risk reorganizations in the conceptual system. They believe that interpretations by a therapist tend to threaten an individual's phenomenal self, and are therefore best avoided. They advocate the establishment of a nonauthoritarian atmosphere, which they believe facilitates the development of self-direction.

Rogers. Rogers, the most influential of the phenomenological self-theorists, has presented his theory of personality in several books which explore its implications for psychotherapy, education, human relationships, and leading a life that is rich and fulfilling (Rogers, 1942, 1951, 1961, 1969, 1972). Rogers acknowledges the influence of Lecky (1969), Snygg and Combs (1949), Sullivan (1953), and Raimy (1943). The most detailed presentation of his theory is in his book *Client-Centered Therapy* (1951), where the theory is set forth in the form of nineteen propositions. The summary that follows is based mainly on this work, but also includes his views on disorganization as elaborated in a later publication (Rogers, 1959).

Rogers assumes that each individual exists in a "continually changing world of experience of which he is the center." An individual's phenomenal field, which defines his or her reality, consists of the total realm of the individual's conscious and unconscious experience at a moment in time. No one can know an individual's phenomenal field as well as the individual can. If we wish to understand another person, we must attempt to reconstruct that person's phenomenal field and to be careful, in doing so, not to confuse it with our own. The individual has one basic tendency, "to actualize, maintain, and enhance the experiencing organism." In addition to maintaining itself physically, the organism strives to develop itself according to its maximum capacity. It grows by expanding, by becoming more differentiated, by becoming more autonomous, and by becoming more socialized.

Emotions and biological needs, such as sex and hunger, must be understood in relationship to their perceived role in maintaining and enhancing the organism. Whether an individual acts to fulfill a sex impulse in a particular setting or decides to inhibit it depends not so much on the strength of the impulse as on the individual's judgment of what is appropriate with respect to self-maintenance and enhancement. Emotions which accompany goal-directed behavior tend to be facilitative of such behavior. The intensity of the emotion is related to the perceived significance of the behavior for the maintenance and enhancement of the organism. Rogers notes that the kind of emotion that is experienced is "related to the seeking versus the consummatory aspects of the behavior," but unfortunately, he does not elaborate on what he means by this.

A key concept for Rogers is the self. The self is defined as "an organized, fluid, but consistent conceptual pattern of perceptions of characteristics and relationships of the 'I' or the 'me,' together with values attached to these concepts" (1951, p. 498). The self includes only those perceptions and values that are conscious or can readily become so. As the result of maturation and learning, part of the phenomenal field becomes differentiated as the self. The young child at first assumes that everything he or she can control, such as arms, legs, milk bottle, and mother are parts of the self. Parts that cannot be controlled, such as a foot that is asleep, are regarded as nonself. With further development, the child gradually forms a more accurate idea of what is self and nonself. Rogers believes that there is an important distinction between values that are acquired directly from experience and those that are introjected, or acquired from others. So long as a child learns directly from experience, the child will correctly label his or her feelings and will not become neurotic. The stage for neurosis is set when the child mislabels experiences because he or she wishes to please significant others. Because the child has a need for positive regard, he or she will do whatever is necessary to please the parents, including adopting their viewpoints about the child's own experiences. When an adult tells a child that it is bad to be angry at a younger sibling, the child learns to avoid labeling its feelings toward the sibling as anger, for it does not wish to think of itself as bad in the eyes of the parent. In order to please the parent, the child learns to misrepresent his or her actual feelings. The conscious self thus becomes out of tune with the organismic self, which produces a feeling of tension and of alienation from the real self. It is such a lack of correspondence between the experiencing organism and the labeled self that establishes the conditions for maladjustment. It does so in two ways. First, the lack of correspondence directly contributes to tension and anxiety. Secondly, because certain perceptions are unacceptable, the individual is forced to misrepresent reality and to resort to exaggerated defense mechanisms.

Experiences in life can be reacted to in three general ways. They can be (a) perceived, symbolized, and assimilated into the self-system; (b) ignored because they are irrelevant to the self-system; and (c) denied symbolization or represented in a distorted way because they are incompatible with the self-system. A process of "subception" allows the individual to unconsciously perceive and evaluate stimuli before they receive conscious recognition. Should subception indicate that perception would be threatening, the individual experiences anxiety, which he or she may react to by either avoiding or distorting conscious recognition of the stimulus.

The greater the threat to the self-structure, the more the self becomes defensively organized to maintain itself. The self will be defended at almost all costs. However, sometimes defense is not possible. "If the self cannot defend itself against deep threats, the result is a catastrophic psychological breakdown and disintegration" (Rogers, 1951, p. 516). This view of Rogers on breakdown is particularly interesting, for it offers a possible explanation of acute schizophrenic disorganization. What are the conditions for breakdown? Rogers (1959) speculates that if an individual were faced with a highly significant incongruity between the self and a new experience, and if the latter occurred with sufficient rapidity so that there was not sufficient time to mobilize defenses, the individual would become conscious of the incongruity, which would produce overwhelming anxiety and lead to a breakdown in "the gestalt of the self-structure." Following such an acute psychotic reaction, a process of defense against awareness of the incongruity would set in. Rogers speculates on the further course of the process as follows:

> Here I would voice my opinion very tentatively as to this process of defense. In some instances perhaps the denied experiences are now regnant, and the organism defends itself against the awareness of the self. In other instances the self is again regnant, and behavior is consistent with it, but the self has been greatly altered. It is now a self-concept which includes the important theme, "I am a crazy, inadequate, unreliable person who contains impulses and forces beyond my control." Thus it is a self in which little or no confidence is felt (p. 230).

Rogers closes his discussion of disorganization with the hope that future work will clarify this important process. Given his overall orientation, which emphasizes a growth principle in human behavior, it is surprising that he does not consider the possibility that disorganization can serve an adaptive function by providing an opportunity for a new, and more effective, reorganization of the self-system to take place. This possibility will be considered later.

The last three postulates of Rogers are concerned with psychotherapy and the conditions for establishing psychological well being. He assumes that if an appropriate atmosphere is established, and the self-structure is not excessively threatened, the organism will spontaneously develop toward health and fulfillment of its potential. However, if there already are deep disturbances, the individual may need aid in the form of an accepting relationship with another person for the growth principle to be manifested. When conditions are established that diminish the individual's feelings of threat, he or she will assimilate past incongruities within the self-structure and will learn to correctly label sensory and visceral experiences. The result will be a unified and integrated self-structure under relatively little stress. The individual will not only be accepting of self, but will become more accepting of others, as he or she will have less reason to be threatened by others. Finally, the individual will replace a value system which was based largely on introjections and distortions from previous experience with a continuing process of learning from ongoing experience.

We have presented the Rogers theory in considerable detail because it is the most thoroughly developed of the phenomenological theories. There is obviously much that is appealing about it, not the least of which is its optimistic view of the nature of man. However, it should be recognized that this optimism is more an act of faith than a conclusion that is unequivocally supported by evidence. The assumption that man is inherently good is, on the face of it, no more defensible than the view that man is inherently evil. Rogers postulates a growth principle that causes the individual to develop in positive directions so long as there are no obstacles and so long as anxiety is not excessive. This process is facilitated by contact with another person who is congruent, i.e. is in accurate contact with his or her own feelings, and who communicates unconditional positive regard and empathic understanding for the individual. Rogers has little more specific to say about the conditions of learning and guidance as he assumes that all growth is motivated from within. The impetus for his theory came from working with disturbed individuals in a counseling setting. It should be considered that the conditions for working out past problems and for developing an integrated self-structure through assimilating previously dissociated material may be quite different from the conditions that would result in optimum development in a psychologically healthy child. We shall return to this issue in the section on research at the end of this chapter.

A problem in the Rogers theory, as in the Snygg and Combs theory, is that maintenance and enhancement of the self are treated as if they are a single need. Rogers apparently assumes that the same underlying process is involved in maintaining the organism as in having it change in a manner that fulfills its potential. Yet, maintenance and change can more reasonably be viewed as opposite processes. This issue will also be considered further in the section on research.

The Self as an Integrative Structure from a Cognitive Perspective

In the phenomenological views presented above, two ideas were combined. One is that the self is an organized conceptual system for assimilating the data of experience. The other is that behavior can only be understood from the viewpoint of the person doing the behaving. Phenomenological approaches have a serious limitation in that they do not take into account reality, as defined from an objective perspective. As will be seen in the theories that follow, the self can be treated as an organized conceptual system without assuming that behavior can only be understood from the viewpoint of the person doing the behaving. Unfortunately, cognitive theories of the self are relatively new and have not been as extensively developed as the phenomenological self-theories. They do not yet include an adequate representation of the objective world, the phenomenological world, and the mediating cognitions between them. Perhaps what these theories best illustrate is that it is possible to have a theory that allows for both the importance of an objective world and the need for a concept of the self as a mediator of experience. It is our belief that such an approach represents the most promising one for the future.[1]

Hilgard. In a paper on the relationship of human motives and the self, Hilgard (1949) notes that most psychological knowledge of motivation is based on research and theorizing on animal behavior. He argues that, while this may be well and good for understanding motives associated with biological drives, it is inadequate for understanding complex human motives. The limitations of generalizing from animal to human motivation become especially clear when one considers the role of defense mechanisms. Anxiety, when experienced by a

[1]We initially planned to include Kelly's (1955) theory of personal constructs in this section. Kelly's theory is, by far, the most highly developed of the cognitive theories, and even includes a method for uncovering the unique dimensions with which individuals construe their private world of experience. In agreement with Lecky, and with our own approach, Kelly assumes that people, in going about the business of leading their everyday lives, function in a manner similar to scientists, formulating and testing hypotheses in the hope of improving their ability to anticipate events. We finally decided to omit Kelly's theory for two reasons. One is that the chapter is devoted to theories that emphasize the self-concept, which is not the case with Kelly's theory. The other is that the chapter, without Kelly, is already at the limit of its space allotment, and to do justice to Kelly's theory, it would have to be considerably lengthened.

It might be noted that although Kelly's theory has much in common with our own theory, there are a number of important differences. Kelly assigns a minor role to the self-concept, to emotions, and to the need to maintain a unified conceptual system, all of which are central in our own theory. Kelly's man is like a computer robot, who construes the world only for the sake of anticipating events, as if the major task of life were to solve an intellectual puzzle for its own sake. Emotions represent little more than a distraction in this game. Our man is a more emotional one who uses his intellect in order to make life as emotionally satisfying as possible. Perhaps this, too, can be viewed as a game; but, if so, it is a game in which emotion and unconscious motivation play as important roles as hypothesis testing and intellect.

subhuman animal, is usually in response to a threat to life or limb. When humans experience anxiety, on the other hand, it is most often in response to a threat to an individual's self, or ego. It is obviously for the purpose of defending the self against such threats that defense mechanisms are developed. Turning this observation around, it could be said that the very fact that people need to defend their egos provides evidence that there is some very important nonphysical aspect of their being that exists and must be protected. The nonphysical aspect of the individual that must be protected Hilgard designates as the "inferred self."

Two aspects of the inferred self can be directly confirmed by self-observation. One is that individuals have a feeling of continuity, which contributes to their sense of personal identity. People, unlike subhuman animals, do not live only for the moment. Their identity is extended in time. They have a sense of connectedness with their past and with their conception of their future. I am who I am because of my wishes for the future as well as because of my memories of the past. Despite changes in my behavior that occur from day to day or from year to year, I feel that I am basically the same person that I was yesterday and that I will be tomorrow. A loss of such a feeling of continuity would produce terror, as it would threaten my psychological existence as a unique human being. The other aspect is that people can readily become aware of an evaluative tendency in themselves. I judge my own and other people's behavior as good or bad, as desirable or undesirable. Not only do I judge specific behavioral acts, but I evaluate my overall self as good or bad. Depending on that evaluation, *all of me* feels good or bad. It is obvious that there is a unity in my self-evaluative feelings. An individual's overall appraisal of self is of central importance, for it influences all other aspects of an individual's valuing processes.

As its name implies, there are some attributes of the inferred self that cannot be observed through introspection, but must be inferred. There are three basic characteristics of the self that must be inferred. First, there is *continuity of motivational patterns,* meaning that central motives and attitudes that are present at earlier periods of life tend to be carried over to later periods of life. The person who is neat and orderly as a child is apt to exhibit similar behavior as an adult, although, as implied by the next characteristic of the self, not necessarily in the same form. A second characteristic of the self that must be inferred is the *genotypical patterning of motives.* Motives that appear different when judged by surface behavior may turn out to be the same when examined on a deeper level, and vice-versa. Expressed otherwise, as behavior is organized around motives and not specific acts, different acts can fulfill the same motive, and the same act can fulfill different motives.

A third important attribute of the inferred self is that *important human motives are interpersonal both in origin and expression.* The self-system is acquired through interactions with others. It is from other people that individuals learn the roles that they need in order to behave effectively in society. Particularly important in this respect are the individual's parents, as they transmit their own values and attitudes as well as those of the broader culture.

Hilgard suggests that the healthy self is more integrative than integrated. By this he means that the healthy self is flexible and capable of adapting to new situations, while the unhealthy self tends to be rigid and unadaptable.

Sarbin. Sarbin (1952) is interested in the development of the self-system from childhood through adulthood. His view of the self is organized around the following seven postulates:

1. The human animal can regard itself as an object in the same way as it regards objects in the external world.
2. Behavior is organized around cognitive structures, the results of responses of the organism to stimulus-objects and residual stimuli. The self is one such cognitive structure. Like other cognitive structures, it includes substructures, which can be referred to as empirical selves and which interact with one another.
3. The self is empirically derived, not transcendental; it is the resultant of experience, that is, interaction with body parts, things, persons, images, and so on.
4. The properties of these substructures at any given moment are determined by the total interbehavioral field of which the substructures are a part. Thus, any of the empirical selves may occupy the focus of the interbehavioral field at any given time.
5. The self (in common with other cognitive structures) is subject to continual and progressive change, usually in the direction from low-order inferences about simple perceptions to higher-order inferences about complex cognitions.
6. Organic maturation and reinforcement of selected responses contribute to changes in the empirical selves (substructure) and concurrently to changes in the total self-structure. Thus, according to Sarbin, changes in the self can occur either through maturation or by means of learning.
7. Change in cognitive structure is a function of (at least) two properties: (a) resistance to de-differentiation and (b) the breadth of the substructures. By resistance to de-differentiation, Sarbin means the inability of a cognitive system to be modified in the direction of finer discrimination. Such resistance occurs as the result of over-learning. By breadth of structures, Sarbin means the range of perception and experience that is relevant to a particular cognitive structure.

In discussing the development of the self, Sarbin assumes that it develops in overlapping stages that are determined by the individual's capacities and experiences. Each stage lays the foundation for the next. The first three stages occur before the development of a true self. To emphasize their continuity with the development of the self, Sarbin nevertheless prefixes them with the word *self.* The first stage, which occurs at about one month of age, is the stage of the "somatic self." In this stage, the infant is aware only of physical sensations. It has only rudimentary cognitions for organizing its sensations. It cannot differentiate itself from objects in the environment, and it regards its own arm, for example, as no different from any other object. The second stage is "the receptor-effector self." It occurs at about the three- or four-month period. The infant's attention in this stage is focused on feelings of tension and on actions that relieve tension, such as eating and voiding the bowels. He or she has cognitions for organizing these tensions and the behaviors associated with them. The infant still cannot tell the difference between self and nonself. The third stage is "the primitive construed self." At this stage, which occurs at about the age of six months, the child is able to discriminate between people and objects, and among different people. The next stage, which occurs at about a year, is labeled "the introjecting-extrojecting self," and marks the beginning of a true self. The child is now able to discriminate accurately between self and nonself, and is also able to employ crude forms of language in forming generalizations. Although the child has not yet learned to say "I", the child can refer to itself by name, is able to imitate others, and has some sense of itself as being similar to, yet different from, others. The final stage, which normally occurs between 13 months and two years, marks the emergence of the "social self." In this stage, the child uses the pronouns *I, me,* and *mine,* and can put together whole sentences. The child then recognizes, and can imitate, not only simple acts of behavior, but organized complex acts, or roles.

In the beginning, the somatic self is the core of the self-structure. With further development, the social self becomes ascendant, the different stages become increasingly differentiated, and organized roles become increasingly important in defining the self. While the early self-concept was organized primarily around biological needs, the adult self-concept is organized primarily around roles and other social influences.

Sarbin believes that much confusion has occurred as the result of considering the self as both a knower, or "I," and as an object of knowledge, or "me." The "me" represents no difficulty, as everyone recognizes that individuals can describe themselves and hold opinions about themselves in the same manner as they can do so about others. The self as an "I" is another matter. It has evoked a great deal of controversy, including the issue of whether it is worth retaining at all. Sarbin believes that the self as an "I" can be understood as a higher-order inference, or cognitive structure, that encompasses all of the empirical selves. This suggests that the "I" is an integrative structure that includes the other selves as subdivisions. Unfortunately, Sarbin does not discuss the nature of this integration or to what extent and in what manner the empirical selves influence and are influenced by the "I." He notes that the consistent use of the concept "I," as a higher order inference, takes longer for the child to develop than other words that refer to the self. The "I" is said to represent a fluid rather than a static state. At any moment in time, a different empirical self may be dominant. Sarbin defines the "I" as the cross-section of the organization of the empirical selves at a moment in time, but does not elaborate on what he means by this.

AN INTEGRATED THEORY OF PERSONALITY

In a book devoted to an intensive study of a single case, Allport (1965) noted that no present theory could adequately represent an individual's personality. He ended the book by stating that "it is a task for the future to blend the approaches so that a systematic eclecticism, a true synthesis of theories will emerge" (p. 211). The following theory is an attempt to do just that. It is a theory that is compatible with learning theory, psychoanalysis, Kelly's theory of personal constructs, other cognitive theories, and, above all, with the self-theories that have been reviewed in this chapter. When the theory has been presented at scientific meetings, it has met with a curious reception. Psychoanalysts have insisted that it is essentially no different from psychoanalytic theory, self-theorists that it is no different from self-theory, and followers of Kelly that it is no different from Kelly's theory of personal constructs. To the extent that they are all right, the theory has, of course, succeeded in synthesizing significant insights from a variety of different viewpoints.

Some Basic Assumptions

A major assumption of the theory is that the human mind is so constituted that it tends to organize experience into conceptual systems. Human brains make connections between events, and, having made connections, they connect the connections, and so on, until they have developed an organized system of higher- and lower-order constructs that is both differentiated and integrated. Whether we like it or not, each of us, because he has a human brain, forms a theory of reality that brings order into what otherwise would be a chaotic world of experience. We need a theory to make sense out of the world, just as a scientist needs a theory to make sense out of the limited body of information he or she wishes to understand.

In addition to making connections between events, human brains have centers of pain and pleasure. The entire history of research on learning indicates that human and other higher-order animals are motivated to behave in a manner that brings pleasure and avoids pain. The human being thus has an interesting lifetime task cut out simply because of his or her biological structure: it is to construct a conceptual system in such a manner as to account for reality in a way that will produce the most favorable pleasure/pain ratio over the foreseeable future. This is obviously no simple matter, for the pursuit of pleasure and the acceptance of reality not infrequently appear to be at cross-purposes to each other. What the world is and what we would like it to be can be quite different. To make the game of life even more interesting, the pursuit of immediate pleasure and the pursuit of long-term pleasure are also often at cross-purposes to each other.

An individual's overall theory of reality includes subtheories of what the individual is like (a self-theory), of what the world is like (a world-theory), and of how the two interact with each other. How the individual views himself or herself is, of course, not independent of how he or she views the world. The individual's conception of the world, to a large extent, is a reflection of his or her self-conception, and vice-versa. In this chapter, we shall concentrate primarily on the individual's self-theory, which is the nucleus of the individual's overall theory of reality.

Like any theory, an individual's self-theory consists of a hierarchical arrangement of major and minor postulates. The lowest level of a postulate is a relatively narrow generalization derived directly from experience. Such lower-order postulates are organized into broader postulates, and these, in turn, into yet broader ones. An example of a lower-order postulate is, "I am a good ping-pong player." An example of a higher order postulate is, "I am a good athlete." A much higher order postulate is, "I am a worthy human being." It is obvious that minor, or lower-order, postulates can be invalidated without serious consequences to the self-system, as they encompass relatively little of the system, but that invalidation of a major postulate has serious consequences, as it affects a whole network of other postulates. Fortunately, as major postulates are broad generalizations, they are removed from the immediate test of experience and are therefore not easily invalidated. Moreover, major postulates exert an important influence on what experiences an individual seeks out and on how he or she interprets the experiences. Thus, major postulates tend to function as self-fulfilling prophecies.

It is important to recognize that an individual's self-theory is not a theory that a person normally is aware of and can describe. Individuals unwittingly construct theories about themselves as a way of dealing with their world. Whether they like it or not, they form concepts about emotionally significant experiences that then serve to organize and guide their future behavior. To the extent that individuals are unaware of their implicit assumptions, significant experiences will appear to be controlled by an external destiny which they are powerless to affect. The destiny, of course, is determined by the need to maintain a familiar world, one that is consistent with their implicit assumptions.

An individual's self-theory does not exist for its own sake, but is a conceptual tool for accomplishing the following purposes: (a) to assimilate the data of experience, (b) to maximize the pleasure/pain balance over the foreseeable future, and (c) to optimize self-esteem. These purposes will be elaborated in the sections that follow.

Development of the Self-System and its Implications for Psychopathology

The development of a self-system will occur so long as cues are available for making the distinction between self and not-self, and so long as it is rewarding to make the distinction. That salient cues are available is readily apparent. The child's body is always present for him or her to see and touch. When the child touches a part of himself or herself, both the part doing the touching and the part that is being touched receive sensation, whereas when the child touches something that is not part of himself or herself, only the part doing the touching feels anything. The child has control over his or her limbs in a way that he or she does not have over objects or over other people's limbs. The child even has a special self-label assigned, a name. The label tells the child that he or she is similar to other people, who also have names, yet is a distinct individual in his or her own right. It is obviously rewarding for the child to distinguish self from not-self. The child receives pleasant sensations when putting a piece of candy into his or her own mouth, but not when placing it into the mouth of another. When the child touches a hot stove, removing the hand immediately diminishes the intensity of the pain. Thus, there are obvious reasons for the child to develop a sense of his or her body, or a "body-self."

As to the development of a "conceptual inner self" that organizes and directs experience, it has already been noted that the individual could not function without such a system. The views of Sullivan, Cooley and Mead are instructive in indicating how the development of such a system is rewarded in social interaction. It will be recalled that, according to Sullivan, an inner self-system is a useful conceptual tool for gaining approval and avoiding disapproval from the mother. According to Mead and Cooley, the self-structure provides the individual with ready-made programs, or roles, for behaving in ways that elicit social approval.

Given evident cues for distinguishing self from not-self, and advantages that follow from developing an integrated conceptual system that contains subdivisions of self and not-self, it is almost inconceivable that a child would fail to develop such a system. Yet, almost inconceivable is not the same as inconceivable. If the child were raised under conditions where becoming aware of self would lead to more pain than pleasure, there would be no reason to develop a self-theory and every reason to actively avoid conceptualizing the self.

Consider the cases of children who, if they were to internalize the parent's evaluations of themselves, would have to carry within themselves a strong measure of self-hatred. In such children, a self-theory could only contribute to low self-esteem and an unfavorable pleasure/pain balance, and would therefore have no reason to develop. Such circumstances could account for some cases of childhood autism in which the child progresses to a point in its language development just short of the use of the personal pronoun *I*, and then either exhibits fixation at that level or regresses and abandons the use of what little language had developed. (This is not to deny that, in other cases, childhood autism may be produced by a biological defect that limits the individual's capacity to establish a complex conceptual system. The same symptoms can obviously occur for different reasons.) In other circumstances where a self-concept would be less completely negative, rather than an absence of a self-system, an unstable self-system might develop, one that is fragile and susceptible to collapse later in life if the individual is exposed to certain kinds of stress. As an example of such an unstable conceptualization of the self, consider the following description of the meeting of a young schizophrenic girl with a psychiatrist: "Ruth, a five-year old, approached the psychiatrist with 'Are you the bogey man? Are you going to fight my mother? Are you the same mother? Are you the same father? Are you going to be another mother?' and finally screaming in terror, 'I am afraid I am going to be someone else'" (Bender, 1950, p. 135).

The development of a theory of reality occurs only if it provides for a net gain in positive emotional experience. For a child, the major source of positive and negative emotional experience is the love relationship with the mother. Thus, it can be expected that feelings of being loveable, and their later internalization as self-love, are intimately associated with the development and maintenance of a theory of reality, and therefore with reality contact. Of particular interest, in this regard, are case histories of schizophrenia in which a close relationship is exhibited between reality contact and feeling loved. The following account by an adolescent schizophrenic girl provides a dramatic example of a rapid alternation between maintaining and losing her capacity for integrating the data of reality in direct synchrony with the perception of warmth in her therapist, whom she refers to as "Mama."

> I perceived a figure of ice which smiled at me. And this smile, showing her white teeth, frightened me. For I saw the individual features of her face, separated from each other. Perhaps it was this independence of each part that inspired such fear and prevented my recognizing her even though I knew who she was. . . . Then I heard this marvelous voice which, like a talisman, could give me again a moment of reality, a contact with life. . . . Warmed again, encouraged, softly repeating Mama's words, I went home. Once in the street, however, I saw again the pasteboard scenery of unreality (Sechehaye, 1970, pp. 37-38).

In addition to a lack of perceptual integration, it is noteworthy that she experiences a loss of depth perception, as revealed in the reference to a "pasteboard scenery of unreality." Depth perception requires inferences to be made from distance and size cues. With the loss of integrative capacity, the ability to make such inferences breaks down and a fundamental perceptual symptom appears.

A related experience, in which perception of reality varies with warmth in a relationship, is recounted in *I Never Promised You a Rose Garden* (Green, 1964).

> When the sign was given, they moved toward each other appearing as elaborately unconcerned as they could. Deborah smiled very slightly, but then a strange thing happened. Into the flat, gray, blurred and two-dimensional waste of her vision, Carla came three-dimensionally and in color, as whole and real as a mouthful of hot coffee (p. 152).

Self-Esteem and the Self-System

Once a rudimentary self-theory is formed, self-esteem becomes the most important influence on an individual's pleasure/pain balance. Although the optimization of self-esteem could be subsumed under the need to maintain a favorable pleasure/pain balance, self-esteem is so important in the functioning of the self-system that it deserves the status of an independent category. The maintenance of self-esteem to the child, and later to the adult, is equivalent in importance to the maintenance of a love relationship with the mother to the infant. Once the child has internalized the parents' evaluative reactions, the child spontaneously loves and withdraws love from himself or herself in a manner similar to the way his or her parents once did. It is known that a child who loses a relationship with a loved one may become severely depressed and lose interest in living (Bowlby, 1973). Correspondingly, a person who suffers a serious blow to self-esteem may become seriously depressed and suicidal. In concentration camps where people were severely humiliated, some were observed to lose interest in living, and to then quickly waste away (Krystal, 1968). Injuries to self-esteem can also produce a psychological death of the personality, as indicated in a complete breakdown in the individual's conceptual system, as in acute psychotic disorganization (Grinker & Holzman, 1973; Perry, 1976).

People with high self-esteem, in effect, carry within them a loving parent who is proud of their successes and tolerant of their failures. Such people tend to have an optimistic view about life, and to be able to tolerate external stress without becoming excessively anxious. Although capable of being disappointed and depressed by specific experiences, people with high self-esteem recover quickly, as do children who are secure in their mother's love. In contrast, people with low self-esteem carry within them a disapproving parent who is harshly critical of their failures, and registers only short-lived pleasure when they succeed. Such people are apt to be unduly sensitive to failure and to rejection, to have low tolerance for frustration, to take a long time to recover following disappointments, and to have a pessimistic view of life. The picture is not unlike that of children who are insecure in their parent's love.

The overall favorableness of self-assessment identifies one of the most basic postulates in a person's self-theory. As a higher-order postulate, self-esteem is resistant to change. Should it change, it has widespread effects on the entire self-system. The resistance to change is illustrated in the manner in which some people, despite unusually high levels of achievement, nevertheless maintain a low opinion of their abilities. It requires a considerable amount of emotionally significant experience in adulthood to counter the emotionally significant experience in childhood from which self-esteem was derived. A further reason why self-esteem is resistant to change is that, as previously noted, once a postulate is formulated, it tends to function as a self-fulfilling prophecy. People with high self-esteem who fail in a task tend to assume that their perfomance was not representative of their ability, and that they will do better next time. If they do well, they accept it as evidence of their adequacy. For people with low self-esteem, failure confirms their inadequacy. If they do well, they question the validity of the test, or assume they were lucky. Moreover, people with high self-esteem, because they are confident of their abilities, are able to work more efficiently and with less strain than people with low self-esteem, and, as a result, are more apt to actually succeed.

Finally, in order to understand why some people tend to maintain an unrealistically low level of self-esteem, it is necessary to consider the effect of a sudden decrease in self-esteem relative to maintaining a low average tonic level to begin with. As sudden decreases in self-esteem are particularly aversive, each person is faced with the task of setting his or her average level of self-appraisal as high as possible without setting it so high that the unpleasant feelings produced by decreases in self-esteem will outweigh the positive feelings gained by a high average level. It can be anticipated that the more sensitive an individual is to decreases in self-esteem, the more likely he or she is to set a low general level. To note that some individuals are motivated to maintain low levels of self-esteem is not to suggest that self-esteem can not be raised, but to indicate that, for good motivational reasons, it tends to be resistant to change.

Not only can unrealistically low self-appraisal be used as a defense against the pain of failure and disappointment, but unrealistically high appraisal can serve the same purpose. In the latter case, however, the appraisal must be insulated from the test of reality. If a person insists he is Napoleon, it may make him feel important, but it also forces him to dissociate himself from reality in order to maintain the delusion. That such extreme reactions do actually occur attests to the critical need humans have to maintain a favorable level of self-esteem.

Maintaining the Organization of the Self-System

In general, any theory is better than none; without a theory for organizing experience, there can be nothing but chaos. A personal theory of reality must therefore be organized not only to assimilate the data of experience, to maintain a favorable pleasure/pain balance, and to optimize self-esteem, but to maintain itself. Obviously, if the theory does not maintain itself, it can not fulfill its other functions. Unlike the views of self-theorists who assume that the individual has one basic need, the maintenance and enhancement of the self-system, the present theory assumes that maintenance and enhancement conflict with each other, as stability and change cannot go on together. As a result, a compromise is effected, so that small positive changes in self-appraisal are more apt to be accepted than larger changes. Research bearing on this issue will be presented later.

To the extent that a self-theory fails to fulfill its functions, it is placed under stress, subjectively experienced as anxiety. If the stress is great enough and cannot be defended against, disorganization occurs. Disorganization is assumed to be a natural adaptive process that has developed in the course of evolution as a means of correcting a poorly organized conceptual system (Epstein, 1973, 1976, 1979a). While correction of specific elements in a self-theory can occur through learning, learning is often an ineffective means for correcting the organization of a conceptual system, as the latter influences what is learned. Before a poorly organized system can be drastically reorganized, it is often necessary to dismantle it. Acute schizophrenic disorganization represents just such a process. This is not the place to discuss the adaptive potential of schizophrenic disorganization in detail. The interested reader can pursue the topic in a number of other sources (e.g., Bowers, 1974, Epstein, 1973, 1976, 1979a; Perry, 1976; Silverman, 1970). Suffice it to note, for the moment, that, as a desperate remedy, disorganization does not always succeed, and is often followed by a poorer organization. There is obviously a need for research to determine the conditions when disorganization is apt to be constructive and when destructive (Epstein, 1979a).

The stability of the self-system is threatened by any experience that challenges its ability to fulfill its functions. When the self-system is threatened, the individual can either assimilate the threatening experience, and thereby expand the self-system at the price of a momentary increase in anxiety, or the individual can employ defenses to protect the self-system and thereby avoid the experience of anxiety. The most general defense against disorganization is constriction of the self-system. The individual then becomes resistant to new information, adheres rigidly to old ways of behaving and thinking, loses emotional spontaneity, and attempts to reduce new assimilative demands on the self-system in all ways possible. Other defenses are those described by psychoanalysts, such as denial, projection, and rationalization. Just as threat to the self-system leads to defensive constriction, enhancement of the self-system, which occurs when the self-system fulfills its functions, leads to increased openness to new experience, positive affect, and increased spontaneity.

Emotions and the Self-System

Although an individual's self-theory is a conceptual system, it is intimately associated with the emotions. It will be recalled that the most rudimentary function of a self-theory is to maintain a favorable pleasure/pain balance, and it was for this purpose that it was initially developed. In the beginning, when the child was mainly responsive to physical needs, the self-theory was subordinate to the emotions. However, in time this becomes reversed, as emotional experience becomes increasingly mediated by the individual's developing conceptual system.

Feelings of exhilaration occur when the self-theory expands through assimilating new information, or when, through discrimination, it resolves inner sources of conflict. Such positive emotional reactions are adaptive in that they provide an inherent motivation for increasing integration and differentiation of the individual's conceptual system. In a comparable but opposite manner, anxiety occurs when the self-theory is unable to assimilate new information or to establish internal consistency. This, too, is adaptive, as it provides a source of motivation for either correcting the self-theory or for mobilizing defenses to protect it against disorganization. Because opposite emotions follow assimilation and a failure of assimilation, the individual is faced with an inherent conflict regarding growth. If the individual exposes himself or herself to new experiences, or to new awarenesses about the self, threat and anxiety will be experienced. Should the person succeed in assimilating the new material, he or she will be rewarded with a reduction in anxiety and with feelings of exhilaration. Moreover, the self-system will become less vulnerable to threat than it previously was, as a potential source of threat has been eliminated. Thus, the individual is caught in a conflict between avoiding anxiety and thereby not growing, and facing anxiety and growing. To further complicate matters, if the threat that is faced is excessive, it will provoke so much anxiety that it will facilitate defensive retrenchment rather than growth. Thus, facing anxiety under certain circumstances can be counter-productive to growth. Two factors must be considered in this respect. One is that it is necessary for an individual to pace his or her exposure to threat so that anxiety does not become excessive. The other is that the more threatened the individual, the more will new sources of stimulation be experienced as stressful. Expressed differently, the more secure the individual, the greater the likelihood that the self-theory will grow and that new experiences will be welcomed as interesting challenges. For this reason, most therapists emphasize the importance of establishing a secure and accepting atmosphere in therapy.

Another way that emotions are related to the self-system is that emotions are aroused whenever anything of significance to an individual's self-theory occurs. Thus, by noting the events that a person reacts to emotionally, important clues can be gained about a person's implicit postulates. For example, if a person becomes upset when someone questions his or her intelligence, it is obvious that it is important for that person to be regarded as intelligent. While this may appear to be self-evident, the person might well deny that impressing people with his or her intelligence is of any concern. Thus, observations of emotions can provide important information about a person's postulates of which the person is unaware. Emotions can thus be regarded as the royal road to an individual's implicit postulates.

Yet another way in which emotions are related to the self-system is that behind almost every emotion there is a hidden cognition. If we believe a poisonous snake is not poisonous, we show no fear of it, although it can kill us. By the same token, if we believe a non-poisonous snake is poisonous, we are terrified of it, although it cannot harm us. Obviously, it is how we interpret events, not the events themselves, that determine the emotions we feel. When we are angry it is apt to be because we have made a judgment that someone has treated us unjustly. When we are depressed, it is apt to be because we have made the interpretation that someone or something important to our happiness will not be available to us. When we are frightened, it is because we have made the interpretation that something may harm us. Once it is recognized that implicit cognitions mediate emotions, it is evident that people who are frequently depressed, anxious, or chronically angry must have certain habitual thoughts that produce a disproportionate incidence of these feelings (Beck, 1976). This observation has led to the development of cognitive therapies by people such as Beck (1976), Ellis (1962), and Meichenbaum (1974), in which an attempt is made to teach people to change their ways of thinking as a way of changing maladaptive emotional states.

Self-Theory and Adjustment

Assuming that all individuals require theories in order to structure their experiences and to direct their lives, it follows that the adequacy of their adjustment can be determined by the adequacy of their theories. Like a theory in science, a personal theory of reality can be evaluated by the following attributes: extensivity, parsimony, empirical validity, internal consistency, testability, and usefulness.

Extensivity. Extensivity refers to the breadth or range of a theory. All other things being equal, the more extensive a theory, the better the theory. An individual with a narrow self-theory can cope with only a limited variety of experiences. Such an individual will be threatened when exposed to events that cannot be assimilated into his or her narrow theory. As a result, the person will tend to be rigid, defensive, and intolerant of different ways of viewing the world. The very existence of other viewpoints will be a source of anxiety, as differences indicate that the person's views may not be the best ones. It is only in a restricted, familiar environment that such an individual can be secure. An individual with an extensive self-theory, on the other hand, can be secure in a wide range of settings. He or she will tend to seek out new experiences, and will find new viewpoints interesting and challenging. As a result, his or her theory of reality will become increasingly differentiated and integrated.

There can be no end-state of adjustment from the viewpoint of self-theory, just as there can be no end-state in the search for truth in science. Adjustment is a process in which there is a continuous expansion and differentiation of an individual's theory of reality as a result of exposure to new data in the experience of living. A characteristic of a good personal theory of reality, like a good theory in science, is that it exhibits such growth.

Parsimony. Parsimony refers to the efficiency of a theory as defined by how much a theory can account for with how few concepts. All other things being equal, the fewer the concepts that are necessary to account for a certain amount of data, the better the theory. Parsimony thus requires postulates of broad generality. However, if postulates are too broad they will lack the specificity that is necessary to relate them to specific events. Thus they must be combined with a network of narrower postulates. Included among the broad postulates in a personal theory are not only descriptive generalizations about the nature of the self and the world, such as "I am a capable person," and "People are not to be trusted," but also motivational postulates, many of which were derived from early childhood experiences, such as "Happiness can only be found by pleasing mother figures." A highly general postulate is not easily confirmed or disconfirmed, as almost any experience can be viewed as an exception or interpreted in a manner that is consistent with the postulate. Broad postulates give stability to the personality. The behavior of a person without broad postulates would be determined almost exclusively by situational factors. Such a person would lack a stable character structure. On the other hand, the behavior of a person who relied excessively on broad postulates would be equally maladaptive, for it would lack flexibility and would not be realistically attuned to variations in situational requirements. Such a person might appear to be excessively ruled by principle and to be lacking in sensitivity.

In sum, a person who is well-adjusted has broad values that give stability to his or her behavior, and has minor, or qualifying, postulates that allow him or her to be flexible and to take into account situational nuances.

Empirical Validity and Testability. When people have experiences that are inconsistent with their theory of reality, they experience anxiety. To protect themselves from such anxiety, individuals learn to insulate their important hypotheses from the test of reality. This can be done by avoiding or distorting perceptions and by formulating postulates in such a way as to make them untestable. Unfortunately, the price one pays for such defensive maneuvers is the loss of the ability to correct faulty hypotheses, and thereby to improve one's self-theory. A postulate such as, "I am a sensitive person who perceives things no one else can see," is almost impossible to disprove. Individuals who are highly threatened can be expected to have many such untestable postulates, as this provides a sure means of protecting their self-esteem and the stability of their self-theories.

Effective adjustment requires a continuous interaction between postulates and experience. The postulates of a well-adjusted person will be influenced by experience, and they in turn will influence experience. This reciprocal process corresponds, of course, to the interaction of theory and data that is characteristic of science.

Internal Consistency. Like any good theory, a good personal theory of reality is internally consistent. To the extent that it is not, the individual will tend to experience anxiety and tension and will be prone to become confused and disorganized. While it is possible for such an individual to avoid anxiety and confusion by dissociating elements of his or her conceptual system from the remainder of the theory, such a reaction makes the person vulnerable to experiences that can activate the dissociated elements, thereby making the dissociation difficult to maintain.

An individual with a theory of reality that is relatively free of inconsistent postulates feels in harmony with himself or herself. There is an absence of conflict between opposing postulates, and, in Roger's terms, his or her verbal system accurately represents organic and sensory experience. An individual with a theory of reality that contains significant inconsistencies has the opposite feelings. In order to reduce the stress produced by internal conflict, such an individual, in addition to utilizing denial and dissociation, will tend to restrict his or her realm of experience and to perceive the self and the world in a biased way in order to avoid becoming aware of the inconsistencies.

Inconsistencies in a theory of reality occur for several reasons. As Rogers and others have pointed out, an important source of inconsistency is the discrepancy between what is learned directly from experience and what is accepted because of the influence of significant others. This produces a tension between two conflicting sources of information. Another source of inconsistency arises from intense emotional experiences which produce excessively broad generalizations that overlap in an incompatible manner. Take, for example, someone who has had warm, loving relationships with significant others in childhood, only to have exactly opposite experiences later in a concentration camp. Such experiences could be expected to produce a deep-seated conflict between higher-order motivational postulates concerning whether significant others should or should not be trusted. For the person with such experiences to achieve internal consistency, he or she would have to sufficiently differentiate the concepts so that they no longer overlap. This would amount to becoming convinced, at a deep emotional level, that some people can, and others cannot, be trusted. Unfortunately, this is easier said than done, as concepts derived from strong emotional experiences tend not only to be broad, but to be firmly implanted and resistant to differentiation.

Usefulness. A person's theory of reality does not exist for its own sake, but is a conceptual tool for solving problems in living. To the extent that the theory accomplishes its purposes, it will be robust and resistant to disorganization. It follows that one way of judging the adequacy of an individual's self-theory is to determine how well the theory is accomplishing its functions of assimilating the data of experience, maintaining a favorable pleasure/pain balance, and maintaining a favorable level of self-esteem. All of these, of course, must be judged in relationship to constraints in the environment. One cannot expect a favorable pleasure/pain balance to be maintained immediately after the death of a loved one. On the other hand, it would be maladaptive if a prolonged depression ensued.

Self-Theory and Psychodynamics

Self-theory is considered by some to be in opposition to psychoanalytic theory. Lecky (1969), for example, states,

> Self-consistency cannot be accepted openly by psychiatry until the way has been prepared by sacrificing the doctrine of a mind divided against itself, conscious versus unconscious, love versus hate, good versus evil . . . . Thus the psychoanalytic pursuit of unconscious complexes, with no stated goal except to destroy them, suggests the superstitious fervor of the witchburner . . . . Not only the doctrine of the unconscious must go, but with it the intolerant dominance of the analytic and mechanistic tradition prevailing in psychology generally (p. 137).

Rogers (1951), while acknowledging the existence of unconscious processes, concentrates on those aspects of the self that can be directly reported. It is understandable that phenomenologically oriented psychologists would de-emphasize the importance of unconscious factors, as their approach focuses on the individual's awareness. Cognitive self-theory, on the other hand, does not contain an inherent bias against psychoanalytic formulations of an unconscious and of psychodynamic processes. The cognitive theory of the self presented here, in fact, has much in common with psychoanalytic theory, including the acceptance of an unconscious and of a mind divided against itself. By reformulating psychoanalytic concepts within a cognitive framework, it is possible to retain the insights of psychoanalytic theory without, at the same time, including some of its more questionable assumptions–such as that behavior can be understood in terms of a distribution of psychic energy; that there is an invariant biologically determined sequence of developmental stages, namely the oral, anal, phalic, and genital stages; that the Oedipus complex is universal; that psychodynamics can profitably be represented by a mechanical or hydraulic model; and that personality can be represented by a conflict between three homunculus-like entities, the id, ego, and superego.

Psychoanalysis emphasizes the importance of inner conflict arising from unacceptable impulses at the expense of recognizing the importance of maintaining a unified conceptual system. Self-theories, on the other hand, emphasize the need to maintain a unified conceptual system at the expense of recognizing the importance of unconscious conflict and psychodynamics. The deficiencies of each can be corrected by incorporating the views of both into a single theory.

As previously noted, individuals will defend their personal theories of reality at almost all costs because they need a theory in order to function. It is important to recognize that defense mechanisms are employed not only to deny unacceptable impulses and to defend self-esteem, but to maintain the unity of an individual's conceptual system.

On occasion, an individual's need to maintain the stability of his or her theory of reality will conflict with the need to enhance self-esteem or to maintain a favorable pleasure/pain balance. When this occurs, the individual may appear to act in ways contrary to his or her own welfare. Examples include masochistic behavior, enduring negative self-appraisals that often accompany depression, and the "repetition compulsion," as exhibited when individuals repeatedly pursue self-destructive goals. Observation of destructive repetition compulsions so impressed Freud that it led him to drastically revise his theory of personality. Seeing no other way of accounting for the phenomenon, he proposed a death instinct which he considered prepotent over the pleasure principle. Without the concept of the need for individuals to maintain a stable theory of reality, he was forced into an awkward theoretical reformulation that most psychoanalysts have since rejected. From the perspective of the cognitive theory proposed here, the daemonic-control-by-fate theme that has appeared in the writings of students of personality from the ancient Greeks to modern times can readily be explained without resorting to mysticism of one kind or another. Namely, individuals formulate broad, self-fulfilling hypotheses, or postulates, as the result of significant emotional experiences. The broader a hypothesis, the greater the need to establish its validity in order to maintain the stability of the self-system. Even the maintenance of a disturbing view of the self or the world is preferable to endangering the stability of a personal theory of reality.

There are similarities and differences between how cognitive self-theory and psychoanalysis treat the unconscious. Psychoanalysis assumes the existance of a dynamic unconscious, meaning that material in the unconscious continuously strives for expression with a psychic energy of its own. The unconscious elements are kept unconscious by a force of repression, which uses up energy. Thus the person with an unconscious conflict has less energy available for other pursuits. Freud was never clear about the nature of psychic energy, which has become one of the most criticized concepts in all of psychoanalytic theory. Psychic energy suggests a steam-boiler analogy, in which the person must either express or repress an impulse; in the latter case, the energy seeks expression through indirect channels. Freud thus came to the pessimistic conclusion that people have a choice between expressing their impulses, and being antisocial, or inhibiting their impulses, and being neurotic. Fortunately, the concept of the unconscious can be reformulated from a cognitive viewpoint in a manner that makes no assumption that psychic energy must be expressed one way or another.

There are two ways in which mental content can be unconscious. First, higher-order postulates, because they are highly general, can influence behavior in a manner that is not apparent to the individual doing the behaving. However, unlike the postulates that will be discussed next, such postulates are not associated with states of inhibition and tension. A person's behavior in any one situation is predominantly determined by the nature of the situation; thus, the subtle biasing effect of higher-order postulates is usually not evident in any one situation, but can be observed only over a sufficient sample of events. It is noteworthy, in this respect, that high levels of stability in personality can be demonstrated when behavior is averaged over occasions, but there is little evidence for stability when behavior is observed on single occasions (Epstein, 1977, 1979b).

The second way in which mental content can be unconscious is through dissociation. Given the existence of inconsistencies in a self-theory, one way in which the unity of the self-theory can be preserved is by isolating, or dissociating, the discrepant elements, which can consist of single memories or of entire integrated complexes as in the case of multiple personality. Given a dissociated memory or complex, the self-system, because it is inherently integrative, will attempt to assimilate the dissociated material. This creates the illusion that the dissociated material has an energy of its own that is seeking expression. If the dissociated complex is effectively isolated from the rest of the personality, it will not be a serious source of stress, precisely because it does not have an energy of its own. However, should events occur that activate the dissociated complex to the point that it is difficult to maintain the dissociation, there will be considerable stress on the assimilative capacity of the self-system.

Implications for Psychotherapy

Limitations of space do not permit a thorough discussion of the implications for psychotherapy of the cognitive theory presented here. However, a few brief comments are in order.

How can an individual's theory of reality that is functioning inadequately be modified? Psychoanalysts believe that significant changes in personality are most effectively brought about by working at the level of the higher-order postulates, while behavior therapists believe that changes can be more efficiently brought about by working at the level of specific behavioral acts. From the viewpoint presented here, both approaches can effect significant change. If changes are made at the level of the fundamental postulates of an individual, they can filter down to changes at the behavioral level. If changes are made at the behavioral level, they can filter up to changes in the higher-order postulates. It is evident that, given a unified hierarchical conceptual system, changes can proceed deductively from the top down as well as inductively from the bottom up. Depending on the nature of the problem, one approach or the other will be more efficient. It is reasonable to assume that problems associated with the overall personality structure can normally most efficiently be treated by producing changes at the general postulate level, while problems that relate to specific behavioral acts can normally most efficiently be treated by behavioral-training procedures.

The kind of therapy that follows most directly from the position described here is cognitive therapy, as described by Beck (1976), Ellis (1962), and Meichenbaum (1974). Such therapy addresses itself to the cognitive process by which an individual interprets his or her world and directs his or her behavior. It recognizes that the emotions an individual experiences depend on how he or she interprets events rather than on the events themselves. By interpreting the illogical and self-defeating mental processes in which an individual engages, cognitive therapy hopes to make the individual aware of how his or her thought patterns contribute to unpleasant emotions and to problems in living. As the individual learns to recognize and then to correct biased hypotheses and maladaptive ways of thinking, he or she should become increasingly able to profit from new experiences.

Experienced clinicians have long been aware of the importance of attending to the subtle expression of emotions. We have been developing a procedure in which individuals attempt to learn about the ways in which they automatically interpret the world by keeping daily records of the events to which they respond emotionally. Students who participate in the project are often surprised to find that their emotions are not simply spontaneous reflections of reality, but are a consequence of their habitual modes of thinking, usually at an intuitive, not conscious, level.

Strange as it may seem, it is a revelation to many people to find that their cognitions, which determine how they subjectively perceive the world, influence how they feel, and that these cognitions are directly under their control. Once an individual recognizes this, the individual can evaluate his or her thoughts as destructive or constructive, rather than passively accept them as automatic reflections of reality. Let us illustrate this with a concrete example. John was very disappointed because he failed an important test. He told himself that he was a fool and that he should have studied harder. Throughout the day, he reprimanded himself, reminding himself of how important the test was. He concluded that he would never amount to anything, and this realization made him feel so hopeless and deeply sad that he could get very little constructive work done. In analyzing his thought processes as destructive or constructive, it is evident that the only constructive thought he had was that he should have studied harder. At least, this has the potential of being constructive, if in fact it leads him to study harder next time. The other thoughts simply reveal John's intolerance of himself, and do nothing other than add to his misery. It is bad enough that he failed the test without having him compound his unhappiness by attacking himself. Ironically, John would probably be sympathetic to someone else in the same plight, and he would more likely offer constructive advice than attack that person. Why then does he attack himself? Most people who think as John does either believe there is some basic virtue in suffering, or feel that dwelling on one's inadequacies is simply acknowledging reality. They do not recognize that they are engaging in a habitual, destructive thought pattern.

In order to convince John of the illogic of his thinking, he might be asked to consider the following: either he is right or wrong in believing he is inadequate. If he is wrong, then the negative self-assessment is clearly inaccurate, and should be discontinued on that basis. If he is right, then he has the choice of being inadequate and miserable about it or being inadequate and not miserable about it. As the latter is clearly preferable, the worrying and self-disapproval again are inappropriate, and should be discontinued. If John could reason this way, and learn to catch himself in the act of producing self-defeating thoughts, he could stop them and, accordingly, feel better, and therefore behave more adequately. He would have learned that thinking in a way that produces self-dislike and misery is not virtuous or realistic, but simply foolish.

One of the weaknesses in current cognitive therapies is that they tend to treat cognitions in isolation. In this respect they are similar to behavior therapies that treat specific behavioral acts in isolation. Like psychoanalysts and behaviorists, most cognitive therapists have not given sufficient attention to the importance to the individual of maintaining a unified, internally consistent conceptual system. Until they do so, the effect of their manipulation of cognitions will be limited, and sometimes even counterproductive, which is not to deny that it can be highly effective under many circumstances. However, it can be anticipated that certain cognitions that are important in maintaining the organization of an individual's self-theory will be extremely resistant to change, and could produce unfortunate results if they were to be changed without adequate consideration of the role they play in maintenance of the individual's conceptual system.

The treatment of depression by cognitive therapists such as Beck (1976) has often involved an attempt to change specific thoughts, such as a belief by a patient that he cannot get out of bed in the morning. While the therapy has been effective in correcting such thoughts, it is one thing to change such a superficial cognition and another to come to grips with people's more basic problems, such as their low self-esteem, and their tendency to have recurrent depressive episodes following disappointments in living. Changing cognitions at deeper levels may require not simply learning to talk to oneself differently, but significant emotional experiences to counteract strong hypotheses that are deeply ingrained because of early emotionally significant experiences. People who have been badly burned in the past by touching hot stoves will tend to be afraid of touching stoves, no matter what they tell themselves. The only remedy may be to have significant experiences that are more compelling than words. Yet, learning to talk to oneself constructively can play a role even here, although an indirect one; for, by changing peripheral thought, it becomes possible to open the way to corrective experience. In conclusion, cognitive therapies appear to be highly promising, but need to consider the role of an integrated conceptual system, not simply to treat isolated thoughts.

Some Controversial Issues in Self-Theory

The Self as an Object of Knowledge Versus the Self as a Knower. Is it useful to regard the self as a knower as well as an object of knowledge? The issue of whether or not it is reasonable to propose a self that is a knower with executive functions can readily be resolved once it is recognized that individuals construct implicit theories of reality as an aid to living their lives. Theories not only contain knowledge but are directive in the sense that they determine what is attended to and what is assimilated. In that they make data meaningful by providing a theoretical context for organizing and interpreting data, they are knowers. In sum, self-theories are objects of knowledge in that they contain knowledge, including knowledge about the self; they are knowers in that they organize and interpret knowledge, and they are executives in that they direct perception and the search for new knowledge.

The Growth Principle. A number of psychologists, including Goldstein (1939), Jung (1953), Rogers (1961), and Maslow (1962) have proposed the existence within humans of a force toward fulfilling their innermost potential. They assume that growth in personality will take place so long as there are no impediments that prevent it from doing so. An analogy is made to a seed that has within its latent structure a beautiful flower. All that is necessary for the seed to fulfill its destiny and become the flower is to provide it with the right environment. No one has to teach a seed how to grow, and too much tending can even interfere with the process. The difficulty with this analogy, appealing as it may seem, is that there are some very fundamental differences between human infants and seeds. Human infants do not simply grow if unimpeded. In addition to a loving environment they need stimulation and have to be taught. The idea that there exists a latent structure that simply unfolds without guidance and direction is untenable. Every culture is compelled to teach its young and to develop sanctions to direct behavior in social channels. It is for such reasons that the idea of an inherent growth principle in the form proposed by humanistic psychologists has not been taken seriously by other psychologists.

A growth principle, however, can be accounted for in a scientifically acceptable manner when it is recognized that people have implicit self-theories. Given a self-theory that assimilates data, the theory will grow so long as it is exposed to appropriate data and so long as the individual is not so threatened as to avoid stimulation and defend the self in preference to pursuing new assimilations. A personal self-theory is no different from a scientific theory in this respect. As we have noted before, self-theories tend to become constricted under high threat and expansive under low threat. Such growth does not mean that what emerges was present in seedling form to begin with. The growth is as much a product of what the environment has to offer as of what the individual brings to it. It is an oversimplification to take into account only one aspect of this equation.

One Self or Many Selves? Some psychologists, such as Lecky, Snygg and Combs, and Rogers stress the unity of the self. Others, such as Cooley, Mead, and Gergen argue that there are many selves. Gergen (1971), for example, makes the following statement:

> The way in which we talk about a person's *concept* or *view* of himself suggests that we largely think of the self in the singular . . . . Yet there are strong arguments against this position of singular conceptualization of self. For one, if a person is asked to describe himself he will typically use a large number of different concepts that have little or no relationship to each other. Former President Lyndon Johnson once described himself as a "free man, an American, a United States Senator, a Democrat, a liberal, a conversative, a Texan, a taxpayer, a rancher, and not as young as I used to be nor as old as I expect to be" . . . . In summary, the assumption of a single, or global concept of self seems misleading. Rather than speaking of *the* self or self-concept, it is much more fruitful to speak of multiple conceptions (pp. 19-20).

The issue of whether there are many selves or one self can be resolved if it is recognized that individuals have self-theories that are both integrated and differentiated. Thus, many selves are incorporated into a unified overall self-system. Since the individual is not aware of his or her self-system, it is pointless to ask the individual whether he or she has a unified self. A unified self must be inferred from other evidence—such as that the same emotional reactions are produced by threats to any aspect of the self, and that disorganization of the entire self-system occurs, as in the case of acute schizophrenic reactions. To assert that there is unity in the self-system is not to deny that there is also differentiation, and even inconsistency, within the system. As was noted before, inconsistencies are a source of stress; and although the self-system aims toward internal consistency, it never succeeds completely. The argument of whether there is one self or there are many selves is, in a way, reminiscent of the older argument of whether intelligence is general or specific. The answer turned out to be that it is both.

Continuity of the Self. How stable is the self-system? Can it be both stable and changeable at the same time? It is evident that a theory can retain its essential stability while it is accommodating itself to new data and is therefore changing, at least peripherally. This is as true of a self-theory as it is of a theory in science. Peripheral changes can, of course, ultimately produce more profound changes; but so long as the more profound changes occur gradually, they will not interfere with the stability of the self-system at any one moment in time. Breakthroughs of significant dissociations, as well as the occurrence of extreme life events—whether constructive, as in a positive love relationship, or destructive, as in a traumatic experience in battle—can produce sudden changes in extremely fundamental postulates. In such cases, the individual will undergo a dramatic change in personality; but normally the self changes through the accumulative effect of many less extreme experiences, and therefore retains its unity.

How can one account for the *feeling* of continuity that people maintain about themselves despite having obviously changed a great deal over a prolonged period of time, such as from childhood to adulthood? It must be considered that any single experience, unless it is of traumatic intensity, is assimilated into the individual's existing self-theory. Compared to the rest of the self-theory, it is apt to add little at any one point in time, and therefore to be hardly noticed. It is like watching a child grow. Only someone who has not seen the child for a long time is apt to be surprised by the change. A further consideration is that the postulates formed early in life become higher-order postulates that assimilate later experiences, and therefore tend to remain as broadly integrative postulates. Thus, while the surface behavior may radically change from childhood to adulthood, many of the early postulates continue to exert their influence into adulthood, although in a form modified by lower order postulates.

Is Behavior Determined by the Past or by the Future? Behaviorists and Freudian psychoanalysts alike have been accused of treating man in a fatalistic way, as a passive creature who has been victimised by his past conditioning. Humanistic psychologists and followers of Jung, on the other hand, argue for a future orientation in behavior. They believe that man's behavior is determined more by a person's vision of the future than by his or her memory of the past.

From the viewpoint of the self-theory presented here, there is room for both positions. Many of the important cognitions that guide an individual's behavior developed in childhood, with the aim of helping the individual cope with his or her present circumstances and conception of the future at that time. It will be recalled that a person's conceptual system is a cognitive tool for helping to adjust to life in the best way possible, as conceived of by the individual. One reason that childhood experiences are particularly important is that the child is apt to make inappropriate generalizations because he or she has strong emotional experiences and has limited conceptual abilities for dealing with them. As previously noted, childhood generalizations become basic postulates that influence the development of the rest of the postulate system. Many of these postulates are prescriptive in nature; that is, they are broad generalizations derived from emotionally significant experiences in the child's past about how to behave in the future in order to maximize the pleasure/pain balance and maintain an optimal level of self-esteem.

The Nature of the Stimulus. According to those self-theorists who are phenomenologists, behavior can only be understood from the viewpoint of the person doing the behaving. As was noted earlier, this presents a problem for treating psychology as a science; for, if each individual responds to his or her private interpretation of stimuli, how can stimuli be objectively classified? What value can there be in the experimental method, in which an experimenter varies specific stimuli in order to investigate their general effect on a sample of people? Phenomenologists would argue that such experiments should be dispensed with, as, given the subjective nature of perception, the objective classification of stimuli is meaningless. There is no doubt but that the phenomenologists are correct in assuming that people respond to stimuli as perceived, and not to stimuli as objectively defined by someone else. Yet, if one ignores the stimulus as objectively defined by a concensus of others, there is no place for a consideration of objective reality. Does one, then, have to choose between studying the subjective reality of the phenomenologists and the objective reality of the behaviorists?

It is obviously necessary to take into account both objective and subjective reality. If orderliness is to be demonstrated in human behavior, it will be necessary to understand the mediating process by which people transform data from the objective world into their subjective world of experience. This is a critical problem for personality theory, and perhaps for all of psychology.

In the study of human personality, it must be considered that people in real life do not respond to stimuli selected for them by others, as in a laboratory experiment, but actively seek out the stimuli to which they respond. Thus, laboratory studies of responses to fixed stimuli are not sufficient; they must be supplemented by studies in which people are free to select their own stimulus situations.

Finally, a word might be said about the issue of whether individuals respond to the world along common stimulus dimensions, or whether the dimensions themselves–let alone the standing of individuals on the dimensions–vary. If the dimensions differ for different individuals, this will considerably complicate the study of personality, because it means that people cannot be compared to each other along common dimensions. It is as if one had to use a different atomic chart for each chemical. Kelly (1955) emphasized the uniqueness of dimensions among people, and he developed an ingenious method for determining the particular dimensions with which an individual construes the world. Allport (1961) has noted that there are both common traits that all people share and unique traits that are specific to individuals. It is reasonable to assume that a similar situation holds for stimulus dimensions, for it is difficult to see how people could be similar in their personality traits if they did not construe the world along similar dimensions. The extent to which dimensions are general or unique is, of course, a question that can only be answered by research. Stimulus dimensions that are unique to an individual when stimulus situations are narrowly defined may well turn out to be common dimensions when stimulus situations are more broadly defined. Thus, not all people are interested in playing tennis well, yet all are very likely responsive in some degree to being competent at something. It follows that, for some, interest in playing tennis could be an indication of their achievement motivation, while for others it could not be. An interesting task for future research is to determine what dimensions that are specific to individuals at one level can be classified into broader dimensions that are common to people at a broader level.

RESEARCH ON SELF-THEORY

Space does not permit a thorough review of research that is relevant to self-theory. Fortunately, an unusually thorough review of this topic is available in a book by Wylie (1974). We shall briefly give some examples of research that has been done by others in a few areas of special interest to self-theory, and then indicate the kind of research we have been pursuing in our own program.

Research on Some Key Issues in Self-Theory

The Unity of the Self-System. According to Lecky, Snygg and Combs, Rogers, and Epstein, there is a tendency for the self-system to seek internal consistency and unity. Perception of a lack of consistency in an individual's conceptual system produces anxiety, which motivates attempts to reduce the discrepancy. According to Rogers, a particularly important discrepancy is that between a person's ideal and actual self. Several students and associates of Rogers have investigated such discrepancies and related them to measures of adjustment and to changes during psychotherapy. Butler and Haigh (1954) reported a significant increase in the correspondence between self and ideal descriptions as the result of psychotherapy. Some studies have confirmed this finding; others have not. Apparently, additional factors complicate the relationship. Friedman (1953), in a study that compared normals, neurotics, and psychotics, concluded that one such complicating factor is defensiveness. He found that psychotics had self-ideal discrepancies that were more similar to normals than to neurotics, and suggested that the psychotics were maintaining internal consistency at the expense of acknowledging reality. Chodorkoff (1954) found that the greater the agreement between an individual's self-description and an objective description of the individual by others, the greater the individual's personal adjustment, and the less the individual exhibited perceptual defense. Such findings support the view of self-theorists that when the self is threatened by perceptions it cannot assimilate into a unified conceptual system, the individual resorts to defenses that deny or distort reality.

Evidence that internal consistency is important is also provided by studies in social psychology. Festinger (1957) and Brehm and Cohen (1962) accumulated considerable evidence to support their thesis that individuals are motivated to avoid and to reduce cognitive dissonance. In a series of studies that are particularly interesting because, unlike most of the others, they demonstrate relatively long-term effects, Rokeach (1973) demonstrated that when individuals are faced with discrepancies in self-related values, they resolve the discrepancies, and, as a consequence, undergo changes in related attitudes and behavior. Such demonstrations provide evidence of the hierarchical arrangement of the self-system. In a study on the maintenance of incorrect beliefs in a course in psychology, Vaughn (1977) found that beliefs that were associated with an individual's important values tended to be resistant to change, and that contrary evidence was either ignored or treated as irrelevant.

The overall evidence strongly supports the view that individuals are motivated to maintain internal consistency in their conceptual systems.

The Need to Enhance the Self. It will be recalled that Lecky, Snygg and Combs, and Rogers argue that the organism has one central need; for Lecky, it is to preserve the unity of the conceptual system, while for Rogers and for Snygg and Combs it is to "maintain and enhance" the self-concept or the organism. Epstein argues that these are actually two separate needs.

Within social psychology, there are two conflicting views, consistency theories and esteem theories. Proponents of each theory argue that the position of the other can be subsumed under their own position. In a review of the literature, Jones (1973) noted that there is support for both positions. In a study of self-esteem as related to reactions to positive and negative evaluations in everyday life, Losco-Szpiler (1977) concluded that neither esteem theories nor consistency theories could alone account for her data. She found that high-self-esteem subjects reported highly positive emotional reactions to favorable evaluations and highly negative reactions to unfavorable evaluations, while low-self-esteem subjects reported relatively mild reactions to both favorable and unfavorable evaluations. These findings can be accounted for by assuming that consistency needs and esteem needs operate simultaneously. For high-self-esteem subjects, favorable evaluations satisfied both needs, hence the very strong positive reactions, and unfavorable evaluations frustrated both needs, hence the very strong negative reaction. For low-self-esteem subjects, favorable evaluations ran counter to their need to maintain a consistent self-view, but appealed to their desire for self-enhancement, hence a compromise reaction. Unfavorable evaluations for low-self-esteem subjects also evoked a compromise reaction, as the negative evaluations supported the need for consistency but frustrated the need for enhancement.

The overall evidence supports the view that individuals have a need to both maintain the stability of their self-systems and enhance themselves, and that the operation of these two needs must be considered together in predicting behavior.

Unconditional Positive Regard as a Condition for Growth. According to Rogers, an optimum condition for fostering growth in personality is one in which an individual rceives unconditional acceptance by another. This idea was suggested to Rogers by his observations of clients in psychotherapy who profited from an atmosphere in which they were treated with unconditional positive regard by the therapist. As a result of such acceptance, clients showed significant gains in psychotherapy in the absence of direction or interpretation from the therapist. It is of course possible that conditions that are optimum in the treatment of disturbed individuals are not necessarily optimum for growth in individuals who are not disturbed. In an extensive study of self-esteem in preadolescent boys and girls, Coopersmith (1967) found that the parents of high-self-esteem children were less permissive than the parents of children with lower levels of self-esteem. The parents with high-self-esteem children set higher standards than parents of lower-self-esteem children. While these parents were respectful of dissent, they were not permissive, but defined the privileges and responsibilities of their children. They showed deep interest in their children, respected their opinions, and guided them rather than treated them as equals. Coopersmith's findings seem to be in direct opposition to Rogers's view that permissiveness combined with unconditional positive regard are the optimum conditions for fostering self-acceptance and personality growth.

Mussen and Eisenberg (1977) investigated the effect of child-rearing practices on producing children who exhibit a helpful and cooperative orientation toward others. According to Rogers, such behavior automatically unfolds when a child receives unconditional positive regard. This was not found to be the case, as parents who cared about their children were found to produce both selfish children and children who were cooperative and helpful to others. To produce children who were concerned over the welfare of others, parents had not only to care for their children but to provide an example in their own behavior that indicated they placed a high value on being considerate and helpful to others. That is, they had to provide role models of considerate and helpful people.

Evidence such as the above casts doubt on Rogers's hypothesis that there is a natural tendency for people to become well-adjusted and socially oriented when they are simply provided with an adequate loving relationship. It appears that specific training and modeling of the desired behavior are also necessary. In psychotherapy, the client observes the therapist's behavior; and it is possible that the increased positive regard toward others that was exhibited in Rogers's clients may have been a response to Rogers as a role model, not a direct consequence of receiving unconditional positive regard. If this is true, were the client to observe the psychotherapist to behave in selfish ways with other people, the client would become more selfish rather than more socialized as a result of the close empathic relationship with the therapist.

Self-Esteem as a Broad Postulate with Widespread Implications. According to self-theorists such as Lecky, Snygg and Combs, Rogers, and Epstein, self-esteem is a central component in an individual's self-system. It is assumed to be resistant to change and to be intimately associated with a wide variety of attitudes and behavior. Thus, it is believed that when self-esteem is affected, there are widespread ramifications throughout the entire personality.

There is evidence that high self-esteem is associated with a variety of positive attributes. For example, it has frequently been noted that acceptance of self is directly associated with acceptance of others (e.g., Berger, 1952; Medinnus & Curtis, 1963; Phillips, 1951; Suinn, 1961). Numerous studies have reported that self-esteem is positively related to effective performance in groups of both sexes and all ages (e.g., Anastasliow, 1964; Coopersmith, 1964; Davis, 1962; Rosenberg, 1965). In Wylie's (1974) extensive review of research on the self-concept, the evidence clearly indicated that self-esteem is directly associated with effective personal adjustment. In a study of people's reactions to evaluations in everyday life by Losco-Szpiler (1977), it was found that following positive evaluations, which can be assumed to produce a temporary rise in self-esteem, subjects reported an increase in feelings of security, kindliness, happiness, energy, spontaneity, calmness, mental clarity, and power. Following negative evaluations, they reported an increase in the opposite feelings. Similar results were obtained in a study by O'Brien and Epstein (1974) in which subjects kept records of their responses to a variety of experiences in everyday life that raised and lowered their self-esteem over a period of six weeks. It was found that increases in self-esteem were associated with increases in all positive emotions, including feelings of integration, in energy availability, in expansiveness and in openness to new experiences. Decreases in self-esteem were associated with increases in dysphoric emotions, including anxiety, with a tendency to become disorganized, and with feelings of being constrained and inhibited. In a study by Epstein (reported in 1977, 1979b, 1979c), subjects kept daily records of pleasant and unpleasant emotions for the space of a month. When the data for unpleasant emotions were factor analyzed, a factor emerged that included feeling unworthy in combination with feeling frightened, tense, and disorganized.

Despite momentary fluctuations in self-assessment, there is evidence that self-esteem is relatively stable. Evidence for stability of self-esteem is reviewed by Brehm and Cohen (1962) and by Rokeach (1973). In studies by Epstein (1977, 1979b), relatively high stability coefficients were found for daily ratings of feelings of worthiness when the data were averaged over an adequate sample of observations.

A Research Program for Investigating Cognitive Self-Theory

An appropriate research program for investigating the theory proposed in this paper would include emotional variables, cognitive variables, and variables related to the extensivity and assimilative capacity of an individual's conceptual system. Changes that are emotionally significant to the individual and that are relatively enduring would be emphasized in preference to laboratory manipulations that produce only transient and trivial effects.

A series of studies, some of which have been reported in the previous section, was conducted with the above requirements in mind. Space does not permit more than a cursory description of these studies. The interested reader is referred to more thorough descriptions elsewhere (Epstein, 1976, 1977, 1979a, 1979b, 1979c; Losco-Szpiler, 1977; O'Brien & Epstein, 1974). In one of the studies (reported in Epstein, 1976, 1979c), subjects kept records of their most pleasant and unpleasant emotional experience each day for a month. They recorded their behavior on special forms on which they rated their emotions; their degree of confusion versus mental clarity; their self-esteem, including competence, likeability, power, and general feelings of worthiness; the situations that gave rise to their emotions; their impulses; and whether or not they expressed the impulses in behavior. The findings indicated that personality variables are stable when averaged over a sufficient sample of observations, but not when based on single observations. This supports the view that personality, although situationally responsive, is also reasonably stable. Of particular interest was evidence of relatively high levels of stability in the organization of variables within an individual. As previously noted, factor analysis of the data revealed a syndrome of low self-esteem combined with a tendency to experience high levels of anxiety and proneness to disorganization. Self-esteem had widespread relationships with other variables, both cognitive and emotional—which is consistant with the assumption that an overall assessment of the self is a concept of central importance in an individual's self-theory. In another study (reported in Epstein, 1976, 1979c), an inventory of self-esteem was constructed with scales on general feelings of worthiness, competence, likeability, power, will-power, moral self-approval, and body self-image. In support of the concept that the self-system is both integrated and differentiated, the results of a factor analysis indicated that there was a general factor of self-esteem that included all scales, as well as individual factors. It was further demonstrated that an individual's assessment of his or her self-worth is reasonably stable over time.

In two studies, subjects kept records of specified kinds of experiences that occurred in everyday life. In one of these studies (Losco-Szpiler, 1977), college students recorded their reactions to favorable and unfavorable evaluations. In the other (O'Brien & Epstein, 1974), students recorded their reactions to experiences that raised and lowered their self-esteem. The results of these studies are reported in the previous section. In a study by Ofria and Epstein (reported in Epstein, 1979c), 200 college students reported the two experiences in their lifetime that produced their most positive and negative changes in self-concept. The findings were consistent with the key assumptions of most of the theories of self reviewed in this chapter, with one exception; namely, not all positive changes in self-concept were produced by a high level of acceptance and positive regard; some were produced by experiences that were regarded as negative at the time of occurrence, such as being negatively evaluated by another or being forced by circumstances to become autonomous or to develop new skills.

The relationship of emotions to cognitions was investigated by studying the development of emotions as a function of increasing information. In one such study (reported in Epstein, 1979c), college students rated their feelings at three points in time: at a control period; after being informed that an examination was about to be returned; and a few minutes after the examination was returned, and they had assimilated the evaluation of their performance as indicated by a letter grade and the reasons for the grade. It was observed that announcement of the return of the examination produced a marked increase in anxiety and a slight increase in feelings of unhappiness and in negative self-evaluation, suggesting that individuals tended to prepare themselves for the possibility of bad news. Upon return of the examination, anxiety *decreased,* and this occurred following both favorable and unfavorable outcomes. Not surprisingly, following favorable evaluations there was an increase in happiness, while following unfavorable outcomes there was an increase in unhappiness, in anger directed toward the self, and in anger directed toward others. It was concluded, in support of hypothesis, that anxiety is associated with uncertainty about a potentially threatening event, while more differentiated emotions occur only following further assessment.

Finally, research has been done on the analysis of case histories of acute schizophrenic disorganization (Epstein, 1976, 1979a). The aim of this research was to examine the disorganization of an individual's conceptual system as a way of learning about the nature of the system, the disorganization process, and the process by which an individual attempts to construct a new system. The findings support the thesis that individuals feel compelled to construct a conceptual system that assimilates the data of experience, that maintains positive self-esteem, and that achieves a favorable pleasure/pain balance over the foreseeable future. Since these three needs often conflict with each other, the restitutive task is a complicated one, and solutions may be less than successful.

SUMMARY

A variety of views on the nature of the self-concept have been reviewed. It has been noted that some self-theorists believe that the self should be considered only as an object of knowledge, while others believe it should be regarded as a "knower," with executive properties. Among those in the latter camp are the phenomenologists, who believe that behavior can only be understood from the viewpoint of the individual doing the behaving, and the cognitive theorists, who allow equal representation of outer reality and the mediating cognitions by which an individual transforms the objective world of experience into a subjective one.

An integrative cognitive theory has been proposed that is compatible with self-theory, psychoanalysis, other cognitive theories, and behavioral approaches to psychology. Like Lecky's and Kelly's theory, it holds that humans, in leading their everyday lives, function like scientists in that they are continuously formulating and testing hypotheses at a subconscious level. It is assumed that the self-concept is actually a self-theory, one that individuals unwittingly develop because they need it to lead their lives. A self-theory together with a world-theory comprise an individual's theory of reality, which identifies the individual's total conceptual system. A theory of reality is not developed as an end in itself, but has three basic functions: (a) to assimilate the data of experience, (b) to maintain a favorable pleasure/pain balance, and (c) to optimize self-esteem. To maintain its other functions, it is obvious that the theory of reality must also seek to maintain itself. Unlike other self-theories that assume that the "need to maintain and enhance" is a single need, the proposed theory regards them as independent needs, often in conflict with each other, resulting in responses that are compromise formations.

Normally, the individual will attempt to defend his or her theory of reality at any cost; for, without the theory, the individual is incapable of functioning. Thus, defense mechanisms are employed not only to defend self-esteem, such as by denying unacceptable impulses, as stressed by psychoanalysts, but also to maintain the unity of the individual's conceptual system, as stressed by self-theorists. Sometimes the need to defend the unity of the conceptual system is prepotent over the need to seek pleasure or to maintain self-esteem, and when this occurs, it may give the appearance that the individual is bent on self-destruction or is behaving in irrational ways.

Emotions are intimately associated with an individual's theory of reality; the theory is initially developed as a conceptual tool for maximizing pleasure and minimizing pain. Once the conceptual system develops, it mediates the emotions. Thus, behind almost every emotion is a hidden cognition. Accordingly, emotions are the royal road to an individual's implicit postulates. Awareness of this relationship can be used to advantage in self-understanding as well as in psychotherapy.

Once it is recognized that individuals have implicit theories of reality, a number of classic issues in psychology can be resolved. Included are the place of an executive self in psychology; the existence of a growth principle; the question of whether there are many selves or one self; the importance of the past versus the future in influencing human behavior; the issue of whether personality is stable or situationally variable; and the attributes of good adjustment.

Some areas of research on key issues in self-theory have been presented, and a research program specially devised to investigate the proposed theory was described.

REFERENCES

Allport, G. *Becoming: Basic considerations for a psychology of personality.* New Haven, Conn.: Yale University Press, 1955.

____. *Pattern and growth in personality*. New York: Holt, Rinehart & Winston, 1961.

___. (Ed.). *Letters from Jenny.* New York: Harcourt, Brace & World, 1965.

Anistasliow, N. J. A report of the self-concept of the very gifted. *Gifted Child Quarterly,* 1964, *8,* 177-178.

Beck, A. T. *Cognitive therapy and the emotional disorders.* New York: International Universities Press, 1976.

Bender, L. Anxiety in disturbed children. In P. H. Hoch & J. Zubin (Eds.), *Anxiety.* New York: Grune & Stratton, 1950.

Berger, E. M. The relation between expressed acceptance of self and expressed acceptance of others. *Journal of Abnormal and Social Psychology,* 1952, *47,* 778-782.

Bowers, M. B., Jr. *Retreat from sanity.* New York: Human Sciences Press, 1974.

Bowlby, J. *Attachment and loss. Vol. 2, Separation anxiety and anger.* New York: Basic Books, 1973.

Brehm, J. W., & Cohen, A. R. *Explorations in cognitive dissonance.* New York: Wiley, 1962.

Butler, J. M., & Haigh, G. V. Changes in the relation between self-concepts and ideal concepts consequent upon client-centered counseling. In C. R. Rogers & R. F. Dymond (Eds.). *Psychotherapy and personality change; Coordinated studies in the client-centered approach.* Chicago: University of Chicago Press, 1954, pp. 55-76.

Chodorkoff, B. Self-perception, perceptual defense, and adjustment. *Journal of Abnormal and Social Psychology,* 1954, *49,* 508-512.

Cooley, C. H. *Human nature and the social order.* New York: Scribner's, 1902.

Coopersmith, S. Relation between self-esteem and sensory (perceptual) constancy. *Journal of Abnormal and Social Psychology,* 1964, *68,* 217-221.

Coopersmith, S. *The antecedents of self-esteem.* San Francisco: W. H. Freeman, 1967.

Davis, R. W. The relationship of social preferability to self-concept in an aged population. *Journal of Gerontology,* 1962, *17,* 431-436.

Ellis, A. *Reason and emotion in psychotherapy.* New York: Lyle Stuart, 1962.

Epstein, S. The self-concept revisited, or a theory of a theory. *American Psychologist,* 1973, *28,* 404-416.

___. Anxiety, arousal, and the self-concept. In I. G. Sarason, & C. D. Spielberger (Eds.), *Stress and Anxiety,* Vol. 3. Washington, D. C.: Hemisphere Publishing Corporation, 1976, pp. 183-224.

___. Traits are alive and well. In D. Magnusson & N. S. Endler (Eds.), *Personality at the Crossroads.* Hillsdale, N.J.: Lawrence Erlbaum Associates, 1977, pp. 83-98.

___. Natural healing process of the mind. *Schizophrenia Bulletin,* 1979a, *5,* 313-321.

____. The stability of behavior: I. On predicting most of the people much of the time. *Journal of Personality and Social Psychology,* 1979b, In press.

____. The ecological study of emotions in humans. In K. Blankstein (Ed.), *Advances in the Study of Communication and Affect.* Plenum, 1979c.

Festinger, L. *A theory of cognitive dissonance.* Evanston, Illinois: Row, Peterson, 1957.

Friedman, I. Phenomenal, ideal and projected conceptions of self, and their interrelationships in normal, neurotic and paranoid schizophrenic subjects. Unpublished doctoral dissertation, Western Reserve University, 1953. Also see Friedman, I. Phenomenal, ideal, and projected conceptions of self. *Journal of Abnormal and Social Psychology,* 1955, *51,* 611-615.

Gergen, K. J. *The concept of self.* New York: Holt, Rinehart & Winston, 1971.

Goldstein, K. *The organism.* New York: American Book Co., 1939.

Green, H. *I never promised you a rose garden.* New York: Holt, Rinehart and Winston. ©1964 by Hannah Green.

Grinker, R. R., Sr., & Holzman, P. S. Schizophrenic pathology in young adults. *Archives of General Psychiatry,* 1973, *28,* 168-175.

Hilgard, E. R. Human motives and the concept of the self. *American Psychologist,* 1949, *4,* 374-382.

James, W. *Psychology: The briefer course.* New York: Holt, 1907.

Jones, S. Self and interpersonal evaluations: Esteem theories versus consistency theories. *Psychological Bulletin,* 1973, *79,* 185-199.

Jung, C. G. *Collected works. Vol. 7. Two essays on analytical psychology.* New York: Pantheon Press, 1953.

Kelly, G. A. *The psychology of personal constructs,* 2 vols. New York: Norton, 1955.

Krystal, H., (Ed.) *Massive psychic trauma.* New York: International Universities Press, 1968.

Lecky, P. *Self-consistency: A theory of personality.* Hamden, Connecticut: The Shoe String Press, 1961.

Losco-Szpiler, J. The relative influence of favorable and unfavorable evaluations on emotional, behavioral and cognitive reactions as a function of level of self-esteem and level of depression. Unpublished Master's thesis, 1977. Also see Losco, J., & Epstein, S. *Reactions to favorable and unfavorable evaluations in everyday life as a function of self-esteem.* Paper presented at Eastern Psychological Association Convention, 1978.

Maslow, A. H. *Toward a psychology of being.* Princeton, N.J.: Van Nostrand, 1962.

Mead, G. H. *Mind, self, and society.* Chicago: University of Chicago Press, 1934.

Medinnus, G., & Curtis, F. The relation between maternal self-acceptance and child acceptance. *Journal of Counseling Psychology,* 1963, *27,* 542-544.

Meichenbaum, D. H. *Cognitive behavior modification.* Morristown, N. J.: General Learning Press, 1974.

Mussen, P. & Eisenberg, N. *The roots of caring.* San Francisco: W. H. Freeman, 1977.

O'Brien, E. J., & Epstein, S. Naturally occurring changes in self-esteem. *Publication of Division-8 Papers,* American Psychological Association Convention, 1974.

Perry, J. W. *Roots of renewal in myth and madness.* San Francisco: Josey Bass Publishers, 1976.

Phillips, E. I. Attitude toward self and others: A brief questionnaire report. *Journal of Consulting Psychology,* 1951, *15,* 79-81.

Raimy, V. C. The self-concept as a factor in counseling and personality organization. Unpublished doctoral dissertation, Ohio State University, 1943.

Rogers, C. *Counseling and psychotherapy: Newer concepts in practice.* Boston: Houghton Mifflin, 1942.

____. *Client-centered therapy: Its current practice, implications, and theory.* Boston: Houghton Mifflin, 1951.

____. A theory of therapy, personality, and interpersonal relationships, as developed in the client-centered framework. In S. Koch (Ed.), *Psychology: A study of a science.* Vol. 3. New York: McGraw-Hill, 1959, pp. 184-256.

____. *On becoming a person: A therapist's view of psychotherapy.* Boston: Houghton Mifflin, 1961.

____. *Freedom to learn: A view of what education might become.* Columbus, Ohio: Merrill, 1969.

____. *Becoming partners: Marriage and its alternatives.* New York: Delacorte, 1972.

Rokeach, M. *The nature of human values.* New York: Free Press, 1973.

Rosenberg, M. *Society and the adolescent self-image.* Princeton, N. J.: Princeton University Press, 1965.

Sarbin, T. R. A preface to a psychological analysis of the self. *Psychological Review,* 1952, *59,* 11-22.

Sechehaye, M. *Autobiography of a schizophrenic girl.* New York: New American Library, 1970.

Silverman, J. When schizophrenia helps. *Psychology Today,* 1970, *4,* 63-65.

Snygg, D., & Combs, A. W. *Individual behavior.* New York: Harper & Row, 1949.

Suinn, R. The relationship between self-acceptance and acceptance of others: A learning theory analysis. *Journal of Abnormal and Social Psychology,* 1961, *63,* 37-42.

Sullivan, H. S. *The interpersonal theory of psychiatry.* New York: Norton, 1953.

Vaughn, E. D. *Teaching of Psychology,* Vol. 4, No. 3. Washington, D. C.: American Psychological Association, 1977.

Wylie, R., *The self-concept* (rev. ed.), Vol. 1. Lincoln, Nebraska: University of Nebraska Press, 1974.

JAMES R. AVERILL

The Emotions

The study of personality is broad and diverse. A perusal of textbooks on the subject might leave the impression that personality does not represent a unified field of study. About the only area of universal agreement is that personality has something to do with human beings (persons) as opposed to infrahuman animals. But not all aspects of human behavior are typically included under the rubric of personality. For example, the study of perception, learning, memory, thinking, problem solving, and other topics related to information processing are not usually considered a part of personality psychology. One reason for this, it might be thought, is that information processing and related topics are concerned with universal "laws" of behavior, while personality is concerned with individual differences—that which makes each person unique. But such a distinction is only partly correct. For one thing, many personality theorists also are concerned primarily with universal processes rather than individual differences. For another thing, not all aspects of individual differences are typically included within the area of personality. The study of intelligence, for example, has traditionally been treated as a distinct area of psychology.

The above considerations suggest that there is a division within psychology between the study of cognitive-intellectual functions on the one hand, and non-cognitive (emotional-motivational) functions on the other, and that an emphasis on the latter is one of the major features of personality psychology. This fact helps explain the inclusion of a rather lengthy chapter on the emotions in a book on personality. However, a caveat must be added. Although the distinction between cognitive and emotional processes represents an historically important division of labor[1], it cannot be accepted uncritically simply because it is tradi-

[1] This division within contemporary psychology reflects a much older division between mental and moral philosophy. Mental philosophy was concerned primarily with questions of epistemology, i.e., the origins and nature of knowledge, while moral philosophy was concerned primarily with questions of motivation, will, emotion, and the like. Stated more colloquially, mental philosophy had to do with truth or falsity, and moral philosophy had

tional. In fact, the orientation of the present chapter might best be described as a cognitive approach to emotion. To adumbrate briefly, the emotions are viewed here as socially constituted ways of solving certain types of problems or conflicts. They differ from other attempts at problem solution, not in terms of the cognitive capacities involved, but in the way they are interpreted by the individual and society, and in the functions they serve.

This chapter is divided into five sections. The first section is devoted to a review and critique of some of the more influential theories of emotion. In the second section, we return to the beginning, so to speak, and examine afresh the nature of emotional phenomena. The third section explores in detail the structure of emotion; that is, the "rules" according to which the emotions are organized, and the reasons why they are interpreted as passions (something which happens to us) rather than as actions (something we do). The emotions, however, represent a very diverse set of phenomena, and no type of analysis is equally applicable to all emotional states. In the fourth section, therefore, three different kinds of emotion are distinguished and several examples of each kind are examined in some detail. Finally, the fifth section takes up the problem of individual differences in emotional reactivity; more specifically, an examination is made of longer-term dispositions to respond emotionally, such as motives, moods, traits, and sentiments.

THEORIES OF EMOTION

Most theories of emotion can be placed into one of three groups—artichoke theories, onion theories, and hybrids. This metaphor refers not to the value of the theories as food for thought, but rather to the structure of emotion which they posit. Consider an artichoke. As the outer petals are peeled away you eventually come to the heart or "essence" of the vegetable. Artichoke theories view emotion in a similar way. As the more superficial aspects of emotional behavior are peeled away, it is presumed, some core feature or essence of emotion will ultimately be revealed. Stated somewhat differently, artichoke theories posit a qualitative difference between the superficial (leaves) and the central (heart) aspects of emotion. By way of contrast, consider an onion. As successive layers are peeled away, the onion is reduced in size until ultimately nothing remains. There is no heart of an onion; by analogy, onion theories do not posit any unique feature which lies at the core of emotional behavior. Hybrid theories represent a cross between the artichoke and onion varieties; they postulate some essential feature of emotion but also emphasize the continuity between emotional and nonemotional processes.

---

to do with goodness or badness. Thus, one might ask of a perception, memory, or problem solution, Is it true (veridical) or false? But one does not usually ask of an emotion or act of will whether it is true or false, although it may be judged right or wrong in a moral sense.

Artichoke Theories of Emotion

Central to artichoke theories of emotion is the assumption that a term such as *emotion* must refer to some specific entity or *thing.* But what could that thing be? The concept of emotion cannot refer simply to behavioral responses. Overt behavior is much too varied for that. A person gripped by anger, for example, might strike his antagonist, make a verbal retort, withdraw affection, tell a third party, or perhaps do nothing at all. The thing to which emotional concepts refer (i.e., the heart of the emotional artichoke) must therefore lie below the surface manifestations of behavior; and here, three main possibilities exist, namely, emotions as feeling, as physiological responses, or as intervening (drive) variables.

Emotions as Feelings. Perhaps the most common variety of artichoke theory defines emotion as a kind of subjective experience or feeling. The famous theory of emotion proposed by William James belongs to this category. "My theory," James (1890) asserted, "is that *bodily changes follow directly the perception of the exciting fact, and that our feeling of the same changes as they occur* IS *the emotion*" (p. 449). In other words, the heart of the emotional artichoke is a subjective experience occasioned by certain physiological changes, primarily visceral activity and postural adjustments. A very similar position was put forward by the physiologist Walter Cannon (1929), but with an emphasis on central neural mechanisms, as opposed to peripheral physiological changes. Specifically, Cannon suggested that the thalamus–one of the major subdivisions of the diencephalon–is the source of emotional experience. Under normal conditions, according to Cannon, the thalamic activity is inhibited by cortical influences. However, when an emotional stimulus is perceived, cortical inhibition is released and thalamic impulses are sent (a) to the muscles and viscera involved in the expression of emotion and (b) to cortical mechanisms involved in the conscious experience of emotion. "The theory which naturally presents itself," Cannon stated, "is that *the peculiar quality of the emotion is added to simple sensation when the thalamic processes are roused*" (1929, p. 369).

Cannon believed that his theory represented an alternative to that of James, and most modern textbooks follow this lead. From a logical point of view, however, the similarities between the two theories are more important than the differences. Both James and Cannon assumed that the essential feature of emotion is a kind of feeling or subjective experience. They differed only regarding the source of that feeling, that is, feedback from *peripheral* versus *central neural* activity. Later in the chapter, we will consider in some detail the role of feedback (self-monitoring) in the experience of emotion. For the moment, let us focus on the assumption common to both James and Cannon–as well as to many others–that the emotions are feelings. The definition of emotions as feelings, whatever the postulated source of those feelings, suffers from three major difficulties. First, the term *feeling* is among the vaguest in the English language. A person may feel a pin-prick, feel ill, feel happy, feel like going to the movies, and so on. To say that the emotions are feelings is, therefore, not very informative. Second, there are over 500 concepts in English which have emotional connotations (Averill, 1975). The contention that each such term refers to a specific feeling reduces to absurdity the argument that emotions are feelings. Third, a person may not be aware of his emotional state at the time of its occurrence. For example, it is perfectly meaningful to say of a person that he is envious, even though that person might sincerely and vehemently deny the fact. Such a statement would not be meaningful, however, if concepts such as envy referred specifically to feelings (since feelings are by definition a matter of conscious awareness).

Emotions as Physiological Responses. A second variety of artichoke theory attempts to overcome difficulties such as the above by identifying emotions with physiological responses per se, and not with any secondary accompaniments (e.g., feelings) of such responses. Perhaps the most explicit statement of this position is that by Marion Wenger (1950), who has defined the emotions as "patterns of visceral change," that is, as activity of the organs innervated by the autonomic nervous system. Wenger considers his position to be a logical extension of one originally put forward by the Danish physiologist Carl Lange (1885), whose name is often associated with that of James in the so-called James-Lange theory of emotion. As we have just seen, however, James considered emotions to *be* subjective experiences; Lange, by contrast, considered physiological change (especially within the cardiovascular system) to be the necessary and sufficient condition for emotion.

The definition of emotion in terms of physiological change would seem to have the advantage of both parsimony and objectivity over the position, say, of William James, who viewed physiological activity as only an intermediate link. There are problems, however. If emotions are defined in terms of peripheral (e.g., visceral) changes, then it is often difficult to distinguish one emotional state from another (e.g., fear from rage) and to distinguish emotional from nonemotional states (e.g., fear from exercise-induced arousal). To overcome this difficulty, the relevant physiological changes might be "localized" within the central nervous system, a move similar to that made by Cannon in the case of James's theory. For example, emotion might be defined in terms of neural circuits located in the thalamus, hypothalamus, limic system, or some other brain structure. But with such a move the position loses much of its parsimony and objectivity, for the relevant brain processes can only be inferred; they cannot be directly observed or measured.

Emotions as Intervening Variables. If the best we can do is make inferences about hypothetical neural mechanisms, then some theorists believe it would be best to dispense with such talk entirely. Instead, emotions could be treated as intervening variables. An intervening variable is basically a logical device introduced to help simplify the description of a functional relationship between two sets of variables. In classical mechanics, for example, the force of gravity (g) is an intervening variable that relates the distance (s) traveled by a falling body to the time (t) of fall ($s = \frac{1}{2} gt^2$). Similarly, in psychology, emotions may be "viewed as intervening variables between meaning of information and bodily changes elicited by it" (Lipowski, 1977).

Of course, the intervening variables postulated by psychologists typically cannot be given precise mathematical expession as in physics. Therefore, an everyday term may be used to label the variable and to describe its properties. "Drive" is the name most often given to the emotions as intervening variables. Fear, according to this view, is the "drive" which motivates avoidance, anger is the "drive" which motivates aggression, and so forth.

A major difficulty with the intervening-variables approach is that it deflects attention away from emotional phenomena per se. Intervening variables, such as drive, are generally regarded as theoretical entities without substantive properties of their own. What is substantive is the behavior motivated by the drive; for example, avoidance in the case of fear. Consequently, instead of investigating fear, psychologists of this persuasion typically investigate avoidance behavior and its antecedent conditions. But this overlooks the fact that not all avoidance behavior is fearful; nor does fear always lead to avoidance.

Some General Observations on Artichoke Theories of Emotion. Each variety of artichoke theory which we have mentioned (i.e., emotion as subjective experience, physiological change, or intervening variable) has its own difficulties. More importantly, however, these theories as a group rest on a questionable assumption, namely, that there is some heart or core to the emotional artichoke, some specific "thing" to which the concept of emotion refers. It would take far too much space to examine the limitations of this assumption as it applies to each kind of artichoke theory. But the nature of the problem can be illustrated quite easily if we change metaphors for the moment and draw an analogy between emotional concepts on the one hand and disease concepts on the other.

Imagine the following situation. A student wakes up one morning feeling miserable. He goes to the university clinic and, after a checkup, is informed that he is suffering from mononucleosis. Being naturally curious, he inquires what *that* is. The physician thereupon describes some of the sensations and feelings which typically accompany this illness. The student finds the information helpful but not sufficient, for his feelings are quite varied, and sometimes he does not even feel ill. Agreeing, the physician lists the major physiological symptoms characteristic of the disease. But the student is still not satisfied. Some of the symptoms mentioned (e.g., an increase in body temperature) are common to many diseases, and even to some non-disease states, while other symptoms are not present in his case. Even more importantly, however, the student has learned from his coursework in psychology not to confuse the symptoms of a disease with the disease itself. To meet these objections, the physician explains the etiology of the disease (its "cause," a viral infection) as well as its prognosis (the expected consequences). But still the student is dissatisfied. He knows perfectly well that many persons can be infected by a particular virus without becoming ill, and also that persons can show the symptoms of a disease without the appropriate etiology (as illustrated by hysterical reactions). What can the physician say now? The student has rejected any definition in terms of subjective experience and/or physiological responses, even when etiological (stimulus) factors are added. Becoming exasperated, the physician might finally assert that mononucleosis is really a theoretical entity or intervening variable which mediates the relationship between the initiating conditions and subsequent responses. But is this answer any more satisfactory than the others? Try to give some meaning to the notion of, say, a mononucleosis "drive" or "mechanism."

This parody, although somewhat silly, illustrates an important point. Both the student and the physician are making what Ryle (1949) has called a category mistake. That is, they are assuming that words which belong to one logical category operate in the same fashion as words belonging to another category. In the case of the student and physician, the confusion is between the concept of a disease syndrome and the concept of an object or thing. In a subsequent section, I shall have much more to say about the concept of a syndrome as it applies to emotional behavior. For now, suffice it to note that a disease–*qua* syndrome–is not something in addition to its etiology, symptoms, and prognosis; but neither can a disease be reduced to, or identified with, any of its aspects. The name of a disease is a higher-order construct which refers to the way certain responses (the symptoms) are *organized* with respect to some object (the etiology) and with predictable consequences (the prognosis). Stated so simply, the point may seem rather trivial. But category mistakes can be extremely subtle and are actually quite common. In the above parody, for example, substitute the term "fear" for "mononucleosis" and "emotion" for "disease," and change the setting from a physician's office to a psychology classroom; the dialogue might not then seem so silly–at least, not to someone who advocates an artichoke theory of emotion.

Onion Theories of Emotion

The analogy between emotional and disease concepts illustrates one of the major features of onion theories of emotion; namely, the view that when various aspects of an emotional response have been peeled away, nothing remains which can be labeled *the* emotion. Onion theories come in a number of different varieties. Two of them will be considered here, the behaviorist approach of B. F. Skinner and the psychoanalytical approach of Roy Schafer.

A Behaviorist Onion. Whereas artichoke theorists find it natural to use nouns (such as anger, fear, etc.) when referring to the emotions, onion theorists typically warn against this way of speech. According to Skinner:

> The names of the so-called emotions serve to classify behavior with respect to various circumstances which affect its probability. The safest practice is to hold to the adjectival form. Just as the hungry organism can be accounted for without too much difficulty, although "hunger" is another matter, so by describing behavior as fearful, affectionate, timid, and so on, we are not led to look for *things* called emotions (1953, p. 162).

Consider the case of anger and aggression. According to a Skinnerian analysis, the probability of aggressive responses may increase when there is an interference with behavior, depending upon whether or not aggressive responses were reinforced under similar conditions in the past. Colloquially, we may describe such responses as "angry," but this should not lead us to assume that they are caused by some feeling or state signified by the noun *anger*. Their cause, and hence the explanation for angry behavior, is to be found in the present circumstances and the past reinforcement of the individual.

Skinner is not very sanguine about traditional theories of emotion. In a bit of hyperbole, he claims that "the exploration of the emotional and motivational life of the mind has been described as one of the great achievements in the history of human thought, but it is possible that it is one of the great disasters" (1974, p. 165). This is because the traditional emphasis on internal states (whether physiological or psychic) has tended to deflect attention away from the environmental antecedents of emotional behavior. In fact, Skinner implies that emotional concepts are used primarily when we are ignorant of the environmental antecedents of a response. In this respect, psychology should emulate the natural sciences: "Physics did not advance by looking more closely at the jubilance of a falling body, or biology by looking at the nature of vital spirits" (1971, p. 15); and neither, presumably, will psychology advance by looking at the jubilance, grief, fear, etc., of a human being.

As we shall see in subsequent sections, there is considerable merit to Skinner's emphasis on eliciting conditions and operant behavior as criteria for the identification of emotional states. It is doubtful, however, whether the full meaning of the emotions can be encompassed within a Skinnerian framework. This is because the meaning of the emotions must take into account their functional significance. Skinner, however, limits the concept of function primarily to the familiar S-R relationship; that is, the response is a function of the stimulus, as mediated by a history of reinforcement.But the concept of function may be used–and will be used in this chapter–in a much broader sense. For example, one may ask of any S-R relationship, what is its function? In this latter case, the concept of function refers to how an element fits into a broader system of behavior on another level of analysis.

Perhaps a physiological example will help clarify these two meanings of function. In a Skinnerian sense, it might be said that there is a functional relationship between changes in heart rate and stimuli originating in the cardiovascular centers of the brain. In a broader sense, however, changes in heart rate can be understood only by reference to the body as a whole; for example, the heart may accelerate in order to provide the tissues of the body with food and oxygen, and to carry away metabolic waste products. Similarly, it may be said that the function, and hence meaning, of an emotion is not to be found by looking at S-R relationships, but rather by identifying the *goals* the emotion serves within a broader system of behavior, either on the individual or social level of analysis.

Skinner would object to this last statement, for it smacks of teleology (an explanation of behavior in terms of goals). His objective is a completely mechanistic explanation of behavior, and within such a framework there is little place for the type of functional relationships just described. But onion theories of emotion need not be so mechanistic, as will be illustrated next.

A Psychoanalytic Onion. Early psychoanalytic theories of emotion were largely of the artichoke variety. Emotions were viewed as drives or forces which could be dammed up, transformed, and discharged in a great variety of ways. But recently, Schafer (1976) has proposed a major revision of the psychoanalytic theory of emotion. In place of the forces (e.g., libido) and mental structures (id, ego, and superego) which cluttered Freud's theorizing, Schafer advocates the use of an "action language." An action is any human behavior that is goal-directed, or is done for a reason. Thinking, as well as overt behavior, can be an action in this sense, although simple sensations and physiological changes typically are not. Some actions, which we might call deliberate or intentional, are recognized by the actor as such. There are other kinds of actions, however, for which the individual may disclaim responsibility. Hysterical reactions—a traditional concern of psychoanalysis—are one form of disclaimed action. The hysterical person may hear voices, or suffer paralysis of a limb, without any organic damage to the nervous system. The voices and paralysis are actions which the hysterical person performs in order to achieve some goal, but for which he disclaims any responsibility, even to himself. The task of psychoanalysis is to uncover the goal—and hence the meaning—of the hysterical response.

Emotions are also disclaimed actions, according to Schafer. That is, emotions are modes of acting, the goals of which are not fully recognized. In a vein very similar to Skinner, Schafer recommends that, when we speak of emotional experiences, we use only verbs (e.g., to love, to hate, to fear) or adverbs (e.g., lovingly, hatefully, fearfully). The use of nouns (e.g., love, hate, fear) fosters the tendency to think of emotions as things we have, rather than as actions we do. But here the similarity between Skinner and Schafer ends. The type of analysis advocated by Skinner relies primarily on eliciting conditions, operant behavior, and contingencies of reinforcement; the type of analysis advocated by Schafer relies primarily on goals and meanings, or what Schafer calls "psychic reality." The usefulness of this latter term, according to Schafer, "resides in its reminding us that psychoanalytic explanation depends on our knowing what an event, action, or object means to the subject; it is the specifically psychoanalytic alternative to descriptive classification by a behaviorist observer" (p. 89).

In short, whereas the behaviorist Skinner searches for the causes of emotion in terms of antecedent conditions, the psychoanalyst Schafer searches for the meaning of emotion in terms of motives and goals. In many respects, the two approaches are complementary and not mutually exclusive, as will become evident in much of the discussion which follows. Moreover, both approaches start with the same assumption; namely, that emotions can be explained in essentially the same terms as other psychological phenomena; that is, emotions are more like onions than artichokes.

An Artichoke-Onion Hybrid

In nature, it is difficult to imagine what a cross between an artichoke and an onion would be like. In our conceptual garden, such a cross is also somewhat fanciful. Nevertheless, with a little imagination we can use the metaphor to describe one of the most fruitful contemporary theories of emotion. The psychologist who achieved this cross-fertilization is Stanley Schachter. Because of its importance, we will review the work of Schachter and his colleagues in some detail.

According to Schachter (1964, 1971), emotions are a joint product of two factors: physiological arousal and cognitive appraisals regarding the source of that arousal. Since in this formulation, physiological arousal is considered a *necessary* condition for emotion, it represents a kind of heart to the emotional artichoke. In fact, Schachter (1971) regards his approach as "neo-Jamesean"—a revision of the James-Lange theory in light of contemporary knowledge. However, unlike James and Lange, Schachter does not place a great deal of emphasis on physiological factors. The major thrust of his theory is, rather, on the cognitive processes which help mediate emotional experience; and these cognitive processes are not viewed as essentially different from those mediating other forms of behavior. In this regard, Schachter's approach bears resemblance to an onion theory of emotion.

To be more specific, Schachter postulates that feedback from physiological arousal provides a nondescript affective tone to experience, while the cognitive appraisal of situational cues determines which, if any, emotion will be experienced. Thus, precisely the same state of arousal might be experienced as joy, anger, sadness, or any of a variety of other emotions, depending upon the kinds of cues present in the situation. If no emotional cues are present, or if the person has a nonemotional explanation for his state of physiological arousal, then no emotion is likely to be experienced.

In an early test of the above assumptions, Schachter and Singer (1962) manipulated physiological arousal by administering to subjects injections of either epinephrine (a hormone secreted by the adrenal gland) or an inert substance (a placebo). Some subjects who received epinephrine were correctly informed about the symptoms they might experience (increased heart rate, etc.). These subjects thus had a nonemotional explanation for their arousal. Other groups of subjects were not given any information at all, or were given inaccurate information (a false list of symptoms to expect). It was hypothesized that the latter groups would search their environment for cues to explain their arousal, not knowing that it was due to the injection.

Through the use of props and trained confederates, subjects were placed in either of two types of situations. In one situation, the props suggested a happy or jocular mood, and the confederate acted in a playful fashion. In the other situation, the props were designed to provoke anger, and the confederate displayed aggressive behavior.

The results of this study showed that subjects who did not have an adequate explanation for their arousal (i.e., the no-information and inaccurate-information groups) tended to rate themselves as more euphoric or angry, depending upon the situational cues, than did subjects who had a nonemotional explanation for their symptoms (i.e., the accurate information group). Also, subjects who received the placebo, and hence who had little physiological arousal to explain, did not report much anger or euphoria as a function of situational cues. These results support the hypothesis that physiological arousal is important for the experience of emotion, but that the quality of the experience also depends upon a person's appraisal of the situation.

In another experiment, Nisbett and Schachter (1966) asked subjects to undergo a series of increasingly intense electric shocks. Presumably, most subjects in such a situation experience the kind of physiological reactions normally associated with mild fear. In this experiment, some of the subjects were given a placebo pill before the shock trials, and were told that the pill might produce fear-like symptoms—hand tremors, heart palpitations, and the like. These subjects thus had a nonemotional explanation for any physiological reactions they might experience. Other subjects were given a list of irrelevant or nonfear-like symptoms to expect; hence, these subjects had no alternative explanation available for their physiological arousal. As predicted, the subjects who received accurate (fear-relevant) information about potential physiological reactions, and who were able to attribute those reactions to a nonemotional source (the pill), were willing to tolerate more shock than were subjects who received an inaccurate list of symptoms. These results suggest that even naturally occurring emotional reactions can be "reinterpreted" in a nonemotional way if the individual has alternative explanations for his arousal; and, moreover, such alternative explanations may facilitate adaptive coping responses (e.g., tolerance for shock).[2]

Numerous other studies by Schachter and his colleagues could be cited, but these two suffice to illustrate the nature and implications of this type of analysis. Perhaps most importantly, the research by Schachter highlights in a dramatic fashion the importance of an individual's appraisal of his immediate situation for the experience of emotion. This is a point about which we will have more to say in subsequent sections. For the present, we may conclude this introductory review of theories by noting briefly several limitations of Schachter's position as a general approach to emotion.

First, Schachter assumes that physiological arousal is a *necessary* condition for emotion. It is certainly true that some physiological change accompanies emotion, as it accompanies all behavior. But the relationship between physiological arousal and the experience of emotion is quite varied. Hope and terror, for example, may be equally intense emotions, and yet they may involve very different levels of arousal. Similarly, a person may be quite aroused when only mildly angry, but cool and calculating when very angry. In short, to single out physiological arousal as a necessary condition for emotion is not very informative, at best, and is somewhat misleading, at worst.

Second, Schachter does not devote a great deal of attention to where the physiological arousal, which is presumably a necessary condition for emotion, comes from in the first place. Under ordinary conditions, a person appraises a situation as dangerous, sexy, insulting, and so forth, and his arousal is based on that appraisal. Schachter's theory finds its most intriguing applications in situations where a person is aroused without knowing why. Although such situations are not infrequent, they do not represent the ordinary state of affairs as far as standard emotional reactions are concerned. Schachter's approach is most applicable to internally generated states of arousal, such as hunger (Schachter & Rodin, 1974), and to situations where the individual is reluctant to acknowledge, even to himself, the source of his arousal. In the latter respect, at least, Schachter's theory overlaps in applicability with psychoanalysis.

Finally, Schachter's approach does not explain why a particular emotional label is used in one circumstance but not another, or why emotional labels are used at all. For example, why should a state of physiological arousal be labeled as "joy" rather than "fury." To say that the selection of labels is based on situa-

[2]Through instructions and the administration of sample shocks of either high or low intensity, Nisbett and Schachter also manipulated the subject's level of fear. The results described above were found only among subjects in the low-fear condition. The high-fear manipulation evidently made it "unreasonable" for subjects to attribute their arousal to the placebo rather than to the shock. While on the topic, the results of an experiment by Calvert-Boyanowsky and Leventhal (1976) might also be noted. These investigators found that simply providing subjects with accurate information regarding typical symptoms in a fear-inducing situation was sufficient to reduce stress and to facilitate coping responses. In other words, the misattribution of arousal to a neutral source (e.g., the placebo) may not be a necessary condition for the kind of results obtained by Nisbett and Schachter.

tional cues is insufficient; for then one must ask, Why are some situational cues considered joyful and others infuriating? And, on a more general level, why should some responses be considered emotional (whether "joy" or "fury") while other responses are considered nonemotional (e.g., deliberate)? In other words, Schachter's theory helps elucidate some of the conditions under which a person will label a response as emotional, but it does not deal with the meaning or functional significance of emotional attributions.

Summary

Emotions often have been treated as things or events. This has led to a variety of artichoke theories, in which emotions are viewed as subjective feelings, as physiological responses, or as intervening (drive) variables. Other theories—the onion variety—attempt to explain emotional phenomena in terms of nonemotional processes. For example, the behaviorist approach of Skinner emphasizes the role of eliciting conditions and instrumental responses, while the psychoanalytic approach of Schafer emphasizes the goals or personal meaning of the response. The two-factor theory of Schachter represents a kind of hybrid, which emphasizes the individual's appraisal of his immediate situation as well as physiological arousal.

Other approaches to the study of emotion could be mentioned, and will be mentioned at appropriate points throughout the chapter. However, enough has already been said to illustrate the complexity of the problem. It is unlikely that any single theory will be able to account for all emotional phenomena. Perhaps the best that can be hoped for is a general framework or orientation which, with appropriate modification, can be applied to most of the phenomena typically classified as emotional. In what follows, an attempt will be made to develop such a framework.

A NEW LOOK AT THE NATURE OF EMOTION

Thus far, we have been tasting the fruit of the labor of others. That is a relatively easy and enjoyable task. Growing the fruit in the first place is a different—and more arduous—endeavor. Yet that is what we must now do. Beginning afresh, as it were, we will attempt to cultivate our own theoretical garden, and see what kind of fruit it bears.

First, let us place some limits on the scope of our endeavor. The term *emotion* is often used in a vague and generic sense to cover a wide variety of experiences, from simple sensations of pleasure and pain to the total breakdown of functioning which sometimes accompanies extreme stress. Such simple feelings and extreme stress reactions fall outside our range of concern. Neither will we be concerned with the "emotions" of infrahuman animals.

Although it is common to speak of animals as being angry, jealous, fearful, and so forth, such use of emotional concepts is primarily metaphorical. As will become evident below, emotional reactions presuppose a degree of intellectual competence which exceeds anything found on the animal level.

With the above limitations in mind, an emotion may be defined as *a socially constituted syndrome which is based on an individual's appraisal of the situation, and which is interpreted as a passion rather than as an action.* There are three key concepts in this definition, namely, *syndrome, appraisal,* and *passion.* In this section, we will examine each of these concepts in some detail.

Emotional Syndromes

In discussing the limitations of artichoke theories of emotion, we drew an analogy between the concept of emotion and the concept of disease. One basis for this analogy is that both *emotion* and *disease* refer to complex syndromes. A syndrome may be defined as a *set* of responses which *co-vary* in a systematic fashion. Each instance of the syndrome (e.g., any given incident of anger) is characterized by a subset of variably weighted responses. That is, some responses may be more symptomatic of an emotion than are others, but there is no single response, or subset of responses, which is *essential* to an emotional syndrome.

The above point may be stated somewhat differently. The various elements which comprise an emotional syndrome (e.g., physiological changes, expressive reactions, subjective experience, and instrumental coping responses) are only loosely coordinated. Each type of response is under multiple control, and hence may be more or less salient–or even absent–in any given emotional episode. The person who is angry, for example, may strike out at his antagonist, or he may withdraw from the situation; he may experience a high degree of physiological arousal, or he may coolly retaliate; his subjective experiences may vary from exhilaration to depression; and, under some conditions, he might not even realize that he is angry. Of course, the individual must do or experience *something,* or else we would not consider him to be angry; and some of the things he might do or experience may be more indicative of anger than others, *but there is no single subset of responses which is an essential characteristic of anger or of any other emotion.*

In view of the above considerations, one of the major problems faced by a theory of emotion is the specification of mechanisms responsible for the formation of, and co-variation among various response elements. For example, what are the ties which bind the elements of anger into a coherent syndrome? As will be explained more fully in the next section, these ties may be conceptualized as social norms which, when internalized, form cognitive systems or rules of behavior. An emotional syndrome, it might be said, represents the enactment of a transitory social role.

In speaking of the emotions as both syndromes and as social roles, it might seem that we are mixing incompatible metaphors. However, even in the case of disease, where the concept of syndrome has its most common application, the symptomatology displayed by the patient may be determined, in part, by the "sick role" he adopts (Segall, 1976). In the case of mental illness, in fact, the role expectations of the patient may far outweigh organic factors in determining the nature of the syndrome. And when we consider neurotic syndromes, such as an hysterical reaction, organic factors are by definition absent or minimal. In the latter case, the syndrome is constituted by the role being played. The same may be said of emotional syndromes. But more of that shortly.

Emotional Appraisals

Thus far we have been considering primarily the response or output side of emotional syndromes. But as we have already noted in our review of Schachter's theory, emotional responses depend upon an individual's appraisal of the situation. Other theorists besides Schachter have also emphasized the importance of emotional appraisals–most notably, Arnold (1960) and Lazarus (1966, 1968). At the core of these "cognitive" theories of emotion is the proposition that all emotions are based upon an individual's evaluation (appraisal) of the situation.

Stated somewhat differently, an emotion is not simply a set of responses joined together in a certain manner; rather, an emotion expresses an evaluative judgment about the situation in which the individual finds himself. The referent of this judgment is commonly called the *object* of the emotion. This last notion is important, and hence requires some additional explanation.

The object of an emotion represents a complex state of affairs as appraised by the individual. For example, if an emotion is directed at a particular individual, then that individual forms part of the object. However, the same individual might become the target of quite different emotions, such as love, anger, and fear. Other aspects of the object must therefore be considered if we are to distinguish among different emotional syndromes. These other aspects have to do with the instigation to, and/or the goal (objective) of the response. In this respect, the object of anger is revenge for wrongdoing; the object of fear is flight from danger; and so forth.

The important point is that each kind of emotion involves its own particular object, distinguishable in terms of the target, instigation, and/or goal of the response. This fact becomes especially evident when we attempt to distinguish among closely related emotional syndromes. Consider the following incident recounted by Schoek (1969). After a local baseball game in New York City, the hero of the winning team was standing on the pavement with his parents and friends when he was struck and killed by an automobile. It was no accident; the driver of the automobile wanted to kill his victim. Was he angry, jealous, or perhaps envious? From the description just given, there is no way to answer this question, for exactly the same responses can be involved in each emotion. (This statement would be true even if we had a more detailed description of facial expressions, physiological reactions, etc.) However, if we were informed that the victim had somehow double-crossed the killer, who now sought revenge, then we would have no difficulty in attributing the response to anger. On the other hand, if we were informed that the victim was having an affair with the killer's wife, then the response might be classified as jealousy. In actual fact, the killer–who was described as a "drab-looking day laborer"–had no personal relationship with the victim and also had no particular interest in the outcome of the ball-game. He simply could not stand witnessing the glamour and success of the victim. His response was thus envy, the object of which is the sheer destruction of the good fortune of another.

It is important to emphasize that the object of an emotion is based on the individual's appraisal of the situation. Thus, in the above example, the day laborer may have had no "real" reason to be envious–the star athlete actually may have had major difficulties which placed him in a more unfortunate position than his killer. In a sense, the good fortune of the athlete was as much a creation of the killer's envy as the envy was the product of the athlete's good fortune. This kind of dialectical relationship between an emotion and its object is even more evident in a case such as love. Love can transform even the most homely and uninteresting person into someone very special, at least in the eyes of the lover. After the ardor of passion has cooled, the lover may rightly wonder what he or she formerly saw in the beloved.

As the above examples illustrate, *the object of an emotion always involves a meaning imposed upon the environment.* Solomon (1976) has expressed this point well:

> An emotion is a (set of) judgment(s) which constitute our world, our surreality, and its "intentional objects." An emotion is a basic judgment about our Selves and our place in our world, the projection of the values and ideals, structures and mythologies, according to which we live and through which we experience our lives (pp. 186-187).

It will be noted that Solomon is defining emotion as a form of judgment, not simply as the consequence of a judgment. In Solomon's view, behavioral responses, physiological changes, and subjective feelings often may accompany an emotional judgment, but they do not form part of the emotion per se. This is a rather extreme position–but no more extreme in its own way than are the definitions of emotion in terms of physiological responses or feeling states.

The Object of an Emotion Distinguished from its Cause. The object of an emotion is often confused with its cause. The cause is what makes an individual appraise the situation in a particular way, thereby creating the object of the emotion along with the response. For example, I may become angry because it is hot and I have been drinking too much. But the object of my anger is not the heat or the alcohol; it is, rather, the individual whom I believe has wronged me.

Similarly, I may fall in love because I am lonely and in a strange place; yet, I love the girl I meet, not my loneliness nor the strange location.

It is the task of psychology, as a scientific discipline, to investigate the causes of behavior. However, any emotional syndrome can have as many causes as there are answers to the question. Why? Any attempt to discuss *all* the causes of emotion is therefore beyond the scope of the present chapter. A brief enumeration of some of the major types of causes will have to suffice. For the most part, the causes of emotion fall into three general classes—historical, environmental, and organismic.

Historical causes refer to events in the past which help determine present behavior. Three types of historical causes can be distinguished, depending upon whether the relevant events occurred during the development of the individual, the evolution of the species, or the evolution of society. Of these three types of historical causes, the present analysis will focus primarily on the last—social evolution. This follows from our definition of emotion as a socially *constituted* syndrome. The emphasis on social evolution should not, however, be taken to mean that individual development and biological evolution are unimportant for the understanding of emotion. That obviously is not the case; and when we discuss specific emotional syndromes in subsequent sections, reference will be made to relevant ontogenetic and phylogenetic factors.

Environmental causes refer to events within the immediate situation which help elicit emotional reactions. Causes of this type can be divided into contextual and focal-stimulus conditions. Among the contextual conditions are such physical and social variables as temperature, crowding, drugs, and anything else which might affect the propensity of the individual to respond emotionally. The focal stimulus, by contrast, is the specific event which the person appraises as infuriating, endearing, depressing, etc. Without a focal stimulus, there could be no object of the emotion. As noted above, however, the focal stimulus is not the same as the object; the latter is a meaning imposed on the former.

Organismic causes refer to the cognitive and/or physiological mechanisms which mediate the emotions. For example, what is the role of perception, attention, and memory—or of subcortical and cortical processes—in the mediation of emotion? The answer to this question is nearly as broad as psychology itself, for there is no convincing evidence that the emotions involve fundamentally different mechanisms (whether cognitive or physiological) than do other forms of behavior. This may seem like a rather cavalier assertion, since the discovery of such differences has been a traditional concern of the psychology of emotion. Consider the long tradition of reifying the distinction between emotional and nonemotional behavior in terms of physiological mechanisms. For James (1890), the distinction was between peripheral and central-neural mechanisms; for Cannon (1929), it was between subcortical and cortical mechanisms; for MacLean (1960), it was between the older paleocortex (limbic system) and the neocortex; and most recently (e.g., Jaynes, 1976) it is between the right and left hemispheres of the neocortex.[3]

Distinctions such as the above cannot be dismissed entirely as irrelevant to the study of emotion. There is considerable evidence that autonomic, subcortical, limbic, and right-hemispheric responses lack the fine control and critical sifting of information characteristic of deliberate, rational behavior; and to that extent, these structures may contribute to the experience of emotion. But there is also ample evidence that these same structures—and the cognitive processes they subserve—enter into nonemotional as well as emotional behavior. And, conversely, emotional behavior could not proceed in any normal sense without the involvement of neocortical and left-hemispheric activity, that is, without the kind of processes that are instrumental in nonemotional responses.

Emotions and Passions

If the emotions are not based on unique physiological or cognitive mechanisms, what distinguishes them from other psychological phenomena? This question brings us to the third main feature of our definition of emotion, namely, emotional syndromes are interpreted as passions rather than as actions. A little etymology may help clarify what is meant by this phrase.

From the ancient Greeks to the middle of the eighteenth century, what we now call emotions were commonly referred to as passions. Both terms, *emotion* and *passion,* emphasize different aspects of emotional phenomena. *Emotion* comes from the Latin, *e + movere,* which originally meant to migrate or transfer from one place to another. It also was used to refer to states of agitation or perturbation, whether physical (as stormy weather) or psychological. The term *emotion* thus emphasizes the often stormy or turbulent nature of emotional reactions. And it is this aspect which finds expression in many current theories of emotion, with their emphasis on activation, physiological arousal, and the disruptive quality of emotional responses.

The term *passion* has a rather different connotation. It derives from the Latin, *pati,* which in turn is related to the Greek, *pathos.* At the root of these concepts is the notion that an individual is undergoing or suffering some change, as opposed to doing or initiating change. Also related to *passion* are such terms as *passivity* and *patient.* Thus, it may be said that emotions are experienced

[3] The tradition of distinguishing emotional from "higher" mental activity, and associating the former with presumably animal-like processes (e.g., instinctive, visceral, sub- and paleo-cortical responses), is quite ancient. Plato, for example, localized rational thought in the head because this was the part of the body which best approximates a sphere, the perfect figure. The emotions were then localized in the trunk of the body, where they could interfere with rational thought as little as possible. In more modern writers, the rationale for localizing the emotions in the viscera and related central neural structures is couched in scientific jargon; nevertheless, as in the case of Plato, such localization is still guided as much by symbolism as by fact. For an historical survey of such "psychophysiological symbolism" as it relates to theories of emotion, see Averill (1974).

passively—not in the sense that emotional reactions lack energy or vigor, but rather in the sense that they are beyond the individual's control.

These two meanings of emotion—to be in a state of agitation and to be in a state of passion—are not unrelated. The person who is highly agitated and perturbed is not likely to have a great deal of control over his behavior. However, not all emotions are characterized by agitation (e.g., hope, sadness, etc.). "Passion" is therefore the broader concept, and the one more pertinent to a comprehensive analysis of emotional phenomena.

Colloquially, the experience of passivity during emotion is expressed in many ways. We "fall" in love, are "paralyzed" by fear, "haunted" by guilt, "torn" by jealousy, "carried away" with joy, "consumed" by envy, "dragged" down by remorse, and so forth. This way of speaking implies that emotions are something which happen to us, not something we do. It is as though emotions were alien forces which "overcome" and "possess" an individual. "I don't know what got into me," is a common explanation for emotional behavior.

But there is another side to the picture. The emotions are, as one maxim has it, "gateways to the soul." If you know what makes a person proud, angry, sad, joyful, fearful, and so forth, then you know what that person considers important about himself, even those aspects of his personality which he may not recognize or admit.

The passions are thus marked by a paradoxical ambivalence: In contrast to actions, passions are regarded as irrational, impulsive, and uncontrollable; and yet they also are considered an integral part of the self. The paradox disappears, however, when it is recognized that actions as well as passions are treated ambivalently. Although reason is often praised as man's greatest asset, the person who is always logical and calculating is also subject to mistrust. How do we know that what he says or does is not a deliberate ploy to achieve the greatest good for himself, perhaps at our expense? In other words, it is precisely because we (supposedly) cannot help responding the way we do when emotional that the emotions are often considered a true reflection of the total self, not just of the self-as-agent.

Summary

The emotions can be conceived of as complex syndromes, consisting of physiological, behavioral, and cognitive elements. Although some elements (e.g., physiological arousal) may be more symptomatic of emotion than others, there is no single response which is essential to an emotional syndrome. This means that any given emotion can be expressed in a great variety of ways, depending upon the individual and the situation.

An important aspect of any emotional syndrome is its object. Each emotion has a different object, identifiable in terms of the target, instigation, and/or goal of the response. However, the object of an emotion is not something "out there," like a stone or a tree. Rather, it is a function of the individual's appraisal of the situation. Through the process of appraisal, the individual imposes meaning on the environment and, in a sense, creates the object of his emotion.

There are many psychological phenomena other than the emotions which could be defined in terms of syndromes and cognitive appraisals. Therefore, another defining characteristic must be added; namely, the emotions are passions. They can be distinguished from rational, deliberate behavior in that the latter (actions) are generally interpreted as being self-initiated. By contrast, the emotions seem to "occur" or "happen" to a person, as though they were beyond self-control.

One of the major problems for any theory of emotion is to explain why emotions are interpreted (and sometimes experienced) as passions rather than as actions. Most traditional theories attribute the passionate element in emotion to biological instincts, to activity of the autonomic ("involuntary") nervous system, or to special structures within the brain (e.g., the reticular activating system, the limbic system, or the right hemisphere.) Such explanations are appealing because they seem to account for the fact that the emotions are both beyond our control and yet are an integral part of ourselves.

In contrast to theories of the above type, we have defined the emotions as socially constituted syndromes. This means that we must account for the emotions as passions in sociological rather than biological terms. In approaching this issue, we will adopt what has been called a dramaturgical standpoint (Harré & Secord, 1973).

A ROLE-MODEL OF EMOTIONAL BEHAVIOR

Some of the more interesting analyses of emotion can be found in books on acting, especially the technique of "method" acting pioneered by the Russian director, Stanislavsky (see, for example, Edwards, 1965; Moore, 1973; Stanislavsky, 1936). Stanislavsky believed that the actor must experience real emotion on stage by identifying with the role he is portraying. Of course, the good method actor always knows that his stage emotions, although real, differ from similar emotions experienced in everyday life. But in what does the difference lie? Primarily in the actor's appraisal of the immediate situation. The insult which arouses his anger is not meant, and the death which evokes his grief is not permanent; and he must control or fashion his emotions accordingly. That is the art of the actor.

What about the art of everyday living. "All the world's a stage, and all the men and women merely players: They have their exits and their entrances; and one man in his time plays many parts." These famous lines by Shakespeare represent one version of a theme which can be traced back at least to the Greek mathematician and philosopher, Pythagoras. It is also one of the most important themes in contemporary social psychology.

Harre and Secord (1973) have described the dramaturgical standpoint in social psychology as follows:

> We ask ourselves how we would perceive what we or other people are doing were we acting deliberately, and following a script in a play and the stylistic instructions of a director. This enables us to discover the appropriate role-rule model, and to produce a commentary consisting of the rules and including the social meaning of the actions performed (p. 14).

Rules and Roles

Before we can analyze everyday emotional behavior from a dramaturgical standpoint, we must define briefly what is meant by social rules and roles.

Rules are guides to behavior. They specify what should and should not be done in a particular situation, and the appropriate way it is to be done. In some cases, such as rituals and ceremonies, the rules may be quite explicit. By contrast, the rules governing most everyday social interactions are generally implicit and difficult to specify with any precision. Indeed, a person may not even realize that he is following a rule until he breaks the rule and is criticized for it. In addition to being implicit and vaguely defined, many social rules are also open-ended. That is, they allow a great deal of improvisation to occur. The rules themselves may even be subject to implicit negotiation and revision as the interaction proceeds.

Roles are parts which specific persons play following an appropriate subset of rules. Some roles are relatively enduring, such as that of a doctor or lawyer. But other roles are transitory or coterminous with a specific behavioral episode. Such transitory roles may, however, be repeated as the situation demands.

The relevance of the above concepts for the analysis of emotional reactions is perhaps best illustrated by considering a concrete example, such as falling in love. In all cultures, there are rules regulating courtship and mating. These rules stipulate, among other things, who is an eligible mate, the proper forms of courtship, when and how sexual intercourse can be performed, what obligations the couple has toward one another and toward any children which might be conceived, and so forth. Through observation and experience in concrete situations (e.g., adolescent play), as well as through formal and informal didactic means (e.g., direct instructions, songs, literature, myths), couples learn how and when to apply the rules, so that their behavior follows an appropriate "script" (Gagnon, 1974; Simon, 1974). In order to complete the script, of course, each participant must play his or her role according to the relevant subset of rules. In the case of falling in love, which is only one of a variety of scripts relevant to mating, these roles are temporary—the young couple typically "recovers." However, if the love-script follows its conventional course within our own culture, it will result in marriage, and a more permanent set of roles, that of husband and wife, will ensue.

In the next section, different kinds of emotional roles, including romantic love, will be examined in more detail. But first, we must consider how some of the general features of emotional syndromes can be explained from a dramaturgical standpoint. We will begin by considering the intensity or depth of emotional experiences in terms of role-involvement.

Role Involvement

An actor may be more or less involved in the role he is playing. At one extreme, his performance may be perfunctory and casual, while at the other extreme, he may become so engrossed in the role that his own identity is momentarily lost. Everyday emotional roles can also be enacted with various degrees of involvement, and this fact helps to explain some of the differences observed in both the expression and the experience of emotion. Although role-involvement varies along a continuum, for ease of discussion only three levels will be distinguished here.

Level I: Low Involvement. Some situations call for an overt expression of emotion with relatively little personal involvement. An example is the teacher who scolds a child for being naughty, while inwardly laughing at the child's antics. The most common expression of emotion at this level of involvement is a simple verbal statement: "Don't do that, it makes me angry"; "I am sad to hear of your father's death"; "the mere thought of that makes me afraid"; and so forth. Such statements are not insincere simply because they lack a great deal of personal involvement; on the contrary, they are typically appropriate to the situation and sufficient to achieve the desired effect. Of course, they would not be effective unless there were not also instances in which involvement was greater.

Level 2: Intermediate Involvement. At this level, the individual's attention becomes focused on the object of the emotion, and it is difficult for the individual to think of other matters. There may also be a good deal of physiological arousal, expressive reactions, and so forth, depending upon the emotion. But in spite of this relatively high degree of involvement, the response is not completely automatic or dissociated from the self-as-agent. Rather, the person knows what he is doing and is sensitive to changes in the situation. On occasion, even, a person may deliberately try to cultivate and "work himself up" to this level of involvement. For example, the angry person may brood about a provocation (real or fancied) until his anger is at just the right pitch; a bereaved individual may wallow in his grief by reminiscing about past pleasures; and lovers may engage in a variety of behaviors in order to stoke the fires of their passion.

Level 3: Total Involvement. At the highest level of involvement, the person becomes completely engrossed in the emotional role. The response tends to be stereotyped, unresponsive to situational constraints, and is often inappropriate.

After the episode, the person may claim that he was completely overcome, that he did not know what he was doing, or that he was not himself. And in a sense, such claims are true. When totally involved in an emotional role, a person's own self-identity may be submerged. In extreme cases, the dissociation of the response from the self may even result in a fugue state or loss of memory.

Interpretating a Response as Emotional

In an earlier section, an emotion was defined as a "socially constituted syndrome which is based on an individual's appraisal of the situation, and which is *interpreted* as a passion rather than as an action." We must now relate this definition to involvement in an emotional role. What does it mean, for example, to say that a person who is overcome by emotion (level 3 involvement) is "interpreting" his response as a passion? And why, at the low end of the continuum (level 1 involvement), should a well-controlled response be interpreted as a "passion" rather than as an action?

In addressing these questions, two aspects of "interpreting" a role must be distinguished. The first aspect is *understanding* the role, and the second aspect is *monitoring* one's own performance in light of that understanding.

Understanding a Role. No role, whether on stage or in real life, has meaning in isolation, for a role is only part of a larger drama. Therefore, in order for a role to be enacted with any degree of authenticity or truth, it must be interpreted and its meaning understood. In their book on improvisation, Hodgson and Richards (1974) describe this aspect of interpreting:

> Acting is an interpretation, an impersonation of aspects of the human situation. . . . This understanding takes place partly on a mental and imaginative level, but if his acting is to portray the situation with truth, [the actor] will have to understand with his whole being (p. 11).

To illustrate this past point, Hodgson and Richards describe the case of a young actress who was told by her producer how to interpret a role. He continued to reiterate the interpretation at almost every rehearsal, until one day the actress suddenly claimed she understood. When the producer complained that he had been telling her for weeks how to interpret the role, she replied, "I know, but I've had to find it out for myself!"

Like the actress in the above anecdote, we come to understand the meaning of everyday emotional roles only slowly and intuitively, during the long process of socialization. As adults, our performance is likely to be so smooth and automatic that we lose sight of the fact that we are interpreting a role every time we become emotional. (However, the interpretative element may become quite explicit in cases where a person is confronted with a new emotional role, such as falling in love for the first time or grieving upon the death of a parent. In such instances, the person may not only wonder, "What should I do?" but also, "Are my feelings true?")

Monitoring the Performance. Not only must a role be interpreted (understood) in the above sense, but the actor must also monitor his own performance to assure that it conforms to the interpretation. This observation is simple enough, but the simplicity is somewhat misleading. In order to appreciate its full implications, we need to distinguish between two orders, or levels, of monitoring.

The first order of monitoring is an aspect of all behavior, from simple reflexes to the enactment of complex social roles, in that all behavior is controlled and corrected through innumerable feedback loops. Much first-order monitoring proceeds outside of conscious awareness. However, as behavior becomes more complex and/or requires the attention of the organism, then such monitoring may be consciously experienced. This is what phenomenological psychologists sometimes refer to as prereflective or "lived" experience. If one could imagine the consciousness of a rat or a kangaroo, say, it would be prereflective—a product of first-order monitoring.

Human beings are not only conscious in the above sense, but they also are able to reflect upon and interpret their conscious experiences. This involves a second order of monitoring, or what we shall call "self-monitoring" for short. In phenomenological terminology, self-monitoring results in reflective as opposed to prereflective experience.

A concrete example may help to clarify the difference between first-order monitoring (prereflective experience) and self-monitoring (reflective experience). When listening to a symphony a person may become completely absorbed in the experience; but subsequently, when describing the experience to a friend, he may analyze the performance, relate it to other performances of the same work that he has heard, and so on. In the latter case, the person is reflecting on his original experience. The reflection in this example is retrospective, but it need not be. If the person happens to be a music critic on assignment, he may analyze the symphony while listening to it; he may reflect upon the experience as it occurs.

Having drawn the distinction between prereflective and reflective experiences for analytic purposes, an important qualification must now be added. Completely prereflective experience is a myth, at least on the human level. All experience is filtered, organized, and given meaning by the categories of reflective thought. Thus, continuing with the above illustration, a music critic listening to a new performance can never completely disregard his past learning and ways of thought, no matter how hard he tries to discard the role of critic and how engrossing he finds the experience to be. In fact, were it not for well-established categories of thought, he probably would not find the experience engrossing at all. (For example, it is almost impossible to become engrossed in the music of another culture with which one is completely unfamiliar.)

The emotions are often taken as the epitome of preflective or lived experience, as though they were the product of first-order monitoring only. But that is not the case. Emotional experiences are reflective, the product of self-monitoring. Moreover, the categories of reflective thought which give an emotional experience its meaning are based upon the individual's understanding of the particular emotional role that is being enacted.

Total Involvement in an Emotional Role. We are now in a position to address the first question raised earlier. How can level 3 involvement, where the person may literally experience being "overcome," "gripped," and "seized" by emotion, be regarded as an *interpretation* of an emotional role? To speak of an "interpretation" in such a context seems to cast doubt on the authenticity of the experience.

A study by Kirshner (1971) provides a good starting point for a discussion of this issue. Kirschner examined all case records of psychiatric admissions to Wright-Patterson Air Force Base Medical Center from 1968 through 1970. Twenty-three cases were found which involved dissociative reactions–that is, "ego-alien behavior accompanied by varying degrees of amnesia." The specific behaviors exhibited by these individuals ranged from assault and attempted rape to relatively minor hypnogogic and trance-like experiences. The following is a specific case:

> A 25-year-old, married sergeant was arrested for attempted rape after his wallet was found in an area where a local girl had reported being attacked by a nude male. When apprehended, he recalled finding himself naked with his arms around the woman, feeling frightened, and running away. He was unable to offer any explanation for the incident. His wife was pregnant with their second child at the time, but he seemed pleased by this. He related having had intercourse with her the very morning of the rape (p. 703).

The behavior exhibited by the sergeant, and by the other patients studied by Kirshner, is an example of an emotional "disorder." Nevertheless, the behavior does represent a passion in the broadest sense. The fact that it is extreme and idiosyncratic is actually an advantage for the purposes of the present discussion. If dissociative reactions of this type involve the interpretation of a social role, then certainly it is not implausible to suggest that the same is true of more standard emotional reactions, such as "falling" in love or being "seized" by anger.

When Kirshner compared the individuals who suffered from dissociative reactions with a control group of psychiatric patients, he could find nothing organic or psychopathologic that might account for the behavior of the former.

There was, however, an important difference between the two groups of patients. Each person who suffered a dissociative reaction had been confronted with an undesirable situation (e.g., an impending transfer to another base) which could not be avoided. Kirshner concluded that the dissociative reactions could best be understood as the assumption of a transitory role. The role called for two elements: (a) some bizarre act which would dramatize the individual's difficulties, while at the same time mustering psychiatric and other services which might facilitate a more adaptive solution; and (b) dissociating the act from the self-as-agent, so that the individual would not be held responsible or punished. Understanding these requirements on an intuitive level, the individual was able to improvise an "appropriate" response, and also to monitor that response so that it was interpreted as a passion rather than an action on the level of reflective experience.

To further illustrate the interpretive element in extreme emotional reactions, consider the response of "being a wild pig." This is the name of a syndrome (loosely translated) that occurs among the Gururumba, a horticultural people living in the New Guinea highlands (Newman, 1964). "Being a wild pig" involves a variety of aggressive acts such as looting, shooting arrows at bystanders, and so forth, but serious harm seldom results. The behavior may continue for several days, until the affected individual disappears into the forest where he destroys his loot. He may then return in a normal condition, not remembering anything of his previous behavior; or he may return still in a wild state. In the latter case, he is captured and subjected to a ceremonial treatment which facilitates recovery.

According to the Gururumba, "being a wild pig" results from the bite of a ghost of a recently deceased individual. However, the actual causes of the syndrome appear to be more mundane. Only males between the ages of approximately twenty-five and thirty-five become "like wild pigs." During this period, a young man must give up considerable freedom, accept economic and social obligations related to marriage (prearranged and often unstable at first), and also must participate in other group-coordinated enterprises. His success in these ventures determines not only his personal prestige and power, but also that of his clan. Sometimes, a young man cannot meet all of the demands placed upon him, but neither can he deliberately renounce them.

Following Newman's (1964) analysis, "being a wild pig" might be viewed as a way of declaring psychological bankruptcy among the Gururumba. That is, when societal pressures become too great for an individual to handle, he may communicate this difficulty by adopting the role of a wild pig. As part of the larger script, other members of the group then re-evaluate the needs and capacities of the individual, bringing expectancies more in line with reality. Thus, by allowing persons to adopt a transitory social role in extreme cases, the society can maintain pressure on individual members to conform *voluntarily* to social norms, while at the same time providing an "out." Of course, if the "out" is to serve its function, it must be symbolically transformed and interpreted as a passion (beyond personal control) rather than as an action.

It will be noted that Newman's analysis of "being a wild pig" is very similar to Kirshner's analysis of dissociative reactions among the American servicemen he studied. Perhaps the major difference is that the role of "being a wild pig" is more formal; that is, it leaves less room for improvisation.[4]

I do not wish to imply by the above examples that all instances of level 3 involvement are characterized by dissociative reactions. That is definitely not the case. For example, a person may be overcome by grief, or fall "madly" in love, without dissociating the experience completely from the self. Dissociative reactions occur primarily when the response is considered (ostensibly, at least) morally wrong or unacceptable by the individual. Such standard emotional reactions as grief, anger, and romantic love will be examined more fully in a subsequent section. The purpose of the present discussion has simply been to illustrate how extreme and even rather bizarre reactions can be viewed as the interpretation of an emotional role.

Low Involvement in an Emotional Role. People are seldom totally overcome by emotion. Most emotional reactions proceed at intermediate or low levels of involvement. And this brings us to the second question raised earlier. How can a response which proceeds at a low level of involvement be interpreted as a passion rather than as an action? When not highly involved, a person may remain in complete control of himself, and the only expression of emotion may be a casual remark. Does such a remark, no matter how sincere, fall outside our definition of emotion?

In addressing this issue, it should first be noted that the distinction between actions and passions is not absolute. Any given response may be interpreted as either an action or a passion depending upon how it is to be understood. For example, if the reprimand I give to a friend turns out to be hurtful, then I may blame my thoughtlessness on my anger. On the other hand, if the reprimand turns out to be helpful, I may interpret the same response as an action, taking credit for being so forthright. Or, to take another example, if I tell my sweetheart that I love her, I may feel quite insulted if she interprets the remark as deliberate or premeditated, no matter how "unpassionate" I happen to be at the moment.

If we go back to the distinction between understanding an emotional role and the self-monitoring of the performance, we can readily comprehend what is happening in instances such as these. The actual behavior exhibited, or remarks made, represents only one factor contributing to the interpretation of a response

[4]For slightly different interpretations of "being a wild pig" and related syndromes, see Langness (1965) and Salisbury (1966, 1967). These alternative interpretations do not, however, alter the basic thrust of the present argument.

as emotional. The other factor involves an understanding of the relevant emotional role. When a person interprets a casual remark as a manifestation of emotion, he is emphasizing the latter aspect. In a sense, he is asking that the remark be understood and judged by the standards typically applied to emotional roles, and not by the standards typically applied to deliberate, rational acts. As will be explained in more detail shortly, these standards have to do with such matters as the attribution of responsibility, degree of commitment, and the like.

Further Observations on Some Theories of Emotion

The idea that the experience of emotion is basically an interpretation of behavior is not novel. Some of the theories reviewed in the introduction to this chapter also have made this assumption. For the most part, however, these theories have emphasized the self-monitoring of behavior and have tended to neglect the individual's understanding of the role being played.

Consider the famous theory of William James. According to James, we do not run because we are afraid; rather, we are afraid because we run, sad because we cry, happy because we laugh, and so forth. In support of James, there is considerable evidence that sensory feedback from visceral activity (Hohmann, 1966), postural adjustments (Bull, 1951), and expressive reactions (Laird, 1974) all contribute to the experience of emotion. But if James had been completely consistent, he would have acknowledged that sensory feedback, by itself, is not sufficient to constitute the experience of emotion. Thus, in another context he noted that nobody "ever had a simple sensation by itself" and that "what we call simple sensations are the results of discriminative attention, pushed to a very high degree" (1890, Vol. I, p. 224). In other words, James recognized an interpretive element in simple sensory experiences, but he did not follow through on the implications of this fact when it came to the emotions. It is therefore not surprising that many followers of James have assumed that certain patterns of bodily activity are automatically experienced as anger, fear, joy, or some other emotional state.

As the work of Schachter (1971) and his colleagues has shown, there is no automatic or one-to-one relationship between bodily activity and the experience of emotion. Schachter has demonstrated that any given state of physiological arousal may be interpreted as joy, fear, anger, etc., depending upon how the individual appraises the situation. But the same question can be asked of Schachter as of James: Why are some situations (even if accompanied by physiological arousal) interpreted as emotional? In other words, the addition of situational cues does not, by itself, clarify the meaning of emotional roles.

This last observation also applies to behavioral cues. Expanding upon the views of Skinner, Bem (1972) has developed a "self-perception theory" to explain emotional and other "private events." The heart of this theory is contained in the following two propositions:

> Individuals come to "know" their own attitudes, emotions and other internal states partially by inferring them from observations of their own overt behavior and/or the circumstances in which this behavior occurs. Thus, to the extent that internal cues are weak, ambiguous, or uninterpretable, the individual is functionally in the same position as an outside observer who must necessarily rely upon those same external cues to infer the individual's inner states (p. 2).

Bem (1972) has reviewed considerable experimental evidence in support of these propositions. There are, however, some difficulties. In a study by Bandler, Madaras, and Bem (1968), for example, subjects were led either to escape electric shocks or to endure shocks of the same intensity. It was found that subjects who "observed" themselves escaping the shocks reported greater discomfort than did subjects who "observed" themselves enduring the shocks. But in a follow-up study, Corah and Boffa (1970) showed that the interpretation of the response as emotional (indicated by self-reported distress) occurred only if subjects believed that they had *chosen* to escape.

As the findings of Corah and Boffa indicate, it is not simply a response to a situation that is interpreted as emotional. The meaning of the response for the individual must also be taken into account. But, as was previously discussed in connection with Skinner's analysis of emotion, the behaviorist position leaves little room for notions such as "the meaning of the response for the individual."

The psychoanalytic approach of Schafer (1976) also treats the emotions as interpretations of behavior or, in Schafer's terms, as "disclaimed actions." Moreover, in contrast to the other positions we have reviewed, Schafer does explicitly take into account both aspects of interpretation, that is, the self-monitoring of behavior and the meaning of the response for the individual. It is fair to note, however, that psychoanalytic theory does not have a great deal to say about standard emotional reactions. Quite understandably, psychoanalysts have focused attention on abnormal reactions, where the meaning of a response (e.g., a conversion hysteria) is idiosyncratic to the individual. Relatively little attention has been given to the social norms and rules which help constitute everyday emotional syndromes.

In short, there is considerable theoretical agreement with, and empirical support for, the assumption that the experience of emotion is basically an interpretation of behavior. However, with the exception of psychoanalysis, the theories mentioned place primary emphasis on only one aspect of the interpretation, namely, self-monitoring. And none of the theories–including psychoanalysis—considers adequately how emotional roles are understood within a larger social framework.[5]

Summary

In this section, emotional syndromes have been analyzed as transitory social roles. This does not mean that the person who becomes emotional is simply acting, like a performer on stage. Nor does it mean that emotional syndromes are *nothing but* social roles. As we shall see in the next section, some emotions (such as grief) also have a strong biological component. Nevertheless, a role-model does provide a useful way of looking at and conceptualizing emotional behavior.

There is a joke about a young woman who, when asked the difference between conjugal and adulterous sexual relations, replied: "I don't know. I've tried them both and they feel pretty much the same." This joke is based on the fact that a response performed in connection with one role (e.g., that of a marriage partner) may be interpreted differently than the same response performed under other conditions, even though in both cases it may feel "pretty much the same." Similarly, emotional responses are interpreted differently than nonemotional responses, but this difference often has more to do with the meaning of emotional roles than with any inherent qualities of the response.

The emotions are interpreted as passions. From a role-model perspective, this means that emotional responses are not judged by the same standards that are applied to actions (e.g., deliberate or rational acts). As we have just noted, however, this fact does not mean that passions necessarily "feel" different than actions. If one could view responses in-and-of themselves, and not as part of social roles, then many emotional responses would also be seen as quite deliberate and rational. This is particularly true when involvement in an emotional role is at a relatively low level. As the level of involvement increases, the individual may become increasingly "caught up" in the role, and in extreme cases, may be completely "overcome." But even in cases involving dissociative reactions, where role-involvement could hardly be greater, there is a sense in which the response is still something the person does (an action) and not something which he suffers (a passion).

[5] Not all theorists would agree, of course, that the experience of emotion is essentially an interpretation. As discussed earlier, some theorists view the emotions as intervening drive variables, while others argue that the emotions can be reduced to physiological mechanisms. (A variation of the latter theme is that the emotions are instincts, or inherited tendencies to respond in a certain manner.) The position being advocated here is obviously quite different. It rests on the assumption that the brain can best be viewed as an information-processing system and not as an energy-distribution system. On this assumption, the basic problem for psychology becomes the structure of behavior, not its activation. And as far as physiological theories are concerned, our position is that the meaning of the emotions is to be found primarily within the social system. Hence, emotions cannot be explained solely in terms of physiological mechanisms.

The above issue can be summarized somewhat differently. From a phenomenological point of view, "action" and "passion" are categories of reflective thought; that is, they are interpretations of experience. As the term *reflective* implies, such interpretations are sometimes retrospective. A person may simply respond and only afterwards (e.g., if the reasons for the response are called into question) is the experience classified as either an action or a passion. Reflective interpretations need not, however, be retrospective. During the long process of socialization, a person learns not only how to respond, but also how to interpret a response as it occurs. It is thus possible for someone to be literally overcome (on the level of reflective thought) by his or her own behavior.

A number of contemporary and traditional theories also have viewed the experience of emotion as an interpretation of one's own behavior. For the most part, however, these theories have emphasized the self-monitoring of the response. But this is only one of the factors involved in the interpretation of behavior. Equally important is the individual's understanding of the role being played. In fact, it is the role which creates the response. Hence, without interpreting the role, there would be no response to monitor.

KINDS OF EMOTION

Up to this point, we have been treating the emotions as though they were all alike. That, of course, is not the case. In the present section, therefore, the emotions will be divided into three kinds–impulsive, conflictive, and transcendental–and several examples of each kind will be examined in detail. These examples will help to illustrate the limitations as well as the advantages of a role-model as applied to the emotions.

The distinction between impulsive, conflictive, and transcendental emotions is based on two major considerations: (a) the social norms which help constitute emotional behavior; and (b) the cognitive structures which help mediate the experience of emotion (Averill, 1979a). These two considerations are not independent, of course, since cognitive structures are determined in large part by the internalization of social norms and values. But rather than dwelling on the bases for the distinction, let us turn directly to a brief description of each kind of emotion.

According to McDougall (1948), human emotions are "clues to the instinctive impulses, or indicators of the motives at work within us" (p. 128). With one important caveat, this description applies well to the class of *impulsive emotions*. The caveat refers to the fact that the impulsive emotions–like other kinds of emotion–are the product of social as well as biological evolution. This is not to deny that certain responses, such as startle to a loud noise or attacking the source of pain, are largely determined by biological predispositions. But such biological impulses do not, by themselves, represent emotional syndromes, at least not until they are further molded by social norms and values. Stated in more cognitive terms, the impulsive emotions can be thought of as states of strong motivation–whether biologically and/or socially induced–which have never been completely identified with the self-as-agent.

Whereas the impulsive emotions represent straightforward desires or aversions, the *conflictive emotions* are the outgrowth of incompatible impulses. In a sense, conflictive emotions are like culturally induced hysterical reactions. In the case of hysteria, the individual wishes to engage in some behavior which conflicts with personal norms or standards. The result is a compromise or symbolic expression, the origins and meaning of which are dissociated from the self-as-agent. In the case of standard conflictive emotions, the source of the conflict and the script for the expression of the response are to be found within the social system, and are not due to intrapsychic conflicts peculiar to the individual. More specifically, conflictive emotions arise when social norms simultaneously encourage and discourage a particular type of response. One way of resolving the conflict is by allowing the response to be symbolically transformed and interpreted as a passion rather than as an action. Since an individual cannot help "suffering" from a passion, the proscribed response can then be made without incurring responsibility.

Both impulsive and conflictive emotions presuppose well-established ego-boundaries, or cognitive structures, so that some responses (actions) may be attributed to the self-as-agent while other responses (passions) are interpreted as beyond self-control. But what happens if the cognitive structures which help define the self-as-agent are disrupted, for example, through the use of drugs, unusual experiences, physical trauma, or the like? If this occurs, there can be no action, only passion. Or, more accurately, the categories of action and passion are transcended, and the individual becomes engulfed in an undifferentiated flood of experience. This defines the class of *transcendental emotions,* of which anxiety and mystical experiences are prime examples.

The nature of this three-fold distinction among impulsive, conflictive, and transcendental emotions will become clearer after we have examined several examples of each kind.

Impulsive Emotions

The two emotions that will be used to exemplify this class are *amae,* a form of emotional attachment fostered by the Japanese, and grief, a relatively universal emotion which results when attachment bonds are broken. These two emotions have been chosen because they illustrate particularly well the interplay between biological and social factors in the construction of emotional syndromes.

Amae. Among the Japanese, *amae* is considered to be a very basic emotion, observable even in animals. Yet there is no equivalent syndrome in Western societies. Roughly translated, *amae* means "dependency." But this translation is not adequate for two reasons. First, "dependency" does not refer to a well-organized emotional state, as does *amae*; and, secondly, "dependency" has a negative connotation, whereas *amae* is regarded as a positive emotion. "Love" might be a better translation. However, *amae* differs from romantic love in that *amae* does not have a sexual connotation. *Amae* can be observed in nearly any kind of close relationship, e.g., between friends, parents and children, employers and employees, and so forth. This might suggest that *amae* is a form of Platonic love. But that concept will not do either, since Platonic love is in many respects the antithesis of emotional involvement. For want of a better term, then, we shall translate *amae* as "affiliative love."

According to Doi (1973), a Japanese psychiatrist who has analyzed *amae* in considerable detail, the prototype of this emotion lies in the infant's relationship to its mother. The syndrome first appears about the age of six months, as the infant becomes aware of its surroundings and seeks after its mother. The prototype of *amae* is thus very similar to what Bowlby (1969) has called attachment behavior. Attachment behavior represents a biological adaptation and is not a specific emotional syndrome. Nevertheless, because of its central importance for the understanding of *amae,* a brief discussion of attachment is necessary.

Among all higher primates, including man, group living is one of the principle adaptations for survival (Wilson, 1975). The group provides, among other things, protection from predators and efficiency in obtaining food. Separation from the group, in turn, greatly diminishes the chances for survival. It is therefore important to members of the group to maintain contact with, or attachment to, one another. What is the mechanism by which contact is maintained? Bowlby (1969) has provided what is probably the most widely recognized (and debated) answer to this question. Very briefly, Bowlby argues that the attachment of an individual to other group members is mediated, in part, by a biological system consisting of a variety of semi-independent responses. In the case of the infant's attachment to its mother, for example, the bond is maintained by such responses as sucking, smiling, crying, clinging, following, and the like. Responses such as these serve to protect the infant from danger by promoting and maintaining proximity to the mother. Bowlby compares the entire process to a complex control system, such as that used in keeping a guided missile on target.

It is important to emphasize that the various elements which comprise attachment behavior on a biological level are not knit together in some invariable fashion. Rather, aspects of attachment may be combined with other responses to form a variety of different syndromes, of which *amae* is one example.

According to Doi (1973), *amae* is "the basic emotional urge that has fashioned the Japanese for two thousand years." Doi sees in *amae* many of the same things that Freud saw in sexual desire or libido. That is, *amae* can be repressed, symbolically transformed, and ultimately expressed in many different ways (including somatic complaints). Most importantly, however, Doi illustrates how *amae* enters into, or forms a part of, Japanese social and political institutions (such as the family and emperor system).

The notion that *amae* has helped fashion Japanese society for 2000 years tells only half the story; it is equally true that Japanese society has been fashioning *amae* into a "basic emotional urge" during the same period. As Doi points out, however, it did not occur to anyone to examine this latter half of the story until the Japanese suffered defeat in World War II. Before then, *amae* was experienced "simply as emotion." After the war, many Japanese institutions underwent profound reexamination, and behaviors that previously were accepted as self-evident, completely natural, or even divinely inspired were now seen to be the manifestation of social roles.

Before leaving this topic, one additional question should be addressed. Why is *amae* experienced simply as emotion–interpreted as a passion rather than as an action? The fact that *amae* is related to attachment behavior on the biological level is only part of the answer. Equally–if not more–important is the manner in which *amae* has become legitimized within Japanese society. A response so fundamental to the society could not be left to the vagaries of individual choice. *Amae* is therefore encouraged and fostered by Japanese customs until it becomes second nature, so to speak. And as part of this socialization, *amae* is legitimized not only as a natural and expected human response, but also as one that occurs in animals. This type of legitimation precludes *amae* from being identified with the self-as-agent, the individual "I" which initiates responses, and places it instead in the domain of the passions.

Grief. An emotional syndrome such as *amae* is relevant primarily when the object of attachment is present or potentially available. Other emotional syndromes, of which grief is a prime example, come into play when social bonds are broken and the object of attachment is permanently lost.

Although grief is one of the most poignant and dramatic of the emotions, until recently it has been relatively neglected by psychologists. In part, this is because the dominant theories of emotion have emphasized activation and drive as theoretical variables. Many of the major symptoms of grief–apathy, withdrawal, fatigue, and the like–simply do not fit into such a theoretical framework. Moreover, it is obviously difficult to investigate grief in laboratory situations, the favorite haunt of academic psychologists. But the fact that grief remained for a long period outside the purview of psychology may have proven to be more of an advantage than a liability, for it allowed the observation of grief to proceed without the restraint of theoretical and methodological blinkers. As a result, there are now more factual observations on grief than on most other emotions (for recent reviews see Averill, 1968, 1979b; Marris, 1975; Parkes, 1972; Rosenblatt, Welsh, & Jackson, 1976).

Grief typically progresses through a series of stages, beginning with protest and yearning for the lost object, followed by despair, and ultimately by a reorganization of behavior with the establishment of new object relationships. These stages may be observed in infrahuman primates as well as across cultures among humans. Many of the symptoms which characterize these stages are thus biologically determined. For example, the protest and yearning which characterize the first stage of grief reflect an attempt to re-establish social bonds; and, since social living has survival value, the predisposition toward this behavior is maintained within the species through natural selection.

But biological reactions to loss do not, by themselves, constitute a syndrome of grief. Bereavement is an event of social as well as biological importance. It is not surprising, therefore, that every society possesses certain mores, beliefs, and customs concerning the appropriate behavior to be displayed upon the death of a significant other. The exact nature of mourning practices varies considerably from one society to the next, but whatever the practice, it must be followed if social stricture is to be avoided. This fact led Durkheim (1915) to declare:

> Mourning is not a natural movement of private feelings wounded by a cruel loss; it is a duty imposed by the group. One weeps, not simply because he is sad, but because he is forced to weep. It is a ritual attitude which he is forced to adopt out of respect for custom, but which is, in a large measure, independent of his affective state (p. 397).

This statement by Durkheim would seem to drive a wedge between grief and mourning—the former being "a natural movement of private feelings" and the latter "a duty imposed by the group." It is true that the concept of grief has a more individual connotation, while the concept of mourning has a more social connotation. However, the two concepts do not refer to different syndromes, only to different aspects of the same syndrome.

Sometimes, of course, the role of the mourner may be enacted with relatively little personal involvement. But that is true of all emotional roles, as was discussed in the previous section. The important point to note in the present context is how biologically based reactions to the disruption of interpersonal bonds may combine with socially determined mourning practices to form a coherent emotional syndrome which may be called either grief or mourning. Stated somewhat differently, the socially evolved expressions of grief (such as wearing mourning garments) may be just as fundamental as are biologically based responses (such as weeping). For the well-socialized individual, both kinds of behavior are experienced as equally compelling.

And what is the meaning of grief and mourning within the social system? Mandelbaum (1959) has suggested that mourning practices can be understood in much the same way as other ceremonies which involve socially important transitions, such as birth, marriage, and the like. Such ceremonies allow the threads of each individual life to be woven into the fabric of society, thus reinforcing the whole. In the case of mourning, this function is perhaps most evident when a prominent figure dies. The nationally televised funeral of President Kennedy, for example, not only elicited sincere mourning in many persons, but it also helped to reaffirm the continuity of American society. National mourning was also encouraged in the USSR following the death of Lenin, and in China upon the death of Mao Tse-tung. In these instances, as following Kennedy's assassination, there was a threat of civil disturbance, and mourning ceremonies helped to unite the population in grief.

This brief discussion of the functions of grief barely scratches the surface of a very complex issue (cf. Averill, 1979b). It does suffice, however, to illustrate the general nature of this emotional syndrome. As a postscript, therefore, let me simply add one further observation. Anyone who has experienced grief, or who has read a firsthand description of grief, such as that by C. S. Lewis (1961), may object that the present account leaves much unsaid, for example, with regard to the personal anguish and suffering involved. The objection is correct, but it misses an important point. A scientific analysis of grief is not intended to represent the experiences of the bereaved any more than a scientific analysis of cancer is intended to represent the experiences of a person suffering from the disease, or a scientific analysis of problem-solving is intended to represent the experiences of a person involved in a game of chess. Grief, like cancer and chess games, can be described in a variety of ways. And, certainly, a scientific description of grief will differ from a poetic or literary description. This does not mean, however, that the scientific analysis is less complete, or that it has left something out, except in the rather trivial sense that the scientific analysis must deal with features which are common to grief in general and not with the intricacies of individual experience.

To summarize briefly, impulsive emotions represent socially constituted syndromes which may (as in the case of *amae* and grief) also incorporate biologically based elements. These syndromes are interpreted as emotional–as passions rather than as actions–because the individual has no freedom of choice. That is, a person does not choose to act with *amae* in the presence of an attachment figure, or to grieve in its absence. On the other hand, neither is one forced to act with *amae* or to grieve by some immediate external reward or punishment. The impulse is thus accepted as stemming from the self, but not from the self-as-agent.

Conflictive Emotions

There is no sharp dividing line between impulsive and conflictive emotions. Both are the product of social evolution, both may have a basis in biological predispositions, and both may be experienced as equally compelling. However, these two kinds of emotion function differently within the social system. Whereas impulsive emotions are like socially based motives, conflictive emotions are like socially based hysterias. A brief discussion of romantic love and anger will serve to illustrate this difference.

Romantic Love. At first, it might seem inappropriate to classify romantic love as a conflictive emotion. But there is more to romantic love than at first appears. Consider the following observations by the anthropologist Linton (1936):

> All societies recognize that there are occasional violent emotional attachments between persons of opposite sex, but our present American culture is practically the only one which has attempted to capitalize on these and make them the basis for marriage. Most groups regard them as unfortunate and point out the victims of such attachments as horrible examples. Their rarity in most societies suggests that they are psychological abnormalities to which our own culture has attached an extraordinary value just as other cultures have attached extreme values to other abnormalities. The hero of the modern American movie is always a romantic lover just as the hero of the old Arab epic is always an epileptic. A cynic might suspect that in any ordinary population the percentage of individuals with a capacity for romantic love of the Hollywood type was about as large as that of persons able to throw genuine epileptic fits. However, given a little social encouragement, either one can be adequately imitated without the performer admitting even to himself that the performance is not genuine (p. 175).

Most anthropologists today would agree that Linton has overstated the case. As Goode (1959) has pointed out, romantic love may be related to the social structure in diverse ways, and it is therefore necessary to forego the dichotomy of "romantic love-no romantic love" in the classification of societies. He argues instead for a continuum or range between polar types. At one cultural extreme, sexual infatuations are viewed as personal aberrations; at the other extreme, romantic love is institutionalized as a rather well defined social role. Contemporary middle-class American society would fall toward the latter pole, as would certain European and Polynesian societies. Traditional Chinese and Japanese cultures might be placed at the opposite extreme where sexual infatuation is frowned upon. Greece after Alexander, Rome of the Empire, and contemporary village and urban India might, Goode suggests, fall somewhere in the middle.

But what is romantic love? How many people actually fall in love in conformance with the romantic ideal? And what is the function of romantic love within the social system? In recent years, research and speculation on issues such as these has burgeoned (e.g., Levinger & Raush, 1977; Murstein, 1974; Otto, 1972; Rubin, 1973). No attempt will be made here to review this literature. The results of a recent study by Averill and Boothroyd (1977) will suffice to provide a focus for the present discussion. In this study, a group of subjects (60 of whom were single, 7 married, and 18 divorced) were asked to describe their attitudes toward, and experiences with, romantic love. Included in the questionnaire was the following newspaper account of a couple who fell romantically in love:

> On Monday, Cpl. Floyd Johnson, 23, and the then Ellen Skinner, 19, total strangers, boarded a train at San Francisco and sat down across the aisle from each other. Johnson didn't cross the aisle until Wednesday, but his bride said, "I'd already made up my mind to say yes if he asked me to

marry him." "We did most of the talking with our eyes," Johnson explained. Thursday the couple got off the train in Omaha with plans to be married. Because they would need the consent of the bride's parents if they were married in Nebraska, they crossed the river to Council Bluffs, Iowa, where they were married Friday.[6]

Subjects were reminded that instances of the above type also can be found in literature (e.g., Romeo and Juliet), and they were asked to indicate on a 10-point scale how closely their most intense experiences of love conformed to the romantic ideal. Thirty-four subjects (40 percent of the sample) indicated that their experiences conformed closely to the ideal (ratings of 8, 9, or 10), while nearly the same number of subjects, 33, rated their experiences as quite dissimilar to the romantic ideal (ratings of 1, 2, or 3). Relatively few subjects fell in between.

Although these results are based on a rather small sample, the subjects involved were quite heterogeneous on a number of variables (e.g., age, sex, and marital status), none of which had a significant effect on the conformity ratings. For example, males were as likely as females to describe their experience as conforming to the romantic ideal; and persons were as likely to have fallen romantically in love following divorce as preceding their first marriage. As a very rough estimate, it therefore seems reasonable to conclude that a large minority (approximately 40 percent) of contemporary Americans interpret their most intense experiences of love as conforming to the romantic ideal.

However, a caveat is in order. Subjects also were asked to give an open-ended description of the experiences they rated. These descriptions allowed an independent—but very rough—assessment of the experiences. From this, it would appear that only between 5 and 10 percent of the total sample had experiences which conformed to the romantic ideal in a literal sense. But regardless of how many subjects "literally" fell in love in accordance with the ideal, it is still worthy of note that 40 percent of them interpreted their most intense experiences as so conforming. As was discussed earlier, the experience of emotion often involves a retrospective interpretation of behavior.

The above results suggest that the romantic ideal as depicted in song and literature is serving as a kind of model or paradigm. The model represents a complex blend of characteristics to which few people actually conform. Rather, it is an abstraction which aids in both the guidance and interpretation of behavior. That is, people may try to emulate the model, and even if they fail, they may still interpret their behavior as being more in conformance than it actually is.

The above line of reasoning does not explain why the romantic ideal was established in the first place, what function it serves within the social system, or why some people interpret their experiences as conforming to it while others react against it. Beigel (1951) has traced the origins of the contemporary Western

[6] This example of romantic love is taken from Burgess and Wallin (1953).

ideal of romantic love to the courtly love of twelfth-century Europe. From then until the present, the romantic ideal has undergone major transformations as a function of changes in socioeconomic conditions. Within contemporary American society, Greenfield (1965) has suggested that the romantic ideal is one way of encouraging couples to marry, even though marriage may be counter to their immediate self-interests. In our culture, for example, the individual is encouraged to be self-reliant, independent, and—in a sense—economically selfish. This is the "rational" way to behave. On another level, however, society also encourages the individual to support a wife and children (or, in the case of the wife, unselfishly to give up a career in the marketplace for a less prestigious domestic role). How can these conflicting demands be resolved? The answer, according to Greenfield, is found in the romantic ideal. One marries because one has fallen in love—an event which cannot be helped.

It is not necessary to agree with the details of Greenfield's analysis in order to recognize the basic ingredients for a conflictive emotion. That is, society has established two conflicting standards (e.g., rational self-interest, and a self-sacrificing commitment to marriage and family). The conflict is resolved by a third set of standards (the romantic ideal) which institutionalizes and encourages an emotional syndrome (falling in love).

A corollary to the above analysis is that persons who have not internalized the relevant though potentially conflicting demands of society also will not interpret their experiences of love as conforming to the romantic ideal. Indeed, they may reject the ideal as unnecessary, at best, and harmful, at worst. In this respect, it will be recalled that approximately 40 percent of the subjects surveyed by Averill and Boothroyd indicated that their most intense experiences of love did *not* conform to the romantic ideal. We cannot say at the present time why these people did not interpret their experiences in terms of the romantic ideal. It was not simply a matter of intensity, for both conforming and nonconforming episodes of love were equally intense (at least as indicated by the duration of the experience). It may be relevant to note, however, that there appears to be a "counter-culture" bias among many recent commentators who reject the romantic ideal (see, for example, the collection of essays edited by Otto, 1972). We do not know whether such a bias also was characteristic of those persons in the Averill and Boothroyd study who interpreted their experiences as dissimilar to the romantic ideal. But one thing is certain: love was not made in heaven; rather, it was fashioned right here on earth, to meet specific societal needs.

Anger. As a second example of a conflictive emotion, let us consider the case of anger. Many writers have treated anger as though it were a species of hate and hence the opposite of love. But according to a recent study (Averill, 1979c), anger is most often directed at loved ones and friends, and relatively seldom at strangers and persons who are disliked. Of course, if the provocations which lead to anger are repeated often enough, then love may turn to hate (McKellar, 1950). That, however, is not the ordinary course of events. More typically, a display of anger helps to strengthen a relationship by preventing the reoccurrence of a provocation and by clarifying misunderstandings.

As the above observations suggest, anger has both good and bad effects. It is therefore not surprising that this emotion has been the subject of considerable debate and conflicting sentiment throughout history. For example, Plato (*The Republic*) believed that anger is fundamental to the organization of the state as well as the individual. On the other hand, the Roman philosopher Seneca (ca. 40-50 A.D./1963) believed this to be "the most hideous and frenzied of all emotions." And although anger often has been condemned as sinful by religious writers, the wrath of God is extolled by some of the world's major religions (Stratton, 1923).

The conflicting sentiments surrounding anger can be understood when it is realized that this emotion is the product of two contradictory sets of norms. The first set of norms has to do with the demand for punishment or retribution against wrongdoing. The second set of norms has to do with the general cultural proscription against deliberately harming another person and, more positively, with the virtues of charity, tolerance, and forgiveness. Both sets of norms find expression in the *Sermon on the Mount*:

> Ye have heard that it hath been said, An eye for an eye and a tooth for a tooth: But I say unto you, That ye resist not evil: but whoever shall smite thee on thy right cheek, turn to him the other also.

How are these conflicting norms—exacting an eye for an eye and turning the other cheek—to be reconciled without forsaking one or the other? One way is to establish permanent roles—such as the military and police—for those who must commit aggression in the service of society. Another way is to establish special occasions—ritual sacrifices, duels, competitive sports, and the like—during which the norms against aggression are temporarily suspended. But formal exemptions such as these do not begin to cover the innumerable (and generally minor) cases of aggression that occur in everyday affairs.

As discussed elsewhere (Averill, 1979c), anger is an institutionalized form of aggression which helps to regulate interpersonal relations through the threat of retaliation. If a person aggresses in anger, the response will not be interpreted as deliberate or intentional. The norms which prohibit deliberate aggression against another are thus preserved. But for aggression to be excused on the basis of anger, it must satisfy certain conditions. For example, the provocation must meet socially accepted criteria of adequacy, and the mode of response must conform to certain standards of legitimacy. If these conditions are not met, the claim of anger may be disallowed entirely; or if some but not all of the conditions are met, the response may be judged as unjustifiable anger and hence subject to punishment.

The above analysis may make anger seem too purposeful, almost like an action rather than a passion. It must be remembered, however, that most emotions proceed at a rather low level of personal involvement. For example, if subjects are asked to keep an *ongoing* record of their experiences, then the average person may report becoming angry once or twice a day (Anastasi, Cohen, & Spatz, 1948; McKellar, 1949; Meltzer, 1933). However, if persons are asked to recall the last time they were angry, they are more likely to report once or twice a week (Averill, 1979c). In other words, most persons simply respond to minor provocations. Only if they are asked to interpret a response are they likely to classify it as an action or a passion; and the longer the delay between the event and the interpretation, the more dramatic the response must be before it will be interpreted as anger (provided it is even remembered). Of course, on occasion the level of personal involvement may be sufficiently great so that the individual is literally "overcome" by anger. However, as we discussed in a previous section, even such extreme experiences are the product of reflective self-monitoring.

Transcendental Emotional Stress

Most standard emotional reactions—whether impulsive or conflictive—presume well-established ego-boundaries; that is, a rather sharp distinction between the self-as-agent and the self-as-patient. These boundaries are built up primarily through experience during the course of socialization. But what is built up can also be dismantled. For example, through physical trauma, psychological conflict, the use of drugs, unusual stimulation, and the like, the cognitive structures which help define the self may be disrupted. The result is a transcendental emotional state. This kind of emotion is called "transcendental," first, because it has its origins in transcendence of the self and, second, because the quality of the experience tends to be indefinite, nebulous, and ineffable. These features will be illustrated by mystical experiences, to take an example of a positive transcendental emotion, and by anxiety, to take a negative example.

Mystical Experiences. As noted earlier in this chapter, one of the historically most important, and still most influential theories of emotion is that put forward by William James. According to James's theory, bodily changes follow directly the perception of an exciting fact, and the feeling of those changes is the emotion. James did not, however, apply this theory consistently to all kinds of emotion. In a discussion of mysticism, James (1902) entertained the hypothesis that there exists within the universe a vast reservoir of consciousness or mind capable of acting directly on the brain from without. Quoting the Canadian psychiatrist, R. M. Bucke, James referred to this reservoir as "cosmic consciousness." In Bucke's (1901) own words:

> The prime characteristic of cosmic consciousness is a consciousness of the cosmos, that is, of the life and order of the universe. Along with the con-

> sciousness of the cosmos there occurs an intellectual enlightenment which alone would place the individual on a new plane of existence—would make him almost a member of a new species. To this is added a state of moral exaltation, an indescribable feeling of elevation, elation, and joyousness, and a quickening of the moral sense, which is fully as striking and more important than is the enhanced intellectual power. With these come what may be called a sense of immortality, a consciousness of eternal life, not a conviction that he shall have this, but the consciousness that he has it already (quoted by James, 1902, p. 398).

We have not followed James in his explanation of standard emotional reactions, and we need not follow his (or Bucke's) speculations regarding a cosmic consciousness in the case of mystical experiences. Nevertheless, it must be recognized that there is something "different" about mystical experiences, and this difference must be accounted for. Therefore, let us consider a little more closely some of the features of mystical experiences.

The first thing to note is that mystical experiences are described as both emotional and cognitive, as a way of feeling and as a way of knowing. On the feeling side, mystical experiences are characterized by heightened consciousness or awareness. If the experience is not complete, as in many drug-induced states, this heightened consciousness may involve little more than vivid and unusual sensory impressions. A full-blown mystical experience, however, is often described as transcending all sense impressions, no matter how vivid or unusual; it is a state of heightened consciousness per se. This is one of the things that makes the mystical experience so difficult to describe.

Another very common characteristic of mystical experiences is a disappearance of self-identity and a sense of unity with all things—not just a state of consciousness, but of *cosmic* consciousness. This sense of unity, together with elation and joyousness, accounts for the fact that the mystical experience is often described as a form of love. It should be evident, however, that the mystical experience is quite different than affiliative love (an impulsive emotion) and romantic love (a conflictive emotion).

As noted above, mystics do not claim that their experiences are "simply" emotional. Rather, the experience is characterized by a sense of realness, not just of the state itself, but also of the ultimate reality which supposedly underlies the experience. While the mystic's claim of direct access to reality must be greeted with skepticism, there is a relationship between transcendental emotional states and creative activity; in both cases there is a breakdown in customary distinctions and an increased fluidity of thought. Greeley (1974) has compared mystical knowledge with the processes by which, say, a musician perceives an entire symphony before he begins to compose, or a novelist intuits a story before he begins to write. Greeley emphasizes that he is not describing something that goes on "inside" the person, but something that the person sees in the world "out there." That is, the mystical experience is a means whereby a person understands the world about him. But unlike other kinds of knowledge, it is more direct, immediate, and intuitive.

Full-blown mystical experiences are relatively rare, although perhaps not as rare as is typically assumed. In a national survey, Greeley (1974) found that 35 percent of the people reported having had at least one mystical-like experience, and about 5 percent had such experiences repeatedly. Maslow (1971) goes even further and claims that almost all persons have had "peak" experiences, or ecstasies, which resemble the mystical experience. And with the recent widespread use of hallucenogenic and other drugs, many persons have experienced altered states of consciousness which contain some of the more dramatic features often described by mystics.

Turning now to an explanation of mystical experiences, three factors must be taken into consideration. The first has already been noted; namely, there is a breakdown in cognitive structures, including those which help define the self. This accounts for the altered state of consciousness and the loss of self-identity. The breakdown is not complete, however, for the altered state of consciousness must still be interpreted. The second factor, then, is the need for some residual cognitive structures by which the experience can be given meaning. The importance of this factor may be illustrated by reference to drug-induced states. The neophyte marihuana user, say, has to learn when he is "high" and even that the experience is pleasurable. Similarly, many of the naturally occurring events which have been found to trigger mystical-like experiences (e.g., a dangerous situation, accident, a brush with death) are also common sources of anxiety and depression. In order to trigger mystical experiences, such events must be interpreted within an "appropriate" framework (Bourque & Back, 1971).

The third factor which must be taken into consideration in explaining mystical experiences follows from the first two. It has to do, namely, with the nature of the residual cognitive structures which provide the framework for the interpretation of the experience. These typically involve some general philosophical or religious system. It is within such a system that the role of the mystic is defined, so to speak. In some instances, as in the case of the saint or the shaman, the role may be quite explicit and formally recognized. In other instances, the role may be more informal. But even the most unorthodox hippy in search of a high has established a role for himself (e.g., as a "priest" within the counter-culture).

Anxiety. The person who attempts to achieve a mystical experience without adequate preparation may find the state more terrifying than blissful. This brings us to the problem of anxiety. Anxiety is an emotional syndrome which is characterized by diffuse feelings of helplessness, uncertainty, foreboding, and dread. The following description by an anonymous surgeon gives some idea of the nature of the experience.

> It is as difficult to describe to others what an acute anxiety state feels like as to convey to the inexperienced the feeling of falling in love. Perhaps the most characteristic impression is the constant state of causeless and apparently meaningless alarm. You feel as if you were on the battlefield or had stumbled against a wild animal in the dark, and all the time you are conversing with your fellows in normal and peaceful surroundings and performing duties you have done for years. With this your head feels vague and immense and stuffed with cotton wool; it is difficult, and trying, to concentrate; and, most frightening of all, the quality of your sensory appreciation of the universe undergoes an essential change (Quoted by Landis & Metler, 1964, pp. 241-242).

A great many explanations have been offered for this syndrome, but among cognitively oriented theorists, at least, one of the most common themes is that anxiety reflects a breakdown in cognitive structures, especially those which represent the self. The causes of such a breakdown may be many, including organic brain damage, the lack of social support, drugs, overstimulation or understimulation, conflicting demands placed upon the individual by the physical or social environment, intrapsychic conflict, and others. But the final result is the same. Unable to impose meaning on the world, and faced with an impending collapse of his own sense of selfhood, the individual becomes terrified; and yet he is powerless to act, for the source of the threat comes from within and not from any well defined external danger.

The above account of anxiety, it will be noted, is in many respects similar to the preceding account of mystical experiences. The major difference is that in the case of anxiety, there is no encompassing framework in which to interpret the experience. Thus, whereas the mystic may interpret his experience as being at one with the universe, immersed in a cosmic consciousness, or united with the Godhead–that is, as achieving a higher plane of reality–the person suffering from an anxiety attack is faced with a loss of reality, a plunge into nothingness.

The above characterization is, of course, overdrawn for illustrative purposes. Full-blown anxiety attacks are about as rare as full-blown mystical experiences, and they are just as difficult to describe in ordinary language. But the mere threat of an anxiety attack can be a powerful motivating force, encouraging a wide variety of defensive maneuvers. This is why anxiety is so often invoked as an explanation for psychoneurotic responses. It is as though the individual were continually trying to shore up the walls of a crumbling edifice (cognitive structures) without ever repairing the edifice itself. The result is a rigid and unyielding personality, encrusted by defense mechanisms, and yet still in peril of collapse.

Some of the above considerations can be illustrated by the work of Kurt Goldstein (1939, 1951) with brain-injured patients. (Since cognitive structures depend on neural functioning, damage to the latter may threaten the former.) By way of background, Goldstein distinguished between two modes of thought, which he called the concrete and the abstract. In the concrete mode, thought lacks an inherent structure of its own; its organization is determined primarily by the structure of the surrounding environment. Experiences which are mediated by this mode of thought are thus under immediate stimulus control. In the abstract mode, by contrast, cognitive structures are internally organized and self-sustaining, so that it is the individual who imposes meaning on the environment, rather than vice-versa.

The brain-injured patients studied by Goldstein suffered from a deficit in the abstract or internally organized mode of thought. To maintain some semblance of order and meaning in their lives, these patients had to arrange their environment down to the most trivial detail. If even minor things were misplaced or out of order, or if the patients were presented with a novel or strange situation, they often would develop what Goldstein called a "catastrophic reaction." Such a reaction is characterized by physiological arousal, behavioral disorientation, and feelings of terror–in short, the kinds of symptoms generally associated with an acute anxiety attack.

States of anxiety are by no means limited to individuals suffering from cognitive deficits. The possibility for anxiety exists whenever an individual is unable to impose meaning on his world because of inadequate or unstable cognitive structures. Such a condition is characteristic of highly creative thought, which tends to be fluid and unstructured in its formative stages. Perhaps this is one reason why anxiety–as well as mystical or peak experiences–is often a central theme in the writings of highly creative individuals. The notion of anxiety is especially common among existentialist writers who, like Sartre (1948), emphasize the absurdity and meaningless of existence.

Of all the emotions considered thus far, anxiety seems to be the one least suited to an analysis in terms of a role-model. If anxiety is complete–as in the catastrophic reactions described by Goldstein–the individual is in a state of psychological disarray. It would be misleading to insinuate that such a reaction represents, even in part, the enactment of a social role. Nevertheless, the role-model is not completely irrelevant to the problem of anxiety. The near total collapse of cognitive structures is rare. Before that occurs, the threatened individual may engage in a wide variety of defensive maneuvers in order to provide some structure and meaning to experience. And in this effort he may be assisted by a variety of formal and informal social roles. Many religious (and political) rituals can be viewed in this way (see, for example, Homans, 1941; Spiro, 1965). "Enlightened" men and women may attribute such rituals to superstition. But this only leaves modern man, in the words of Becker (1969), "to contrive his defiances in petty, lonely, and ingenious ways: and so in order to understand his efforts, we need to invent a psychiatric category instead of a ritual-religious one" (p. 26).

Summary

A response may be interpreted as a passion rather than as an action for three general reasons, and this helps to define three kinds of emotion. In the case of *impulsive* emotions, the response is so important from a biological and/or social point of view that it cannot, in a sense, be left to deliberate choice. Rather, during the course of socialization, responses of this kind are made "second nature," "instinctive", or, as we have labeled the class, "impulsive." Impulsive emotions can be distinguished from *conflictive* emotions in terms of their social evolution and function, as well as in terms of underlying cognitive mechanisms. Within any complex social system, there are bound to be norms or rules which place conflicting demands on the individual. An emotional role may then evolve which helps resolve the conflict. Specifically, by interpreting the compromise solution as a passion rather than as an action, the individual may engage in the proscribed behavior without incurring responsibility.

Both impulsive and conflictive emotions can be distinguished from *transcendental* emotional states in that the former presume well defined ego-boundaries, whereas the latter involve a breakdown in cognitive structures. Some transcendental emotions may be encouraged by society, for example, in the form of mystical and aesthetic experiences. More frequently, however, transcendental emotions represent a kind of mental anarchy due to neurological disease, unusual stimulation, intrapsychic conflict, and/or the lack of social support. Anxiety is a prime example.

It should be emphasized that this threefold distinction among kinds of emotion is primarily analytical. Any actual emotional episode may involve impulsive, conflictive, and transcendental aspects. Moreover, the common name for an emotion is often a poor guide as to which aspect predominates. We have already noted this fact in the case of love, which may be predominantly impulsive (affiliative love), conflictive (romantic love), or transcendental (mystical love). "Fear" also illustrates this same point. Many fears are impulsive; they involve straightforward responses to natural or socially defined dangers. But what begins as an impulsive fear may be transformed into a conflictive emotion. This may occur, for example, when a person comes to fear an object, not because of any realistic danger or past history of traumatic conditioning, but as a means of resolving some social or intrapsychic conflict. Fear can also be closely associated with anxiety, a transcendental emotional state. This association stems, in part, from the fact that both kinds of emotion have certain elements in common (e.g., a feeling of dread); but perhaps even more importantly, fear is frequently used as a defense against anxiety. That is, when an individual is faced with uncertainty, and normal cognitive processes prove to be inadequate, the "cause" of the problem may be projected on some external source. The latter then becomes the object of fear, which helps relieve anxiety by providing structure to the experience.

In spite of the above qualifications, the distinction among impulsive, conflictive, and transcendental emotions is of both theoretical and practical significance. This fact is somewhat difficult to demonstrate in a short space without gross oversimplification. Nevertheless, a few observations along these lines may be helpful, if for no other reason than to further illustrate the nature of the distinction among the three kinds of emotion.

On reading theories of emotion, one often gets the impression that different authors are discussing different phenomena. To a certain extent, the impression is correct. Learning and instinct theories, no matter how else they may differ, are both most applicable to impulsive emotions; psychoanalytic and related theories, on the other hand, are most relevant to conflictive emotions; and, finally, existentialist theories are most pertinent to transcendental emotional states.

Of course, each type of theory mentioned is not limited to only one kind of emotion. As already described, every emotion contains impulsive, conflictive, and transcendental aspects. Hence, each type of theory is applicable to all kinds of emotion, albeit to a greater or lesser extent. Also, some theories make implicit allowances for different kinds of emotion. For example, psychoanalysis recognizes instinctual impulses, intrapsychic conflict, and primary-process, highly fluid, nonlogical thought; with some modification, notions such as these can be used to account for impulsive, conflictive, and transcental emotional states.

Some practical consequences also follow from the above theoretical considerations. Although much of psychotherapy deals with emotional problems, there is little aggreement regarding the effectiveness of different types of therapy. To a certain extent, this is due to the fact that a particular type of therapy may be more relevant to one kind of emotion than to another. Again recognizing the oversimplification involved, it may be said that some combination of behavior therapy (counter-conditioning, desensitization) and cognitive therapy (altering a person's cognitive appraisals) is most appropriate in cases that involve impulsive emotions, where there are no hidden motives or goals. On the other hand, some form of depth analysis (e.g., psychoanalysis) may be the treatment of choice when conflictive emotions are involved, for in these cases the response has more than one level of meaning. Finally, some form of existential analysis might be most appropriate in cases of transcendental emotional states, such as anxiety, when the individual has lost a sense of meaning and purpose.

INDIVIDUAL DIFFERENCES IN EMOTIONAL REACTIVITY

We have now examined some of the processes involved in the experience of emotion (e.g., the self-monitoring of behavior and the understanding of an emotional role), and we have distinguished among various kinds of emotion. But there is still one issue which we have not touched upon, namely, individual differences in emotional reactivity. Imagine a large class in psychology where, say, 10 percent of the students fail an important examination. If one were to interview the students who failed, some would be angry, others sad, and still others fearful, envious, or ashamed. Some might even dismiss their failure in a jocular fashion, as though it were a bad joke.

In attempting to account for such individual differences, two general approaches are possible. The first approach is to examine the antecedent conditions (e.g., prior learning and physiological state) that might influence the individual's appraisal of the situation and ability to respond. This approach is the most "respectable" from a scientific point of view. However, it represents an ideal that is seldom attainable in practice. We are seldom in a position to know or evaluate all the antecedent conditions that help determine a person's behavior on any given occasion. A second approach is therefore often adopted, namely, the assessment of "higher-order" variables from which the response in question can be inferred as a special case. These higher-order variables, or predispositions to respond, are themselves the product of complex–and often unknown–antecedents. Hence, they do not explain behavior in a rigorous sense, although they may allow for a good deal of prediction and control.

In this section, we will examine briefly four kinds of emotional predispositions: motives, moods, traits, and sentiments. These four do not exhaust the list of relevant variables, but together they do illustrate most of the difficulties involved in this approach to the problem of individual differences. There is also another reason for selecting these particular variables for further analysis. In theoretical psychology as well as in ordinary discourse, a term which generally refers to a specific emotional episode may also be used to refer to a motive, mood, trait, or sentiment. For example, it may be said of a person that he is motivated by jealousy, is in a sad mood, has a trait of anxiety, and loves his wife (in the sense of a long-enduring sentiment). All of these descriptions may be true of the same person at the same time, whether or not he is experiencing at the moment any particular emotion (e.g., jealousy, sadness, anxiety, or love). It is easy to see how this state of affairs can lead–and frequently has led–to much confusion and fruitless debate about what emotions *really* are. Indeed, entire "theories" of emotion have been based on the identification of, or the distinction between, emotional episodes, on the one hand, and motives, moods, traits, and/or sentiments, on the other (e.g., Leeper's, 1970, motivational theory of emotion, and Spielberger's, 1966, state-trait theory of anxiety).

Motives

The emotions may be related to motives in two ways: first, an emotion may be said to motivate behavior, and second, an emotion may itself be motivated by broader concerns. The first of these aspects has received considerable attention from psychologists, many of whom have defined emotions as motives or drives. The second aspect–the motives for emotions–has received less attention; but because it is the one most relevant to individual differences in emotional reactivity, it will be emphasized in the present discussion.

An analysis of motivation which is applicable to both the motivating and motivated aspects of emotional behavior has been adumbrated by Chein (1972). He begins by noting that all behavior forms a hierarchy. To use one of Chein's own examples, I am now holding a pencil; this is a subsidiary or low-order response which is embedded in a superordinate act, writing a sentence. Writing a sentence is, in turn, embedded in a still higher-order unit, preparing a chapter on the emotions. According to Chein, a superordinate act can be regarded as the motive for a subsidiary response if the latter is necessary for the completion of the former. Thus, preparing a chapter on the emotions is the motive for writing this sentence, and writing this sentence is the motive for holding the pencil.[7]

In the above sense, all behavior is both motivating (when treated as a superordinate act) and motivated (when treated as a subsidiary response). This is true of emotional as well as nonemotional behaviors. For example, an episode of anger may be considered the motive for a variety of subsidiary responses (e.g., yelling, striking, etc.). But looking upward rather than downward in the behavioral hierarchy, one might also ask, What is the motive (superordinate act) of which the episode of anger is a subsidiary part?

At first, this last question might seem somewhat odd. We are used to thinking of the emotions as though they were self-contained units of behavior. This way of thinking stems from the fact that the emotions, as passions, are ostensibly beyond personal control. However, simply because a response is interpreted as a passion does not mean that it is divorced from the remainder of a person's behavior. This point may be illustrated by several anecdotal examples.

As a class exercise, ten students kept a diary record of each time they became angry or annoyed during a two-week period. At the end of that time, they wrote a brief description of anger based on their experiences. One student, who described himself as "quick to anger," made the following observations:

> Quick to anger persons have found that anger works. Most people dislike displays of temper and cater to such persons to avoid the embarassment or discomfort that such a display would cause. This quick to anger person—in contrast to the "walking bomb" [who inhibits his anger until he "explodes"]—may not be dissatisfied or even very angry, but has found a mode of behavior which is effective.

Another student observed:

> What I now find myself doing when I get angry is stopping and dissecting the situation into definitions, causes, actions, effects, etc. I feel like a psychoanalyst who can't avoid psychoanalyzing everyone he meets. I'm

[7]In referring to motives as acts or behavior, Chein does not mean to imply that motives can be defined solely in terms of bodily reactions. Behavior, as he conceives it, is a unit of analysis which takes into account the transaction between the person and the environment. Thus defined, a motive involves a *system* of potential responses directed toward some object. Another common way of defining motives, and one which also is compatible with the present analysis, is in terms of *dispositions.* Specifically, a motive may be defined as a higher-level disposition to respond in such a way that some objectively definable end-state or goal is likely to be achieved (cf. Atkinson, 1964). For reasons already stated, the frequently held notion that motives—and emotions—as intervening drive or energy variables is not consistent with the present analysis.

> not sure that this academic approach is applicable to studying an emotion, especially for me. My anger is irrational and illogical, and I'm trying to study it in a rational logical manner. By doing this I have undermined my anger's usefulness, because I use anger as a defense mechanism, and now that I realize it, it has become much less effective.

After analyzing their anger, these students came to realize that many of their responses were not so uncontrollable and irrational as they had previously assumed. On the contrary, both students noted the usefulness and effectiveness of their anger in achieving goals which often were only tangentially related to the precipitating incidents.

Similar observations could be made with regard to other emotions. Thus, a Don Juan may repeatedly "fall" in love in the service of his amorous adventures; a bereaved person may grieve, not only over the loss of a loved one, but also for the sympathy it brings; a student may engage in hilarity in order to diminish the threat of an impending exam; and so forth.

In short, any emotional episode can be viewed as part of behavioral hierarchy, and hence as motivated by the broader concerns of the individual. In this respect, the emotions are no different than other forms of behavior. However, there is a sense in which the emotions are special. Throughout this chapter, it has been emphasized that emotional responses are *interpreted* as passions rather than as actions. To interpret something is itself to make a response, and the attribution of emotion may thus be subsidiary to other behaviors. This is most obvious when the attribution is retrospective, as in a series of experiments by Averill, DeWitt, and Zimmer (1978). In these experiments, students were asked to work on some problems which ostensibly were part of a culture-free test of academic ability. The problems were presented together with photographs of mutilated corpses and playboy-like nudes. It was predicted that a photograph would subsequently be evaluated as more emotionally arousing if it were associated with failure than if it were associated with success. This prediction was confirmed. Subjects rated the corpses more disturbing and the nudes more beautiful following failure than following success. This tendency was most marked among subjects who were highly ego-involved in the task.

In the above experiments, it may be assumed that subjects who judged a photograph as more arousing also considered themselves (retrospectively) to have been more aroused by that photograph during the problem-solving task, thus accounting for their failure. Of course, self-attributions which are retrospective on one occasion may become prospective on other occasions. For example, a child who fails on an examination might be told not to feel bad, as he was too nervous and upset to do well. If such comforting advice is internalized, the child may come to apply it to himself on future occasions. In the extreme, he might even adopt the strategy of becoming so nervous *beforehand* that he "blocks" on an examination. Such a strategy would provide an excuse for failure, but at the high cost of precluding success.

In the above examples, the motive for the attribution of emotion was the abnegation of responsibility for failure. Of course, this is not the only motive for interpreting a response as emotional. Emotional attributions also imply a degree of commitment and sincerity that makes them useful in many situations. Interpreting a response as emotional is, in a sense, like offering a guarantee; it implies that there will be an appropriate follow-through. And it should go without saying that each emotional syndrome (anger, grief, love, fear, hope, disgust, etc.) has its own meaning which helps determine the motives that it may subserve.

These brief observations on the purposive and defensive use of emotional reactions should not lead to cynicism. They are meant only to illustrate one of the factors–motivation–which must be taken into consideration when trying to account for individual differences in emotional reactivity. During the normal course of socialization, the child (and adult) learns both how to respond and how to interpret the response in an appropriate fashion.[8] In this way, individual motives are made consonant with social norms. And when they are not consonant (as in the case of a crime of passion, a Don Juan, or a student who continually "blocks" on an exam), the attribution of emotion may be disallowed and/or the response punished. But socialization is never complete, and even if it were, social norms only set broad and vaguely defined limits on behavior. There is thus considerable latitude for individual differences in motivation to influence who will and will not become emotional on any given occasion.

Moods

Everyone knows what it is like to be in a happy, irritable, or depressed mood, and how this may affect emotional reactivity. But what is a mood? There is no simple answer to this question. Some theorists attach profound significance to moods. For example, the existentialist philosopher Heidegger (1927) suggests that a person's mood reflects his mode of "being-in-the-world" or *Dasein.* On a less grandiose–but still somewhat grand level–the psychoanalyst Jacobson (1957) argues that a mood represents "a cross section through the ego, lending a particular, uniform coloring to all its manifestations for a longer or shorter period of time" (p. 75). She further contends that moods serve a useful, though primitive, function by allowing a repetitive affective discharge on a wide variety of objects. Such a prolonged discharge supposedly allows the release of psychic energy to proceed in conjunction with reality testing, rather than in a dangerous, explosive fashion.

[8]In order to prevent misunderstanding, it should again be emphasized that there is a close dialectical relationship between a response and its interpretation; that is, each helps determine the other. This issue was discussed earlier in connection with the interpretation of emotional roles. Here, as in that earlier discussion, the distinction between a response and its interpretation is made primarily for analytical purposes.

Although formulations such as the above provide some indication of the importance of moods, they are not very meaningful when taken out of their respective theoretical contexts. For our purposes, a more limited and theoretically neutral definition of mood is required. Succinctly put, a mood is a temporary state which predisposes the individual to repond in a certain way. Expressed in terms of the role-model outlined earlier, it might be said that a mood facilitates or hinders involvement in a given emotional role. (Of course, not all moods refer to affective states; but our concern is only with those that do.)

As the above definition implies, the explanation of behavior by reference to a mood indicates that the response in question is in keeping with a temporary but somewhat unusual state of the individual. For example, to say that John became angry because he was in an irritable mood suggests that John would *not ordinarily* have become angry in such a situation. However, John has been short-tempered all morning, and his anger is consistent with the remainder of his behavior during this period. In many everyday contexts, such an explanation often settles the matter. In fact, reference to a mood may sometimes be made explicitly to stop further inquiry ("I don't know why I did it; I was just in a bad mood"). From a psychological point of view, however, reference to a mood is typically only the beginning rather than the end of the inquiry. What still must be explained is the presence of the mood.

Moods may be induced in a great variety of ways. A mood may be the product of naturally occurring bodily changes, especially on the part of the endocrine system (e.g., premenstrual irritability and depression). A wide variety of drugs may also affect mood, including the caffein in coffee, the nicotine in cigarettes, the alcohol in liquor, not to mention such less common (but still prevalent) drugs as marihuana, barbiturates, tranquilizers, and amphetamines. Moods also may be altered by such general environmental factors as temperature, humidity, noise level, the presence or absence of other people, the color and shape of the room, to mention but a few of the more obvious variables. The good and bad things which happen to a person, such as receiving a surprise gift or unpleasant news, can also affect mood. Even our memories influence our moods. In fact, one of the most frequently used ways of inducing a mood in the laboratory is to ask subjects to recall some happy (or sad, infuriating, etc.) event of the past.

In many cases, the factors responsible for an individual being in a particular mood are obvious, or at least easily determined. In other cases, the responsible factors may be unknown. But even in the latter cases, knowledge of a person's mood may allow us to predict (if not explain) behavior. This is true in the laboratory as well as in everyday affairs. For example, Zuckerman (1976) has summarized a number of studies indicating that moods are better predictors of behavior than are, say, personality traits. This suggests that even when we do not know the origins of moods or understand the mechanisms by which they exert their effects, it may still be possible to discover lawful relationships between moods and other forms of behavior on a molar level of analysis.

The reader who is interested in investigating the relationship between mood and behavior should consult Nowlis (1965, 1970) and Cattell (1973) for information regarding assessment. In concluding this brief discussion of mood, I would simply like to add a cautionary note. In the past, there has been a tendency to underestimate the importance of mood as a determinant of individual differences in reactivity. However, one must also be careful not to *over*interpret the influence and significance of moods. The changes in mood which accompany the premenstrual phase of a woman's cycle are a case in point. Such mood changes probably have no functional significance in their own right; moreover, they do not ordinarily influence performance on cognitive and behavioral tasks, especially if the woman is aware of their source (Golub, 1976; Rodin, 1976).

Traits

Conceptually, traits are in many respects like moods. But whereas moods are short-term dispositions to respond, traits are long-term or enduring characteristics of the individual. Gordon Allport, who until his death in 1967 might be considered the dean of American personality theorists, regarded traits as the natural unit of analysis for the study of persons. He defined a trait as *"a generalized and focalized neuropsychic system (peculiar to the individual), with the capacity to render many stimuli functionally equivalent, and to initiate and guide consistent (equivalent) forms of adaptive and expressive behavior"* (1937, p. 292). Many contemporary personality theorists (e.g., Cattell, 1965; Eysenck, 1967) would tend to agree with Allport's definition, at least as it concerns basic or "source" traits. There are other theorists, however, who believe that traits exist primarily in the mind of the observer—that they are a kind of fiction or myth imposed upon the individual—and hence that traits can have little predictive or explanatory value (Mischel, 1968; Jones & Nisbett, 1971). Still other psychologists, including some of those most heavily involved in test construction and use (e.g., Gough, 1969; Hogan, DeSoto, & Solano, 1977), take a more neutral stand on the issue. They note that tests can be constructed and used for predictive purposes without making assumptions regarding underlying mechanisms.

There is not space here to go into the details of this debate regarding the ontological status and usefulness of trait concepts. Suffice it to say that there are no logical grounds for excluding personality traits (or dispositional variables in general) as explanatory constructs (Averill, 1973). Moreover, there is increasing empirical evidence (e.g., Block, 1977; Epstein, 1979; McGowan & Gormly, 1976) for *stable* personality differences in emotional responsivity. To demonstrate such stability, however, two conditions must be met. First, the criterion variable must be sampled adequately. That is, the relationship between a trait-measure of hostility, say, and a single instance of anger may be low; on the other hand, the relationship between the trait-measure and behavior averaged over time may be quite high.

The second and theoretically more interesting issue has to do with how personality traits are conceptualized and measured. In general, ability traits (such as intelligence) have shown a much higher correlation with criterion variables than have emotional traits. Wallace (1966) has suggested that this may be due, in part, to the way these two kinds of traits are measured. In the case of abilities, test items are usually clear, the subject knows what is expected, and he is asked to respond as best he can. In the case of emotional traits, the questions are often ambiguous (in projective tests, especially), the subject is told there are no "correct" answers, and he is asked to indicate how he usually or typically responds (as opposed to how capable he is of responding if he tried hardest). Wallace suggested that if emotional traits were conceptualized and measured in the same manner as abilities, then the relationship between personality tests and behavior might be correspondingly increased. In line with this suggestion, Willerman, Turner, and Peterson (1976) asked subjects to describe how capable they were of responding to an emotional situation (i.e., to describe their maximal possible, rather than usual, response). Such descriptions proved to be better predictors of emotional behavior than did more traditional tests of emotional traits.

At first, it might seem somewhat strange to conceptualize emotional traits as abilities. This strangeness stems, in part, from the fact that the emotions are interpreted as passions (as something which happens to us), rather than as actions (as something we do). It is more natural to speak of susceptibilities in the case of passion, and of abilities in the case of actions. However, if the analysis of emotion offered in the preceding sections has any validity, then the emotions are also things we do, and, hence, abilities are as important for emotional reactions as for other forms of behavior.[9]

The question which logically follows from the above considerations is, What kinds of abilities are important for emotional responsivity? Factor-analytic studies of personality traits have typically yielded a broad dimension that has variously been called "emotionality," "neuroticism," or "anxiety." This suggests that there may be a general ability to become emotional, analogous to general intelligence in the cognitive domain. Additional support for such a notion comes from the study of psychopaths, who are, in a sense, emotional imbeciles. The psychopath, in the words of Cleckley (1964), "fails to know all those more

[9]I do not wish to imply that emotional reactions are not often the result of an *inability* to cope with a situation. However, an inability is never absolute. The person with a low IQ must still have some ability to solve whatever problems he can. Similarly, the experience of fear, say, presupposes certain abilities as well as weaknesses. "Fools rush in . . . ."

serious and deeply moving affective states which make up the tragedy and triumph of ordinary life, of life at the level of important human experience." Cleckley goes on to note that "such capacities [for emotional experience] vary widely, of course, among normal people and are perhaps proportionate to the general personality development, or, in a far-reaching sense, to true cultural level" (p. 409).

But before we accept the notion of a general emotional ability or capacity, two facts should be noted. First, most situations do not require a great deal of involvement in emotional roles. Nearly everyone, even psychopaths, have the capacity to enter into emotional roles with at least some degree of involvement. Second, a general emotional ability, if it exists, is not sufficient for the enactment of specific emotional roles. This is because each emotion places unique demands upon the individual. Anger, for example, requires skills different from those involved in romantic love or grief.

Pursuing this last line of reasoning even further, it may be said that any given emotion requires a variety of different abilities (either in addition to, or as components of, a more general emotional capability). Thus, to become angry, a person must be able to appraise situations as provocative and to respond accordingly. This distinction between appraisal and response capabilities is often recognized in ordinary language. A trait such as "hostility," for example, refers primarily to the appraisal side of the emotional syndrome, while a trait such as "aggressiveness" refers primarily to response characteristics. Knowledge of both kinds of traits is important for the prediction of behavior.

To complicate matters even further, a third kind of trait or ability is relevant to emotional reactivity. This kind has to do with the cognitive processes that intervene between the appraisal of an emotional stimulus and the response output. The use of "defense mechanisms" (e.g., repression, projection, sublimation, etc.) falls into this category. Within psychoanalytic theory, the defense mechanisms are ways of coping with threat, for example, by avoidant thinking and selective attention (repression), displacing the danger onto another source (projection), transforming the danger into its opposite (reaction formation), retreating to an earlier mode of coping (regression), and so forth. As these descriptions suggest, defense mechanisms are extensions of common cognitive processes. We all, for example, tend to avoid thinking about unpleasant events, and focus our attention instead on more comforting aspects of a situation. In the case of repression, such cognitive responses have simply become compulsive, rigid, and reality distorting. Defense mechanisms are not just defensive, however. When the "danger" being defended against represents some unacceptable impulse on the part of the individual (e.g., sexual or aggressive desires), then the defense may also provide gratification by subterfuge. For example, through projection and reaction formation, a person may engage in a fight against obscenity which allows—even requires—him to view every new pornographic film that arrives in town. Such a feat obviously requires a good deal of intellectual dexterity.

To summarize briefly, emotional traits involve the ability to perceive, think, and respond in certain ways. The actual emotional response displayed by an individual is determined by a combination of such traits in interaction with situational variables and other personal dispositions (e.g., motives and moods). For example, the character of Uriah Heep in Dickens's novel *David Copperfield* could be described in terms of such traits as hostility, timidity, and reaction formation. Uriah was continually seeing wrongdoing where none existed, and he interpreted even kindly gestures as personal affronts; at the same time, he was too timid to express anger, for fear of reprisal. When threatened, he frequently responded with humility, but it was a humility that barely masked a display of aggression.

The above example illustrates how a combination of traits helps to account for the emotional life of a person such as Uriah Heep. But yet another kind of predisposition must still be added if we are to account for individual differences in emotional reactivity.

Sentiments

Consider two Uriah Heeps, both of whom are equally hostile, timid, and prone to use similar defense mechanisms. One might be a super-patriot and the other a confirmed revolutionary; hence, events that would make the former rejoice might make the latter furious. The characteristic that distinguishes these two individuals is not any trait but, rather, their sentiments—that is, the way their emotional tendencies are organized with respect to certain objects. In a way, sentiments are to emotional traits what interests are to intellectual traits.

Sentiments may vary greatly in their degree of complexity. The simplest kind of sentiment is one where a single emotional response is associated with a single object. Fear of a domineering parent would be a case in point. Such a sentiment might develop in complexity as the object becomes associated, perhaps under different circumstances, with a variety of different response tendencies. Thus, if the feared object (e.g., a domineering parent) is also the source of affection and security, the sentiment might develop into one of reverence.

A sentiment may also become more complex through elaboration or differentiation of the object, as when reverence for a parent is extended to one's forefathers, clan, or nation. In this way, the objects of sentiments may range from the very concrete (a specific person or object) to the highly abstract (an idea or value).

When the object is abstract, certain sentiments may be shared by a large number of people within a given society. Using factor-analytic techniques, Cattell and Child (1975, p. 46) have identified 27 common sentiments within our own society.[10] The most important of these center about a person's profession, home (family), spouse (sweetheart), religion, superego, and self. Although these sentiments are identified primarily in terms of the objects involved, the relevant response tendencies are intuitively obvious. Only the meanings of the superego sentiment and self-sentiment require brief elaboration. The superego sentiment reflects a person's attitudes toward moral values or ideals. Of course, a person need not—and seldom does—live up to these ideals, and hence there typically is a discrepancy between the superego and self-sentiment. The latter is defined primarily by attitudes and responses designed to maintain the person's physical, psychological, and social well-being. We shall have more to say about the self-sentiment shortly.

As defined above, sentiments reflect the way emotional responses are *organized* about particular objects. However, sentiments can also be a source of conflict or disorganization, as when the sentiment toward one's profession conflicts with the sentiment toward one's family, or when there is a marked discrepancy between one's superego sentiment and self-sentiment.

The conflict resulting from incompatible sentiments has been especially emphasized by psychoanalytic writers. Within psychoanalysis and related disciplines, the term *complex* is typically used instead of *sentiment*, but the idea is basically the same. The Oedipal complex postulated by Freud, for example, describes the way a child's emotional life is structured around the opposite-sexed parent; and the inferiority complex popularized by Adler represents a person's attitudes and responses toward his own (presumed) inadequacies.

Jung, even more than Freud, did much to stimulate interest in emotional complexes. Jung (1948/1960) defined a complex as "the *image* of a certain psychic situation which is strongly accentuated emotionally and is, moreover, incompatible with the habitual attitude of consciousness" (p. 96). In noting the incompatibility of complexes with the "habitual attitude of consciousness," Jung emphasized the tendency for behavior to become organized about the images (or objects) of complexes, much like iron filings become organized around the poles of a magnet. In extreme cases, this can result in a dissociation of consciousness, or a split personality. In fact, Jung referred to complexes as

[10] In applying factor analysis to the problem of the sentiments, Cattell begins by assessing the attitudes of people toward a variety of common objects, activities, and social institutions. These attitudes are then intercorrelated. When a number of attitudes co-vary in a systematic fashion, they are said to represent an underlying "factor" or, in this case, a sentiment. For example, attitudes toward God, organized religion, and certain social practices (e.g., regarding birth control) tend to be correlated with one another and hence define a factor which Cattell calls the "religious sentiment."

"splinter psyches." This is an apt phrase, for it emphasizes both the integrative and divisive nature of emotional sentiments and complexes.[11]

People are sometimes known by the sentiments that dominate their lives. A religious fanatic, for example, may sustain for years an unending round of activities directed toward the object of veneration; the "homebody," by contrast, directs an inordinate amount of attention toward his family. Of all the sentiments, the one that dominates the life of most persons is the self-sentiment. An enhancement of the self leads to joy; a diminution of the self is a source of sadness; an offense against the self is a provocation to anger; and a threat to the self is an occasion for fear. But what is the self? This is a question that has long plagued psychologists, and no satisfactory answer can be given here. Suffice it to say that the self is an abstract object, an inference based on knowledge of one's own physical and mental assets, of past actions and accomplishments, and of the reactions of others toward us. Epstein (Chapter 3) has likened the self to a theory. The analogy is appropriate. Like any theory, a person's self-concept may be poorly or well articulated, its scope may be narrow or broad, and its basic assumptions may be discrepant or unified. Be that as it may, as the object of a kind of "master sentiment," the self provides the focal point about which much of a person's emotional life is organized. Hence, if we wish to understand individual differences in emotional reactivity, we must first of all understand how a person conceives of his own self.

Summary

This brief discussion of motives, moods, traits, and sentiments (complexes) has been primarily descriptive rather than theoretical. Its major purpose has been to illustrate the kinds of variables that psychologists have traditionally used—and undoubtedly will continue to use—to explain and predict individual differences in emotional reactivity.

The immediate situation is the most important determinant of whether or not an emotion will be elicited and, if so, which emotion it will be. Some theorists would therefore like to place all the burden of explanation for individual differences on the person's appraisal of the situation and/or on the past history of reinforcement in similar situations. However, outside of an intimate friendship, or a clinical setting, we are seldom in a position to specify with any confidence the beliefs and attitudes on which a person's appraisals are

[11] Jung searched for complexes not only on the individual, but also on the species level. The latter, he suggested, are the inherited residue of remote human experiences, and they form part of our "collective unconscious." Speculating further, Jung suggested that these universal complexes are centered on certain ideas or "archetypes" which appear to have special significance for human beings—for example, because they have to do with universally important events in almost any human's life (such as birth, puberty, and death). These archetypes presumably can be recognized in the myths and religions of most—if not all—cultures.

based, or the history of reinforcement that would lead to an emotional response in any given situation. In view of this, descriptions in terms of motives, moods, traits, and sentiments may serve as useful halfway stations between ignorance and understanding. That is, knowledge of a person's motives, moods, and so forth, may allow a great deal of prediction and control in a practical sense, but the question may still be asked, How was the disposition acquired and by what mechanisms (e.g., cognitive and physiological) does it influence behavior? Until we can answer this last question, we do not have true understanding.

CONCLUDING OBSERVATIONS

This chapter has been divided into five sections: theories of emotion, the nature of emotion, a role-model of emotion, kinds of emotion, and individual differences in emotional reactivity. Since each section has been accompanied by its own summary, no attempt will be made here to review again the contents of the chapter. Rather, these concluding observations will be limited to a few comments on how the present analysis relates to other approaches to the study of emotion.

Generally speaking, there are three main types of scientific inquiry. The first type, epitomized by taxonomy, is concerned primarily with the description and classification of phenomena. The second type, represented by much of classical mechanics, searches for the causes of events. These first two types of inquiry are applicable to all phenomena, inanimate as well as animate. The third type of inquiry is limited primarily to the human sciences. It attempts to explain behavior, not in terms of mechanisms or causes, but by showing how the behavior in question conforms to certain rules or standards of conduct.

With regard to the first type of inquiry, many theories of emotion represent little more than attempts at description and classification. This is true, for example, of Wundt's (1897) famous tridimensional theory, which attempted to classify all emotions in terms of the three dimensions of pleasantness-unpleasantness, excitement-depression, and strain-relaxation (for modern extensions of this theory, see Osgood, May, & Miron, 1975; Russell & Mehrabian, 1977; Schlosberg, 1954). Suggestions, such as that by Wenger (1950), that emotions be regarded as patterns of physiological activity can also be viewed as proposals for description and classification.

In the present chapter, the section on the nature of emotion was concerned primarily with the criteria for describing and classifying the emotions. In that section, the emotions were distinguished from other psychological phenomena in terms of three characteristics; namely, emotions are (a) socially constituted syndromes that are (b) based on cognitive appraisals and (c) interpreted as passions rather than as actions. In an expanded discussion, these three criteria could be used as the basis for a classification scheme. Thus, emotions could be contrasted in terms of their symptomatic expression, the appraised object, and/or the reasons why a response is interpreted as a passion. Based on this last criterion, a threefold distinction among impulsive, conflictive, and transcendental emotions was presented in the section on kinds of emotion. Any finer classification would, however, have to take into account the first two criteria, that is, the symptomatic expression of emotion and the appraised object (especially the latter).

The second type of scientific inquiry mentioned above has to do with the analysis of causal mechanisms. Among traditional theories of emotion, causal analyses have taken three forms: historical, dispositional, and mechanistic. These three types of causal analyses are not independent. For example, historical analyses refer to events which occurred during the evolution (development) of the species, the society, and/or the individual. Such historical events result in dispositions on the part of persons to respond when appropriately stimulated. Of course, dispositional variables do not "cause" behavior in the ordinary sense. Rather, they exert their influence through underlying cognitive and/or physiological mechanisms.

In the present chapter, relatively little attention has been devoted to the analysis of historical causes, although the general thrust of the argument has been to highlight the importance of social as well as biological evolution in the development of standard emotional syndromes. With regard to the analysis of emotional dispositions, the identification and assessment of motives, moods, traits, and sentiments has been a traditional concern of personality psychologists; and that concern is reflected in the section on individual differences in emotional reactivity. When we turn from molar dispositions to underlying mechanisms, it may seem that there is a gap in the present analysis. Aside from an emphasis on the appraisal of emotional objects and the interpretation of emotional roles, relatively little has been said about the cognitive and physiological mechanisms which mediate emotional behavior. But this gap merely reflects the belief that the emotions depend upon the same mechanisms (i.e., in terms of perception, memory, attention, symbolization, etc.) as do other forms of behavior. An analysis of causal mechanisms would thus encompass much of psychology—or, at least, it would far exceed the compass of this chapter.

This brings us to the third type of scientific inquiry mentioned above, namely, the explanation of behavior in terms of rules or standards of conduct. The section on a role-model of emotional behavior represented an attempt to explain the emotions from a dramaturgical standpoint. Within such a theoretical framework, emotional syndromes are analyzed as transitory social roles. This type of analysis has two major implications. First, to explain the individual's own experience of emotion, we must consider (a) how he interprets (understands) the emotional role and (b) how he monitors his own performance. The experience of emotion is a product of these two processes, together with the individual's involvement in the role. Second, to understand the meaning of emotion in general, we must consider how emotional roles fit into the broader "drama" represented by society. The section on kinds of emotions touched upon this issue. In it, we described three ways in which emotional roles may relate to the social system as a whole, as well as to the self-system of the individual. These three ways help define the three classes of emotion mentioned earlier, namely, impulsive, conflictive, and transcendental.

It is obvious that there is still much that has not been covered in this chapter. We have not, for example, discussed whole topics that are often included under the rubric of emotion–such as undifferentiated stress and arousal, feelings of pleasure and pain which accompany simple sensory stimulation, among others. Our concern has been primarily with specific emotional syndromes recognized and named within a given culture, such as grief, anger, and romantic love within our own society, *amae* in Japan, and "being a wild pig" among the Gururumba.

Even with the above limitation in scope, the present analysis has necessarily been sketchy, but hopefully not oversimplified. If there has been one central theme to the chapter, it has been this: the emotions are passions. But the passions are not, as the word implies, something we suffer. Rather, the emotions are something we do; they are responses which we make, but for which we do not–or cannot–accept full responsibility. The reason we cannot accept responsibility is different for each emotion. But for the most part, it has to do with the functions the emotions play within the social system. The emotions are among the roles societies create and individuals enact, seldom realizing their full significance.

REFERENCES

Allport, G. *Personality: A psychological interpretation.* New York: Henry Holt, 1937.

____ **& Odbert, H. S.** Trait-names: A psycho-lexical study. *Psychological Monographs,* 1936, *47* (1, whole No. 211).

Anastasi, A., Cohen, N. & Spatz, D. A study of fear and anger in college students through the controlled diary method. *Journal of Genetic Psychology,* 1948, *73,* 243-249.

Arnold, M. B. *Emotion and personality.* New York: Columbia University Press, 1960. 2 Vols.

Atkinson, J. W. *An introduction to motivation.* Princeton, N.J.: Van Nostrand, 1964.

Averill, J. R. Grief: Its nature and significance. *Psychological Bulletin,* 1968, *70,* 721-748.

———. The dis-position of psychological dispositions. *Journal of Experimental Research in Personality,* 1973, *6,* 275-282.

———. An analysis of psychophysiological symbolism and its influence on theories of emotion. *Journal for the Theory of Social Behavior,* 1974, *4,* 147-190.

———. A semantic atlas of emotional concepts. J.S.A.S. *Catalogue of Selected Documents in Psychology,* 1975, *5,* 330 (Ms. No. 421).

———. Emotion and anxiety: Socio-cultural, biological, and psychological determinants. In M. Zuckerman & C. D. Spielberger (Eds.), *Emotion and anxiety: New concepts, methods and applications.* New York: LEA-John Wiley, 1976.

———. A constructionist view of emotion. In R. Plutchik & H. Kellerman (Eds.), *Theories of emotion.* New York: Academic Press, 1979a, in press.

———. The functions of grief. In C. Izard (Ed.), *Emotions in personality and psychopathology.* New York: Plenum Press, 1979b.

———. Anger. In H. Howe & R. Dienstbier (Eds.), *Nebraska symposium on motivation:* 1978. Lincoln, Neb.: University of Nebraska Press, 1979c, in press.

———, & **Boothroyd, P.** On falling in love in conformance with the romantic ideal. *Motivation and Emotion,* 1977, *1,* 235-247.

———, **DeWitt, G. & Zimmer, M.** The self-attribution of emotion as a function of success and failure. *Journal of Personality,* 1978, *46,* 323-347.

Bandler, R. J., Jr., Madaras, G. R., & Bem, D. J. Self-observation as a source of pain perception. *Journal of Personality and Social Psychology,* 1968, *9,* 205-209.

Becker, E. *Angel in armor.* New York: Braziller, 1969.

Beigel, H. G. Romantic love. *American Sociological Review,* 1951, *16,* 327-335.

Bem, D. J. Self-perception theory. In L. Berkowitz (Ed.), *Advances in experimental social psychology,* Vol. 6. New York: Academic Press, 1972.

Bourgue, L. B., & Back, K. W. Language, society, and subjective experience. *Sociometry,* 1971, *34,* 1-21.

Bowlby, J. *Attachment and loss. Vol. 1: Attachment.* New York: Basic Books, 1969.

Brown, J. S. *The motivation of behavior.* New York: McGraw-Hill, 1961.

Bull, N. The attitude theory of emotion. *Nervous and mental diseases monographs* (No. 81). New York: Collidge Foundation, 1951.

Burgess, E. W., & Wallin, P. *Engagement and marriage.* Philadelphia: Lippincott, 1953.

Calvert-Boyanowsky, J., & Leventhal, H. The role of information in behavioral responses to stress: A reinterpretation of the misattribution phenomenon. *Journal of Personality and Social Psychology,* 1975, *32,* 214-221.

Cannon, W. B. *Bodily changes in pain, hunger, fear, and rage* (2nd ed.). New York: Appleton, 1929.

Cattell, R. B. *The scientific analysis of personality.* Baltimore: Penguin Books, 1965.

____. *Personality and mood by questionnaire.* San Francisco: Jossey-Bass, 1973.

____, **& Child, D.** *Motivation and dynamic structure.* New York: John Wiley & Sons, 1975.

Chein, I. *The science of behavior and the image of man.* New York: Basic Books, 1972.

Cleckley, H. *The mask of sanity* (4th ed.). St. Louis: C.V. Mosby, 1964.

Corah, N. L., & Boffa, J. Perceived control, self-observation, and response of aversive stimulation. *Journal of Personality and Social Psychology,* 1970, *16,* 1-4.

Doi, T. *The anatomy of dependence.* Tokyo: Kodansha International, 1973.

Durkheim, E. *The elementary forms of religious experience.* New York: Macmillan, 1915.

Edwards, C. *The Stanislavsky heritage.* New York: New York University Press, 1965.

Epstein, S. The stability of personality: On predicting most of the people much of the time. *Journal of Personality and Social Psychology,* 1979, in press.

Eysenck, H. J. *The biological basis of personality.* Springfield, Ill.: Charles C Thomas, 1967.

Gagnon, J. H. Scripts and the coordination of sexual conduct. In J. K. Cole & R. Dienstbier (Eds.), *Nebraska symposium on motivation:* 1973. Lincoln, Neb.: University of Nebraska Press, 1974.

Goldstein, K. *The organism: A holistic approach to biology.* New York: American Book Co., 1939.

____. On emotions: Considerations from the organismic point of view. *Journal of Psychology,* 151, *31,* 37-49.

Golub, S. The effect of premenstrual anxiety and depression on cognitive function. *Journal of Personality and Social Psychology,* 1976, *34,* 99-104.

Goode, W. J. The theoretical importance of love. *American Sociological Review,* 1959, *24,* 38-47.

Gough, H. G. *Manual for the California Psychological Inventory* (rev. ed.). Palo Alto, Calif.: Consulting Psychologists Press, 1969.

Greeley, A. M. *Ecstasy: A way of knowing.* Englewood Cliffs, N.J.: Prentice-Hall, 1974.

Greenfield, S. M. Love and marriage in modern America: A functional analysis. *Sociological Quarterly,* 1965, *6,* 361-377.

Harré, R., & Secord, P. F. *The explanation of social behavior.* Totowa, N.J.: Rowman & Littlefield, 1972.

Heidegger, M. *Being and time.* New York: Harper, 1962. (Originally published, 1927).

Hodgson, J., & Richards, E. *Improvisation.* London: Eyre Methuen, 1974.

Hogan, R., DeSoto, C. B., & Solano, C. Traits, tests, and personality research. *American Psychologist,* 1977, *32,* 255-264.

Hohman, G. W. Some effects of spinal cord lessions on experienced emotional feelings. *Psychophysiology,* 1966, *3,* 143-156.

Homans, G. C. Anxiety and ritual: The theories of Malinowski and Radcliffe-Brown. *American Anthropologist,* 1941, *43,* 164-173.

Jacobson, E. Normal and pathological moods: Their nature and functions. *Psychoanalytic study of the child.* Vol. XIV. New York: International Univer-sities Press, 1957.

James, W. *Principles of psychology,* 2 vols. New York: Henry Holt, 1890.

——. *Varieties of religious experience.* New York: Longmans, Green & Co., 1902.

Jaynes, J. *The origin of consciousness in the breakdown of the bicameral mind.* Boston: Houghton Mifflin, 1976.

Jones, E. E., & Nisbett, R. E. *The actor and the observer: Divergent perceptions of the causes of behavior.* New York: General Learning Press, 1971.

Jung, C. G. A review of the complex theory. In *The collected works of Carl G. Jung. Vol. 8. The structure and dynamics of the psyche.* New York: Pantheon Books, 1960. (Originally published, 1948.)

Kirschner, L. A. Dissociative reactions: An historical review and clinical study. *Acta Psychiatrica Scandinavica,* 1973, *49,* 698-711.

Laird, J. D. Self-attribution of emotion: The effects of expressive behavior on the quality of emotional experience. *Journal of Personality and Social Psychology,* 1974, *29,* 475-486.

Landis, C., & Meltler, F. A. *Varieties of psychopathological experience.* New York: Holt, Rinehart & Winston, 1964.

Lange, C. The emotions. In C. G. Lange & W. James, *The emotions.* Baltimore: Williams & Wilkins, 1922. (Originally published 1885.)

Langness, L. L. Hysterical psychosis in the New Guinea highlands: A Bena Bena example. *Psychiatry,* 1965, *28,* 258-277.

Lazarus, R. S. *Psychological stress and the coping process.* New York: McGraw-Hill, 1966.

——. Emotions and adaptation: Conceptual and empirical relations. In W. Arnold (Ed.), *Nebraska symposium on motivation*: 1958. Lincoln, Neb.: University of Nebraska Press, 1968.

Leeper, R. W. The motivational perceptual properties of emotions as indicating their fundamental character and role. In M. B. Arnold (Ed.), *Feelings and emotions: The Loyola symposium.* New York: Academic Press, 1970.

Levinger, G., & Raush, H. *Close relationships: Perspectives on the meaning of intimacy.* Amherst, Mass.: University of Massachusetts Press, 1977.

Lewis, C. S. *A grief observed.* London: Faber & Faber, 1961.

Linton, R. *The study of mean.* New York: Appleton, 1936.

Lipowski, Z. J. Psychosomatic medicine in the seventies: An overview. *American Journal of Psychiatry,* 1977, *134,* 233-244.

Lundsgaarde, H. P. *Murder in space city.* New York: Oxford University Press, 1977.

McDougall, W. *An introduction to social psychology.* (23rd ed.). London: Methuen, 1936.

McKellar, P. The emotion of anger in the expression of human aggressiveness. *British Journal of Psychology,* 1949, *39,* 148-155.

____. Provocation to anger and the development of attitudes of hostility. *British Journal of Psychology,* 1950, *40,* 104-114.

Mandelbaum, D. G. Social uses of funeral rites. In H. Feifel (Ed.), *The meaning of death.* New York: McGraw-Hill, 1959.

Marris, P. *Loss and change.* Garden City, N.Y.: Anchor Press/Doubleday, 1975.

Maslow, A. H. *The farther reaches of human nature.* New York: Viking, 1971.

Meltzer, H. Students' adjustments in anger. *Journal of Social Psychology,* 1933, *4,* 285-309.

Mischel, W. *Personality and assessment.* New York: Wiley, 1968.

Moore, S. *Stanislavski today.* New York: American Center for Stanislavski Theatre Art, 1973.

Murstein, B. I. *Love, sex, and marriage through the ages.* New York: Springer, 1974.

Newman, P. L. "Wild man" behavior in a New Guinea highlands community. *American Anthropologist,* 1964, *66,* 1-19.

Nisbett, R. E., & Schachter, S. Cognitive manipulation of pain. *Journal of Experimental Social Psychology,* 1966, *2,* 227-236.

Nowlis, V. Research with the mood adjective check list. In S. S. Tompkins & C. Izard (Eds.), *Affect, cognition and personality.* New York: Springer, 1965.

____. Mood: Behavior and experience. In M. B. Arnold (Ed.), *Feelings and emotions: The Loyola Symposium.* New York: Academic Press, 1970.

Osgood, C. E., May, W. H., & Miron, M. S. *Cross-cultural universals of affective meaning.* Urbana, Ill.: University of Illinois Press, 1975.

Otto, H. A. (Ed.). *Love today.* New York: Association Press, 1972.

Parkes, C. M. *Bereavement: Studies of grief in adult life.* London: Tavistock Publications, 1972.

Rodin, J. Menstruation, reattribution, and competence. *Journal of Personality and Social Psychology,* 1976, *33,* 345-353.

Rosenblatt, P. C., Walsh, R. P., & Jackson, D. A. *Grief and mourning in cross-cultural perspective.* New Haven: HRAF Press, 1976.

Rubin, Z. *Liking and loving: An invitation to social psychology.* New York: Holt, Rinehart, & Winston, 1973.

Russell, J. A. Evidence for a three-factor theory of emotions. *Journal of Research in Personality,* 1977, *11,* 273-294.

Ryle, G. *The concept of mind.* London: Hutchinson, 1949.

Salisbury, R. Possession on the New Guinea highlands: Review of literature. *Transcultural Psychiatric Research,* 1966, *3,* 103-108.

____. (Reply to L. L. Langness). *Transcultural Psychiatric Research,* 1967, *4,* 130-134.

Sartre, J. P. *The emotions: Outline of a theory.* New York: Philosophical Library, 1948.

Schachter, S. The interaction of cognitive and physiological determinants of emotional state. In L. Berkowitz (Ed.), *Advances in experimental social psycology.* Vol. 1. New York: Academic Press, 1964.

____. *Emotion, obesity, and crime.* New York: Academic Press, 1971.

____, **& Rodin, J.** *Obese humans and rats.* Hillsdale, N.J.: Lawrence Erlbaum Associates, 1974.

____, **& Singer, J. E.** Cognitive, social, and physiological determinants of emotional state. *Psychological Review,* 1962, *69,* 379-399.

Schafer, R. *A new language for psychoanalysis.* New Haven: Yale University Press, 1976.

Schlosberg, H. Three dimensions of emotion. *Psychological Review,* 1954, *61,* 81-88.

Schoeck, H. *Envy: A theory of social behavior.* New York: Harcourt, Brace & World, 1969.

Segall, A. The sick role concept: Understanding illness behavior. *Journal of Health and Social Behavior,* 1976, *17,* 162-169.

Seneca. On anger. In J. W. Basore (Trans.), *Moral essays.* Cambridge, Mass.: Harvard University Press, 1963. (Originally written about A.D. 40-50.)

Simon, W. The social, the erotic, and the sensual: The complexities of sexual scripts. In J. K. Cole and R. Dienstbier (Eds.), *Nebraska symposium on motivation:* 1973. Lincoln, Neb.: University of Nebraska Press, 1974.

Skinner, B. F. *Science and human behavior.* New York: Macmillan, 1953.

____. *Beyond freedom and dignity.* New York: Knopf, 1971.

____. *About behaviorism.* New York: Knopf, 1974.

Solomon, R. C. *The passions.* Garden City, N.Y.: Doubleday Anchor, 1976.

Spielberger, C. D. Theory and research on anxiety. In C. D. Spielberger (Ed.), *Anxiety and behavior.* New York: Academic Press, 1966.

Spiro, M. E. Religious systems as culturally constituted defense mechanisms. In M. E. Spiro (Ed.), *Context and meaning in cultural anthropology.* New York: Macmillan, 1965.

Stanislavski, C. *An actor prepares.* New York: Theatre Arts Books, 1936.

Stratton, G. M. *Anger: Its religious and moral significance.* New York: Macmillan, 1923.

Wallace, J. An abilities conception of personality: Some implications for personality measurement. *American Psychologist,* 1966, *21,* 132-138.

Wenger, M. A. Emotions as visceral action: An extension of Lange's theory. In M. L. Reymert (Ed.), *Feelings and emotions: The Mooseheart symposium.* New York: McGraw-Hill, 1950.

Willerman, L., Turner, R. G., & Peterson, M. A comparison of the predictive validity of typical and maximal personality measures. *Journal of Research in Personality,* 1976, *10,* 482-492.

Wilson, E. O. *Sociobiology: The new synthesis.* Cambridge, Mass.: Harvard University Press, 1975.

Wolfgang, M. D. *Patterns of criminal homicide.* Philadelphia: University of Pennsylvania Press, 1958.

Wundt, W. *Outlines of psychology.* New York: Gustav E. Stechert, 1897.

Zuckerman, M. General and situation-specific traits and states: New approaches to assessment of anxiety and other constructs. In M. Zuckerman and C. D. Spielberger (Eds.), *Emotions and anxiety: New concepts, methods, and applications.* New York: LEA-John Wiley, 1976.

HERBERT M. LEFCOURT

Locus of Control and Coping with Life's Events

5

INTRODUCTION

When life events seem to be overwhelming, we can sometimes reassure ourselves by recalling examples of certain rare persons who have not only survived equally tumultuous events, but have done so with grace. While some individuals appear ready to succumb to the slightest of life's challenges, there are others who display great fortitude in encounters with tragic and horrifying circumstances.

Though literature and history abound with examples of courage and heroism, familiarity with real persons who have survived extreme stresses nearly always provides us with compelling stories and information regarding the nature of man. This writer had the good fortune to have become acquainted with a recent survivor of extreme stress, one who was able to return to active participation in his life with grace, though he endured extreme hardship for a considerable period of time, and was still recovering from resulting disabilities two years after the event.

The case is fascinating because it exemplifies the role which a person's orientation toward his own life has for altering the events in that life. This "orientation" which pertains to the belief that one can or cannot effect the course of his life is the focus of this chapter, and will be described in terms of the personality construct, locus of control. Though we begin with a description of severe trauma, the relevance of locus of control to coping with more ordinary obstacles should become apparent later in this chapter.

The protagonist, whom we shall refer to as Richard X, is a middle-aged financially comfortable engineer and president of a manufacturing company. He has a warm close-knit family, a devoted and affectionate wife, and four children in their early adult years who seem to care a great deal about their parents and each other.

Among his various talents, Richard X flew his own twin-engined plane from one place to another throughout North America, visiting friends and business acquaintances at will. During one such trip, Richard was in the process of taking off from the municipal airport of a large U.S. midwestern city when he began to experience some difficulty in controlling his plane. While his description of the problems was technical, he summed up his flying conditions as "messy", and he knew that he would have to return to ground level immediately. However, he had just taken on a full tank of fuel, the weight and flammability of which, coupled with his plane's malfunctioning, made a dangerous crash-landing close to inevitable. As he viewed it, his choice was between types of disasters, his best hope being to crash as high as possible into the levee which surrounded the end of the runway. With an exhibition of determination and courage until the fateful moment, Richard steered the plane so that it came near to clearing the levee. However, the plane did crash, killing Richard's best friend who sat beside him, and critically injuring Richard and the two other passengers seated at the rear.

The crash began an ordeal that would provide a near ultimate test of Richard's mettle. Hospitals were places that he had always sought to avoid. However, following the accident, Richard X was to spend several months in a hospital undergoing various surgical procedures during which he lost one eye, was totally immobilized, had his shattered bones reset, his gum linings sewed back into his mouth, had to be treated for ulcers and pneumonia, and received plastic surgery to regain the appearance of being a whole human being.

His first moments of awareness about what had occurred were confused, and his consciousness fleeting. His first week in the hospital consisted of feeling probed at, and slowly discovering the extent of his own enfeeblement. Even though he was barely able to speak and could maintain only intermittent consciousness, Richard X began to show one primary characteristic–a wish to participate in the events that would help to shape the course of his recovery. When a surgeon informed him that his right eye would have to be removed, Richard insisted on a second opinion. When the second surgeon concurred with the judgment of the first, Richard agreed to the operation. Nevertheless, he stated that he would agree to the surgery only if the nerves and muscles were left intact so that, if it became possible to have an eye transplant someday, then he would be able to do so. When the surgeon informed him that such a procedure was light years away, he nevertheless insisted, reflecting upon all the other changes that would have seemed impossible to his grandfather such a relatively short time ago.

In essence, Richard X demonstrated an unwillingness to become a passive recipient of his fate. At several points during his hospitalization he insisted on participating in his treatment, and often incurred pain in the process. An example of his willingness to suffer pain as a price for recovery involved his self-imposed exercises for regaining the use of his hands. At one point, his hands were "barely a collection of twisted muscle tissue and bones" most of which were visible to the eye. From a friend, Richard X learned about someone who had recovered the use of his hands after a serious debilitating injury to them.

Richard's hands had been limp and immobile for about a month when he requested a lump of plasticene to squeeze, beginning the exercises which the other person had found useful in the regaining of manual functioning. It is notable that he initiated these exercises. The nursing staff did not encourage him and he was warned about the pain and probable futility that he would experience. Richard did suffer severe pain when he began his hand exercises. Nevertheless, he winced and went on with it.

In addition to his bodily pain, Richard experienced a "mental phenomenon" that he referred to as "isolation hallucinations," the contents of which were rather interesting. During the first weeks of hospitalization, Richard's rather vivid dreams focussed upon the events that had immediately preceded the plane crash. Richard relived the crash repeatedly, an experience well-known in the literature concerned with traumatic stress (Janis, 1958). One interesting characteristic of these early dreams which was to be found in subsequent "hallucinations" pertained to Richard's role in his dreams. In each repetition he sought to actively alter the event—that is, he tried to pilot the plane in such a way as to avoid the crash. As time wore on, his vivid dreams shifted to other topics. However, the theme to be repeated among most of these dreams was that of responsibility and active coping processes. Early among these post-crash-concerned dreams was one in which Richard suffered considerable guilt as the primary perpetrator of the debacle involving the infamous thefts at the Watergate Hotel. News of the Watergate break-in had just surfaced at the time of Richard's plane crash, so his knowledge of it was limited. However, in his dreams he participated in a set of scenarios in which he was the accountable individual who held the blame for the break-in. Another vivid dream that became the cause of some mirth and concern for his family was one in which he excitedly told his wife, while in a seeming fugue state, that he had invented a machine that would turn the tide of the war (World War II)—a machine that would efficiently produce long johns (winter underwear). The manner in which Richard communicated his excitement prompted his wife to speak with a psychiatrist, who wisely suggested that Richard needed more "real world" involvement. Interestingly enough, the psychiatrist, who was a family friend, described Richard to his wife as a man accustomed to activity, to pressing buttons and making things happen. Enforced passivity was seen as being destructive to his more customary tendencies and thus to his sense of himself. Daily readings of the *Wall Street Journal* were prescribed, with some therapeutic effects.

One other vivid dream also reflected upon the ways in which Richard customarily operated upon his problems. Richard dreamed that he was in a desert that was scorching and dry. The entire world around him, including himself and the camel upon whose back he was riding, was constituted of talcum powder. As such, he tried to avoid breathing so as to escape the suffocating effects that talcum powder could create in his lungs. Now, even in his dream, Richard began to do what was customary for him—he began to consider the consequences of not breathing and the alternatives available to him. He reasoned, "if everything is talcum powder, and I am talcum powder, then it should be possible to breathe in talcum powder." Given this set of statements, Richard then inhaled deeply. Fortunately, his breath caused an audible gurgling noise and cough, as his lungs had been in the process of filling up with fluid. His thrashing about alerted the hospital staff to these signs of developing pneumonia, for which he then received care. In this latter dream in which his actions may have saved his life, Richard revealed himself as a person who is likely to reason with himself as he considers plans and decisions. In each dream Richard appeared as *the actor* who must somehow operate upon the circumstances before him. As the pilot relanding his plane, as the perpetrator of the Watergate burglary, as the inventor of machinery that would alter the course of World War II, and finally as the curious desert traveler who could reason that talcum powder could be inhaled, Richard appeared to be at the center of his dreams—as the actor who determined the course of events in each of them.

Toward the end of an evening in the course of which Richard X told me about his experience, I asked him to tell me how it was possible that he could survive his ordeals with such magnanimity and humor. In response, Richard offered his "methods" and his way of understanding them, as follows:

> When I found myself so damaged and hurt, it was like discovering that I had fallen to the bottom of a very deep well shaft approximately four feet in diameter. It was very dark at the bottom, and upon looking upward the opening seemed very high up and far away. There were people up there looking down. But they were far away and couldn't reach me or even hear me. In that darkness I realized that I was going to have to help myself, though I knew that I had been very badly hurt. So, it was like wedging myself between the sides of the well and moving myself very slowly upward, one step at a time. If I moved too quickly I could have slipped and fallen to the bottom, and then I would have had to start all over again. Even if you should fall though you just don't give up hope—you don't give anything away.

At this point I probed Richard X as to the nature of these "steps." They consisted of each of the myriad decisions and acts that he had undertaken during his hospitalization—from acquiescing to eye surgery to self-imposing physiotherapy. His unwillingness to give anything away referred to his remaining the active chooser, not allowing himself to become the passive object—the patient. To that end, Richard noted that he rarely slept for more than an hour at a time during the first month of hospitalization, going, as he put it, on "nervous energy." Though consciousness was intermittent, he never felt comfortable about "letting go" and indulging himself in lengthy sleep, though he ached for such rest. When questioned if he might not have been afraid that he would die in his sleep, Richard denied such feelings: "I wasn't afraid that I was going to die. I wanted to make damn certain that I was going to survive." Though fear of death and desire to survive are similar, the slight variation in phrasing is quite revealing of Richard X's vantage point. Rather than fearing his possible failure to be able to solve his immediate problems, Richard primarily focused his attention upon the ways in which he might operate upon his problems.

As a postscript, it should be mentioned that one year after his nearly fatal accident Richard X did not look or act like a person who had been severely debilitated. He was wired together in many places, and according to his physicians, he had healed very rapidly from the large number of operations that he underwent. He was still anticipating further surgery at the time, for a dislocated hip that necessitated his use of a cane. However, he had resumed most of the normal roles of his life in business and at home. He was looking forward to driving his car again, to the purchase of a new plane and the resumption of flying, and to various projects including the design and building of a new home. In other words, he had returned from the edge of death with a degree of vitality unknown to many persons throughout their whole lives, though with a wisdom borne of that near confrontation with his demise.

Richard X provides us with considerable material for thought. His very survival and quick return to active functioning, albeit with much accommodation and compromise, leaves us with some wonder and with a desire to comprehend the sources of his strength. Within his reflections we are provided with some clues as to the characteristics that may have aided him in his confrontation with stress. As we have noted throughout the commentary, Richard always seemed ready to assume an active stance toward the crises that befell him within both his dreams and his daily actions. As disabled as he may have been after the accident, he would not simply accept others' ministrations, but seemed to remain alert to the possible roles he could play in meeting the demands of his crisis.

In lay language, many words could be used to describe Richard X's stance toward life. Terms such as *courage, hope,* or *self-reliance* easily come to mind. However, more relevant to the subject matter of this chapter is what can be described as his sense of "can-ness". For Richard X, stressors are translated into hurdles, problems which *can* be analyzed and attacked. While *can-ness* is the term used by Heider (1958) to describe this belief about the ability to effect live events, in social-learning theory (Rotter, Chance, & Phares, 1972), the personality construct *locus of control* has been used to describe such beliefs. Though we will return to definitions of terminology later in this chapter, let it suffice at present to state that locus of control refers to the ways in which causation is attributed. An internal locus of control refers to a belief that outcomes of interactions between persons and the events that befall them are, at least in part, determinable by the acts of those persons. An external locus of control refers to the belief that events occur for reasons that are irrelevant to a person's actions, and thus are beyond attempts at controlling them. Richard X, as we will see, represents those who are at the extreme internal end of a continuum ranging from external to internal with reference to locus of control.

COGNITIONS AND STRESSORS

Implicit throughout the introductory section above is the suggestion that particular cognitions alter the ways in which stressors are experienced. Such an emphasis upon cognitive mediation has not always been popular in psychology, despite its continuing acceptance in common sense lay thinking. Beginning perhaps with Kurt Lewin's (1935) theoretical contributions in the area of personality, in which internal events and field forces or external conditions received equal emphasis, and continued by social-learning theorists such as Julian Rotter (1954), Walter Mischel (1973), Albert Bandura (1971), and others, a resurgence of interest has developed in the cognitive mediators, or thought processes, that intervene between raw stimulus events and subsequent actions. This revival of concern with cognitive mediation follows a fairly long period in which observable stimuli and observable responses comprised the core of psychologists' formulations for predicting behavior.

With particular regard to the study of stress, however, interest in cognitive mediation was never entirely eclipsed by radical behaviorism, as it had been in other areas such as learning. Given the clinical interest in stress and coping processes, theorists and researchers with less laboratory-based orientations contributed much to that literature. In psychoanalytic theories—for instance, reality anxiety—the perception of actual oncoming stressors received continuous attention, especially in view of the high incidence of traumatic neuroses that occurred during wartime. In dealing with traumatic neuroses, psychoanalytically oriented clinicians were apt to speculate in terms of awareness and repression, or other descriptors of cognitive structures and processes, that could account for individual differences in the response to stressors.

Prominent among psychologists who emphasized the cognitive mediation involved in the response to stressors were Irving Janis (1958) and Richard Lazarus (1966). From their unique positions, these two theorist-researchers have explored the roles that cognition can play in mediating a host of potential stressors.

Janis's work, deriving from the Hull-Hovland formulations combining drive and habit strength, illustrated the utility of those constructions in predicting responses to social influences in general, and to stresses in particular. Briefly, Janis found that persons who engaged in the "work of worry," who gave some thought to the possible negative experiences that they might suffer before undergoing surgery, were less apt to exhibit inappropriate extremes of distress or anger subsequent to surgery than were persons who had failed to consider potential pain and discomfort. Janis's work revealed how awareness, cognitive processing, or the quiet internal role-playing of possible occurrences, could lower drive levels, and thus could account for some of the differences in distress observable among persons as they responded to stressors.

Where Janis described the facilitative nature of "thinking through" a problem and considering its ramifications for coping in "real" field settings, Lazarus and his colleagues were able to demonstrate similar findings within the confines of the laboratory. In a series of studies using filmed presentations of stressful events, Lazarus found that autonomic responses indicative of arousal could be "short-circuited" by the induction of intellectualization, or a more detached "intellectual" framework through which the stressful event could be interpreted. A more detailed description of this work may be found in this book within the chapter by Averill. Both Lazarus and Janis's work can be described in terms of an idealized dimension of awareness wherein some individuals are said to characteristically avoid information pertinent to their lives (repressors), while others, at the opposite extreme, seem overly vigilant about threat-related events (sensitizers).

While there are differences between Janis, Lazarus, Goldstein (1973), Luborsky et al. (1965), Byrne (1964), and others who have used the terms *repression-sensitization* or their facsimiles, it suffices for us to be aware that there has been a tradition of research concerned with the ways in which individuals experience potential stressors as a function of their cognitive styles and processes.

Most pertinent to our developing discussion about the locus of control are Lazarus's terms *primary appraisal* and *secondary appraisal.* Primary appraisal refers to the process in which an individual makes a judgment regarding the presence or absence of threats or stressors. Secondary appraisal pertains to the consideration of possible responses if there is a threat anticipated. It is in the use of secondary appraisals that we draw near to a discussion about locus of control. Secondary appraisal consists of a screening of available alternative responses that could be made in order to cope with oncoming stressors, and of assessments of one's own attributes relative to coping with those stresses.

At this point it may prove helpful to return to our narrative about Richard X. Upon becoming cognizant of his incapacities, Richard X may be said to have engaged in primary appraisal. With the realization of his endangered state, he became vigilant, so much so that he slept only in brief spurts—"living on nerves" during his first weeks of hospitalization. Subsequently, Richard X began considering his choices, what he should do—a response to adversity and challenge that was apparently habitual for him. With these secondary appraisals, he revealed a point of view that he held about himself—that he was to be the source of some actions that might serve to effect his recovery. Richard X evidently believed that there was always to be some choice available to him; and, though he was severely immobilized, he could still decide to act, if only cognitively, to somehow alter the ultimate outcomes of his crisis.

While it is possible to describe aspects of Richard X's behavior under duress in terms of appraisal processes, it will be one of the purposes of this chapter to illustrate the equally useful formulations deriving from social-learning theories for predicting variations of responses to stress. The locus-of-control construct, in particular, will be shown to provide us with a keener appreciation of how cognitions alter the nature of our experiences.

Epidemiological researchers such as Holmes and Rahe (1967), the Dohrenwends (1974), and others have recently provided evidence as to which life events will most likely prove to be stressful for most people. Even within their work, however, variability has always been evident, despite the high magnitude and seeming universal character of the stressors explored. As it has been suggested above, psychoanalytic theorists, social learning theorists, and others as well have implicated cognitive processes and styles as mediators of stress, and therefore as sources of that variance noted in stress research. In the subsequent section, a brief description of social-learning formulations will be presented from which various cognitive-mediational constructs such as locus of control have derived.

SOCIAL LEARNING AND COGNITION

Among statements of social-learning positions, a relatively clear exposition may be found in the text by Rotter, Chance, and Phares (1972) and in articles by Mischel (1973) and Bandura (1971). Each theorist has emphasized, in his own manner, the importance of both internal-cognitive processes and field conditions for predicting behavior. By internal processes is meant personal interpretations as to the valuing of particular events and the understanding as to how those events may be brought about. That is, social-learning-oriented psychologists are not content with research in which rewards or punishments are assumed de facto to be rewards or punishments. Rather, the personal evaluation of those events by the person experiencing them would be more satisfying information. Recent research by Klinger (1975) has clearly described an attempt to assess what "really matters" to individuals. Klinger terms "what matters" as *current concerns*. In Klinger's system, an event can serve as an incentive or reinforcement only insofar as that event is a current concern for an individual–*reinforcement* meaning an event that has the power to shape behavior. However, it is not enough to know that something matters to a person to be able to guess what it is that he will do in pursuit of that end. A second variable of importance would be one that explicates the person's "cognitive map"–his beliefs and expectancies regarding the ways in which desired ends are best attained or odious ones are best avoided. In Rotter's terminology, the construct *expectancy* is aimed at defining such cognitive maps. The term *expectancy* refers to the individual's beliefs that given behaviors will cause given outcomes. With such internal-cognitive variables, social-learning psychologists can be said to be interested in personal values and concerns, and the ways in which persons believe that they may cause valued outcomes to occur.

With regard to "field variables," the social-learning theorist emphasizes situational cues that are likely to effect the occurrence of reinforcements. Whether through the presence of models for particular behaviors or by the awareness of reinforcement availability (opportunity), or in the knowledge that the attainment of particular reinforcements is appropriate at given times and places, social-learning theorists attempt to include the "realities" of the field within their behavioral predictions.

It is within the realm of generalized expectancies that we encounter the construct *locus of control.* Rotter has differentiated between specific and generalized expectancies. The former are, as the term suggests, expectancies about specific behaviors and specific outcomes. If, for instance, one hopes to succeed on a particular mathematics examination, then studying may be viewed as the direct instrumental route to the outcome desired. Thus the precise formulation of the expectancy would be, "If I study hard, then I should do well on that examination." This specific expectancy, in turn, may derive from a more generalized expectancy or rule by which an individual lives—academic success results from diligent studying. Even this generalization may be a particular example of one's highest generalization—that "one gets out of his enterprise what he puts into it," or some facsimile. To anyone familiar with human nature, however, it may be evident that, as admirable as such statements might seem to be, there will be many persons to whom such verities might not be plausible. Some persons may be found to hold rather divergent conceptions with regard to specific expectancies about a mathematics examination, or about each of the subsequent generalizations regarding achievement activity, or about activity per se. For example, some individuals may believe that courses involving mathematics are unlearnable by ordinary mortals. Consequently, studying might be thought to be of little worth for improving one's grades. What we are discussing here is the relatively specific expectancy regarding one's educability in quantitative matters. If one were to step back and speak in greater generality, it is possible that certain persons feel that they are not educable in any formal sense, such that school in toto is associated with ineffectuality and frustration. Such, of course, are the highly prevalent beliefs among persons labeled as borderline retarded. Very often, mildly retarded persons are those who hold little hope that they can effect achievement-related outcomes. Consequently, little effort may be elicited from such individuals even when, in an observer's judgment, they might be capable of mastering certain challenges (Cromwell, 1963). Recent research by Dweck (1973, 1975) offers confirmation of this association between beliefs about causality and achievement efforts, which will be described in detail in a later section.

If we were now to take one step further back, an even greater generalization would be that we are not able to effect important outcomes in a whole range of life's pursuits. Locus of control is a generalized expectancy which pertains to such generalizations about causality. It concerns the belief about how one's conduct and the outcomes of experiences are associated one with the other.

To become aware of possible extremes with regard to locus of control, one need only consider the apathy and hopelessness commonly observed among impoverished and disenfranchised persons who believe themselves to be entirely at the mercy of fate. On the other hand, an extreme statement of contingency is well represented by the Horatio Alger myths that were so prevalent in the United States during the early decades of the twentieth century. All one needed to do was to work hard, and one's fortunes improved, or so the myth went. The locus of control, the source of outcomes, was held to be largely internal to the actor. External events had little bearing upon the fates one experienced. It is possible, then, to consider extremes of causal beliefs–from that of excessive fatalism, "what will be will be," to extreme beliefs of potency, that events occur largely as a function of how one acts.

Realistically, each individual may be said to have varied loci of control for various outcomes. One may not feel able to influence the outcomes in particular academic pursuits, but feel highly adept at managing one's affiliative affairs. Nevertheless, if one were to draw generalizations across potential reinforcement areas that matter to individuals, differences may be observed in the degree to which persons believe that those outcomes are amenable to their efforts at effecting them. Certain persons may feel more helpless about creating desired ends than do others; and, as we shall see, such differences may have considerable ramifications for the ways in which such persons cope with problems that befall them.

EMPIRICAL FINDINGS WITH LOCUS OF CONTROL

In 1962 the first of many papers concerned with locus of control was published in an obscure collection of research papers (Rotter, Seeman, & Liverant, 1962). Since the publication of that first introductory paper, the reports of research pertaining to locus of control have been so abundant that *Current Digest,* the abstracting journal, concluded that in 1975 the locus-of-control construct had come to be the central preoccupation in personality research.

As indicated in the previous section, locus of control concerns the expectancies of individuals regarding the causes for their experiences. Internal control refers to the generalized expectancy that life experiences are contingent upon one's actions, whether those experiences are positive or negative. Likewise, external control refers to generalized expectancies that life experiences are not contingent upon one's own behavior, but are determinable by a host of external causes–luck, fate, other people, or even perhaps by invariant characteristics of one's self, for example, beauty or intelligence.

Among a wide range of research areas under investigation, one that has proven to be compelling in its reliability and convergent validity is that which has connected locus of control to the ways in which people contend with aversive events. Research from laboratories that focus upon animal learning, social behavior, and personality functioning have produced congruent information with regard to the ways in which the effects of aversive events are modified by the perceived causes of those events. To begin the discussion of this literature, we shall first review the research that has derived from situationally determined perceptions of control, and then the more personality-focused research bearing upon the response to aversive events.

Situationally Determined Locus of Control and the Response to Stress

As was noted above, social-learning psychologists rely upon both internal-cognitive and field-derived variables in their predictions of behavior. If high-magnitude predictions of behavior are desired, then assessments of values, expectancies, and situation characteristics would all be deemed necessary. However, in demonstration research, in which the simple presence of an effect may be all that is required, more often than not only one variable at a time is explored. In the earliest research with the locus-of-control construct, the largest number of studies relied solely upon situation manipulations. That is, subjects were led to believe that outcomes during given tasks were determined either by luck, and therefore were uncontrollable, or by skill, and therefore were controllable. The ensuing performances were then observed. Generally, the results proved to be encouraging. If tasks were construed as skill-demanding, subjects were more likely to use their experiences for making estimates of their future performances than if the tasks were viewed as chance-determined. For reviews of this early literature, see Lefcourt (1966) and Rotter (1966).

In the last few years, there has been a resurgence of research in which causal perceptions have been investigated through situational contrivance. Much of this research has derived from Heider's (1958) original papers on causal perception, and has come to comprise an area of interest referred to as *attribution theory* (Harvey, Ickes, & Kidd, 1976). Rather than emphasizing the skill or chance nature of a task, as had social-learning researchers, these more social-psychological experimenters have stressed controllability per se, often presenting tasks wherein the presence or absence of controllability is obvious.

Most extensive of the research programs focusing upon control has been that of Glass and Singer (1972). Among the results reported in their monograph, *Urban Stress,* are the relatively consistent findings that aversive events are experienced in accord with the degree of control that subjects believe they can exercise over those events. In one typical investigation, subjects were presented with loud blasts of noise while they were engaged in a series of routine tasks. Subsequently, the subjects had to perform two other tasks which demanded attention and engendered frustration. The first was a task requiring subjects to trace patterns without crossing any previously drawn lines and without raising their pencils from the paper. As it was, certain designs were impossible to do. Ignorant of the inevitability of their failure, the subjects were allowed to persist at it for as long as they wished by simply taking additional copies of each design from a pile and beginning anew. Glass and Singer were thus assessing their subjects' tenacity at problem solving in the face of repeated failure. The second task was simple but demanding—copyreading. Subjects had to read quickly and locate embedded spelling errors. The crucial element in these studies pertaining to control inhered in the manner in which the previously administered noise had been presented to the subjects. Unpredictable loud noise had proven to have the most deleterious effects upon subjects' subsequent willingness and/or ability to persist and to copyread with competence. Unpredictable loud noise was then presented to another group of subjects, with one major difference—the presence or absence of a button which could terminate the noise. Half of the subject sample were shown a button on the side of their chair and were told that if the noise were to become too bothersome, a push on the button would cause it to stop. This simple device, which in fact was never used, had dramatic effects. Subjects who were informed about the use of the button attempted to complete the impossible designs five times more than did their peers who were not informed about a means of controlling the noise. Likewise, the former made fewer omissions of misspelled words than did the latter.

Apparently the *mere knowledge* that one can exert control can alter the impact of an aversive event. Not a single subject actually used that control. However, knowing it was there proved to be enough to change the character of the situation for the subjects in that experiment. These findings of Glass and Singer have been replicated with other aversive stimuli and with other means of access to control. In each instance, when control was made available in some way, aversive stimuli failed to have as much impact as when no means of control were available.

More dramatic are a host of studies which have reported upon the effects of an absence of control among rats or dogs. Curt Richter (1959) reported upon a strange phenomenon that had occurred in his laboratories with some regularity. Richter had noticed that a number of his rats were dying during an experiment in which they were subjected to a turbulent bath. Now, rats can swim for long periods of time. But many of Richter's rats failed to even try, and after a downward corkscrew motion, expired. Strangely enough, autopsies revealed that the rats had not drowned but had died what was referred to as a parasympathetic death. Richter, after much close observation and experimentation, found that this sudden death phenomenon could be attributed to physical restraint upon the movements of *wild* rats, the restraint occurring as the animals were held and placed into the turbulent bath. Tame, laboratory-reared rats did not succumb to the effects of the constraining manipulations; only those animals who would experience passive restraint as an aversive event succumbed during the experiment. It is not possible to convey the sense of mystery and excitement that Richter creates in his article, which was reprinted in Herman Feifel's (1959) book *The Meaning of Death*, without too much digression. However, his conclusions are dramatic enough. Eliminating a host of alternative hypotheses, Richter concluded that the loss of hope, generated by the failure of previously effective behaviors to terminate an aversive experience, was the cause of death.

Other research with subhuman primates has provided us with similar data and conclusions. Mowrer's (1948) classic study of the "fear of fear" and Brady's (1958) work with the "executive monkey" each indicated that the nature of an aversive event varied with the animal's position regarding control of that event. In the latter study, the animal that could respond to a conditioned stimulus and shorten the length of a subsequent electric shock developed ulcers, whereas the passive, yoked recipient of shock did not. To have had some control in that study by Brady seemed to have created worse effects than being a passive victim. More extensive research by Weiss (1971), however, offered strong refutation of the Brady study. Noticing that Brady had preselected his four pairs of monkeys for their respective roles on the basis of activity levels previously measured, Weiss conjectured that Brady had confounded genetic propensities with the assigned roles vis-a-vis control. With extensive samples of rats matched for genetic characteristics pertaining to activity, Weiss found that the "executive rat" did not reveal ulceration after a series of trials in which shock was presented in similar fashion as in Brady's experiment. Rather, the passive recipient of shock who could do nothing to terminate shock became the ulcerous rat, and—most significant—the longer the number of trials as a passive recipient of shock, the larger was the ulcerous lesion in the rat.

Martin Seligman (1975) has also provided a most interesting set of data regarding helplessness and depression. In brief, Seligman created dysfunctional dogs—dogs that would not actively protect themselves from an aversive situation—by having them undergo inescapable shocks. That is, by preventing dogs from being able to effectively avoid shocks administered to their feet, Seligman created dogs that were highly atypical among canines—dogs that would not pick themselves up and run away when it later *became possible* for them to escape from another aversive situation.

Seligman subsequently compared clinical symptoms of depression and observed behaviors associated with learned helplessness, and suggested that the two phenomena may actually be one. Work among humans by Lewinsohn (1972) lends some credence to this position. Lewinsohn defines depression in terms of the loss of instrumentality through loss of ability or opportunity. In essence, when previously effective behaviors no longer generate desired reinforcements to which actors have been accustomed, or when effective behaviors are no longer possible for the person, depression is likely. The similarity to Seligman's work is strong. Seligman's dogs likewise found themselves unable to rescue themselves, unable to use the skills dogs are granted in the scheme of things, and consequently became inert in the face of challenges—much as the depressive human.

Each of these aforementioned explorations into the effects of situation-determined locus of control indicates that aversive events have a more negative impact when the individual experiences them in a state of helplessness. Whether through a failure of previously effective acts, or through a dearth of opportunity to act in one's own behest, the organism that perceives an absence of causal connection between his actions and his success at avoidance or escape from stressful events will exhibit more distress in those encounters. It is in the light of such findings that we may come to understand the severity of emotional responses that we humans are prone to as we become afflicted by illnesses, accidents, natural catastrophes, and death. Each commonly occur in a non-contingent fashion, seemingly inevitable and unalterable by personal efforts.

At this point it is salutary to recall the case of Richard X with which we began this chapter. Not everyone, it would seem, perceives non-contingency between acts and outcomes at the same points in time. Given the sort of accident that Richard X suffered, many individuals would believe that they were entirely at the mercy of medical caretakers and whatever deities they held sacred. Some persons would assume such passive postures after much less upsetting experiences. On the other hand, some individuals, like Richard X, seem to disbelieve that there is ever a point at which their own efforts can become entirely useless. It is in the consideration of such individual differences that we will now examine the research focused upon locus of control as a personality characteristic, or in social-learning terms, as a generalized expectancy.

Locus of Control as a Personality Attribute and the Response to Stress

The most widely used tool for assessing individual differences with regard to locus of control has been a forced-choice scale that was constructed by Julian Rotter (1966) and his colleagues. While there are at least ten other assessment devices that have been employed with more or less success for particular purposes (Lefcourt, 1976a), Rotter's scale is still the most common in use. It consists of 23 items in which subjects are asked to choose the more accurate statement reflecting their own beliefs. Examples are as follows:

11. a) Becoming a success is a matter of hard work; luck has little or nothing to do with it.

    or

    b) Getting a good job depends mainly on being in the right place at the right time.

23. a) Sometimes I can't understand how teachers arrive at the grades they give.

    or

    b) There is a direct connection between how hard I study and the grades I get.

The scale is scored for the total number of items to which a person indicates that the more external choice is the truer statement of his beliefs. Agreement with *b* for item 11 and *a* for item 23 would be scored as instances of external-control expectancies. Generally, the mean scores obtained on Rotter's scale are approximately 10, meaning that 10 out of 23 items are answered with agreements to external causal statements.

The customary strategy in studies using Rotter's scale has been to classify subjects as internal or external, and to observe subsequent behavior in tasks and situations pertinent to locus of control. Subjects are often classified as internals if their scale scores are below the mean or median (less than 10), and as externals if their scores are higher than the average. Some experimenters, however, use more divergent cutting points for their classifications; above 12 for externals, below 8 for internals.

With regard to the response to stress, we may begin by reviewing research that has examined the relationship between locus of control and reactions to illness, in keeping with our previous discussion and case study.

Among the earliest investigations using a variation of Rotter's scale, Seeman and Evans (1962) found that hospitalized tuberculosis patients who were classified as internals knew more about their illness and were more inquisitive with the hospital staff about tuberculosis and their own health status than were those patients who were classified as externals. This finding indicated that internals were more active in their pursuit of information relevant to their illness than were externals, a finding which has proven to be an instance of a greater generality–internals have commonly been found to be more eager assimilators of personally relevant information than externals, whether that information pertained to obtaining parole (Seeman, 1963), to influencing others (Davis & Phares, 1967), or to understanding another person (Lefcourt & Wine, 1969).

With pertinence to illness, diabetic internals have been found to be better at maintaining diets and keeping appointments for dialysis than have external diabetics (Weaver, 1972). Similarly, internals have been found to resort to preventative dental care and to use seat belts while driving more than externals (Williams, 1972a, b). With a health-focused locus-of-control scale, Wallston et al. (1976) found that persons who were concerned about their health and held themselves responsible for their health were more apt to seek information regarding hypertension than were their less concerned and fatalistic peers.

In each instance, then, internals have been found to be more ready to encounter potentially negative experiences, and to prepare themselves so that they might avoid accidents and illnesses, while externals seem to be more oblivious or fatalistic with regard to possible negative events.

When aversive events can no longer be ignored, however, externals have been found to suffer from those events more than internals. In our own laboratories we have observed such differences in response to failure experiences in achievement-relevant tasks (Lefcourt, Hogg, Struthers, & Holmes, 1975); to role enactments of failure in social and achievement situations (Lefcourt, Antrobus, & Hogg, 1974); and in the response to embarrassment in social interactions

(Lefcourt, Gronnerud, & McDonald, 1973; Lefcourt, Sordoni, & Sordoni, 1974; Lefcourt, 1976b).

In most of these latter studies, we have not dealt with subjects' responses to highly aversive or painful stimuli. What we have examined are the ways in which persons cope with uncertainty during the course of an experiment in which embarrassment and feelings of being abused are likely. An example of one such study may help to illustrate our procedures and findings.

In the study by Lefcourt, Gronnerud, and McDonald (1973), our primary concern was to observe the manner in which subjects behaved when becoming aware of the fact that the experimenter had not been honest with them about his intentions. The task was one that gradually "turned fishy," containing an increasing number of dissonant cues that eventually had to arouse suspicion that the experimenter had been less than totally honest in his description of the task.

Subjects had originally been solicited for participation in a study that nominally involved verbal facility. To legitimize this claim, a number of verbal-facility tasks were administered. The last test to be administered was a word-association procedure to which subjects were instructed to give evidence of their speed of verbal productivity. Throughout the administration of this test, the experimenter recorded the subject's response times and verbal answers, and videotape recordings were made of the subject's head and upper torso through a one-way observation mirror.

The list of words was no ordinary one, however, but was derived from a word-association test containing sexual double entendres that had been used for the study of sex guilt by Galbraith and Mosher (1968). The beginning of the list administered in this study consisted of a series of decidedly non-sexual words. Subsequent to the thirteenth word (rubber) double entendres occurred at every third word: (16) *bust*; (17) fire; (18) watch; (19) *snatch.* After the 24th word, double entendres alternated with non-sexual words; and from the 40th word until the end of the list all of the words were double entendres. Therefore, the uncertainty regarding the sexual nature of the list may be seen to have steadily diminished so that what may have produced a vague suspicion among subjects early in the list became almost unavoidably explicit as the list progressed.

Our initial intention was to study the differences in ability of internals and externals to discern the changes occurring throughout the word association list. We anticipated that internals would require fewer trials with double entendres than externals before drawing inferences about the investigator and/or the investigation. In addition to the cognitive differences that were found, a second concern focused upon the ways in which subjects behaved in response to their discovery of our duplicity. Toward that end, we began examining the videotaped recordings of the subjects' facial expressions that accompanied "the discovery."

At this point, our thinking was as follows: The experiment was changing in character for subjects such that the experimenter's intentions were now ambiguous. If the subject was correct in perceiving a shift in our purposes, then obviously we had been deceiving him in our description of the task. If so, what was he expected to do? How might this reflect upon his self? Some individuals will respond to such uncertainty with apprehension, others perhaps with bemusement. We reasoned that persons who felt more vulnerable before others' judgments were more likely to feel disconcerted by this uncertainty than would individuals who felt less threatened by such judgments. Since externals have more often been found to be susceptible to suggestions offered by prestigious authorities (Lefcourt, 1972), and such susceptibility may be attributed to feelings of vulnerability and a resulting need for certainty, we hypothesized that externals should become more apprehensive than internals in the double-entendre task in which uncertainty steadily increases. It was with this chain of reasoning that we began to re-examine the videotape recordings for humor responses as an indication of the subjects' lack of apprehension on discovery of duplicity. This second set of data derived from these recordings of facial expressions has been described in detail elsewhere (Lefcourt, Sordoni, & Sordoni, 1974).

Our first data analyses consisted of general indications of mirth–smiles and laughter which suggested lesser apprehension. Internals were found to both laugh and smile more often than externals throughout the word-association task, producing statistically significant main effects or interactions with particular segments of the list.

In addition to these general differences, we were able to reliably rate three kinds of mirth expression–social, tension, and superiority humor. It was the latter, superiority humor, which was of primary interest to us. This is the sort of humor that exudes awareness and seems to indicate "a laughing down at one's previous stupidity at taking all this seriously" (see Lefcourt, Sordoni, & Sordoni, 1974). It was superiority humor which we believed would most reflect the comfortable coming to terms with awareness of our duplicity; and we anticipated that internals would exhibit this less stressed demeanor while confronting uncertainty more than would externals.

During the third and fourth segments of the list, when the fourth to thirteenth double entendres were presented, internals were found to exceed externals significantly in the display of superiority humor. There was an increasing curve for the incidence of superiority humor as the task progressed among internals. Externals, on the other hand, exhibited a decline in the exhibition of superiority humor during the same segments in which internals presented more humor displays.

At this point we tentatively concluded that externals were more likely than internals to respond with gravity to uncertainty in evaluative situations. The latter were perhaps more disposed to take our experimental tasks with a grain of salt. Subsequent investigations were then planned to ascertain whether these results were reliable, that uncertainty had a more negative impact upon externals than upon internals. As noted above, in this series of studies, internals were found to be less apt to become upset than externals, often relying upon humor as a means of softening potentially abrasive events.

These findings with reference to humor are of some importance when we consider the ways that humor can modify human responses to crises. Rollo May (1969) has written a rather compelling description of the role that humor can play, which converges with our own interest in examining the association between locus of control and the experiencing of aversive events:

> Another example of how the sense of the self has been disintegrating in our day can be seen when we consider humor and laughter. It is not generally realized how closely one's sense of humor is connected with one's sense of selfhood. Humor normally should have the function of preserving the sense of self. It is an expression of our uniquely human capacity to experience ourselves as subjects who are not swallowed up in the objective situation. It is the healthy way of feeling a "distance" between one's self and the problem, a way of standing off and looking at one's problem with perspective. One cannot laugh when in an anxiety panic, for then one is swallowed up, one has lost the distinction between himself as subject and the objective world around him. So long as one can laugh, furthermore, he is not completely under the dominance of anxiety or fear–hence the accepted belief in folklore that to be able to laugh in times of danger is a sign of courage. In cases of borderline psychotics, so long as the person has genuine humor–so long, that is, as he can laugh, or look at himself with the thought, as one person put it, "What a crazy person I've been!"–he is preserving his identity as a self. When any of us, neurotic or not, get insights into our psychological problems, our spontaneous reaction is normally a little laugh–the "aha" of insight, as it is called. The humor occurs because of a new appreciation of one's self as a subject acting in an objective world (May, pp. 61-62).

If we are correct that humor is more commonly to be observed among individuals who perceive contingent relationships between their outcomes and their actions, and if May is correct that humor prevents the feeling of being overwhelmed by anxiety, then it may be possible to conclude that persons who hold internal-control beliefs are more insulated against potentially stressful events. Consequently, internals should be less likely to exhibit depression or anxiety than externals in response to stressful events.

As noted in this author's book (Lefcourt, 1976a), there have been many investigations reporting reliable correlations between locus-of-control scale scores and indexes of anxiety and depression. In our own laboratories we have conducted one investigation bearing upon this issue (Lefcourt, Hogg, Struthers, & Holmes, 1975). In this study we presented our subjects with some inevitable failure experiences as well as some successes throughout an extended anagram test. During the test performance, we recorded nonverbal gestures as well as declarations of expectancies and attributions. As we had hypothesized, externals were more apt to make external attributions than were internals, and this was especially the case during failure trials. More pertinent to the present discussion, however, were our findings with body movements. Adaptors—the movements of hands over the surface of one's body, which have been used as indicators of tension and depression (Ekman & Friesen, 1972)—were most commonly found during trials when subjects experienced failure. While all subjects displayed an increase of adaptors when suffering failure, there was a consistent difference in the rate at which these tension-indicating body movements occurred. Externals exhibited more adaptor movements throughout the anagram procedure, a difference which became the more marked when failure trials were encountered.

In essence, externals looked more distraught and vulnerable than internals during this achievement-relevant experiment. In addition to the anagram procedure, we had our subjects complete a profile of mood states. The three moods that we evaluated were "tension," "depression," and "vigor." The former two were assumed to be negative, and the latter, a positive, instrumentality-facilitating mood. As others have reported, we found that externals acknowledged more frequent tension and depression and less vigor than internals.

Our final empirical datum is of like interest. The same subjects were asked to complete a shortened version of Jerome Singer's daydreaming questionnaire (Singer & Antrobus, 1966). For our purposes, two groups of daydream factors were of interest. The first, which bears likeness to "resultant achievement motivation," were daydreams concerning successful achievement versus those dwelling upon the fear of failure. When we compared the incidence of each type of daydream reported, we found a crossover interaction with locus of control. Internals reported a higher frequency-of-achievement and a lower frequency of fear-of-failure daydreams than their external opposites.

Secondly, daydreams of past, present, and future events differed in incidence with locus of control. Internals dwelled less upon the past and more upon the future, while the reverse characterized externals. Insofar as daydreams are concerned, then, internals seem to engage in the sort of mentation that could facilitate goal-directed activity. In contrast, externals seem more apt to fantasize about negative experiences, dwelling upon failures and past events rather than upon successes and future events which might facilitate them in their strivings.

These data involving daydreams bear some similarity to Richard X's reflections, noted previously. Richard X also did not dwell as much upon the fearsome aspects of his hospitalization as upon the ways that he could act that would be of aid in his recuperation. As he stated it, he did not fear death, but wanted to assure his survival. His dreams focused upon problem solving and responsibility, and according to his family, his demeanor exuded more humor and sympathy for others than pity for himself.

Richard X's case provides us with a living example that lends vividness to the various findings with locus of control as a stable attribute of personality. Richard X can be said to be the sort of person who leaves little to fate. In most instances, he believes that his valued reinforcements in family life, work, and social relationships are contingent upon his actions, or subject to internal control. Upon encountering the sudden shift in his fortunes that began with his plane crash, this tendency to view events as responsive to his efforts was found to have salutary consequences for his recovery. It is here, in the way that people experience traumatic crises, that we can more clearly see the intricate workings of various orientations toward life events.

It is fitting toward the end of this section to be able to report one last empirical datum in support of the above anecdotal material. Bulman and Wortman (1977) recently completed an interview study with 29 survivors of severe misfortunes. Most were victims of traffic accidents, and all were extensively paralyzed. The investigators elicited attributions of blame and causality for the accidents from the patients. At the same time, they obtained judgments of each patient's success at coping with recuperative procedures from the nurses and social workers who worked with them. The findings suggested that the tendency to blame others, and to feel that the accident could have been avoided, were associated with less adequate coping behavior. Self-blame, on the other hand, the attribution of responsibility for one's difficulties to one's self, proved to be more adaptive.

These findings could seem paradoxical. To blame one's self is often thought to have maudlin and self-pitying consequences. However, persons who hold themselves responsible for their accidents may also regard themselves as being responsible for their recovery, and thus be more apt to cooperate with necessary procedures. Therefore, the unwillingness to become despondent and apathetic despite misfortune may be as comprehensible a concomitant of an internal locus of control as is the preventative, information-seeking behavior designed to avert misfortune.

At the end of the previous section concerning situation-derived perceptions of control, we had returned to the case of Richard X to establish the point that individuals differ in their responses to stresses. Though the negative effects of stressors may be predicted on the basis of the victim's state of helplessness, it is important to remember that people differ in their readiness to believe that they are helpless. Though the hypothesis has not been tested, it seems reasonable to presume that persons who hold highly generalized expectancies of internal control, such as Richard X, will require considerably more trauma and shock before believing in the futility of their efforts than will externals, for whom a state of helplessness confirms their prior beliefs.

Not all theorists, however, are in agreement that an internal locus of control necessarily offers a better prognosis for coping with aversive events. Cohen and Lazarus (1973), for example, have conjectured that such illnesses as myocardial infarctions that initially require a response of rest and passivity may present more difficulty for internals than for externals. They have provided some limited data to the effect that externals recover more quickly from heart attacks than internals, and that recovery is associated with acceptance of enforced passivity.

Although the evidence is slight, it nevertheless serves to remind us again that if highly accurate predictions are desired it is necessary to consider the interaction of all relevant variables. The nature of the situation–in the latter case, the kinds of demands that a heart attack places upon a person–is as essential a variable for predicting behavior as are the expectancies and values of the person engaged in that situation.

THE SOCIAL ORIGINS OF LOCUS OF CONTROL

Given the importance of locus of control as a personality characteristic, it is appropriate to inquire as to how such expectancies are formed. Common sense would suggest that experience with reinforcements following instrumental activity is the source of locus-of-control cognitions. The toddler who beams when he discovers that a hand movement on his part results in the onset or termination of illumination presents a model of the sorts of experience with contingencies that result in cognitions about causation.

John Watson (1966, 1967, 1972) has presented a series of investigations that focus upon what he has referred to as "contingency awareness." Using the available responses of infants, he has established games by which happenings occur in response to the child's voluntary efforts. Mobiles are set in motion in response to an infant's head motions on a pillow, or hands are moved in conjunction with the infant's eye movements. In each case, some rudimentary response within the capacity of an infant becomes instrumental so that the infant is provided with evidence for contingency. Watson proposed that such experiences could result in an early awareness of causation, with a consequent increase in attempts at other instrumental activity. Watson found evidence to support his position. Infants who were granted contingency experiences displayed more positive affect, cooing, laughing, and remaining in their cribs for longer periods of time without complaint, and performed other motoric acts that might not have been expected had the child not been so stimulated.

While Watson's explorations are intriguing, they are limited to the hyper-specific motoric acts of infants. When examining possible source routes for generalized expectancies that are assessed later in life, one is more apt to want to describe home and social atmospheres in which a host of possible instrumental acts can occur. It is possible, however, to extrapolate from Watson's work and to describe the home milieu in terms of the degree to which contingency awareness is fostered.

If we were to envisage a home in which children would increasingly perceive themselves as effective individuals, we might expect to find that home to be offering encouragement, challenge, and standards for achievement. That is, where children are encouraged and aided in making efforts toward increasingly greater accomplishments, we might expect to find a more highly developed awareness of contingencies between action and outcomes. Anecdotal evidence for the connection between warm encouragement, increasing demands and challenges, and the development of an internal locus of control is available in the biographies of former President Harry S. Truman (Miller, 1973) and former Supreme Court Justice William O. Douglas (Douglas, 1974). Both of these men had to overcome challenges imposed upon them by deaths, illness, and impoverishment in their families (Douglas suffered from a severe case of polio), and therefore had to assume responsibilities to help in sustaining their families. In the case of both men, there were also devoted and encouraging mothers who helped to set high expectancies for their children. As children, these men were not left to feel pitiable despite their circumstances, but were encouraged to overcome the handicaps present in their family settings.

Empirical research directed toward an examination of the origins of locus of control does not provide conclusive evidence regarding childhood antecedents. Warmth, supportiveness, and parental encouragement have been found to be essential for the development of an internal locus of control (Lefcourt, 1976a). However, most of the studies from which such conclusions are derived have relied upon descriptions of child-family relationships obtained during the respondent's young adult years. As Crandall (1973) has reported, there had been but 16 studies directed toward child-rearing practices associated with locus of control by 1973; and of those 16, only 4 were based upon observed parental behavior. Crandall has had access to a greater range of measures and observations than have most investigators: locus-of-control measures assessed during young adulthood, home observations of maternal behavior during the subject's first ten years, and interviews with subjects during early adolescence.

From her longitudinal data, Crandall has obtained some findings that offer a more dynamic, or changing, view of family atmosphere and locus of control. Simple warmth and support were not found to bear a stable relationship with later assessments of locus of control. Rather, independence training, the push toward self-assertion, seemed to be a more important element in the development of an internal locus of control. Warmth and support were not irrelevant, however. Early rejection or suffocation by overindulgent, pampering parents obviously should not help to produce internal-control expectancies. Nevertheless, warmth untempered by a "push from the nest" did not result in the later development of "internality." As Crandall (1973) suggested, the function of independence training is to

> put the child into more active intercourse with his physical and social environment so that there is more opportunity for him to observe the effect of his own behavior, the contingency between his own actions and ensuing events, unmediated by maternal intervention (Crandall, 1973, p. 13).

From Crandall's research and that which preceded it, it is possible to surmise that the ideal home atmosphere for producing children that will grow up with an internal locus of control is one that changes with the child's needs; warm and nurturant when the child is helpless, but increasingly challenging and encouraging of independent pursuits as the child becomes of age to test his developing powers. Accelerating demands for competence as the child's abilities mature may be a necessary ingredient that supplements the security created by the initially supportive, dependency-gratifying home.

In contrast, the family origins of an external locus of control may be described in terms similar to those used by Alfred Adler (Ansbacher & Ansbacher, 1956). Adler believed that if children were overindulged or neglected they were equally likely to develop misguided "fictions" about life, and these were frequently in the form of feelings of inferiority and helplessness. Pampered children were said to be as thwarted in their development as were neglected children in that they were deprived of the opportunity to learn how to act so as to cause the occurrence of desired outcomes. Both pampered and neglected children, then, through lack of experience with contingent reinforcement, may fail to explore and discover the relationships between acts and outcomes from which beliefs in the order of causal sequences develop. Nonreinforcement, for one, and indiscriminate reinforcement, for the other, may result in exaggerated feelings of helplessness, or an extremely external locus of control.

In homes where nurturance and dependency gratifications continue unabated into early adolescence, it is possible that children will not sufficiently encounter challenges from which they can assess their own developing abilities. As such, Crandall's findings with regard to the negative impact of nurturance for internality development merges with the Adlerian focus upon pampering, the granting of reinforcements on a non-contingent basis.

From one other source of information it is possible to ascertain the role of experience with contingent reinforcement upon the development of locus of control. Among many social groups, the opportunities to achieve desired ends have been limited by prejudice, discrimination, and/or deficits produced by earlier deprivations. Children who are reared in a non-literate household, for instance, will experience considerable difficulty when confronting challenges in school that require understanding and the use of the written word. Consequently, the attainment of reinforcements for effort should be relatively rare; and if the child does not receive encouragement and special help, he may easily develop fatalistic beliefs, or external control expectancies.

A fair amount of research has been conducted in which various ethnic and racial groups have been compared with regard to scores on measures of locus of control. Those groups which, at the time of testing, were reputed to be deprived of reinforcement opportunity because of prejudice (blacks, Mexican-Americans, American Indians) or deprivations (lower economic classes) were most often found to acknowledge holding external control expectancies (Lefcourt, 1966; 1976a). A most compelling correlation was reported by Jessor et al. (1968) in which a measure of locus of control correlated strongly with objective access to opportunities available in a particular community. The $r = .50, p < .001, N = 221$, indicated that the less access to opportunity that an individual had, the more external was his locus-of-control score.

In sum, families or larger social settings that offer attainable challenges, responsiveness to instrumental activities, and encouragement to aid children to accept these challenges are more likely to facilitate the growth of internal control expectancies. On the other hand, when a child's efforts go to naught, through neglectful or pampering parents or through hostile milieus offering minimal opportunities, the likelihood of externality increases with its outward signs of helplessness and apathy.

OTHER CORRELATES AND CONSEQUENCES OF LOCUS OF CONTROL

Thus far, we have discussed the ramifications of locus of control with regard to the ways in which people cope with stresses. In this section we will briefly summarize other general correlates of locus of control, and will present an example of how a more detailed analysis of an individual's perceptions of causality can increase our understanding of achievement behavior.

Response to Social Influences

A sizeable number of studies have examined the ways in which locus of control relates to social responsiveness. It has often been assumed that persons who view outcomes as determined by their own machinations will be less likely to accept others' prescriptions for their behavior without giving their choices due deliberation. This reasonable hypothesis has been supported in several studies with differing methodologies such that conclusions are offered with a degree of confidence.

For example, externals, defined by scores on Rotter's scale, have been found to be more influenced by communications from prestigious sources than have internals (Ritchie & Phares, 1969). The internals, on the other hand, have been found to be more attentive to the content of persuasive arguments per se than to the prestige and status of their sources. This finding has been replicated in various ways. Externals, for instance, have been found to be more accepting and readily responsive than internals to the instructions given by experimenters in psychological investigations. The behavior of internals seems to be less predictable by situation characteristics than by their more idiosyncratic constructions of those situations. This work derives from a series of studies that have been described in some detail elsewhere (Lefcourt, 1976a). In addition to the "prestige suggestion" phenomenon, there is some evidence to suggest that externals are less resistant to temptations such that they are more apt to cheat (Johnson & Gormly, 1972) and more easily led into violations of social norms than are internals (Johnson, Ackerman, Frank, & Fionda, 1968).

These findings relevant to the response to social influences have been extended further by research indicating that externals are facilitated, and internals impeded, by the mere presence of social stimulation when they are engaged in various tasks (Baron, Cowan, Ganz, & McDonald, 1974; Baron & Ganz, 1972; Pines, 1973; Pines & Julian, 1972). This difference has also been observed by Lefcourt, Hogg, and Sordoni (1975) who found that internals were more at ease, as indicated by a low frequency of fidgeting, when working on a task in isolation than when "feeling observed" by a video camera operating behind a mirror. In direct reverse, externals were found to fidget less when feeling observed than when they were alone.

These findings suggest that as internals become engaged in various problem-solving tasks, their involvement in the pursuit is more "complete" than is that of external subjects. The latter seem to require more social feedback during a performance, with the possible evaluative information that such feedback may offer. Internals, in contrast, seem to be distracted by such moment-to-moment responsiveness and may prefer such feedback after the completion of a task. While this linkage between locus of control and temporal orientation requires further research, some related findings have been reported to the effect that externals are more oriented toward present and immediate events than they are to those more removed in time (Lefcourt, 1972).

Regardless of the reasons, the overall evidence consistently suggests that externals are more attentive and positively responsive to social cues, and are facilitated in task performances by their presence. Internals, on the other hand, seem more resistant to social influences and are, at the least, distracted by social cues as they attempt to cope with various tasks.

These findings may have been reflected in the "resistance" displayed by Richard X, despite his seeming state of helplessness. He had refused to accept the verdict of authorities with regard to impending eye surgery until he was able to obtain additional opinions; and even then, he only consented "with conditions." Likewise, he did not accept the discouraging response to his interest in physiotherapy. In essence, he was critical of advice and remained cautious and planful about any major decisions that pertained to his welfare.

Cognitive Activity

A second research area, which has been alluded to previously, is that which has examined the cognitive processes associated with locus of control. Internal tuberculosis patients, as described earlier, were more likely to become knowledgeable about their illness than were external patients (Seeman & Evans, 1962). Internals have generally been found to be more attentive than externals to information that bears relevance to valued goals. This attentional difference has been assessed in some instances by the amount of time that persons require for making difficult decisions and choices. In such studies, internals have been found to deliberate for a longer time than have externals when the choices have been more difficult to choose between (Rotter & Mulry, 1965; Julian & Katz, 1968; Lefcourt, Lewis, & Silverman, 1968). In the latter study, externals were also found to be more distractable during a task that seemed to require skill–looking away, daydreaming about irrelevancies, and so on–whereas internals were more likely to behave in that fashion when they believed that the task was more chance determined.

In another set of studies described previously (Lefcourt *et al.*, 1973; Wolk & Ducette, 1974), internals were found to be more alert and less in need of outside cues to know when certain events in their milieu were changing in character. In both of these studies, internals were found to be more discerning of shifts in an experimenter's intentions than were externals. Internals have been found to be more rapid in their assimilation of information, and, therefore, are more quick to transform a state of uncertainty into one of comprehension.

Again, these results are illustrated in Richard X's behavior. Though badly hurt and suffering all sorts of disability, Richard X remained alert to his choices. As he expressed it, "You don't give anything away," indicating that he had to be involved in each major decision, knowing the options and prognoses of each choice. Richard X's struggle to remain awake during his first weeks in the hospital may have reflected his need to remain aware, to know what was about to happen to himself.

Anxiety and Depression

A third area of research that has produced congruent evidence bears enough similarity to the section concerning stress that a presentation of details might be redundant. It suffices to note, then, that externality has been found to be associated with the acknowledgement of anxiety and depression. These consistent correlational data have been tabulated elsewhere (Lefcourt, 1976a). One interesting study that may add color to the stark correlational figures involved the recall of mood states by suicidal patients. Melges and Weisz (1971) asked patients to reconstruct their states of mind immediately prior to their suicide attempts. Subjects were left by themselves with a tape recorder into which they spoke aloud of the events and feelings that were going through their minds at this time. Both before and after the soliloquy, subjects completed a number of tests which included a version of Rotter's locus-of-control scale.

The findings indicated that increases in suicidal ideation were associated with changes toward a more negative evaluation of the future, toward greater external control, and toward a lesser extension of awareness into the future. The correlations between the measures indicated that increasing externality was associated with an increasingly negative outlook and a diminishing awareness of the future.

When Richard X denied fearing death but asserted that he had a strong urge to survive, he provided us with another rich illustration, this time pertaining to affect. As internals have differed from externals in previous investigations, Richard X did not dwell upon fears and the anxiety-arousing circumstances that were inherent in his immediate situation. Rather, he focused his energies on the tasks at hand, the striving to recuperate and to survive into the future. His appreciation of the future never dimmed in expectation or awareness, and his sense of himself as the responsible actor remained intact.

Achievement Behavior

One last area of interest to be mentioned is that of achievement behavior. Though the results of research in this area indicate that various achievement behaviors are predictable by locus-of-control orientations, some recent developments have raised intriguing questions regarding more precise relationships between causal attributions and achievement performances.

Bernard Weiner and his associates (1971, 1972) have brought the work of attribution theorists to bear upon the relationship between locus of control and achievement behavior. Weiner has contended that if the large variety of reasons people offer for their achievement outcomes were to be examined, it would become apparent that a simple dichotomous classification of causes into internal and external would be insufficient. As an introduction to complexity, Weiner advocates the use of at least two dimensions for classifying causes: locus of control and stability of cause. If a person were to attribute his achievement successes and failures solely to his abilities—stable-internal attributes—then it would be less likely that he would change in the amount of effort he expends after encountering failure experiences. "After all," he might reason, "if I'm *incapable* of comprehending physics regardless of the time I spend studying, why should I waste further time in trying to improve my grade." On the other hand, if a person believed that effort was a prime determinant of his successes and failures—an internal-variable attribute—then he might be more apt to work harder after experiencing failures. In other words, stable-internal attributes, such as intelligence or ability, might prove to be less predictive of *changes* in behavior following adverse outcomes than would variable-internal characteristics. The latter afford hope, since there is something one can do about one's outcomes if they are responsive to changes in personal behavior. Belief in the causal power of intelligence, on the other hand, might lead to resignation when one is failing and he believes that he simply lacks the intelligence to succeed.

Weiner has also differentiated among external attributes. Luck is described as an external-variable cause; the level of difficulty or task circumstances are described as external-stable causes. Weiner has argued that it is not enough to know whether a person holds himself accountable for his outcomes; rather, one must know *which* personal attributes or *which* external attributes are viewed as causal in order to make precise predictions of achievement behavior.

Two investigations by Dweck (1973; 1975) illustrate the utility of Weiner's approach. Both in laboratory-like tasks and with real academic difficulties, Dweck has demonstrated that precise causal attributions can be used to assess problems and to effect therapeutic changes. For example, children who were experiencing difficulty in learning to read improved markedly when they were taught to reassign the cause of their difficulties to effort rather than to ability. In other words, when children believed that their failures were due to a lack of ability, a stable internal cause, little effort was given to overcoming their deficits. However, when cause for failure was attributed to a lack of effort, an unstable internal attribute, the children increased in their attempts at learning and enjoyed some consequent successes. In these studies, two internal attributes were found to have differing impact upon the subsequent behaviors of children as they performed achievement tasks.

Dweck's findings may help toward the creation of understanding and of ameliorative attempts with the achievement-related difficulties of particular slow learners. As noted earlier, Cromwell (1963) has suggested that many borderline retarded individuals may suffer more from expectancy deficiencies than from ability deficits. Conceivably, such persons have all too readily accepted a lack of ability as cause for academic failures, and consequently have surrendered any ambitions in this direction. On the other hand, if such persons were to be encouraged to attribute cause for their failures to more variable sources such as effort, attitudes, or study habits, the likelihood of exertions that could increase the probability of successes might become greater.

OVERVIEW AND FUTURE DEVELOPMENTS

If we were familiar with only the few findings discussed within this chapter, we could conclude that locus of control is a powerful construct, one that has meaning for the ways in which people function. Nevertheless, as has been intimated in the preceding section, work with locus of control is not about to become static. Weiner's theoretical contributions and Dweck's research are but two advances in this area of personality investigation that are raising new questions.

When Rotter and his colleagues began their speculations about locus of control, they did not envisage the construct as one that would lend itself to the development of a typology. To divide the world into "internals" and "externals" is clearly an error; and although, in the use of the terms, there is that ready temptation to think of people as types, it was never the intention of social-learning advocates to do so. The predecessor of Rotter's 23-item locus-of-control scale contained a large number of items that sampled from a wide range of reinforcement areas. It was hoped that goal-specific locus-of-control scores could be obtained so that individuals could be characterized by profiles of their expectancies regarding achievement, affiliation, love and affection, and so forth. In essence, the investigators who were responsible for creating much of the interest in the locus-of-control construct did not envision it as being unidimensional. However, the psychometric properties of the early scales were such that specific goal-locus-of-control subscales failed to materialize, and a broad, assumedly unidimensional measurement tool came into use. As was noted in this chapter, this instrument, Rotter's locus-of-control scale, has had extensive use, and even with its many psychometric shortcomings, has generated much in the way of provocative research. Nevertheless, it is important to bear in mind that the construct is not meant to define a typology, but pertains to the ways in which people construe reinforcements or goals as occurring. It should therefore be possible to speak of someone holding internal-control expectancies for successes and/or failures in one sphere–love and affection, perhaps–while perceiving himself to be helpless in another, such as social recognition at his work setting. In other words, previous research has demonstrated the utility of the construct for predicting a range of behaviors, and we are now approaching a stage where research will become more refined and complex. Dweck's focus upon specific internal-causal attributes opens our purview to one such refinement. Her research encourages us to ask when particular attributes can lead to specific ends. Ability or intelligence as a cause of outcomes may lead to different behaviors, for instance, when people experience successes as opposed to failures. If successes in academic work are ascribed to ability, a continuous high output of work may be evident as individuals seek confirmatory evidence of that ability. If, however, failure were one's common lot, and a *lack* of ability were the ascribed cause, withdrawal and apathy might be a more likely response to achievement demands. Internal characteristics such as ability, then, may operate differently when used as an explanation of success than when it is held to be a cause of failure. In the latter case, intelligence may actually be viewed as an external attribute, a "given" which must be accepted as one's fate.

Other developments in locus-of-control research that offer promise of more complexity are evident in the construction of goal-specific locus-of-control scales. The Intellectual Achievement Responsibility Scale constructed by the Crandalls (Crandall, Katkovsky, & Crandall, 1965) was the first of such specific devices. Their scale focused upon achievement among children and differentiated between success and failure experiences. More recently, scales constructed by Kirscht (1972) and the Wallstons (1976) have assessed the locus of control for health. This author has also constructed a measure for differentiating between the locus of control for achievement and affiliation, with subscales assessing ability, effort, chance, and situation (Weiner's four causal attributes) as causal factors. Though these scales, with the exception of the Crandalls' measure, have not been used extensively thus far and have not been tested in many validity studies, there is little reason to doubt their eventual value, if only as a model for other investigators. Rotter's scale has been factor analyzed repeatedly and found to contain separate factors. Given the "multidimensional" nature of even this short locus-of-control scale, theoretically derived measures containing "planned" factors should prove to be valuable.

Between the attempt to ask when particular attributes will effect given outcomes and the attempt to construct goal-specific measures, there is considerable room for future developments in research. Another inquiry that has been made by some investigators pertains to whether it is always beneficial to view one's self as a cause of outcomes. One may ask whether control is actually possible in many circumstances, and may question what are the reasonable limits for a belief in internal control.

Few answers to these questions can be found in the research literature. However, it is possible to contend first that, by definition, locus of control does not refer to delusions of omnipotence evident among persons enveloped in a manic state; rather, it refers to the roles that persons perceive for themselves in their pursuits of valued goals. Death, birth, illness and taxes, some would assert, are inevitable and must be accepted fatalistically. Political happenings, natural catastrophes, and the like will more often be viewed as being beyond personal control, resulting in the well-known "Why me?" response. On the other hand, certain life events are assumed to be responsive to human efforts in particular cultures. It is with regard to these events, normatively considered controllable, that differences in control expectancies should provide differential predictions of behavior, and that an internal locus of control may be said to be the more optimal belief.

It has been contended by some (Gurin, Gurin, Lao, & Beattie, 1969) that oppressed minorities would do well to place blame for negative experiences upon oppressors, and that such attributions are more apt to lead to constructive efforts for change. While this argument is appealing, one can wonder at the personal price that may have to be paid for overgeneralized blaming of others for one's failures. After a struggle to redress grievances, it may be rather difficult to eschew the habit of holding others responsible for one's misery.

Beyond politics, it is conceivable that external attributions may afford better prognoses for recovery from some sorts of difficulties. A benign, philosophical acceptance of life's twistings and turnings may be more beneficial in some instances than would a continuous struggle resulting from beliefs about one's personal responsibilities. The death of a loved one is one such event to which a fatalistic view of life and its vicissitudes would seem to be a more appropriate response.

Nevertheless, the overall data accruing from a wide range of research investigations leaves us with the conclusion that to know that one has causal impact on valued reinforcements bodes well for the ways in which one will cope with experiences pertinent to those reinforcement areas.

It should also be noted that a literature focusing upon self-control and self-regulation in behavior modification has recently attained prominence (Mahoney & Thoresen, 1974; Goldfried & Merbaum, 1973). While much of this research has been technique oriented, a guiding proposition has been that the exercise of self-control allows one a sense of freedom, a feeling that one can correct one's difficulties; and it is this sense of "can-ness" which seems to be an aim of these forms of therapy.

As we have indicated in this chapter, "can-ness" refers to the sense that one can effect the course of one's life. We have referred to that "sense" as one's locus of control; and it is our conclusion that when one loses the belief that important events are to some degree controllable by one's actions, one loses that vitality and courage that humans can display in their encounters with hardships. Richard X might never have struggled so effectively had he been passive and resigned to his fate.

REFERENCES

Ansbacher, H., & Ansbacher, R. *The individual psychology of Alfred Adler.* New York: Basic Books, 1956.

Bandura, A. *Social learning theory.* New York: General Learning Press, 1971.

Baron, R. M., Cowan, G., Ganz, R. L., & McDonald, M. Interaction of locus of control and type of performance feedback: Considerations of external validity. *Journal of Personality and Social Psychology,* 1974, *30,* 285-292.

Baron, R. M., & Ganz, R. L. Effects of locus of control and type of feedback on the performance of lower-class black children. *Journal of Personality and Social Psychology,* 1972, *21,* 124-130.

Brady, J. V., Porter, R. W., Conrad, D. G., & Mason, J. W. Avoidance behavior and the development of gastroduodenal ulcers. *Journal of Experimental Analyses of Behavior,* 1958, *1,* 69-72.

Bulman, R. J., & Wortman, C. B. Attributions of blame and coping in the "real world". *Journal of Personality and Social Psychology,* 1977, *35,* 351-363.

Byrne, D. Repression-sensitization as a dimension of personality. In B. A. Maher (Ed.), *Progress in experimental personality research.* New York: Academic Press, 1964.

Cohen, F., & Lazarus, R. S. Active coping processes, coping dispositions, and recovery from surgery. *Psychosomatic Medicine,* 1973, *35,* 375-389.

Crandall, V. C. Differences in parental antecedents of internal-external control in children and in young adulthood. Paper presented at the American Psychological Association Convention, Montreal, 1973.

____, **Katkovsky, W., & Crandall, V. J.** Children's beliefs in their control of reinforcements in intellectual academic achievement behaviors. *Child Development,* 1965, *36,* 91-109.

Cromwell, R. L. A social learning approach to mental retardation. In N. R. Ellis (Ed.), *Handbook of mental deficiency.* New York: McGraw-Hill, 1963, pp. 41-91.

Davis, W. L., & Phares, E. J. Internal-external control as a determinant of information-seeking in a social influence situation. *Journal of Personality*, 1967, *35*, 547-561.

Dohrenwend, B. S., & Dohrenwend, B. P. (Eds.), *Stressful life events: Their nature and effects.* New York: Wiley, 1974.

Douglas, W. O. *Go east, young man.* New York: Random House, 1974.

Dweck, C. S. The role of expectations and attributions on the alleviation of learned helplessness. *Journal of Personality and Social Psychology*, 1975, *31*, 674-685.

____, **& Repucci, N. D.** Learned helplessness and reinforcement responsibility in children. *Journal of Personality and Social Psychology*, 1973, *25*, 109-116.

Ekman, P., & Friesen, W. V. Nonverbal behavior and psychopathology. In R. J. Friedman & M. M. Katz (Eds.), *The psychology of depression: Contemporary theory and research.* U.S. Govt. Printing Office, 1972.

Feifel, H. *The meaning of death.* New York: McGraw-Hill, 1959.

Galbraith, G. G., & Mosher, D. L. Associative sexual responses in relation to sexual stimulation, guilt, and external approval contingencies. *Journal of Personality and Social Psychology*, 1968, *10*, 142-147.

Glass, D. C., & Singer, J. E. *Urban stress: Experiments on noise and social stressors.* New York: Academic Press, 1972.

Goldfried, M. R., & Merbaum, M. (Eds.), *Behavior change through self-control.* New York: Holt, Rinehart & Winston, 1973.

Goldstein, M. J. Individual differences in response to stress. *American Journal of Community Psychology*, 1973, *1*, 113-137.

Gurin, P., Gurin, G., Lao, R. C., & Beattie, M. Internal-external control in the motivational dynamics of Negro youth. *Journal of Social Issues*, 1969, *25*, 29-53.

Harvey, J. H., Ickes, W. J., & Kidd, R. F. (Eds.), *New directions in attribution research.* Hillsdale, N.J.: Lawrence Erlbaum Associates, 1976.

Heider, F. *The psychology of interpersonal relations.* New York: Wiley, 1958.

Holmes, T. H., & Rahe, R. H. The social readjustment rating scale. *Journal of Psychosomatic Research*, 1967, *11*, 213-218.

Janis, I. *Psychological stress.* New York: Wiley, 1958.

Jessor, R., Graves, T. D., Hanson, R. C., & Jessor, S. *Society, personality, and deviant behavior.* New York: Holt, Rinehart, & Winston, 1968.

Johnson, C. D., & Gormly, J. Academic cheating: The contribution of sex, personality, and situational variables. *Developmental Psychology*, 1972, *6*, 320-325.

Johnson, R. C., Ackerman, J. M., Frank, H., & Fionda, A. J. Resistance to temptation and guilt following yielding and psychopathology. *Journal of Consulting and Clinical Psychology*, 1968, *32*, 169-175.

Julian, J. W., & Katz, S. B. Internal versus external control and the value of reinforcement. *Journal of Personality and Social Psychology,* 1968, *76,* 43-48.

Kirscht, J. P. Perception of control and health beliefs. *Canadian Journal of Behavioral Science,* 1972, *4,* 225-237.

Klinger, E. Consequences of commitment to and disengagement from incentives. *Psychological Review,* 1975, *82,* 1-25.

Lazarus, R. S. *Psychological stress and the coping process.* New York: McGraw-Hill, 1966.

Lefcourt, H. M. Internal-external control of reinforcement: A review. *Psychological Bulletin,* 1966, *65,* 206-220.

____. Recent developments in the study of locus of control. In B. A. Maher (Ed.), *Progress in experimental research in personality, Vol. 6.* New York: Academic Press, 1972.

____. *Locus of control: Current trends in theory and research.* Hillsdale, N.J.: Lawrence Erlbaum Associates, 1976. (a)

____. Locus of control and the response to aversive events. *Canadian Psychological Review,* 1976, *17,* 202-209. (b)

____, **Antrobus, P., & Hogg, E.** Humor response and humor production as a function of locus of control, field dependence and type of reinforcements. *Journal of Personality,* 1974, *42,* 632-651.

____, **Gronnerud, P., & McDonald, P.** Cognitive activity and hypothesis formation during a double entendre word association test as a function of locus of control and field dependence. *Canadian Journal of Behavioral Science,* 1973, *5,* 161-173.

____, **Hogg, E., & Sordoni, C.** Locus of control, field dependence, and conditions arousing objective versus subjective self-awareness. *Journal of Research in Personality,* 1975, *9,* 21-36.

____, **Struthers, S., & Holmes, C.** Causal attributions as a function of locus of control, initial confidence and performance outcomes. *Journal of Personality and Social Psychology,* 1975, *32,* 391-397.

____, **Lewis, L., & Silverman, I. W.** Internal versus external control of reinforcement and attention in decision-making tasks. *Journal of Personality,* 1968, *36,* 663-682.

____, **Sordoni, C., & Sordoni, C.** Locus of control and the expression of humour. *Journal of Personality,* 1974, *42,* 130-143.

____, **& Wine, J.** Internal versus external control of reinforcement and the deployment of attention in experimental situations. *Canadian Journal of Behavioral Science,* 1969, *1,* 167-181.

Lewin, K. *A dynamic theory of personality.* New York: McGraw-Hill, 1935.

Lewinsohn, P. M. *Clinical and theoretical aspects of depression.* Paper presented at Georgia Symposium in Experimental Clinical Psychology, 1972.

Luborsky, L., Blinder, B., & Schimek, J. Looking, recalling and GSR as a function of defense. *Journal of Abnormal Psychology,* 1965, *70,* 270-280.

Mahoney, M. J., & Thoresen, C. E. *Self control: Power in the person.* Monterey, California: Brooks/Cole, 1974.

May, R. *Man's search for himself.* New York: W. W. Norton, 1953.

Melges, F. T., & Weisz, A. E. The personal future and suicidal ideation. *Journal of Nervous and Mental Diseases,* 1971, *153,* 244-250.

Miller, M. *Plain speaking.* New York: Berkley Pub. Corp., 1973.

Mischel, W. Toward a cognitive social learning reconceptualization of personality. *Psychological Review,* 1973, *80,* 252-283.

Mowrer, O. H., & Viek, P. An experimental analogue of fear from a sense of helplessness. *Journal of Abnormal and Social Psychology,* 1943, *43,* 193-200.

Pines, H. A. An attributional analysis of locus of control orientation and source of informational dependence. *Journal of Personality and Social Psychology,* 1973, *26,* 262-272.

____, **& Julian, J. W.** Effects of task and social demands on locus of control differences in information processing. *Journal of Personality,* 1972, *40,* 407-416.

Richter, C. P. The phenomenon of unexplained sudden death in animals and man. In H. Feifel (Ed.), *The meaning of death.* New York: McGraw-Hill, 1959.

Ritchie, E., & Phares, E. J. Attitude change as a function of internal-external control and communicator status. *Journal of Personality,* 1969, *37,* 429-443.

Rotter, J. B. *Social learning and clinical psychology.* Englewood Cliffs, N.J.: Prentice-Hall, 1954.

____. Generalized expectancies for internal versus external control of reinforcement. *Psychological Monographs,* 1966, *80* (Whole No. 609).

____, **Chance, J. E., & Phares, E. J.** *Applications of a social learning theory of personality.* New York: Holt, Rinehart & Winston, 1972.

____, **& Mulry, R. C.** Internal versus external control of reinforcements and decision time. *Journal of Personality and Social Psychology,* 1965, *2,* 598-604.

____, **Seeman, M., & Liverant, S.** Internal versus external control of reinforcement: A major variable in behavior theory. In N. F. Washburne (Ed.), *Decisions values and groups, Vol. 2.* London: Pergamon Press, 1962, 473-516.

Seeman, M. Alienation and social learning in a reformatory. *American Journal of Sociology,* 1963, *69,* 270-284.

____, **& Evans, J. W.** Alienation and learning in a hospital setting. *American Sociological Review,* 1962, *27,* 772-783.

Seligman, M. *Helplessness.* San Francisco: W. H. Freeman, 1975.

Singer, J. L., & Antrobus, J. S. *Imaginal processes inventory.* New York: City College of CUNY, 1966.

Wallston, B. S., Wallston, K. A., Kaplan, G. D., & Mardes, S. A. Development and validation of the Health Locus of Control Scale. *Journal of Consulting and Clinical Psychology,* 1976, *44,* 580-585.

Watson, J. S. The development and generalization of "contingency awareness" in early infancy: Some hypotheses. *Merrill-Palmer Quarterly of Behavior and Development,* 1966, *12,* 123-135.

____. Memory and "contingency analysis" in infant learning. *Merrill-Palmer Quarterly of Behavior and Development,* 1967, *13,* 55-76.

____. Smiling, cooing and "the game". *Merrill-Palmer Quarterly of Behavior and Development,* 1972, *18,* 323-339.

Weaver, R. Internality, externality, and compliance as related to chronic home dialysis patients. Unpublished Master's thesis, Emory University, 1972.

Weiner, B., Friese, I., Kukla, A., Reed, L., Rest, S., & Rosenbaum, R. M. *Perceiving the causes of success and failure.* New York: General Learning Press, 1971.

Weiner, B., Heckhausen, H., Meyer, W. U., & Cook, R. E. Causal ascriptions and achievement motivation. *Journal of Personality and Social Psychology,* 1972, *21,* 239-248.

Weiss, J. M. Effects of coping behavior in different warning signal conditions on stress pathology in rats. *Journal of Comparative and Physiological Psychology,* 1971, *1,* 1-14.

Williams, A. F. Factors associated with seat belt use in families. *Journal of Safety Research,* 1972, *4,* 133-138. (a)

____. Personality characteristics associated with preventive dental health practices. *Journal of American College of Dentists,* 1972, *39,* 225-234. (b)

Wolk, S., & DuCette, J. Intentional performance and incidental learning as a function of personality and task directions. *Journal of Personality and Social Psychology,* 1974, *29,* 90-101.

ERVIN STAUB

Social and Prosocial Behavior: Personal and Situational Influences and Their Interactions

6

As I crossed Harvard Square one day, I noticed a young woman waving her arms and shouting in the middle of the street. She was standing in front of a car, demanding that the driver run her over. Just before I reached her, a policeman appeared and escorted her to the sidewalk. She sobbed, said that she did not want to live, that life is miserable. A local professor-typc tried to take her into the restaurant that we happened to be standing in front of, offering her a cup of coffee, presumably wanting to give her a chance to calm down. I was trying to talk to the policeman–who began to disentangle himself from this scene, busily giving information to a driver who stopped near us–telling him that we need to take some action, that the woman needs psychiatric attention. The woman suddenly turned, walked away and disappeared around the bend of the street. An older man and I started to walk after her. Not wanting to seem to chase her, we did not run; and by the time we turned the bend, she was nowhere to be seen. I looked into a couple of stores and a restaurant further down the street, but could not see her.

What happened to this young woman that lead to her actions? How would other people, with different personal characteristics, have reacted to the same experiences? What influences guided her behavior and the behavior of those of us who responded to her, however ineffectively?

A major goal of psychology has always been to study and come to understand human behavior. In this chapter, I am concerned with two large questions. First, what determines the way people behave toward each other; what influences guide their social behavior? Second, what influences guide *positive* interactions among human beings? Can we understand why people do or do not behave toward each other in a positive fashion–why they do or do not help each other,

The dissertations described in this chapter, and my own research since 1973, as well as the preparation of this chapter, were facilitated by Grant MH 23886 from the National Institutes of Mental Health.

share with each other, show sensitivity and kindness to each other? Can we predict the occurrence of such behavior?

These two questions are related. In order to understand positive social behavior, we have to consider how social behavior in general is determined. Frequently, people face conflicts between benefiting others and engaging in behavior that promotes their own interests. They may want to reach a high level of achievement in some activity, gain social approval, enjoy others' company, or enrich themselves. What determines how they resolve their conflict and how they act? In this chapter I will attempt to develop a conception of how social behavior is determined, while focusing on the more specific question, examining influences on positive social behavior. Some of the same principles are likely to account for how varied social behaviors are determined, although specific types of behaviors will also have special or unique influences on them.

By positive social behavior I refer to actions that benefit other people. Usually, such behavior demands some form of self-sacrifice. Helping, sharing, cooperation, sensitivity, and responsiveness to other people can all be considered positive acts. In order for an act to be positive behavior, it has to be voluntary and intended to benefit another person. However, the reasons or motives for intending to benefit others can vary. Concern with others' welfare and the desire to enhance their welfare may be one reason. Personal values and norms may be the source of such concern, or the source may be an affective involvement with others and the experience of empathy. The reason for positive acts may also be the desire for social approval or the avoidance of social disapproval, or the desire for other forms of self-gain, including the hope of material rewards that a person can gain by inducing other people to reciprocate their kindness or generosity. In cooperative activities, a person can benefit himself or herself while benefiting others.

A person's tendency to behave positively is important even if the positive behavior intends to gain benefit for the actor. After all, attempting to further the interest of the self through positive acts, in contrast to aggressive, harmful acts, promotes everyone's welfare. The philosopher Hume suggested that human beings are capable of learning through their experience in social living to promote their self-interest in an enlightened fashion, by considering the interrelationship between their own and others' interests. Some current theories and research seem in agreement with this conception. For example, exchange theories assume that social systems and personal relations are guided by exchange relationships, in which people exchange goods and services, and engage in a give-and-take that is mutually beneficial (Chadwick-Jones, 1976; Homans, 1961; Staub, 1972, 1978; Thibaut & Kelley, 1959).

A number of years ago I talked to a Carnegie Hero, someone who received a medal from the Carnegie Hero Foundation for having endangered his life in the course of saving someone else's life. This happened 10 days after his combined gallbladder and appendectomy operations, on his first day out of the house.

He went to the beach with his girlfriend. Hearing the cries of a drowning woman, he jumped into the water, swam to her, and pulled her toward the shore, keeping her afloat until a rescue boat arrived. When pulled from the water, he himself was in a state of collapse.

Many questions can be asked that highlight our inquiry. What motivated him to act? Why was it he, a man still recovering from surgery, rather than others on the crowded beach? Would he help people in other ways too? Would he give money to a needy person, or try to console someone who is sad or upset? Is he usually kind and generous with his friends and acquaintances? Is it reasonable for us to expect that he would be helpful in any of these ways? What do we have to know about him to predict whether he will behave positively in these ways and/or whether he will show consistency in positive behavior?

To state these issues in a general way, to what extent are people consistent in their behavior? Can people be characterized by tendencies to behave one way or another? Is it possible to gather information about people that enables us to predict how they will behave on specific occasions? Can we develop a theoretical model to make such predictions? What do we have to know about people, about their environment, and about the relationship between individual characteristics and environments to understand (and predict) social behavior?

The purpose of this chapter is to examine these and related questions and to describe a conceptualization, or theoretical model, for understanding and predicting (positive) social behavior. Research findings about influences on positive social behavior are too extensive to review here in detail. Instead, generalizations derived from the research findings will be presented, based on this author's recent elaborate reviews of this literature (Staub, 1978, 1979). Some examples of the research on which these generalizations are based will be presented. Research that is specifically relevant to the theoretical model will be reviewed.

Like most writers in this book, my purpose is not only to present existing knowledge but to develop and present a conception relevant to an important domain in personality (as well as in social psychology). I will attempt to show how theoretical concepts were arrived at, and to indicate how some of the basic concepts of the theory may be tested.

BACKGROUND: SITUATIONS, PERSONS AND THEIR INTERACTIONS

The Issue of Consistency

To what extent is behavior consistent across many situations? The concept of personality assumes the existence of stable individual differences. Most personality psychologists assume consistency at some level of people's functioning, although not necessarily at the level of behavior. Consistency may be assumed in the domain of perception, of interpretation of events, of motives, or in other domains. Although consistency in behavior has frequently been assumed, even Gordon Allport (1937), the most avid promoter of trait theory, clearly recognized the limitations of consistency in behavior. He enumerated several important sources of inconsistency: personality traits may contradict each other; the environment constantly changes, activating one trait and then another; and, usually, several traits act together.

The existence of consistency in behavior has been repeatedly questioned in the past (see Bem & Allen, 1974). Recently, the assumption that people behave consistently across varied circumstances has been vigorously questioned by several writers (Mischel, 1968, 1969, 1973; Jones & Nisbett, 1971; Gergen, 1968, 1976). Mischel (1968, 1969) reviewed evidence suggesting that people tend to perceive others as consistent and to view themselves as consistent. Seemingly, we are motivated to believe that the world around us is predictable and hence to perceive the behavior of others as well as our own as consistent. But does this reflect reality? On the basis of research findings that he reviewed, Mischel concluded that there is a fair degree of consistency in cognitive, intellectual functioning. Performance on intellectual tasks, and on varied cognitive tasks (e.g., tests of field differentiation, such as matching familiar figures), tends to be reasonably highly correlated. However, consistency in interpersonal and social behavior is limited. Correlations among behaviors performed under different circumstances, or between personality test scores and behavior, seem to reach a maximum of about .30. Greater consistency in behavior is to be found only when the situations in which behavior is tested are highly similar. But when the characteristics of situations vary, behavioral similarity declines. Mischel's review and his conclusions imply that we cannot expect that a person who is helpful at one time will be another time. People have idyosyncratic histories of reinforcement and experiences with their environments, and they will respond to circumstances in a differentiated manner. (Conditions under which consistency can be expected will be discussed at a later point.)

Gergen (1968, 1976), based on his research, questioned consistency in the self-concept. The self-concept of mature individuals has usually been regarded as highly consistent (see Epstein in this volume). In varied experiments, Gergen and his associates showed that relatively minor experiences, or even the nature of the surrounding environment, frequently affect how positively or negatively people evaluate themselves. Self-esteem, or self-evaluation, has been regarded, however, as an important aspect of the self-concept. For example, Gergen (1968) has shown that when subjects wait for a job interview, the presence of an immaculately dressed and apparently extremely well organized person, who is also waiting for the job interview, leads people to describe themselves on a test of self-esteem in less favorable terms than they did at a previous administration of the self-esteem measure. The presence of a poorly dressed and apparently disorganized person leads to increase in the positivity of self-descriptions. There is also evidence, in research on prosocial behavior, that seemingly limited positive and negative experiences, including success and failure experiences, affect people's willingness to help others or share with others. It has been assumed that a person's mood and temporary level of self-esteem are affected by such experiences and in turn affect subsequent positive acts (Rosenhan et al., 1976; Staub, 1978).

Most likely, self-esteem has both stable and variable components. A person's moods and current feelings about himself or herself are the result of varied influences. Just as behavior is multidetermined, a person's feelings about the self at any one time must be multidetermined. Consistent with Epstein's views, the self-concept may be regarded as consisting of hypotheses about the self—as well as about the relationship between the self and the outside world. Some of these hypotheses are likely to be more firmly held, others less so. When less firmly held but important hypotheses are questioned or disconfirmed by current experiences (I am intelligent; I am handsome; I am likeable or liked; I am competent—can be such hypotheses), self-concern may arise or temporary negative self-evaluation may result. Confirmation of such hypotheses would induce temporary positive states. At the same time, if a person is asked to respond to the question of how he or she usually feels about or evaluates himself or herself, to provide a self-evaluation of a stable kind, greater consistency may result. Whatever their temporary state, people are likely to know how they usually feel about themselves.

Some writers (Bowers, 1973) describe the position of those who question consistency in behavior as "situationism." Situationism presumably minimizes or ignores the characteristics of organisms as the determinant of their conduct, and emphasizes the impact of external stimuli (Harré & Secord, 1972). It has been long assumed, by most psychologists, that behavior is a function of the person, the situation, and the interaction between the two. Traditionally, personality psychologists emphasized the influence of individual characteristics. Social psychologists tended to emphasize the influence of situations: the social group, other people, specific circumstances and the pressures exerted by them. A number of psychologists emphasized the interactive influence of persons and situations which led to a renewed interest in how persons and environments jointly—interactively—affect behavior (Bowers, 1973; Magnusson & Endler, 1977; Mischel, 1973, 1976; Staub, 1978). The questioning of consistency, gave rise to controversy (Lewin, 1948; Murray, 1932).

What does person-situation interaction refer to in real-life terms? Let's assume that our Carnegie Hero who saved the drowning woman was genuinely motivated to help—that he responds strongly to the need of people whose life is in danger, or to those who suffer physical pain. However, let's also assume that he very much believes in the American ideal of individuality and competitiveness (purely an assumption, not based on any information I have), and therefore he strongly believes that people should work hard and earn a living. Consequently, when there is an opportunity to share with someone who is deprived, or when he is approached to donate for the poor, believing that such people should help themselves, he will not be motivated to help. Depending on the nature of the *stimulus* for prosocial behavior, his motivation to help will or will not be activated. Sometimes, when his motivation to help is activated he will actually proceed to act; at other times (for reasons that will be discussed later) he may not. Thus, the nature of circumstances and his characteristics jointly determine his motivation to help and whether or not he will be helpful. In another person, neither type of situation may give rise to the desire to help or benefit others, while in a third person both types of situation may do so.

Most, if not all, personality (and social) psychologists would agree that characteristics of persons and of the environment join in affecting behavior. However, differences exist in how much importance different psychologists have assigned to the influence of situations, to persons, and to their interactions in their theory and research.[1]

Situational and Personal Influences

When will the external environment or situation exert primary influence on behavior? While situations exert influence, they do so as a function of their meaning to people, of the thoughts and feelings they give rise to, and of the motives they arouse. It is people, not situations, who act. Under certain circumstances most people may act similarly because the situation activates very basic common goals or needs. Sometimes, such goals or needs may be common to most of humanity, such as the desire for survival, perhaps aroused by a wild animal, or by a fire, or by someone with a gun. When someone pulls a gun on us and demands our money, most of us will hand it over. Other times, communality among people in basic goals or needs, and the manner in which they try to satisfy goals, will be a function of similarity in socialization and of norms and rules that guide social behavior in particular cultures. For example, the desire for respect by one's peers may be strongly inculcated in one culture and less so in another. The ways to gain respect may also vary. Usually, circumstances do not exert such a powerful influence that most people who face them would behave in a similar way. Particularly in a culture like ours, in which great variability in values and motives exists across subcultures and individual families, there will be variations among people in how they interpret and react to most situations.

[1]Maddi, in Chapter 8, notes that personality situation interaction is a foregone conclusion: Naturally the two interact. That seems to me a reasonable view. He also implies that the current rediscovery of interactionism is like a rediscovery of the wheel. I believe, however, that the "rediscovery" is important. While, as an expression of faith, most personality psychologists would have agreed 15 or 20 years ago with a statement of interaction, this would have been like saluting the flag. Such a belief gained little or no expression in research and theory. Currently, we are moving from an abstraction to genuine concern with an investigation of the nature of person-situation interactions.

People not only respond to events, but seek them out and create opportunities for varied kinds of conduct. Here, personal–in contrast to environmental–influences are even more important. Obviously, some people like to go to the movies, and frequently do so, while others who like football may spend endless hours in the stadium or in front of the television set. People also shape their environment, and the circumstances they create will in turn influence their own behavior. For example, Kelley and Stahleski (1970) found that some subjects believed that people in general are competitive rather than cooperative, and these subjects behaved competitively from the start in a prisoner's dilemma game. This resulted in competitive reactions by their partners. By their own behavior, they apparently brought about the competitive behavior they expected, which then confirmed their original belief and further affected their behavior. Cross-cultural research with children showed cultural differences in degree of competitiveness, and showed that patterns of interaction develop within particular pairs that affect the continued interaction of the pair even more than cultural origin or other conditions. Some children act so competitively that they provoke competition in even potentially cooperative partners (Toda, Shinotsuka, McClintock, & Stech, 1978). A substantial body of research shows reciprocity in human interactions: by what we do, we shape others' reactions to us (Staub, 1978). Our relationship to the world is usually transactional. We continuously shape our environment. The influence of the environment, whether we ourselves shaped it or not, in turn interacts with our characteristics in affecting our further conduct.

The Meaning and Nature of Interaction

The controversy about the relative influence of persons and situations on behavior led to renewed interest in their interaction. The concept of interaction has a long history (Ekehammar, 1974). Magnusson and Endler (1977) presented a recent view of interactionist approaches. In this view, "persons and situations are regarded as indispensibly linked to one another . . . . Neither the person factors nor the situation factors per se determine behavior in isolation; it is determined by inseparable person by situation interactions" (Magnusson & Endler, 1977, p. 4). This view is consistent with my own, implying that a major concern we must have is not the relative influence of persons versus situations–to what *degree* it is the characteristics of the person and to what *degree* it is the situation that determines behavior. Instead, we must be concerned with how personal characteristics and situations *join,* how they each enter, and how they combine. What will result from particular personality environment combinations, and why?

In spite of the long history of the interaction concept, most personality research employed a single measure of some personal characteristic and correlated it with behavior in a specific instance. Interactions were usually not tested. When situation-personality interactions were tested, researchers usually explored the influence of a single personality characteristic in conjunction with limited situational variation. For example, one study explored how persons who vary in their feeling of responsibility for others' welfare are affected by the number of people who are present when someone needs help—a variation in one personal characteristic and one aspect of the environment each. Generally, the presence of a greater number of people allows the diffusion of responsibility for others' welfare, and results in less help. People with a stronger sense of personal responsibility were less affected by such variation in the number of bystanders (Schwartz & Clausen, 1970).

Perhaps the limited influence of interactionist approaches on empirical research may partly be explained by the theoretical nature of "classical" interactionism (Ekehammar, 1974). However, theoretical notions have been proposed that may be useful in understanding the manner in which personal characteristics and environments relate to each other in guiding perception, thought, affect, and behavior. Murray (1938) described personal needs and environmental presses that are relevant to these needs and would activate them. Lewin (1938, 1948), who was perhaps the most powerful advocate of behavior being a joint function of persons and their environments, suggested the importance of goals, and of valences or forces within persons that move them toward relevant environmental "regions" where the goals may be satisfied.

If the current, more research-oriented interactionist approaches are to be fruitful and ultimately successful, several conditions must be fulfilled. It is certainly not a single characteristic of a person that guides his or her actions on any one occasion, that determines how he or she reacts to circumstances. We need to specify the classes of personality characteristics and situations that we regard important in determining particular types of behavior. We need to consider interrelationships among personal characteristics, and their joint influence. Situations not only activate relevant characteristics, but must affect their relationships. That is, the organization of personality characteristics is not static; it is dynamic, changing, active (Carlson, 1971, Chap. 1). Further we have to specify the psychological processes that are aroused by varied situations, as a function of personal characteristics. Situations give rise to meanings; they activate personal values, norms and beliefs, empathic reactions toward other persons, and other thoughts and affects. We have to provide a theoretical model that will specify the interrelationships among personal characteristics, situations, the psychological processes that result, and behavior. Finally, we have to develop elaborate measures of both persons and situations. Without their proper measurement, no theoretical model can be tested.

Consistency Revisited

The assumption that stable personal characteristics will manifest themselves in behavior has been one major reason for concern with consistency in behavior. However, psychologists are sufficiently sophisticated to realize that personal characteristics, such as motives, do not always directly manifest themselves in behavior. In the Freudian view, for example, unconscious motives often express themselves in barely detectable ways, such as in slips of tongue or in jokes, or even manifest themselves in behavior or feelings seemingly contrary to the unconscious motive. Anger may be projected into others, so that a person feels and acts persecuted, the object of anger. Such views have led to a distinction between genotypic characteristics—what people are *really* like—and phenotypic ones, apparent or surface characteristics.

The expectation of consistency may have been enhanced by the popularity of the trait concept. Traits refer to distinguishable and relatively enduring ways in which individuals differ from each other. Traits are not observable: they are inferred on the basis of the recurrent quality of observable acts of behavior (or some substitute, such as self-report). Since traits are inferred from recurrent acts, they imply future recurrence and thus consistency. Traits are descriptive concepts—they offer no reasons or explanations for behavior. They do not tell you *why* a person behaves in certain ways, what psychological processes contribute to the resulting behavior. Allport (1937) extended the trait concept, suggesting that traits motivate action and lead to a tendency to perceive stimuli in "functionally equivalent" ways. However, it seems more useful to separate motives, perceptual tendencies, and behavior, and to identify the nature of interrelationships among them.

In this section I will consider under what circumstances, using what measurement procedures, we might find some consistency in behavior, and will discuss some research that showed consistency or coherence (the latter referring to a meaningful relationship among parts or aspects of personality and behavior). An understanding of how social behavior comes about, as a result of what influences, should enlighten us to what extent and in what domains of behavior particular people might behave consistently. Since behavior is multidetermined, consistency will usually be limited. However, slight to moderate consistency can be expected in most people's behavior, with greater consistency in activities relevant to important goals.

To briefly preview some elements of the theory I will propose, a person's motives, which will be conceptualized as personal goals, together with a few other characteristics, are primarily important in affecting conduct. Individuals with strong prosocial goals, with a belief that they can influence events, and with the capacity to generate plans of action are likely to behave more prosocially across varied situations in which such behavior is required or needed than are persons who do not possess these characteristics. Across varied circumstances, the likelihood that other, conflicting motives or goals will dominate behavior should be smaller for such prosocially motivated individuals, and their prosocial motivation would tend to gain expression in behavior. The tendency not to act prosocially would also become apparent. Similar consistency across many situations may be found when other dominant personal motives and related supporting characteristics are considered, such as achievement or affiliation. I am suggesting that when people's behavior is considered on a few occasions, no consistency may be found, because other motives may be predominant, or the competence required for action may be lacking, or, for other reasons, the motive does not gain expression. However, considering behavior across many situations that have similar psychological meaning for people, consistency may be apparent.

One relevant contrast is between adaptability—people responding to varied elements of their environments in the spirit of their varied needs and goals—versus extreme (and thus rigid) consistency. Taking positive behavior as an example, absolute consistency—a person always behaving positively—would be maladaptive. Always favoring others when the interests of the self and of others conflict would be self-destructive. Even highly prosocial people, if they are capable of reasonable adjustment, would have ways to evaluate the intensity and legitimacy of others' needs in contrast to their own, and to respond in a discriminative fashion.

Why has there been so little consistency in behavior demonstrated in research? Or has it been so little? Magnusson and Endler (1977) differentiate among four types of data. Self-report (*S* data) is represented by varied forms of self-descriptions by people, by verbal-interview type of information. Standardized tests (*T* data) represent another type of information. Ratings by observers or by people familiar with a person (*R* data) is a third type of information. Objective measures, of specific acts, of physiological reactions, of adrenalin secretion, and so on, represent a fourth type of data (*O* data). Block (1977) suggests that while consistency in behavior across laboratory situations (where objective measures of specific acts are taken) is limited, with *R* data and *S* data both consistency and stability over time have been found.

With regard to prosocial behavior, in laboratory research where only two or three samples of behavior have been taken, either at different times or in somewhat different situations, the relationship among these behaviors is usually limited, and not significant (Midlarsky & Bryan, 1972; Staub, 1971c; and many others). In laboratory research, investigators usually expose participants to circumstances which, in the researchers' view, have certain properties and would instigate particular kinds of acts. However, the manner in which these situations are perceived by the subjects is rarely determined. Consequently, apparent inconsistency in behavior across several situations may result from differences in the meaning of the situations to the experimenters and the subjects. Moreover, most situations have varied elements and place varied demands on people, even if similarities (e.g., people face some type of human need) can be identified. Only when many samples of behavior are taken would the influence of certain propensities, as noted above, become apparent. Even then, consistency may be expected primarily in domains of activities that are important for people, not in just any domain.

While there is consistency and stability in the domain of self-report data—people describing how they behave, think, or feel, or what attitudes they hold—

this may tell us little about actual behavior, if we tend to organize our perception of the world and ourselves so that they are consistent and orderly. Consistency in self-ratings may be a manifestation of perceptual consistency or of consistency in self-presentation, rather than of behavior. In some areas where the stability of self-perception is substantial, self-perception is likely to have a close relationship to behavior. For example, people appear highly consistent in their vocational goals. In one study, Strong (1955) reported that vocational goals of college seniors, after a 22-year time interval, related .75 to their original vocational goals.

Even if, in general, self-reported consistency or stability represents primarily a person's manner of perceiving himself or herself, a person's mode of categorizing his or her experience and behavior, it still has substantial significance. That a particular person has consistently high self-esteem, while another's is consistently low, may be a matter of self-perception; but it significantly affects the meaning of experiences and the emotions generated by them. It is also likely to affect behavior. For example, a person with low self-esteem may be less certain of the correctness of his judgment that someone needs help—particularly when the signs that a need exists are mild and therefore ambiguous—and of his ability to actually provide help. For both of these reasons, such a person may frequently not initiate help.

Some writers also claim evidence of consistency provided by *R* data. That is, they claim that ratings of characteristics of persons by other people—based on their behavior or even on varied sources of information such as interviews, tests, as well as behavior—show strong relationships. Ratings by teachers and peers, or by any kind of observers, of a person's behavior presumably represent a summary of the observers' perceptions of how a person behaves across varied occasions and situations. On the basis of the above discussion, one would expect such data to show consistency; but this consistency may be artificially enlarged by halo effects. For example, teachers, peers, and observers' ratings of varied forms of positive behavior may partly represent a perception or evaluation of the child on a general dimension of positivity-negativity. As a result, sometimes ratings can be misleading. In one study (Staub, 1971a), teachers' ratings of children on several dimensions (initiation of activities in interaction with others, competence on tasks, expression of affection toward other children, and need for approval) were highly interrelated, suggesting that the ratings reflected the teachers' general evaluations of the children. The teachers' ratings of boys was positively related to their attempts to help in response to sounds of distress from another room, but somewhat negatively related to girls' attempts to help. Possibly, boys who are preferred and thus highly rated can be active—which is important for initiating help—while girls who are preferred are less active, more quiet and well behaved, making it less likely that they would initiate help. Observers may often make generalizations about behavior from dominant characteristics that they perceive in individuals, or from their evaluation of persons according to their implicit personality theories. More accurate indices of behavior would be provided by sums of actually observed acts of certain kinds. Consistency may be tested by relating such sums to independently derived sums of the same kinds of acts.

There is evidence of consistency in behavior from data collected in these fashions (Bem & Allen, 1974; Block, 1977; Epstein, 1979; Mussen & Eisenberg-Berg, 1977; Magnusson & Endler, 1977; Staub, 1978, 1979). Bem and Allen proposed that at least some people may be consistent in some areas of their behavior. They tried to identify college students who either would or would not be consistent on the traits of friendliness and conscientiousness. They simply asked people to identify themselves as either consistent or not consistent in these domains. They collected ratings of their subjects' behaviors from mothers, fathers, and peers, and observed their friendliness in a waiting room and in a small group discussion. People who identified themselves as consistently friendly showed a greater degree of intercorrelation among their friendly behaviors than did people who did not indicate consistency in this characteristic. Similar findings were apparent with conscientiousness, although the generality of the latter was more limited. Some people who indicated consistency on this "trait" were more conscientious in keeping order in their room and their environment, while others were more conscientious in their school-related academic activities.

Perhaps, as earlier suggested, people will be consistent in domains of activities that are important for them. We may need to specify the *domains of situations* in which particular persons tend to behave in a particular way. The tendency for prosocial behavior may not generalize across all different circumstances in which prosocial behavior is possible or appropriate. Staub and Feinberg (1977) observed and coded children's interactive behaviors. A factor analysis of girls' positive behaviors led to the emergence of a factor on which varied behavior that may be called "responsive" had high loading, showing that they tended to be performed by the same children. They included expression of positive emotion toward others, responsiveness to others' needs, and cooperation. However, engaging in helpful behavior had a somewhat negative loading on this factor. These children tended to act prosocially, but not in all possible ways. That people shape their own environments is also suggested by the kinds of behaviors directed at these children. Others behaved in a generally positive manner toward them, but directed few requests for help at them. Apparently, an accommodation developed between these children and their peers.

In their frequently quoted research on honesty, Hartshorne and May (1928) found relatively low correlations among behaviors such as cheating in a classroom, on a take-home examination, or during a game, and stealing money, lying, and falsifying records of athletic performance. The average intercorrelations among 23 measures was only .25. Hartshorne and May concluded, and many authors later quoted them, that honesty in any one situation implies little about honesty in other situations. Later, Burton (1963) factor analyzed their data and concluded that honesty had greater generality than Hartshorne and May originally indicated. However, Hartshorne and May themselves performed analyses that indicated consistency in behavior. They combined several tests of honesty into a single score and found that the relationships between this sum score and other measures of honesty were substantial, reaching a coefficient of .73. They wrote: "One test of deception is quite incapable of measuring a subject's tendency to deceive . . . . If we use ten tests of classroom deception, however, we can safely predict what a subject will do on the average whenever ten similar situations are presented" (1928, p. 134).

A variety of studies have shown both stability and a combination of stability and consistency in behavior. (Some of these are described in Meichenbaum's chapter in this volume.) Briefly, Block (1971, 1977) examined the relationship in the behavior of people who were in the Berkeley longitudinal study when they were in junior and senior high school and when they were in their mid-thirties. A great deal of data was available on each subject, different types of data at each age period, including ratings of behavior during the two earlier time periods and verbal interviews at the last time period. Block had trained judges to independently rate the information available about subjects at each of the three time periods. Judges used the *Q*-sort technique: from a group of statements describing characteristics and behavioral tendencies, they selected those that indicated their perception of the participants on the basis of all the data available at a particular time period. Between junior and senior high school, 58 percent of the *Q*-sort items correlated at least as high as .35 (significant at the $p < .001$ level), with some as high as .70. Between senior high and the last time period, 29 percent of 114 *Q*-sort items were related to each other at least at the .35 level, with some as high as .61. Notice that these findings show substantial stability, but also instability, since many of the *Q*-sort items had negligible relationships.

As noted, some of the relationships reported above may be inflated because ratings may result from an emphasis on some dominant characteristics and generalization from them as to what a person is like. However, in order for the relationships to exist in the Block study, people had to have the same dominant impression at different ages, based on different data. Clearly, stability exists in some domains, but the manner in which it gains expression in behavior is not clear from such data. Block suggests that his data show the coherence of personality.

Other studies also indicate that there is consistency and/or stability in individual characteristics as expressed in behavior. Olweus (1973, 1974, 1977) found both substantial stability over a three-year interval of ratings of aggression by classmates, and found that peer ratings, teachers ratings, and self-ratings of aggression on an aggression inventory were significantly correlated.

In a study described by Epstein (1979), pairs of undergraduates at Smith College served as subjects and observers of each other. The correlation between behaviors observed on days one and two were low. However, correlations among behaviors observed during even- and odd-numbered days, over an extended period of time, showed substantial magnitude. The relationships gradually increased with increase in the number of observations. This may mean that over a limited time period people behave variably, as demanded by their circumstances, but that there is consistency and stability in some of their behavioral tendencies, which, over time, will be demonstrated in their behavior. Alternatively, it is possible that biases develop in what observers see, that they increasingly tend to categorize persons and then perceive their behavior according to the categories they established. To some degree, both may be true. If observations collected by different observers who *succeed* each other over time show similar consistency and stability in behavior, the former conclusion would become convincing.

Some studies of positive behavior showed both consistency, in the form of significant relationships among somewhat different types of positive behaviors, and stability. In the first phase of a longitudinal study (Block & Block, 1973, as reported by Mussen & Eisenberg-Berg, 1977), nursery-school children were extensively observed. Nurturance toward other children, expressions of sympathy toward them, and understanding of others' perspectives were significantly related to each other. Five or six years later, in elementary school, observationally based indices of socially responsible and altruistic behaviors were again significantly related. Of special interest is that significant relationships were found between indices of social responsibility and altruism in nursery school and in elementary school, over five- to six-year intervals ($r = .60$ for boys; $r = .37$ for girls). These behaviors showed surprising stability.

In another longitudinal study (Baumrind, unpublished data, as reported by Mussen & Eisenberg-Berg, 1977), nursery-school teachers' ratings of generosity, helpfulness, empathy and other prosocial characteristics were significantly associated with the amount of rewards the children shared a year later. The children earned their rewards by their performance on a task, and could share with another child who did not have time to finish the task and consequently did not earn rewards. Children who were rated the year before as aggressive, and as having trouble with delaying gratification, shared less.[2]

There is some evidence of increased consistency with increasing age. Hartshorne, May and Shuttleworth (1930) found that older children were more consistent than younger ones in their performance on various measures of honesty. Moreover, those older children who were consistent tended to be honest, while those who were inconsistent tended to be dishonest. This latter finding may mean that some children developed personal values or motives that guided them to honest conduct. Others may have developed such values to a lesser degree, and behaved honestly only under circumstances when honesty served the satisfaction of some other personal value or goal, such as testing their skill on a task, or because of their concern about being caught and punished. A

[2]The last two studies that were described are unpublished. They were briefly reported by Mussen and Eisenberg-Berg, and no detailed report of them was available to this writer.

further study showed that the degree to which children's values and behavior correspond increases with age. Henshel (1971) found, with female participants, increased consistency between values about honesty and the degree to which children acted honestly with increasing age. Although this study is somewhat flawed procedurally (see Staub, 1979) the findings are suggestive. Children's responses to questions about the value of honesty, and their cheating as measured by the number of errors that children did not report in correcting their own spelling tests, increased with age from .02 at fourth grade to –.78 at seventh grade.

What determines how persons behave on specific occasions? What determines whether particular individuals will or will not show a tendency to behave in certain ways–that is, consistency in some type of behavior? What determines the range of situations across which behavior is consistent? What conception of personality-situation interaction will enable us to understand and predict behavior in specific instances, and to understand the existence of behavioral tendencies or their absence? The theoretical model presented below attempts to answer these and related questions.

A THEORETICAL MODEL FOR PREDICTING PROSOCIAL BEHAVIOR

A Brief Outline of the Theory

In this section I will discuss each component of the theory in some detail. To provide a coherent picture, I will start with a brief outline. The theory presumes that people are purposeful organisms who develop varied motivations, which will be called *personal goals,* in the course of their growth and development. Personal goals can be activated by characteristics of the environment, either the external environment or a person's internal environment, his thoughts or imagination. The environment can be described in terms of its activating potential for particular personal goals. Depending on the activating potential of the environment and on the extent that a person possesses various personal goals, an environment may activate no goal, or one, two, or more goals. When two or more goals are activated, they may conflict with each other, when their satisfaction cannot be pursued by the same course of action. Alternatively, one of the goals may be dominant; or the goals may join with each other, when a particular course of action can lead to the satisfaction of all of them. Sometimes, helping another person can satisfy a prosocial goal, an approval goal–since helping others is a socially valued activity that often leads to approval and praise by other people–and even an achievement goal, since, in the course of helping, a person can show skill, competence, or excellence. When two or more goals conflict with each other, action may be inhibited, or the conflict may be resolved. Whether a goal is activated or not, and whether an activated goal will be pursued in action, depends also on personal characteristics other than goals. Perceptual tendencies—which include the speed of defining events and role taking, the capacity of viewing events from others' points of view—can affect the interpretations of events. Varied types of competencies may affect the likelihood that a person will take action. Lack of competence may also interfere with the activation of goals.

Personal Goals

There has been a long history in psychology of concern with and emphasis on motivational constructs in attempting both to understand why people behave as they do and to predict how they will behave. The names of constructs have varied: *drive, need, reinforcement, reward value,* and other terms have been used. The purported properties of these constructs has also varied.

Long ago, McDougall (1908) suggested that people's behavior can be best understood by the goals they pursue—in contrast, for example, to the means by which they pursue their goals. Other writers echoed this belief (Murray, 1938; Lewin, 1938, 1948). Why have many writers stressed needs, or goals, as primary influences on human behavior? In addition to those cited, motivational constructs are included in many writers' theories of human behavior. For example, both Rotter (1954) and Mischel (1966) stressed the subjective value of outcomes as important determinants of behavior: people are inclined to move toward outcomes that are valued by them. Others have stressed the importance of specific motives such as need for approval, need for achievement, or need for affiliation.

A primary characteristic of human beings seems to be their purposefulness (see Deci's chapter in this volume). We do not go about the world in a random fashion; nor do we simply follow rules all the time. Our adherence to rules itself probably, to a large extent, depends on our motives. While the nature of motivation that characterizes the social behavior of specific human beings varies across cultures, varies as a function of socialization in specific families and personal experiences in life, and perhaps varies due to heredity, the existence of motivation seems universal. Anthropologists and psychologists have found, for example, that cultures differ in the extent to which they lead members to be cooperative, competitive, or individualistic in their interactions with each other (Mead, 1937). In some cultures, people come to prefer to bring about mutual gain, to interact with others in a cooperative fashion. In other cultures, members come to prefer competition, to enhance their own gain in comparison to the gains of others, to increase their relative advantage over others. In either case, motivation exists, but its nature is different.

I assume that personal goals, the construct I will use to denote motivation, exert strong influence in directing our behavior, and that many other personality characteristics that need to be considered are primarily important in determining whether personal goals are activated and/or whether their satisfaction is pursued or not. The word *goal* implies a preference for certain outcomes or end states, or an aversion for certain outcomes and the desire to avoid them. It also implies a striving toward or away from these outcomes. The word *personal* refers to the fact that different people have different goals, and that the organization of goals within persons—their relative importance—varies. The same goal may be high in one person's hierarchy of goals and low in another's. Further, each person's goals have a special individual character, partly because of differences in cognitive elaboration and ranges of applicability (see below). Nonetheless, there is likely to be enough similarity among goals or different individuals that people can be grouped on the basis of communality in goals.

While people appear idiosyncratic in the outcomes they value (Mischel, 1973; Mischel & Mischel, 1976), for each individual there is probably a range of similar-valued outcomes. Certainly, all past conceptions of motives imply classes of outcomes that can reduce or satisfy a motivated state, or outcomes at which motivated behavior aims. Research findings on need approval (Crowne & Marlowe, 1964), and on other motives, provides some support. People with a strong need for approval desire and/or seek varied forms of approval, and are concerned about and want to avoid disapproval by people in general. With regard to outcomes related to a prosocial goal, minimally, a person who values diminishing others' physical pain is likely to hold this value with varied sources of pain. Certain classes of outcomes are likely to be valued by many people who grow up and live in a particular culture. Most people in our culture probably value, to varied degrees, positive evaluation and approval (and want to avoid negative evaluation and disapproval—the latter might be regarded as a negative goal), physical safety, and material welfare, among other goals.

Internalized values, norms, beliefs, and the tendency to react empathically to others' needs can all increase the value or desirability of benefiting other people, and thus contribute to a prosocial goal. Depending on the nature of the values, the extent to which empathy is involved, and so on, the specific character of the goal may differ. For some people, the desired outcome might be to improve others' welfare; for others, acting in a helpful manner might itself be the desired outcome. However, neither the component values and norms nor the exact nature of the desired outcomes which enter into defining goals have a piecemeal character. In order to qualify as a motivational orientation that is represented by the term *personal goal*, they have to combine into some kind of organized whole. In the case of prosocial goals, this organized whole may have the form of broad value orientations.

Variation in the nature of personal goals is likely to be found in most domains, not only the prosocial one. Some individuals who are characterized by a strong achievement goal may want to do well in comparison to some standard of excellence when their goal is activated; others may want to experience success; and so on. Regardless of their exact quality, when such achievement goals are activated, they may all gain expression in hard work and attempts to do well in varied activities.

I am implying that a family of personal goals of a particular kind may exist. However, the primary members of the family may be few. In the case of prosocial goals, two types of value orientations may give rise to two primary prosocial goals; and even those two can frequently be related to each other, or occur together. One value orientation I will call *prosocial orientation*; it emphasizes concern about the welfare of other human beings. I will discuss this in greater detail below. Another value orientation focuses on *duty and obligation* toward other human beings, on societal rules and/or abstract moral principles that prescribe positive behavior, rather than on the persons themselves who are to be helped. As I noted elsewhere, (Staub, 1978, 1979) persons who are characterized by a prosocial orientation are likely to perceive, interpret, and think about events in a manner that gives rise to feelings of empathy. Thus, in the case of most people, the capacity for empathy, for vicariously experiencing others' feelings, is coded in the form of a value orientation. The arousal of empathy can, in turn, motivate prosocial acts.

Defining Characteristics of Goals. Personal goals are likely to have a number of defining characteristics. One I already noted is the desirability of certain outcomes. Another is a network of cognitions that is usually associated with a goal. It does happen, of course, that the inclination to reach some goal—or the desire to avoid an outcome, a negative goal—is primarily emotional, that a person has few conscious thoughts, beliefs, or values that are associated with the goal. Phobic reactions are not regarded as based on reason, as the result of thinking and evaluation.[3] The tendency to react with empathy or sympathy to another's fate can also be primarily a "gut reaction." Usually, however, we have varied thoughts, beliefs, and values associated with outcomes that are desirable (or aversive) to us. These cognitions function, in part, to tune us perceptually to the kind of circumstances that make it possible to satisfy our goal. They are also applied to the interpretation of situations. The manner in which events, situations, or outcomes are interpreted is likely, in turn, to determine our emotional reactions to them. This view is consistent with current cognitive theories of emotion (Arnold, 1960; Lazarus, 1966; Leventhal, 1974; Averill, this volume). Thus, the cognitive network presumably leads to interpretations that give rise to emotions, which make the goal desirable and motivate attempts to reach the goal. Over time, many circumstances may acquire well-developed meanings and give rise to strong emotions without much cognitive elaboration. Seeing a child standing in the path of an onrushing car will give rise to strong emotion, in most

[3]This is a debatable issue, however. Whiie phobic individuals frequently say "I know that this (the object the person is afraid of) is not dangerous," they sometimes hold beliefs that can understandably give rise to strong fear. It is possible to argue that at some level they must evaluate the object of their fear as dangerous or terrifying, or, depending on one's theory, they use the object as a symbol for something that is terrifying to them. Providing people with information can, in fact, reduce fear and even the experience of pain produced by electric shocks (Staub & Kellett, 1972).

people, with little or no thinking about or processing of the meaning of the event.

Personal goals can lead to experiences that help people learn to perceive the relevance of events to their goals. If our Carnegie Hero possessed a prosocial goal, the range of applicability of which extended to people in physical distress or at risk, he may have had past experience in responding to cries for help. In the course of his experience, he may have come to take such cries of distress seriously. He may have come to believe that when people call for help they are in trouble. One reason for his responding before others did may have been that he did not need to think about the meaning of those calls for help to decide whether or not they were serious. If so, he did not need to engage in cognitive work to determine the meaning of the event, and thus could respond faster.

A third related characteristic of personal goals is the arousal of tension upon the activation of the goal, which continues to exist until either the goal has been reached or it has been deactivated in some manner. The notion that tension is aroused and maintained by the activation of a goal has been proposed by Lewin (1948; see also Deutsch, 1968) and currently extended to the realm of prosocial behavior by Hornstein (1976). The limited evidence that is available about tension systems and their properties supports the concept. An example is the well known Zeigarnick (1927) effect. Consistent with Lewinian assumptions, Zeigarnick found that interrupted tasks are remembered better than completed ones. Tasks that are interrupted nearer their completion—nearer to reaching the outcome—are remembered better than tasks interrupted further from completion (Deutch, 1968). The latter finding provides support for another Lewinian concept, that of a goal gradient.

The concept of personal goal implies some generality of the motivation, a class of outcomes that are valued, rather than a single outcome.[4] Still, among people with similar personal goals—such as the goal of benefiting other people—the *range of applicability* of goals can vary. Some people might have learned to apply their concern about others' welfare at times when another person was in physical need but not in psychological distress; others might have learned to apply such concern only to people of certain kinds, perhaps people whom they think of as similar to themselves or as coming from the same ethnic or racial background. Thus, the personal goal that motivates prosocial action might have different specific ranges of applicability. The range can be relatively narrow, or it can be broad, applicable to varied circumstances, varied needs. We have to

[4] Although personal goals usually point to classes of outcomes, seemingly it can happen that a single end satisfies a personal goal. Consider, for example, that a major personal goal for someone may be finding and experiencing love. This person may focus his or her energies on satisfying this goal. Let's assume that he or she encounters someone who perfectly satisfies the goal, for a lengthy period of time. What happens to a goal once so fulfilled (whether by a single outcome, or by repeated experiences or cumulatively, e.g., when someone whose goal is wealth feels sufficiently wealthy)? Presumably, it will be replaced by others in a person's hierarchy of goals. The goal would not be an activated state, and would not be pursued in action.

develop devices to measure not only the existence of various personal goals and their intensity, but also the specific ranges in which they are applicable, and their breadth or narrowness.

Further specifications of the range of applicability of goals is also possible. We can specify domains to which each goal is *likely* to be applied. The desire for excellence, as it is embodied in achievement goals, may be applied to intellectual activities, to a person's work and/or profession, to interpersonal interactions, to sports, or to several of these domains. In Feinberg's (1977) study, for example, which will be described later in detail, high-achievement women applied themselves to consoling, advising, and generally extensively talking to another (distressed) female. With regard to prosocial goals, domains of applications may be divided into physical distress and psychological distress, or into family and friends versus others—the latter further subdivided into potential ingroups and outgroups (people with the same or different religion, race, etc.).

The range of applicability of a prosocial goal can also be affected by specific values and norms that people ascribe to, which qualify or further define the general goal. A prosocial orientation implies concern about other people's welfare; still, people with a strong prosocial orientation may differ in the importance of the value of equity (people should receive benefits as a function of their inputs or accomplishments) and equality (people should receive benefits equally) to them. Those who value equity more may apply their prosocial orientation less to people who they feel are less deserving—on the basis of their characteristics, or due to lack of effort, or to some prior wrongdoing. People who value equality, in contrast to equity, may discriminate less in the application of their prosocial goals as a function of deserving. People who believe that the world is a just place where people get what they deserve (Lerner & Simmons, 1966) may sometimes not react to others' suffering, believing (or rationalizing) that, since the world is just, the suffering must be deserved (Rubin & Peplau, 1973; Staub, 1978).

Would any outcome that a person tries to reach be an expression of a personal goal? Presumably not. Some outcomes or end states may reflect a temporary desire evoked by particular conditions, neither recurrent nor of a class of outcomes valued by the person, nor an expression of the person's cognitive network. Such desires would best not be considered examples of personal goals.

The Activating Potential of Situations and Goal Conflict

Every person has varied goals, which can be arranged in a hierarchy according to their importance to the person. These goals, as described so far, represent potentials. At any one time, the desire for a certain outcome or end state, which is the primary defining component of the goal, may be dormant. Alternatively, goals may be in an activated state. Sometimes, thoughts, images, or internal stimuli can activate a goal; at other times, aspects of the environment can activate it.

In a particular situation, varied motives or personal goals may be aroused in a person. Sometimes when a person is faced with another's need for help, that is the only force acting on him or her: given some degree of motivation to be helpful, the person will act. At other times, a person might be faced with a situation which potentially activates a variety of motives: to be helpful, to achieve well on some task, to affiliate with other people, to pursue adventure, or to behave in proper social ways. Whether such goals are activated will depend on the nature of the situation and on its activating potential, as well as on the characteristics of the person and the degree to which the person possesses the personal goals that might be activated by the situation. For example, someone might be working on a task, or might be simply sitting in a room waiting. Somebody in another room seems to be in distress. If it is important for this person to both do well on tasks and to help other people, he will experience conflict when he is working on the task. His two goals conflict with each other. This will not happen when he is simply waiting, because then his goal of achievement will not be activated. Neither will this happen if doing well on tasks is unimportant to him.

What is the utility of the conception of personal goals and activating potentials? Their utility lies in the recognition that, frequently, circumstances activate varied personal goals. If we are to understand how prosocial behavior in particular and social behavior in general are determined, we have to consider the joint influence of varied motives. Different goals may sometimes conflict, and may sometimes join and support each other. The goal to achieve may lead a person to work hard on a task and diminish helping; or it may be applied to helping someone in need, adding to the influence of a prosocial goal. Using motivational constructs that apply to varied motives and classes of outcomes can improve our ability to understand and predict social behavior. For this to happen, we will have to be able to measure personal goals, ranges of applicability, and the activating potentials of situations.

A retrospective analysis of an extreme form of helpful behavior can provide an example of how personal goals affect helping, and of the match that is required between personality and the situation for help to occur (Staub & Feinberg, 1980). This example draws on a report by London (1970). He concluded, on the basis of extensive interviews with "rescuers"—people who were involved in an underground system of saving Jews and other persecuted individuals in Nazi Germany—that they had three characteristics in common. These were: a strong conscious identification with moral parents; adventurousness; and a sense of marginality in relation to the community. Presumably, strong moral identification led to personal values promoting helpful behavior, thus to the motivation to help. The costs of helping in this situation were potentially extremely high—with the loss of life likely and the loss of liberty certain—if discovered. A sense of adventurousness, gaining satisfaction from dangerous activities and perceiving them as exciting, which apparently led these individuals to also participate in other dangerous activities in the course of their lives, seems important. This characteristic might have not only have enhanced the likelihood that they would carry out their prosocial goal, but might be thought of as an additional goal that could be satisfied by helping. Marginality might have helped rescuers in not accepting the definition of their environment of the persecution of Jews and others, a definition which would have minimized the perception of the need or the justification for involvement.

The study of conflicts among goals that are activated in specific situations has been surprisingly neglected. While psychoanalytically oriented writers, and Dollard and Miller (1950), in translating psychoanalytic concepts into a behavioral framework, clearly recognized the importance of goal conflict, even they stressed the role of conflict between approach and avoidance tendencies toward a single goal. Frequently, multiple goals are activated by circumstances; and the manner in which one or another comes to predominate, or the extent to which they mutually inhibit (or sometimes promote) each other, needs to be considered.

What determines which personal goal in a particular situation will exert dominant influence on behavior? The strength of intensity of an activated personal goal must be a joint function of the strength or importance of the personal goal to the individual and the strength of the activation potential of the environment for that goal. As an initial assumption, I will suggest that the intensity of the activated goal will be a function of the multiplicative relationship between intensity of the personal goal and the activating potential. The greatest sum that results from this multiplication will determine which activated goal will be dominant and will influence behavior. When the intensity of two or more activated goals is nearly identical, action required to pursue any of them may be inhibited, and/or various processes may be involved in conflict resolution. One of these, justification processes, will be discussed below.

The Nature of Prosocial Goals and the Measurement of Goals

How can personal goals be measured? One possibility is to ask people to rank order their goals, similar to Rokeach's (1973) method for rank ordering values. Values and goals are quite similar concepts, in fact, in that values also imply the desirability of certain outcomes. Rokeach presents people with two lists of 18 values. They are asked to rank order each in their order of importance for them. The rank ordering has reasonable stability over time intervals of a year and a half. In measuring personal goals in a similar manner, we must recognize that the hierarchy of personal goals may not only change over time, but may vary over the circumstances of a person's life. For example, such a hierarchy may be different for students during the academic year and during their vacation.

A second index of personal goals can be the cognitive network associated with them. With regard to prosocial goals, varied research findings suggest to me that the important aspects of the cognitive network of a prosocial goal of some generality and breadth are: a) positive orientation toward other people—positive evaluation of human beings; b) concern about—value placed on—others' welfare; and c) a feeling of personal responsibility for others' welfare. These three dimensions are interrelated. Clearly, these are dimensions of both thought and affect: they will be regarded here as cognitive dimensions, which represent a cognitive network, since even when we collect information about affects, we tap a person's perceptions and cognitive representations of his or her emotions. The information that we receive consists of people's cognitive representations of their beliefs, values, feelings, and desires, and of relevant portions of the world around them.

The importance of the second and third cognitive components listed above is suggested both by findings of research that explored situational influences on helping (which show that the degree of another's need or dependence affect helping, and that circumstances that focus responsibility on a person enhance helping; Bar Tal, 1976; Rosenhan et al., 1976; Staub, 1978) and by findings of research that explored personality correlates of positive behavior (which show that people who have a sense of personal responsibility for others' welfare, or hold values or personal norms that favor helping, tend to help more; Huston and Korte, 1976; Schwartz, 1977; Staub, 1974, 1978). The first component is likely to be a basic, important, but generally neglected influence (Staub, 1976, 1978). In one study, Wrightsman (1966) found that subjects' evaluations of human nature were related to their trust and trustworthiness in a laboratory game. Christie's test of Machiavellian orientation has many items testing beliefs about human nature and human beings: scores on this test were found to be associated with helpful conduct (Staub, Erkut & Jaquette, as described in Staub, 1974; Feinberg, 1977; Grodman, 1979). A test Midlarz (1973) developed to measure trust also explored this basic orientation toward others (e.g., people's evaluation of human beings, the extent of their positive regard for them). Scores on this test were significantly related to the acceptance of another's need as real, when there were reasons to question it, and to the resulting helping behavior. Positive orientation to people is likely to be a basic element, a precondition for the other two cognitive components of the prosocial goal.

The above three central dimensions of the cognitive network are characteristic of a value orientation that I called *prosocial orientation*, which gives rise to one kind of prosocial goal (Staub, 1978, 1979). Earlier, I suggested that a second primary prosocial goal centers on feelings of duty and obligation—imposed by society, by principles that one has adopted or developed, or by the commandments of God. Duty or obligation is clearly related to a feeling of responsibility for others' welfare—the third cognitive component discussed above. To what extent are the two goals different, and what reason is there to believe that there are two such separable goals? Prosocial orientation is more person centered; duty orientation is based more on norms and principles. The first and second cognitive components may be less important for orientation toward duty or obligation, or may be different in quality. Consider, as an extreme, that a person feels obligation or duty to help people even if he or she assumes that people are basically selfish and untrustworthy. A person may believe on religious grounds that human beings are sinful and bad, but that it is nonetheless one's obligation to do good to others. Or a person may feel that, while people are basically unworthy, and though he has little liking for them and even fears them, the social contract demands that one helps others. The two types of prosocial goals may be regarded as distinct: people may be characterized by one or the other to varied extents, but also by some mixture of the two.

A relevant differentiation between value orientations was suggested by Hoffman (1970b). He found that children's thinking, as measured primarily by story completions, can be characterized by either an external orientation (judgments of right and wrong based on what might be punished or rewarded by people in authority) or by two different "internal" orientations. Children who have internalized certain values–who accepted them as their own, and tended to evaluate conduct not in terms of positive or negative reactions by other people but in terms of these internalized values–were regarded as having an internal orientation. One of the two internal orientations Hoffman called humanistic, the other conventional. Humanistic children seemed concerned with others' welfare and were willing to deviate from conventional rules and standards if this would benefit another person. Conventional children tended to give legal and religious bases for moral judgments and tended to ignore extenuating circumstances for wrongdoing. Moreover, they would indicate that story characters experienced guilt not so much because of harm that they actually caused to other people, but as a result of awareness of an unacceptable impulse in themselves. Hoffman's stories concerned themselves with moral judgment–the resolution of some type of moral conflict–and with reactions to having harmed someone or not having helped someone, and with transgressions of rules. They provide little direct information about thoughts and feelings about positive actions. Nonetheless, the findings are relevant to the distinction between the two types of prosocial goals. They indicate, however, that conventional children are concerned not only with acting according to societal rules (a duty or obligation type of orientation), but also with the inhibition of their impulses.

Other relevant discussion comes from Durkheim (1961), who believed that some people are concerned with promoting the "good" and are inclined to respond to others' need even if that demands a break with conventions, while other people are concerned with the maintenance of the social order.

In discussing prosocial or other goals, one cannot assume universality across cultures in any of the aspects of goals that I specified. Cultures vary in how much certain outcomes of behavior are valued. In some cultures, benefiting other people is apparently not valued–as indicated by the absence of such behavior and by the contrary behavior seemingly promoted by the culture (Benedict,

1934; Turnbull, 1972). Even if similar types of outcomes are valued in different cultures, the nature of the goal, as represented by the cognitive network associated with it, may differ. The form or circumstances of relevant conduct may, therefore, also vary. Cohen (1972) states that the idea of unselfish helpfulness (which is embodied in prosocial orientation and is an ideal in Western cultures) is alien to most social groups. It is assumed that when you do things for other people, you do it for self-gain. In hunting-and-gathering societies, for example, where cooperation and mutual help was essential and food sharing was obligatory, the person who contributed the most gained thereby the greatest power and prestige.

In different societies–and in different families, which may be regarded as small societies–the extent of cognitive elaboration of goals can vary. In some groups, the affective components–perhaps of great intensity–of goals may be directly socialized, and the network of relevant beliefs and thoughts restricted. This makes it important to include intensity measures of the desire for outcomes or end states.

A third way of establishing individual differences in personal goals, which may be done after people rank order their personal goals and provide information about their cognitive networks, is experimental. We can examine the extent to which the importance of goals, and the presence of relevant thoughts and feelings, can be affected by varying conditions of activation. That is, if a prosocial goal moves up in a person's hierarchy of goals, and/or a person's thinking shows greater evidence of the cognitions characteristic of a prosocial goal when circumstances are expected to activate the prosocial goal, that would provide further evidence for the importance of the goal for that person. We can expose people to activating conditions and then, rather than examining their behavior, provide them with opportunities to describe what they think (and how they feel).

The Measurement of Cognitive Networks. How could the cognitive network be measured? In preliminary testing that will be further described in the section on supporting research below, we administered to people existing questionnaires that to some extent tapped the domains of cognitions described above. Next, we factor analyzed scores on these measures. The factor analysis produced a factor on which these tests had high loading, while other kinds of tests did not. The participants' scores on this factor were related to their positive behavior.

Following this exploratory measurement of a prosocial goal, more direct, thorough, and differentiated measures are needed. The kind of measures that are described below seem applicable to any kind of goal. First, questionnaires can be developed that attempt to assess cognitive networks relevant to goals–in the case of the prosocial goal, the three dimensions of thought described above. Items can ask people: whether they evaluate others positively or negatively, consider human beings good or bad, whether people are a source of satisfaction for them; whether they value and are concerned about the welfare of other people and/or different categories of other people; and the extent to which they feel responsible for not harming others and for contributing to their welfare.

Can answers to direct questions about such matters be regarded as true representation of what people think? Would people not represent their thoughts as prosocial simply because such answers are socially desirable? The tendency to say socially desirable things has long been regarded as a major problem in testing. At the same time, it is questionable whether tests can effectively hide their purpose. Moreover, there is evidence that when people are directly asked to either predict their behavior (Mischel, 1976, 1977) or to provide information about their behavioral tendencies (Bem & Allen, 1974), their responses represent them quite accurately–seemingly more accurately than standardized tests that ask indirect questions. As described earlier, Bem and Allen found that people who were asked how consistently friendly or conscientious they were, gave answers that accurately represented them–as judged by ratings of friends and relatives and observations of their behavior. This was true even though people were not asked what friendliness and conscientiousness meant to them; such terms may have different meanings and behavioral referants to different people. In addition to this apparent accuracy of some direct self-reports, the questionnaires I discussed would measure cognitive networks through many questions, in an elaborate way: false self-presentation of a whole system of thought may be difficult.

The validity of answers on the questionnaire can be partly tested, and further information can be collected by adding another method of measurement: brief stories that are completed by the subjects. Either someone's need for help, or a missed opportunity to act prosocially can be described in each story. Story completions may indicate people's conceptions of the meaning of helping or not helping others in need, may indicate their notions about the rewarding, self-reinforcing nature of helpfulness or about guilt produced by not helping, and may provide additional indications of their values, standards, and beliefs. This method is usually called projective testing: the person who completes the story is assumed to put himself or herself into the role of the protagonist in completing the story. Whether that assumption is correct or not, completions would express relevant thinking and thus represent the cognitive network. Further, respondents can be asked to imagine that they are in the position of the protagonist of the story. Such stories have frequently been used in measuring children's internalized values and norms (see Hoffman, 1970a, b) as well as in measuring achievement and other motives in adults and children (Atkinson, 1958).

From the theoretical assumption I made that cognitive networks are central elements of motives (which is yet to be adequately tested), it may seem that I consider all important personal goals to be conscious. There is little question that unconscious motives frequently exert influence. The exact nature of unconscious motives is debatable. Are they simply desires for outcomes, without awareness that the outcomes are desired? If so, it is still possible that there is a relevant, elaborate, cognitive network that guides thinking and feelings and is involved in giving rise to the desire, but that people are simply unaware of the connection which is indirect or is somehow obscured by conflicting values or goals. In this case, our measures of the cognitive network may provide useful information and may enable us to deduce the relevance of certain outcomes for a person. Are unconscious motives, as Freud conceived of them, repressed impulses that are so unacceptable to people that cognitions that are directly relevant to these impulses or desires would also be repressed, or be altered in significant enough ways that they would be unlikely to betray the existence of the impulse? In this case, our measures would have less value; they may pick up some relevant cognitions, but special methods of examining the data would be necessary to understand their meaning. Certain cognitive elements may be present on projective measures but not on direct self-report measures; or, conflicts among cognitive elements may be apparent.

It is also possible that a person consciously values some outcome or end state, but (unconsciously) is highly conflicted about it. Lack of consistency among cognitive components may indicate this. A person who proclaims his or her desire to help others, and who states responsibility for others' welfare, but evaluates people negatively and expresses little concern about their welfare on indirect (story completion) measures when their need is not obvious, may have such conflict. (Psychoanalytically oriented writers suggest that true altruism—help motivated by the desire to benefit others—does not exist (Freud, 1963). Altruism is an expression of neurotic tendencies. According to this view—with which I and most contemporary writers on altruism disagree—apparent altruism is based on intrapsychic conflict.)

The Measurement of Activating Potentials

This model implies a *relational classification* of situations. The significance of a situation is a function of its relationship to personal characteristics of the individual—particularly (but not only) to his or her personal goals. Depending on personal characteristics, people will attend to, perceive, evaluate, and emotionally and behaviorally respond to a situation to different extents and in different ways. There is some evidence of a meaningful relationship between personal needs, as measured by the Edwards Personal Preference Scale, and the perceptual dimensions that people employ in describing other people (Cantor, 1976). Implicit personality theories that people hold also affect the manner in which they perceive other people (Schneider, 1973).

Although people who do not possess a certain goal may perceive a particular situation as relevant to that goal, they may do so to a smaller degree than a person for whom that goal is important. Even with identical perception of the relevance of particular situations to particular goals, a person for whom a certain goal is important will evaluate the situation, and the importance of pursuing that goal in that situation, quite differently from one who is unconcerned about that particular goal. We can test this assumption by asking people who possess personal goals to varied degrees to evaluate the meaning of situations which we believe vary in their activating potential for those goals, and by asking them to describe what they would do in those situations, and why. As presented here, personal goals and activating potentials would be measured and validated–in part–in relation to each other. Measures of activation potentials would also have to be validated by differences in the behavior of people with the same and with different personal goals, under varied conditions of activation, as well as by other criteria.

With such "relational" measurement, personal goals and activating potentials are not independent predictors of behavior. While in *reality* they are intertwined, in that situations have activating potentials for certain goals only to the extent that persons possess those goals, it may be advantageous to separate them in measurement. But can activating potentials be independently measured? Is activation not so much a function of personal goals, that their independent measurement is impossible? We can ask people to evaluate the meaning of various situations, to describe how they would act and why, without considering differences among them in personal goals. Probably, this measurement will give similar, but weaker differentiation among situations than would the evaluation of situations by people varying in goals. Without considering differences in people's goals, it is still those who possess relevant goals who can be expected to give evaluations of situations that indicate their activation potential.

The necessity to conceptualize, categorize, and classify situations, for understanding the manner in which situations and personality interact in determining behavior, has been increasingly recognized (Fredericksen, 1972; Mischel, 1976; Moos, 1974). But so far, little progress has been achieved in doing so. Environments have been classified in varied ways: as "behavioral settings" such as school, church, or home; by the characteristics of inhabitants, their age, status, and occupation; by perceived social climate, such as the "nature and intensity of personal relations"; and by functional properties such as the "reinforcement consequences for particular behaviors in that situation" (Mischel, 1976, p. 496). I suggested here that a meaningful classification of situations is in terms of their relevance for, or relationship to, various personal characteristics, particularly goals; that is, a "relational classification." Later in this chapter, dimensions of situations that, on the basis of past research, appear to represent variations in activating potentials for prosocial goals will be described.

How can we assess the activating potentials of situations? First, a series of stories can be created, describing situations that are expected to activate specific goals, to varied degrees, and combinations of goals. Then, perceptions of these situations–their meaning, preferred actions and reasons for them–may be assessed. The stories can be based on research findings suggesting the activating potential of certain dimensions of situations, on hypotheses we hold on conceptual bases, or on the basis of research that has established some determinants of behavior in specific situations.

For example, in a series of studies (Staub, 1970, 1971b), children, particularly sixth and seventh graders, felt inhibited from attempting to help, in response to sounds of distress of another child from an adjoining room. Prior permission to enter the adjoining room for an irrelevant reason resulted in substantially greater frequency of attempted help, in the form of subjects entering that room. This situation may have had a high activating potential for several goals: a prosocial goal; an approval goal that led subjects to want to behave appropriately by not entering a strange room; and also an achievement goal, since children were working on a task. For measurement purposes, the description of this basic situation, with certain variations, could be used (e.g., children simply waiting in the room, de-emphasizing achievement; children working on an important task, emphasizing achievement). Children can be asked to respond to a story with a description of what it is that they would choose to do in this situation, and why, (what it is that they would want to accomplish, what outcome to reach, etc.). In addition to having children freely respond to the stories, they could also be asked to respond to the same stories by rating different alternative courses of action on varied scales, and to statements about the reasons for choosing each action. From knowledge of what behavior children regard important and/or believe they would engage in, and why, scores can be derived that indicate the intensity of the activating potential of the situation for various goals. Progressively, descriptions of situations can be developed in which one, combinations of two, or all three relevant goals are activated at the same time, and in which the different activating elements have about the same intensity.

Exposing people to such situations can help us validate both measures of personal goals and measures of activating potentials. Obviously, people should behave more helpfully in a situation when someone needs help than in one when no one appears to be in need. However, classifications of people by personal goals will improve prediction of behavior.

Predictions made on the basis of classifying persons by personal goals, and classifying the situations that they are exposed to by their activating potentials, can also help us confirm or disconfirm the theoretical model, as well as to progressively develop it and refine it. For example, imagine that people with varying strengths of achievement and prosocial goals are working on a task and are also exposed to a person who seems very upset. To make proper predictions, we would have to previously evaluate whether the achievement goal can also be satisfied by doing a good job in responding to the distressed person. If it can be, people with a strong prosocial and a strong achievement goal might be most helpful. If it cannot be, a conflict will arise for such people. If we are able to make very precise measurements, of both goals and activation potentials, we may determine the relative strength of a person's achievement and prosocial goals; and by multiplying each with the strength of the corresponding activating potentials, we may be able to determine which goal would be dominant. If our prediction is incorrect, on the basis of the behavior that resulted, we may state new hypotheses about how conflict is resolved, and make predictions on that basis for future experiments. The careful measurement of all the behaviors of the participants may provide indications of their conflict and may improve our understanding. People in conflict often behave inappropriately. Some may simply be inhibited by their conflict in all their activities; others may try hard to both work on the task and help the distressed person. Again, the information we collected can lead to adjustments in theoretical assumptions about conflict resolution, and provide confirmation or disconfirmation of hypotheses.

A recurring problem in testing theories has been how to decide, when the research findings do not disconfirm important hypotheses, whether the reason was inadequate or incorrect measurement, or incorrect hypotheses, or incorrect theoretical concepts from which specific hypotheses are derived. If people with strong prosocial goals do not help more than those with weak prosocial goals, even when no conflict should exist, was our evaluation of the activation potential of the situation, or our measurement of prosocial goals inadequate or incorrect? Is a cognitive network–and, in general, verbal information that people provide–an inadequate way of measuring their motivation? Or are the theoretical notions and hypotheses derived from them incorrect? Usually, investigators persist with their theory, particularly in their initial stages; but repeated disconfirmation, even following some modification of the theory, should lead to its abandonment. However, appealing theories, particularly well established ones, often persist; as Hall and Lindzey (1970) suggest, theories often persist until they are supplanted by other theories.

A number of writers have suggested that person measures and situation measures should be in the same units (Murray, 1938; Rotter, 1954). The concepts of personal goal and goal-activating potential of a situation are consistent with this view. While a great deal of current interest has developed in an interactionist view, theories about the aspects of individuals and of situations that are particularly important to consider, although not absent (Mischel, 1973; Bem & Funder, 1978), have been minimal. Using concepts somewhat similar to those suggested by Murray (1938) and Rotter (1954)–who emphasized, respectively, needs and the value of outcomes–and in some ways similar to those of Lewin (1948), the present conception proposes basic dimensions along which personality and situations interact.

OTHER PERSONALITY INFLUENCES

A variety of personal characteristics, in addition to personal goals, can affect social behavior, primarily by affecting the likelihood that motivation for action will be aroused, or that it will be expressed in behavior.

Perceptual Tendencies

Several perceptual tendencies can contribute to the activation of prosocial goals. The capacity for *role-taking,* which was mentioned earlier, may be an important one. Sometimes, another person's need is so obvious that no special skill or sensitivity is needed to perceive it. This is usually the case in emergencies, when suddenly the need emerges to respond to someone's physical distress or to danger to a person's life. At other times, the need is subtly expressed, and well-developed role-taking capacity is needed for perceiving it, particularly for perceiving it accurately. Role taking affects not only perception but also the manner in which what is perceived is then processed. Role taking varies in kind (perceptual, communicative, affective), and, of course, not all kinds are equally involved in the activation of prosocial goals (Staub, 1979).

The capacity to accurately perceive how another feels can certainly exist without concern about others' welfare. However, the likelihood that a person takes another's role will itself be increased by a prosocial orientation or values which increase the sensitivity to others' welfare. Providing people with different perceptual orientations–instructing them to impersonally observe another person, or to imagine what an experience might be like for him or her, or to imagine what it would be like for the observer to have that experience (imagine the self in the other's place), or to simply watch the other person–results in different degrees of physiological reactions, and in different emotional experiences and/or behavior (Stotland, 1969; Aderman & Berkowitz, 1970; Aderman et al., 1974). Prosocial values and empathic capacity may, in everyday life, lead to such differences in perceptual orientation toward others' experiences. That is, values, empathy, and role taking are likely to be related to some degree. There are, in fact, research findings which show that a positive relationship exists between certain types of role-taking capacities and level of moral reasoning (see Staub, 1978).

Another relevant perceptual-cognitive tendency is the speed of making judgments about the meaning of events in one's environment. People seem to vary in this (Denner, 1968). By suspending judgment, the opportunity for taking action may frequently pass. Role taking is a perceptual tendency primarily relevant to prosocial goals. Other perceptual tendencies may exist that are relevant to other specific goals. The speed of making judgment can be relevant to varied goals. The opportunity to gain approval or avoid disapproval, or the possibility of taking initiative in beginning a relationship with other people, can depend on the speed of assessing circumstances and events. The speed of judging events itself appears to be related to, or be a function of, other characteristics. Denner suggests, on the basis of his discussion with subjects, that people who are slow in judging events distrust their own judgment, and perhaps also the world, in that they do not want to be taken in by the appearance of things. Self-esteem and belief in one's competence may be involved.

Competencies and the Execution of Goals

A person's competence is probably a crucial determinant of whether he or she will take action in executing personal goals. Lack of the subjective experience of competency may also inhibit the activation of personal goals.

Assume that you are walking across a deserted bridge. You see a person ahead of you who appears to begin to climb up the railing. As he notices you, he stops and remains standing there, looking at the water. You assume that he intended to jump—to commit suicide—and that he is waiting for you to pass by and disappear from sight. You believe that you ought to intervene in some fashion. Depending on how you feel about your capacity to intervene, the chances that you will take action, and the kind of action you will take, would be greatly affected. If you trust your ability to initiate a conversation, to talk to another person, and to exert an influence on another person's thoughts, feelings, and behavior, you may start a conversation, and continue until you establish some kind of contact with this person. It may then become possible for this person to talk about his problems and his reasons for being on the bridge, or for you to introduce the question. Alternately, you may feel that you cannot start a conversation with a stranger, who probably does not want to have anything to do with you anyway. If you feel sufficiently strongly this way, the feeling may even interfere with the activation of your prosocial goal, your awareness of the need, and your desire to help.

Competence refers to a person's subjective evaluation of his capacities as well as to his possession of skills and capacities in an objective sense. Here, competence is a summary term that refers to a class of variables. The most general one is the person's belief in his or her ability to influence events, to bring about desired outcomes—described by the concept of locus of control (and extensively discussed in Lefcourt's chapter in this volume). Belief in their ability to influence events and to bring about desired outcomes makes it worthwhile for people to initiate action and actively pursue their goals.

Existing plans or strategies for action in various situations, and the capacity to generate plans, seem another important aspect of competence (Miller, Galanter, & Pribram, 1960; Mischel, 1973). When the behavior that is required is clearly specified by someone's need or by the existing circumstances, such competence is not needed. However, the kind of action that would be helpful is frequently unclear, and the need to generate plans is great. One may even move further back along the chain of events and consider that cognitive competencies are involved in deciding whether values and beliefs that one holds are applicable to a current situation. Values and beliefs tend to be relatively general: when one cannot rely on past experience with similar situations, one needs to derive standards and norms of conduct ("In this situation, I ought to help") which are applicable to the specific situation that one faces.

Schwartz (1970, 1977) suggested that a person's awareness of the possible consequences of his behavior on other people is an important determinant, in combination with other characteristics, of helping behavior. Awareness of potential consequences of one's action may be the result of joint variation in role taking, in a person's sense of his ability to exert influence over events, and in the capacity to generate plans of action. It is the combination of these characteristics that would lead a person to consider what consequences his behavior may have, and to realize and appreciate its potential beneficial consequences. Schwartz found that persons who scored high on a paper-and-pencil measure of awareness of consequences were more helpful under some circumstances than those who scored low on this measure. Under other circumstances–for example, in an emergency, where the potential consequences of action may have been clear to everybody–scores on this measure did not affect helping. I would expect that a strong personal goal combined with awareness of consequences–or more generally, with awareness of and belief in one's capacity to affect others' welfare–would lead to most help for a person in need.

A further aspect of competence is the possession of behavioral skills and/or a person's belief in possessing the skills that are necessary for prosocial action on a particular occasion. One has to swim in order to pull someone out of the raging river. One has to have certain interpersonal skills or believe that one possesses them, in order to attempt to help a person distressed about some aspect of his life and, certainly, to actually be helpful to him.

Varied aspects of competence contribute to the expectations of success in reaching a desired outcome (Rotter, 1954; Mischel, 1966), which in turn affect the likelihood of taking action to reach that outcome. All of these competencies may contribute to a feeling of control on a particular occasion. The feeling of control over aversive events increases tolerance for them and diminishes both the physiological arousal they produce and their negative effects on task performance (Glass & Singer, 1972; Staub et al., 1971; Staub & Kellett, 1972). Lack of control produces a sense of helplessness (and/or lack of hope), which reduces the likelihood of subsequent attempts at taking action and exerting influence (Lefcourt, 1973, and chapter 5 in this volume; Seligmen, 1975). Lack of competence, subjective or objective, may not only diminish attempts to reach the outcomes implied by personal goals, but may also diminish the likelihood that goals are activated, since a goal activated but not pursued is likely to create distress and discomfort. Lack of competence may exert its influence by minimizing attention to activating stimuli, or by creating a desire to avoid the activating stimuli. That is, subjective incompetence may be a source of motivation itself, a negative goal that gives rise to the desire to avoid situations where competence is called for.

Related to competence, to some extent an outcome of variation in competence, is a person's capacity to take initiative, to engage in action under ambiguous or difficult conditions–his or her "action tendency." Variation in subjective or objective competence is certainly not the only determinant, however, of action tendency; independence, impulsiveness, courage, adventurousness, and anticonformity may all contribute to a person's tendency to initiate action consistent with his goals. Depending on circumstances, some of these characteristics may be more important than others. In one study, for example, we found a significant positive correlation between subjects' ranking of *courageous* on Rokeach's test of values (a term that was defined as standing up for one's beliefs) and their entering an adjoining room in response to mild sounds of distress coming from there (Staub, Erkut, & Jaquette, in Staub, 1974).

Our Carnegie Hero had served as a parachutist during World War II. To do his job as a parachutist, he had to deal with physical danger and must have possessed physical coordination and skill. I do not know how parachutists were selected during World War II; if he volunteered, that would suggest that he liked to face physical challenge. All these characteristics could be important in leading him to take action and to be successful in saving the drowning woman. A liking of danger and of the exercise of his physical capacities may have also contributed (in spite of his weakened condition) to his motivation to help.

Disposition Toward "Justifications"

Frequently, people engage in cognitive activities to minimize the activating potential of certain conditions on themselves. To different degrees, people will hold beliefs and values that can be applied to inhibit the arousal of a personal goal, as well as to deactivate an already activated goal. Certain cognitions, when used in this manner, will be called *justifications.* Many conditions make the inhibition of a personal goal, or its deactivation, desirable. They include foreseeing or experiencing conflict among goals. A high cost of helping–when, in order to benefit someone, a person has to sacrifice a great deal of time or valued material resources, to expand substantial energy, or to risk his or her safety–frequently results in conflict between a prosocial goal and the goal of promoting the interests of the self. Both high cost and lack of competence in pursuing a goal may lead to justifications. Conflict can also be inherent in the quality of a person's goal itself. When a person experiences goal conflict, it can be disturbing to simply proceed with the pursuit of the strongest, activated goal. Justifications can minimize the activating potential of certain conditions, or can deactivate goals, and thereby decrease the experience of conflict and distress about not pursuing some goal.

Not all thoughts that lead to not helping or to not acting according to some goal are properly called justifications. The analysis of how personal goals affect behavior suggests that a person can decide that he or she wants to pursue one goal rather than another, for good reasons. A person may weigh the degree of another person's need, or the legitimacy of another person's request, and decide that his or her own needs or goals are more important to pursue. However, a person may use reasons for not helping (or not acting according to some other goal) that rationalize, that justify the decision or the fact that one has not helped. Often we have no objective criteria to differentiate between good reasons and justifications; the distinction can be a matter of judgment or point of view, and can be argued. A potential helper may think that a person in need does not deserve help—because of the kind of person he is (and a little suffering may even be good for him), or because his own actions brought about the need for help—and thus may think that his suffering is deserved. If a man is lying on the street, someone may think he is a bum, probably drunk, and that he either needs or deserves no help (Staub & Baer, 1974). While the passerby who thinks this way is likely to not check out his judgment, which is then used as justification, he or she can approach this person and see if he is drunk, or sick and in need of help. If a person believes that there is no need for civil-rights action, and does nothing to promote such action or legislation, claiming that blacks are poor and "disadvantaged" not because of the way society treated them but because they are not interested in education and do not work as hard as whites, direct "checking out" of the correctness of such beliefs is more difficult. This can make it relatively easy to use such thinking for justifications. A person with a strong prosocial goal, who frequently uses justifications to eliminate the need for help, either has strong conflicting motives or has conflict inherent in his or her prosocial goal.

Justifications can also be applied to goals other than prosocial ones. When they are applied to a goal that conflicts with a prosocial goal, they can contribute to helping. For example, a person may justify not trying to do well on a task, by judging it a poor task or by devaluing the people who gave the task, thereby decreasing conflict about helping someone.

There seem to be certain beliefs and values that make justifications of not helping easier. Lerner (Lerner & Simmons, 1966; Lerner, 1971) proposed that people believe that the world is just. When they see an innocent person suffer (innocent in the sense that this person has not *done* anything to bring about or deserve suffering), in order to maintain their belief in a just world, people will devalue the suffering victim. They will assume that, due to his character or personality, this person deserves to suffer. Rubin and Peplau (1973) found that people greatly vary in their belief that the world is just. Individuals who more strongly hold the just-world view are more inclined to devaluate people who suffer, members of minority groups who are discriminated against, or others whom the world apparently does not treat in a just fashion.

Reactance and Sensitivity to Pressure

Another person's need for help can arouse resentment about the imposition that it represents (Berkowitz, 1973; Staub, 1978). Brehm (1966) proposed that people are sensitive to demands placed on them that either limit their freedom of action or imply or threaten a limitation on their freedom. Frequently, people respond against such pressures by acting contrary to them. People may be particularly sensitive to such pressure in the realm of prosocial behavior. Others' need for help invokes societal norms that make it an obligation to help. The obligatory nature of these norms may often create psychological reactance. The feeling of reactance can also be used as a justification: "I will not let my freedom be limited; I am not going to oblige with demands placed on me."

There is evidence that children, particularly boys, respond to some conditions that aim at increasing their helping behavior with opposition, presumably arising out of reactance. Boys respond with opposition to verbal communications about the desirability or usefulness of help or about its beneficial consequences for the recipients (Staub, 1971c, 1975a, 1975b, 1979). Since, in our culture, boys are trained to be independent, it is understandable that they would respond more negatively than girls when such demands are placed on them. Boys, and males in general, evidence less concern about others' welfare on various paper-and-pencil tests than do girls and women, at least in our culture (Hoffman, 1977; Staub, 1978); this would also increase the likelihood of oppositional reactions to requests for help.

Sensitivity to pressure, and an oppositional tendency, may be dominant characteristics of some individuals. Under many circumstances, people may respond differently to conditions that potentially activate a prosocial goal, or other goals, as a function of variation in this characteristic. The desire to not be unduly influenced by other people, to not be controlled by them–independence or self determination–may be an important personal goal for many people.

DIMENSIONS OF SITUATIONS RELEVANT TO HELPING

A staggering amount of research, considering that almost all was conducted within the last decade, shows that varied aspects of situations affect positive behavior. The findings of this research can help us specify dimensions of situations that vary in activating potential for prosocial goals. Variations along some of the dimensions can also determine whether personality characteristics other than goals–for example, the feeling of competence in reaching an outcome–will be important. Still other variations can affect the activation of goals that conflict with a prosocial goal. The summary of situational dimensions below was derived from Staub, 1978. These dimensions are conceptual: many different actual characteristics of stimuli can specify their location on one of these conceptual dimensions, or on several of them at the same time.

1. The extent to which the nature of stimulus for help (someone's physical or psychological need, its degree, nature, and manner of presentation), the surrounding conditions, or social influence that is exerted by other people provide an unambiguous definition of someone's need for help. The less ambiguity, the more help will follow. Ambiguity diminishes the likelihood that the stimulus is interpreted as representing someone's need, and thereby diminishes activating potential. Ambiguity can also give rise to concern that a helpful act would be inappropriate or appear foolish, and thus may activate an approval goal.

Yakimovitch and Saltz (1971) had a workman fall off a ladder in front of the subject's window—an event enacted to provide a stimulus for help. The frequency of help substantially increased when, in addition to other indications of distress, the workman eliminated ambiguity by calling for help. Other studies also found that clearly defining a situation as one in which someone needs help increases helpful responses by people (Bickman, 1971; Staub, 1974).

2. **The degree of need for help.** Usually, the greater the need for help, the more help will follow (Staub & Baer, 1974). However, exceptions may exist, partly because when someone's distress, discomfort, or the danger to a person are great, which make the need for help great, the costs associated with helping—the sacrifices demanded from, or the potential danger for a helper—are frequently also great.

3. **The extent to which responsibility for help is focused on a particular person rather than diffused among a number of people.** The more clearly the circumstances focus the responsibility on a particular person, the greater the likelihood that this person will provide help. Responsibility is focused on a person if he or she is the only witness to another's need; if he or she is the only person who is in a position to help, although not necessarily the only witness; if he or she has special skills that are required for helping; if he or she has a special relationship to the person in need; if a leadership position makes this person the natural one to take charge; and in other ways.

In the well-known studies by Latane and Darley (1970), the number of people who witnessed emergencies varied. As the number of witnesses who were present, or whom participants believed were present, increased, the likelihood that a participant would respond to sounds of distress coming from another room decreased. Presumably, diffusion of responsibility was one reason for this. People who were alone when they heard the sounds were most likely to attempt to help. In a study by Korte (1969), the subject, who witnessed through an intercom an ostensible asthma attack by the experimenter, was led to believe either that another person who also witnessed the emergency was in a position to help, or that the other person was tied to electrodes and thus could not leave. In the latter condition, which appears to focus responsibility on the subject to a greater degree, participants helped more.

Conditions that strongly focus responsibility to help on a person can lead to helping, even if that person has little personal motivation to help. Societal norms strongly prescribe that we help people with certain kinds of needs. When responsibility is focussed on a person, compliance with these norms is more likely. When a need exists, but responsibility is not directly focused on particular individuals, people with personal motivation to help should be more likely to do so. In one study, female subjects who (in responding to questionnaire items) ascribed more responsibility to themselves for others' welfare helped more and were less affected by variation in the number of bystanders in an emergency (Schwartz & Clausen, 1970). The findings of another study also showed that personal characteristics modify the influence of other witnesses (Wilson, 1976). Esteem-oriented individuals who (on the basis of sententence-completion tests) appeared to have feelings of strong personal adequacy, the belief that "they can master situations in realistic and functional ways" (Wilson, 1976, p. 1079), and a need for efficacy in interpersonal relationships, responded more in an emergency, and were unaffected by variation in the number of bystanders–in comparison to "safety-oriented" subjects or a mixed group. Safety-oriented subjects appeared dependent and mistrustful, characterized by feelings of personal incompetence and a view of the world as uncontrollable. The difference in helping was particularly great when subjects witnessed the emergency with two passive bystanders. In addition to being more action-oriented and more resistant to external influence, more concern about the distressed person's welfare may have been aroused in esteem-oriented individuals. The presence of others–and particularly that of bystanders who, by their passivity, defined the situation as one in which no action was necessary–may have created fear of disapproval and self-concern in safety-oriented persons. Self-concern, however, appears to strongly interfere with the capacity to respond to others' needs (Staub, 1978).

4. The degree of impact of the instigating stimuli. Closeness in space and the length of exposure to a distressed person, and the ease or difficulty of getting away from his or her presence (affecting length of exposure) seem to be conditions that affect the impact of the stimulus for help on a potential helper. In studies where people were exposed to an emergency on the subway, somebody usually helped, regardless of the number of people who were present (Piliavin et al., 1969; 1975). In some cases, the emergency occurred on the express train that did not stop for several minutes. Although several influences may be at work, the impact of continued exposure to a person in physical need was probably important in leading people to initiate help.[5] In another study (Staub & Baer, 1974) bystanders helped a distressed person on the street, who fell down in their path, substantially more than they helped a person who fell down on the other side of the street. In the latter instance, the impact of the stimulus was smaller, and the opportunity for bystanders to escape from its presence greater. Greater impact presumably embodies a greater activating potential for

[5] In one study, Piliavin *et al.* (1975) attempted to test the effects of length of exposure by having the emergency occur either four stops or one stop before the end of the line. While they found no effect of length of exposure, in both conditions the emergency occurred right after the subway train left a station. Thus, length of exposure till the next station, where bystanders *could* leave the train, was equal. "Escape" from the situation was possible in both conditions, although inconvenient in one treatment condition for passengers who intended to travel beyond the next station.

prosocial goals. However, the social cost of not helping and the attendant desire to avoid social punishment can also increase with greater impact.

5. The extent to which circumstances specify the response to someone's need for help or leave the required response undefined. Sometimes, the stimulus for help and/or surrounding conditions clearly indicate not only that help is needed, but also the kind of action that is required; a potential helper may even receive a specific request for a specific act. At other times, a person may have to decide both that help is needed and what needs to be done. In such cases, more decision making and greater initiative are required, and varied competencies are involved in helping. For example, Schwartz and Clausen (1970) found that when a person in need asked for a pill that he had in his coat pocket, he received help much more frequently than in another condition, where the need was presented, but ways of helping were not specified.

6. The "direct" costs of helping. How much effort, time, energy, material goods, or risk to oneself is demanded? The greater such costs, the less help can usually be expected. Greater costs create conflict between a goal that is powerful for most people, to protect and promote one's interests, and other goals that may promote helping.

7. Indirect costs. In everyday life, it is a common occurrence that in order to help others, one has to sacrifice the pursuit of goals that one is actively pursuing. There has been little research about how attention to others' needs is affected, what kinds of conflicts are created, and how they are resolved when a person is engaged in the pursuit of some activity or personal goal and has to sacrifice that pursuit in order to help another person. It is one thing to talk to a seemingly upset neighbor who stops by, when one has free time; it is a somewhat different thing when one is about to go to play tennis, or to meet one's lover, or has only a couple hours to finish some important work for a deadline. In a study that is relevant to this kind of conflict, Darley and Batson (1973) found that seminary students who were to deliver a lecture were less helpful to a person lying on the ground, whom they passed by on their way to the lecture, if they were told that they were late and had to hurry to get to their lecture on time. Being engaged in the pursuit of goals must frequently diminish people's willingness to help others.

8. The social appropriateness of the behavior required for help. Circumstances can suggest that the type of action that is required for help is socially acceptable or that it may be undesirable, inappropriate, or socially unacceptable. For example, implicit or explicit rules–that a child is to continue working on a task, or that going into a strange room in a strange environment is inappropriate (Staub, 1970, 1971b, 1974)–may inhibit responses to another person's apparent distress. When circumstances activate approval goal on, it may promote helping by inducing people to act according to social norms or specific situational rules that prescribe help for others, or it may inhibit helping, depending on the nature of the circumstances.

9. Temporary psychological states of a person that result from positive or negative experiences concurrent with or just prior to the opportunity to benefit others. Such experiences can result in positive or negative moods, different levels of temporary self-esteem, or differences in other internal states. Positive states usually enhance, negative states frequently (although not always) diminish, help for others. Presumably, a person's own psychological state affects his or her capacity to perceive or seriously consider others' needs and affects the feeling of connection between the self and others: both would affect the activation of prosocial goals. Notice that the conceptual-stimulus dimension here is a person's own internal state.

I proposed a theory of "hedonic balancing" which specifies how people balance their own and other people's states of well-being at any particular time (Staub, 1978). In the course of this "balancing," people consider how they themselves feel at the moment, how much better or worse they feel than their usual state of well being. They compare this to how the other person feels, how much better or worse than the other might usually feel. The outcome or hedonic balance can affect both the activation of prosocial goals and whether activated goals will be acted upon. Many hedonic balance conditions are possible. A person who had a success experience and feels good would be more likely to show positive behavior, according to this conception, if his usual state of well-being is neutral rather than highly positive, so that his current feelings represent a positive hedonic discrepancy. He may show even more positive behavior if the person who need help appears to experience a negative hedonic discrepancy, a state worse than his usual state–if he is usually healthy but now sick, rather than if he is usually sick and is now sick as well.

Researchers found that even seemingly minimal experiences, such as finding a dime in a telephone booth or receiving a cookie from someone, can increase people's subsequent willingness soon afterwards to help a person who appears to need help (Isen & Levin, 1972). Providing information to people about their competence on a task (whether or not this competence is relevant to the kind of action that needs to be taken to help another person); their success and failure on tasks; children thinking about past positive or negative experiences; communications to people that they will be evaluated on some task (this perhaps arousing self-concern);–all have been found to affect prosocial behavior (for reviews, see Rosenhan et al., 1976; Bar-Tal, 1976; Staub, 1973, 1978). However, the extent to which persistent individual differences in self esteem and/or characteristic moods of individuals modify the influence of the momentary experiences has remained largely unexplored (although not completely–see Staub, 1978). Such persistent characteristics may directly influence the activation of prosocial goals or the feeling of competence in executing positive action. They may also affect what internal states are created by everyday experiences.

10. Past experience with the potential recipients of positive behavior. A person's sense of relatedness to or connectedness or identification with another person seems to be an extremely important determinant of whether this person will take action to benefit another (Hornstein, 1976; Reykowski, 1975; Rosenhan et al., 1976; Staub, 1978). This connection between others and the self may be a function of a person's orientation toward other people in general, an aspect of a prosocial goal, or an aspect of past experience with or knowledge about particular others.

The existence of a relationship to a person in need, its degree and kind, will affect the extent to which the interests of the self and others are regarded as identical or unrelated or opposing, and will affect the kind of special rules or principles that guide the relationship. Our relationships to other people frequently place special obligations on us to respond to their needs, to promote their welfare. The existence of a close relationship, as well as certain other conditions (knowledge of shared group membership, or of similarities of opinions, beliefs, and personality) can lead to identification with another person; and this makes the arousal of a prosocial goal, or specifically of empathy and of other motives that promote help, more likely. Other conditions, those which give rise to antagonism, may make help less likely. An ongoing relationship also provides others' needs with greater impact, since it makes it difficult to physically remove oneself, to escape from the presence of another's distress or need.

Principles that guide positive social behavior among people in close relationships probably differ somewhat from those that guide positive behavior among strangers or acquaintances. In responding to a stranger's need for help, the prior behavior of that person toward us is not an issue; we may anticipate future reciprocity, but we do not respond to the past behaviors of this person. However, reciprocity does guide our behavior toward people with whom we had past interactions: we return favors, and frequently retaliate harm. Interpersonal relations and positive interactions are certainly transactional. Past actions by one person affect subsequent responses by another, which in turn influence the next behavior of the first actor, and so on. Reciprocity applies less in relationships among friends than among acquaintances and strangers who are participating in a "minimal interaction," a limited exchange of behaviors (Floyd, 1964; Staub & Sherk, 1970; Staub, 1978). Presumably, in close relationships, benefits that people provide for each other and sacrifices that they make can be balanced over a longer time interval.

In sum, the existence of a positive relationship with another person may not only increase the likelihood of the activation of prosocial goals, but can invoke varied obligations and special principles that guide positive (and negative) interactions. Finally, people in continuing relationships can develop norms, rules, standards, and values that are applicable to that relationship, which guide their behavior toward each other. Unfortunately, our knowledge of principles of interaction in close relationships are quite limited, as yet.

SUPPORTING RESEARCH

What research findings exist that provide support for the theoretical conceptions described above? Some of our own research attempted to explore both the influence of a prosocial goal as a function of its activation by stimulus conditions, and/or the joint influence of several goals, on positive behavior. Some previously existing research is also relevant.

Research Conducted to Test the Theoretical Model

The findings of one of our studies provided one impetus to the conception advanced above; it also provides support for it (Staub, Erkut, & Jaquette, as reported in Staub, 1974). In this study, responses to sounds of distress, and help for the distressed person in the course of subsequent interaction with him, were affected by a combination of the characteristics of the situation and personality characteristics of subjects. Male participants worked on a number of personality tests, some of which measured values and beliefs relevant to a prosocial goal. In a second session, while working on a personality measure, the subject heard sounds of distress from an adjoining room. Previously he either received permission to enter the adjoining room, or was told not to interrupt work on the task (prohibition), or received no information about rules that might affect freedom of action. If the subject did not enter the adjoining room in response to the sounds, the "distressed" confederate entered the subject's room. An interaction followed in the course of which the confederate presented the subject with several sequences of behavior, each providing a separate opportunity for a helping act. The final sequence presented the subject with a choice between going to a pharmacy to fill a prescription, and thereby help the confederate's stomach problem, or calling the confederate's roommate—which demanded less effort but would result in much slower help—or refusing to help.

Subjects with a more advanced level of moral reasoning (Kohlberg, 1969), or those who tended to ascribe responsibility to themselves for others' welfare, (Schwartz, 1970) helped more, but only when the experimenter previously indicated that it was permissible to interrupt work on their task and to enter the adjoining room for an irrelevant reason—to get a cup of coffee (permission condition). As in other experiments (Staub, 1971b), permission presumably reduced concern about disapproval. People who held prosocial values such as helpfulness or equality—as indicated by their ranking of these values on Rokeach's (1973) measure—tended to help more in the permission condition.

In the prohibition condition, where subjects were told that their task was timed and were asked to work on it without interruptions, and in the no information condition where the experimenter said nothing, only slight relationships existed between scores on these varied value-related measures and subjects' behavior. Values that conflicted with helping, such as ambition, reduced helping. The negative relationship between valuing ambition and helping was particularly strong in the prohibition condition, which would be expected to activate ambition or the desire for achievement by subjects on their tasks.

A factor analysis of measures that expressed positive values about people or about helping produced a strong factor with a high loading of most of the measures on this factor. These included the measures mentioned above, as well as scores on a measure indicating negative evaluation of human beings and manipulativeness (Christie & Geis, 1968), which had negative loading. Scores on this "prosocial-orientation" factor were related to most of the helpful actions that the subjects had opportunities to perform, and the relationship was relatively unaffected by situational variation.

The findings of this study showed that situations and prosocial values and beliefs interact in affecting behavior, but people characterized by a combination of these beliefs and values were less affected by situational variation. Since in all treatments a need existed, a prosocial goal could be activated in all conditions. The findings also suggested that a number of existing measures can be used together as a preliminary index of a prosocial goal.

In two dissertations, Feinberg (1977) and Grodman (1979) further tested the theoretical model. In both of these studies, a little explored but extremely important type of helping was studied: people's reactions to someone's psychological distress. We all have the frequent experience that someone we know or interact with is upset, frustrated, sad, or disappointed. What determines our willingness to attempt to console, advise, or in other ways help?

In both studies, female participants were administered most of the value-related personality measures, and a couple of additional ones, that in the above study had a high loading on the prosocial-orientation factor. In addition, in Feinberg's study the subjects also filled out a group of measures to test values and beliefs related to an achievement goal. A factor analysis of scores on the measures of prosocial values and beliefs provided a strong factor in both studies: factor scores were used to divide subjects into high and low prosocial groups. In Feinberg's study the factor analysis of achievement-related measures also provided a strong factor, and subjects divided by factor scores were assigned to high and low achievement groups.

In Feinberg's study these divisions resulted in groups of subjects who were either low in both achievement and prosocial goals, high in both, or low in one and high in the other. In a second session, each subject was working together with another person—a confederate—on a personality test. In response to a story that was part of this test, the confederate began to tell the subject about a very upsetting experience that occurred the night before (*high need*). She described how her boyfriend of two years standing, with whom she had talked about marriage, suddenly broke up with her. Not only did he not explain why, but he refused to discuss the matter. The confederate presented several pieces of information, if the subject allowed, and additional information if the subject elicited it by what she said, all in a carefully prepared and structured manner. In a *low need* condition the confederate provided the same information, but reported that the event occurred a year ago, and did not act upset. She seemed to reminisce rather than need help.

Varied behaviors of the subjects were recorded, either by observers or on a tape recorder, and were later categorized. These included verbal behaviors such as the total amount that subjects talked, their expression of sympathy, giving advice, and others; nonverbal behaviors such as working on or looking at the task, or looking at and smiling at the confederate; ratings by the confederate and the observer following the interaction of the subjects' helpfulness and orientation toward the confederate; and an index of the subjects' willingness to continue the conversation after the experimental participation was over. Subjects also provided information on a post-experimental questionnaire about their feelings about the confederate, and about other aspects of their experience.

As expected, people helped more in high need than in low need, both verbally and nonverbally. Contrary to expectations, persons who valued achievement more helped more than those who valued achievement less, particularly in verbally responding to the confederate. It was originally expected that achievement orientation would be expressed in task-related activity, not recognizing that an achievement goal can also be satisfied by doing well in helping a distressed person. This points to the importance of carefully evaluating the activating potential of situations for varied goals. High-prosocial subjects helped less in low need than did low-prosocial subjects, but more in high need. This difference was particularly strong in nonverbal responses, attention to the confederate rather than the task. Responses on the post-experimental questionnaire indicated that in low need, the high-prosocial subjects felt an obligation to help the experimenter by completing the task. High need apparently activated their desire to help the confederate, which was expressed by a moderate degree of verbal help and by substantial nonverbal interest and responsiveness, and a willingness to later continue the interaction.

Contrary to expectations, persons with high achievement and low prosocial goals talked substantially more to the confederate than did any other group of subjects. This happened both under high need and low need, suggesting that these people were not simply responding to a strong need, but to any claim on their attention. People high on the prosocial goal and low on the achievement goal tended to behave as high prosocial subjects in general, but showed the same trends toward helping somewhat more strongly. Under high need, high-prosocial low-achievement subjects paid more attention to the confederate than did subjects in any other condition. Finally, answers on the post-experimental questionnaire indicated that when faced with strong need, high-prosocial subjects, particularly high-prosocial, low-achievement ones, tended to like the confederate more and perceive her distress as more genuine than did low-prosocial subjects, particularly low-prosocial, high-achievement ones. The latter group of subjects, in addition to talking a substantial amount and paying moderate attention to the confederate, also worked a substantial amount on their task. Seemingly, they wanted to do a great deal, but they indicated—although generally not to a significant degree—that they gained less gratification from helping behavior than did any other group of subjects. The findings of this study provide some support for the theory. However, they also point to certain issues—for example, that *assumptions* by researchers about the meaning (activating potential) of stimuli for people can be incorrect. Moreover, they show that people are highly discriminative in their behavior, which is a complex function of their personality and the existing conditions.

In another study, Grodman (1979) used the high-need condition described above. In addition to dividing subjects by their prosocial goal into low and high groups, on the basis of their performance on personality measures (see Feinberg's procedure described earlier), she varied the costs associated with helping the distressed confederate. By attending to the confederate and helping her, and thereby neglecting their task, people provided less information about themselves to the experimenter—who, in the high-cost condition, promised to give the subjects information about their personality on the basis of test results. No such promise was made in the low-cost condition. Thus in high cost, by helping, people diminished the value of the feedback that they would receive about themselves.

In this study, subjects with a strong prosocial goal helped more than those with a weak prosocial goal. The difference was not only significant on varied measures of help, verbal and nonverbal, but was also quite substantial. On several measures, this was true regardless of costs. On other measures, prosocial goal and cost each affected helping; and on still others, only the interaction between the two affected behavior. In the latter case, usually the high-prosocial subjects helped significantly more than the low-prosocial ones, verbally or by showing interest, in the low-cost condition. Frequently, they also helped numerically more in the high-cost condition, but the difference was insubstantial.

The differences in helping that are associated with a prosocial goal are consistent with, but stronger than, Feinberg's findings, whose high-prosocial subjects were more helpful than low-prosocial ones in the high-need condition, but mainly in nonverbal ways. Conflict between helping and the possibility of acquiring knowledge about themselves reduced helping by high-prosocial subjects. Grodman noted, on the basis of responses by subjects on a post-experimental questionnaire, that acquiring knowledge about themselves seemed very important for high-prosocial subjects, more important than for low-prosocial ones. This is consistent with research findings showing that among young adolescents those who are more sensitive and responsive to others are more concerned about their interaction with others and about their effects on other people (Reese, 1961). To such individuals, information about themselves and about how they appear to other people would be important. Consequently, Grodman's high-cost condition may have created greater conflict for high-prosocial subjects than some other kinds of costs would have.

Other Relevant Research

A few existing research studies seem relevant to the theoretical model described in this chapter. In one study, Schwartz and his associates (1969) provided subjects with an opportunity to cheat on a task on one occasion, and with an opportunity to be helpful on another occasion. Subjects could cheat in solving multiple-choice vocabulary problems; and while working on a puzzle they could help someone who had trouble putting the puzzle together and had made requests for help. Before either activity, three personality characteristics were measured: the participants' need for achievement, their need for affiliation, and their level of moral reasoning. The authors made differential predictions about the relationship between personality characteristics and behavior in the two situations. Stronger need to achieve was expected to be positively related to not cheating, because the desire for excellence cannot be satisfied by getting the right answers through cheating; but it was expected to be negatively related to helping, because helping would interfere with solving the puzzle. Need for affiliation was expected to be unrelated to cheating, which is an impersonal activity, but positively related to helping, which involved a positive interpersonal interaction. More advanced moral reasoning was expected to be positively related to both honesty and helping, since both can be regarded as moral behaviors. Essentially, the hypotheses were confirmed by the data. At the same time, the two behaviors, cheating and helping, were unrelated to each other.

From the perspective of our theory, these researchers considered the activating potential of each of two situations with regard to three values or motives, and measured individual differences in these values or motives. By doing so they could correctly predict the relationship between these personal motives and behavior.

In another study, Liebhart (1972) measured some form of a prosocial motive or goal of eleventh- to thirteenth-grade German male high-school subjects, by administering a projective test of "sympathetic orientation." The subjects' disposition to take instrumental action to relieve their own distress was measured by a Lickert-type scale that the author devised. Subjects with a sympathetic orientation helped more quickly in response to sounds of distress from the adjoining room–a bang followed by cries and moans–if they were also disposed toward instrumental action. This finding supports the notion that when personality characteristics which make it a desirable goal to assist another are activated, a person is likely to help if he is characterized by an orientation toward taking action.

Also relevant are findings of a study by Gergen and associates (1972), and their discussion of their findings. Members of an undergraduate class could indicate their willingness to aid the psychology department with five ongoing projects–counseling male students from a nearby high school; counseling female students; helping with a faculty research project on deductive thinking; with a research project on unusual states of consciousness; or collating and assembling materials for further use by the class. In the preceding class session the students completed a battery of personality tests, measuring a variety of characteristics or "traits."

Gergen and associates found that different personality characteristics were significantly related to volunteering help with different tasks. Also, the pattern of correlations differed for males and females. The findings are consistent with the present model: people selected tasks to help with that seemed to satisfy some personal goal or lead to some outcome desirable for them. For example, need for nurturance in males was significantly related to their willingness to help with counseling other males (r = .41), but not to volunteering with other forms of help. Presumably, students with a strong need for nurturance expected to experience satisfaction in the course of a nurturant relationship that they anticipated in counseling. Sensation seeking as a personality characteristic was positively related to helping with research on unusual states, but negatively related to volunteering for research on deductive thinking. The correlations between personality and volunteering showed a similar kind of specificity among female subjects. The authors stressed that helping behavior is determined by specific situational payoffs. People have different payoff preferences, and depending on them, they will move toward one or another social context. They discourage the notion that certain trait dispositions or individual differences will be found to account for variability in prosocial behavior.

Helping behavior was not measured in this study: rather, the subjects' stated intentions to help were evaluated, in a group situation. The relationship between measures of the intention to help and actual helping is poor (Staub, 1978). However, for the purposes of considering the theoretical meaning of the data, this is not a prohibitive problem. Since subjects were not confronted with someone's immediate need for help, and since the class consisted of 72 people, the students probably did not feel an obligation to provide substantial help with most of the five tasks. Our theoretical model suggests that they would choose the kind of help that, either in terms of the activities inherent in them or the outcomes they lead to, would be satisfying and meaningful from the standpoint of their personal goals.

A further important consideration is that no attempt has been made in this study to evaluate personality characteristics that are relevant to helping per se, that make helping a desirable activity; that is, the kinds of characteristics that enter into or might be components of a prosocial goal. Only a high degree of motivation for prosocial behavior can be reasonably expected to lead to any generality in helping behavior or generality in the expressed intention to be helpful, and only under certain conditions. An "irrelevant" characteristic, such as sensation seeking, would be expected to sometimes add to, other times detract from, the influence of a prosocial goal. When considered by itself, it can be expected to lead to helping only when it so happens that the helping behavior satisfies sensation seeking; that is, for accidental reasons. However, given the existence of a strong prosocial motivation, a positive relationship between such motivation and several helping acts can be expected, at least when other personality characteristics are supportive and no conflicting goals are active.

In conclusion, both our own initial research efforts and research conducted by others, based on varied theoretical conceptions, provide findings that can be viewed as encouraging initial support for the theoretical model (see also Schwartz & Clausen, 1970; Wilson, 1976; both reviewed above). In most of this research, the joint, interactive influence of some personality variables and environmental variation led to behavior in a specific setting that can be meaningfully explained in terms of the theoretical model. In addition to further research of this kind, future studies can also explore the extent to which people with certain personal goals and/or related competencies will seek out situations in which they can pursue their goals, and the extent to which they behave consistently across varied circumstances in pursuing their goals. The conditions under which such consistency can be expected has been specified at earlier points in the chapter.

Self-Regulation in the Pursuit of Goals

How do personal goals, stimulus conditions and associated activation potentials, competencies, and other relevant personal characteristics jointly affect behavior? As noted earlier, a precise formulation of the interrelationship among these determinants of behavior may be premature. The intensity of a personal goal and of the activating potential of the situation may join to determine the intensity of an activated goal in a multiplicative fashion. Competencies may affect the expectancies that one can or cannot successfully pursue an outcome that would satisfy a goal. As a function of the specific nature of their competencies, people may carry with themselves such expectancies toward certain outcomes, this affecting goal activation. Such expectancies may also arise (may be constructed) on specific occasions as a function of circumstances following the activation of a goal, and may inhibit or promote the pursuit of goal satisfaction. In the initial stages of testing the theory, it is sufficient to assume that strong competencies for pursuing some outcomes may be promotive, weak ones may be prohibitive of goal-directed behavior. Either an analysis-of-variance model or a regression model can be used to test the joint influence of goals and competencies.

How does self-regulation of behavior take place? Several authors, writing about determinants of helping behavior, propose that people progress through a series of decisions; their nature determines whether they will help others or not (Latane & Darley, 1970; Schwartz, 1970, 1977; Pomazal & Jaccard, 1976). Latane and Darley proposed a decisional sequence in emergencies. In their view, people first have to notice an event, then they have to decide that it means that someone needs help, then they have to assume that they are responsible for providing help. Given all these positive decisions, they still have to execute some action.

Such a specification of decision steps is useful. By varying the nature of the environment—for example, providing people only with the stimulus for help, or providing them with that as well as with a definition of its meaning, or also focusing responsibility on them, and so on—we can affect where people will be along the decisional sequence. By also considering personality characteristics, and by measuring the joint effects of situational variations and personality on thought and feeling—before behavior could have taken place—as well as on behavior, we can progressively elaborate on what takes place internally, on how varied influences affect thinking and feeling.

At the same time, this conception of decisional steps is likely to be an oversimplification. Our actual flow of consciousness is probably more formless, with less definite junctures, without definite decision points. This flow is likely to include interpretations of events and the considerations of what actions one might take. If there is no conflict due to great demands on the helper, or to conflicting goals, or to other thoughts and feelings that block the flow of consciousness, a person's "will" may gain uninhibited expression in action (William James, 1890).

The flow of consciousness can include thoughts about the ease or difficulty of interpreting an event and dealing with it, verbal self-reinforcements or self-punishments that accompany action (a person thinking about how well or poorly he is doing, how good, clever, and skillful, or how bad, stupid, and incompetent he is) with corresponding feelings. There is substantial evidence that the way people "speak to themselves," their internal dialogue, affects their behavior (see Meichenbaum's chapter in this volume). Mischel, Ebbesen, and Zeiss (1972, 1973) showed that, with young children at least, whether or not children have in front of them valued material objects that function as rewards, and instructions that lead them to engage in varying cognitive processing of such stimuli, affects their delay of gratification, their capacity to wait for delayed, larger rewards, in contrast to accepting immediate but smaller rewards. Masters and Santrock (1976) demonstrated that asking children to think varied positive or negative thoughts while they were working on tasks affected their persistence, whether these thoughts were relevant to the task itself or not.

I have suggested all along that personal goals are the primary organizers of a person's thinking about, feelings toward, and actions related to the pursuit of varied classes of outcomes. Personal goals provide general orientations. I suggested that ranges of applicability of goals can be different for different people. Schwartz (1977) elaborated a decisional model that is based on the assumption that specific moral norms that people hold will determine whether they behave prosocially on specific occasions (e.g., "It is my obligation to donate blood"). I believe that specific norms are likely to be one determinant of the range of applicability of more general personal goals. While personal goals are more basic and general in their applicability, both would enter into guiding the flow of consciousness. By setting standards of conduct for specific occasions, they will affect self-reinforcement, self-punishment, and other elements of the flow of consciousness which guide people's behavior. The specification of the nature of self-regulation, of the flow of thoughts and feelings and their relationship to conduct, is an important task.

REFERENCES

Aderman, D., & Berkowitz, L. Observational set, empathy and helping. *Journal of Personality and Social Psychology,* 1970, *14,* 141-148.

——, **Brehm, S. S., & Katz, L. B.** Empathic observation of an innocent victim: The just world revisited. *Journal of Personality and Social Psychology,* 1974, *29,* 342.

Allport, G. W. *Personality: A psychological interpretation.* New York: Holt, Rinehart & Winston, 1937.

Arnold, M. *Emotion and personality.* New York: Columbia University Press, 1960.

Atkinson, J. W. *Motives in fantasy, action, and society.* Princeton: D. Van Nostrand Company, Inc., 1958.

Bar-Tal, D. *Prosocial behavior: Theory and research.* Washington, D.C.: Hemisphere Publishing Company, 1976.

Bem, D. J., & Allen, A. On predicting some of the people some of the time. The search for cross-situational consistencies in behavior. *Psychological Review,* 1974, *81,* 506-520.

——, **& Funder, D. C.** Predicting more of the people more of the time: Assessing the personality of situations. *Psychological Review,* 1978, *85,* 485-501.

Benedict, R. Anthropology and the abnormal. *Journal of General Psychology,* 1934, 59-82.

Berkowitz, L. Reactance and the unwillingness to help others. *Psychological Bulletin,* 1973, *79,* 310-317.

Bickman, L. The effect of another bystander's ability to help on bystander intervention in an emergency. *Journal of Experimental Social Psychology,* 1971, *7,* 367-380.

Block, J. *Lives through time.* Berkeley, Calif.: Bancroft Books, 1971.

____. Advancing the psychology of personality: paradigmatic shift of improving the quality of research. In Magnusson, D. and Endler, N. S. (Eds.), *Personality at the crossroads: Current issues in interactional psychology.* Hillsdale, N.J.: Lawrence Erlbaum Associates, 1977.

____, **& Block, J. H.** Ego development and the provenance of thought: A longitudinal study of ego and cognitive development in young children. (Progress report for National Institute of Mental Health, No. MH 16080, January, 1973.)

Bowers, K. S. Situationism in psychology. An analysis and a critique. *Psychological Review,* 1973, *80,* 307-336.

Brehm, J. W. *A theory of psychological reactance.* New York: Academic Press, 1966.

Burton, R. V. Generality of honesty reconsidered. *Psychological Review,* 1963, *70,* 481-499.

Cantor, J. H. Individual needs and salient constructs in interpersonal perception. *Journal of Personality and Social Psychology,* 1976, *34,* 519-525.

Carlson, R. Where is the person in personality research? *Psychological Bulletin,* 1971, *75,* 203-219.

Chadwick-Jones, J. K. *Social exchange theory: Its structure and influence in social psychology.* New York: Academic Press, 1976.

Christie, R., & Geis, F. (Eds.) *Studies in Machiavellianism.* New York: Academic Press, 1968.

Cohen, R. Altruism: human, cultural or what? *Journal of Social Issues,* 1972, *28,* 39-57.

Crowne, D. P., & Marlowe, D. *The approval motive: Studies in evaluative dependence.* New York: Wiley, 1964.

Darley, J., & Batson, C. "From Jerusalem to Jericho": A study of situational and dispositional variables in helping behavior. *Journal of Personality and Social Psychology,* 1973, *27,* 100-108.

Deutsch, M. Field theory in social psychology. In G. Lindsey & E. Aronson (Eds.), *Handbook of social psychology,* Vol. I. Addison Wesley Publishing Company, 1968.

Denner, B. Did a crime occur? Should I inform anyone? A study of deception. *Journal for Personality,* 1968, *36,* 454-466.

Dollard, J., & Miller, N. E. *Personality and psychotherapy.* New York: McGraw-Hill, 1950.

Durkheim, E. *Moral education.* New York: The Free Press, 1961.

Ekehammar, B. Interactionism in personality from a historical perspective. *Psychological Bulletin,* 1974, *81,* 1026-1048.

Epstein, S. The stability of personality: On predicting most of the people much of the time. *Journal of Personality & Social Psychology,* 1979, in press.

Feinberg, H. K. Anatomy of a helping situation: Some personality and situational determinants of helping in a conflict situation involving another's psychological distress. Unpublished doctoral dissertation, University of Massachusetts, Amherst, 1977.

Floyd, J. Effects of amount of reward and friendship status of the other on the frequency of sharing in children. Unpublished doctoral dissertation, University of Minnesota, 1964.

Fredericksen, N. Toward a taxonomy of situations. *American Psychologist,* 1972, *27,* 114-124.

Freud, A. The infantile instinct life. In H. Herma & G. M. Karth (Eds.) *A handbook of psychoanalysis.* New York: World Publishing Co., 1963.

Gergen, K. J. Personality consistency and the presentation of self. In C. Gordon & K. J. Gergen (Eds.), *The self in social interaction, vol. I.* New York: John Wiley & Sons, 1968.

____. The decline of character: Socialization and self-consistency In G. DiRenzo (Ed.) *Social change and social character,* Greenwood Press, 1976.

____, **Gergen, M. M., & Meter, K.** Individual orientations to prosocial behavior. *Journal of Social Issues,* 1972, *8,* 105-130.

Glass, D. G., & Singer, J. E. *Urban stress. Experiments on noise and social stressors.* New York: Academic Press, 1972.

Grodman, S. M. The role of personality and situational variables in responding to and helping an individual in psychological distress. Unpublished dissertation, University of Massachusetts, 1979.

Hall, C., & Lindzey, G. *Theories of personality* (2nd ed.). New York: Wiley, 1970.

Harré, R., & Secord, P. F. *The explanation of social behavior.* Oxford: Blackwell, 1972.

Hartshorne, H., & May, M. A. *Studies in the nature of character. Vol. I: Studies in deceit.* New York: Macmillan, 1928.

____, **& Shuttleworth, F. K.** *Studies in the nature of character. Vol. III: Studies in the organization of character.* New York: Macmillan, 1930.

Henshel, A. M. The relationship between values and behavior: A developmental hypothesis. *Child Development,* 1971, *42,* 1997-2007.

Hoffman, M. L. Moral development. In Mussen, P. H. (Ed.), *Carmichael's manual of child development.* New York: Wiley, 1970. (a)

____. Conscience, personality, and socialization technique. *Human Development,* 1970, *13,* 90-126. (b)

____. Sex differences in empathy and related behaviors. *Psychological Bulletin,* 1977, *84,* 712-720.

Homans, G. C. *Social behavior: Its elementary forms.* New York: Harcourt, Brace & World, 1961.

Hornstein, H. A. *Cruelty and kindness. A new look at aggression and altruism.* Englewood Cliffs, N.J.: Prentice-Hall, Inc., 1976.

Huston, T. L., & Korte, C. The responsive bystander: Why he helps. In T. Lickona (Ed.), *Moral development and behavior.* New York: Holt, Rinehart, & Winston, 1976.

Isen, A. M., & Levin, F. Effect of feeling good on helping: Cookies and kindness. *Journal of Personality and Social Psychology,* 1972, *21,* 384-388.

James, W. *The principles of psychology.* Vols. I and II. New York: Henry Holt, 1890.

Jones, E. E. & Nisbett, R. E. *The actor and the observer: Divergent perceptions of the causes of behavior.* New York: General Learning Press, 1971.

Kelley, H. H., & Stahleski, A. J. Social interaction basis of cooperators' and competitors' beliefs about others. *Journal of Personality and Social Psychology,* 1970, *16,* 66-91.

Kohlberg, L. Stage and sequence: The cognitive-developmental approach to socialization. In D. Goslin (Ed.), *Handbook of socialization theory and research.* Chicago: Rand McNally, 1969.

Korte, C. Group effects on help-giving in an emergency. *Proceedings of the 77th Annual Convention of the American Psychological Association,* 1969, *4,* 383-384.

Latane, B., & Darley, J. M. *The unresponsive bystander: Why doesn't he help?* New York: Appleton-Century-Crofts, 1970.

Lazarus, R. S. *Psychological stress and the coping process.* New York: McGraw-Hill, 1966.

Lefcourt, H. The function of the illusions of freedom and control. *American Psychologist,* 1973, *28,* 117-125.

Lerner, M. J. Observer's evaluation of a victim: Justice, guilt, and veridical perception. *Journal of Personality and Social Psychology,* 1971, *20.*

____, **& Simmons, C. H.** Observer's reactions to the "innocent victim": Compassion or rejection? *Journal of Personality and Social Psychology,* 1966, *4,* 203-210.

Leventhal, H. Emotions: A basic problem for social psychology. In C. Nemeth (Ed.), *Social psychology: Classic and contemporary integrations.* Chicago: Rand McNally, 1974.

Lewin, K. The conceptual representation and measurement of psychological forces. *Contributions to psychological theory,* 1938, *1.*

——. *Resolving social conflicts.* New York: Harper, 1948.

Liebhart, E. Empathy and emergency helping: The effects of personality, self-concern, and acquaintance. *Journal of Experimental Social Psychology,* 1972, *8,* 404-411.

Loban, W. A study of social sensitivity (sympathy) among adolescents. *Journal of Educational Psychology,* 1953, *44,* 102-112.

London, P. The rescuers: Motivational hypothesis about Christians who saved Jews from the Nazis. In J. Macauley & L. Berkowitz (Ed.), *Altruism and helping behavior.* New York: Academic Press, 1970.

Magnusson, D., & Endler, N. S. *Personality at the crossroads: current issues in interactional psychology.* Hillsdale, N.J.: Lawrence Erlbaum Associates, 1977.

Masters, J. C., & Santrock, J. W. Studies in the self-regulation of behavior: Effects of verbal and cognitive self-reinforcement. *Developmental Psychology,* 1976, *12,* 334-348.

McDougall, W. *Social psychology.* London: Methuen, 1908.

Mead, M. *Cooperation and competition among primitive peoples.* New York: McGraw-Hill, 1937.

Midlarsky, E., & Bryan, J. H. Affect expressions and children's imitative altruism. *Journal of Experimental Research in Personality,* 1972, *6,* 195-203.

Midlarz, S. The role of trust in helping behavior. Unpublished masters thesis, University of Massachusetts, Amherst, 1973.

Miller, G. A., Galanter, E., & Pribram, K. H. *Plans and the structure of behavior.* New York: Holt, Rinehart & Winston, 1960.

Mischel, W. Theory and research on the antecedents of self-imposed delay of reward. In B. A. Maher (Ed.), *Progress in experimental personality research,* Vol. III. New York: Academic Press, 1966.

——. *Personality and assessment.* New York: Wiley, 1968.

——. Continuity and change in personality. *American Psychologist,* 1969, *24,* 1012-1018.

——. Towards a cognitive social learning reconceptualization of personality. *Psychological Review,* 1973, *80,* 252-283.

——. *Introduction to personality* (2nd ed.). New York: Holt, Rinehart & Winston, 1976.

——. On the future of personality measurement. *American Psychologist,* 1977, *32,* 246-254.

——, **Ebbesen, E. B., & Zeiss, A. R.** Cognitive and attentional mechanisms in delay of gratification. *Journal of Personality and Social Psychology,* 1972, *21,* 204-218.

____. Selective attention to the self: Situational and dispositional determinants. *Journal of Personality and Social Psychology,* 1973, *27,* 129-142.

____, & **Mischel, H. N.** A cognitive social-learning approach to morality and self-regulation. In T. Lickona (Ed.), *Moral development and behavior.* New York: Holt, Rinehart & Winston, 1976.

Moos, R. H. Systems for the assessment and classification of human environments. In R. H. Moos & P. M. Insel (Eds.), *Issues in social ecology.* Palo Alto, California: National Press Books, 1974.

Murray, H. A. *Explorations in personality.* New York: Oxford University Press, 1938.

Mussen, P. & Eisenberg-Berg, N. *Roots of caring, sharing and helping.* San Francisco, Calif.: W. H. Freeman & Company, 1977.

Olweus, D. Personality and aggression. In J. K. Cole & D. D. Jensen (Eds.), *Nebraska symposium on motivation.* Lincoln, Nebraska: University of Nebraska Press, 1973, 261-321.

____. Personality factors and aggression: With special reference to violence within the peer group. In J. de Wit & W. W. Hartup (Eds.), *Determinants and origins of aggressive behavior.* The Hague: Mouton Press, 1974.

____. "Modern" interactionism in personality psychology and the analysis of variance components approach: A critical examination. In D. Magnusson & N. S. Endler (Eds.), *Personality at the crossroads: Current issues in interactional psychology.* Hillsdale, N.J.: Lawrence Erlbaum Associates, 1977.

Piliavin, I. M., Rodin, J., and Piliavin, J. A. Good samaritanism: An underground phenomenon. *Journal of Personality and Social Psychology,* 1969, *13,* 289-299.

____, **Piliavin, J. A., & Rodin, J.** Costs, diffusion and the stigmatized victim. *Journal of Personality and Social Psychology,* 1975, *3,* 429-438.

Pomazal, R. J., & Jaccard, J. J. An informational approach to altruistic behavior. *Journal of Personality and Social Psychology,* 1976, *33,* 317-327.

Reese, H. Relationships between self-acceptance and sociometric choices. *Journal of Abnormal and Social Psychology,* 1961, *62,* 472-472.

Reykowski, J. Introduction. In J. Reykowski (Ed.), *Studies in the mechanisms of prosocial behavior.* Wydaevnictiva Universytetu, Warszawskiego, 1975.

Rokeach, M. *The nature of human values.* New York: Macmillan Publishing Co., 1973.

Rosenhan, D. L., Moore, B. S., & Underwood, B. The social psychology of moral behavior. In T. Lickona (Ed.), *Moral development and behavior.* New York: Holt, Rinehart & Winston, 1976.

Rotter, J. B. *Social learning and clinical psychology.* Englewood Cliffs, N.J.: Prentice-Hall, 1954.

Rubin, Z., & Peplau, L. A. Belief in a just world and reactions to another's lot: A study of participants in the national draft lottery. *Journal of Social Issues,* 1973, *29,* 73-93.

Schneider, D. J. Implicit personality theory: A review. *Psychological Bulletin,* 1973, *79,* 294-309.

Schwartz, S. H. Moral decision making and behavior. In J. Macauley & L. Berkowitz (Eds.), *Altruism and helping behavior.* New York: Academic Press, 1970.

____. Normative influences on altruism. In L. Berkowitz (Ed.), *Advances in experimental social psychology,* Vol. 10. New York: Academic Press, 1977.

____, & **Clausen, G. T.** Responsibility, norms and helping in an emergency. *Journal of Personality and Social Psychology,* 1970, *16,* 299-310.

____, **Feldman, K. A., Brown, M. E. & Heingarter, A.** Some personality correlates of conduct in two situations of moral conflict. *Journal of Personality,* 1969, *37,* 41-57.

Seligman, M. E. P. *Helplessness: On depression, development, and death.* San Francisco, Calif.: W. H. Freeman and Company, 1975.

Staub, E. A child in distress: The influence of age and number of witnesses on children's attempts to help. *Journal of Personality and Social Psychology,* 1970, *14,* 130-140.

____. A child in distress: The influence of modeling and nurturance on children's attempts to help. *Developmental Psychology,* 1971, *5,* 124-133.(a)

____. Helping a person in distress: The influence on implicit and explicit "rules" of conduct on children and adults. *Journal of Personality and Social Psychology,* 1971, *17,* 137-145. (b)

____. The use of role playing and induction in children's learning of helping and sharing behavior. *Child Development,* 1971, *42,* 805-811. (c)

____. Instigation to goodness: The role of social norms and interpersonal influence. *Journal of Social Issues,* 1972, *28,* 131-151.

____. *Children's sharing behavior: Success and failure, the "norm of deserving", and reciprocity in sharing.* Paper presented at the Symposium: Helping and Sharing: Concepts of Altruism and Cooperation, at the meeting of the Society of Research in Child Development, Philadelphia, Pennsylvania, March, 1973.

____. Helping a distressed person: social, personality, and stimulus determinants. In L. Berkowitz (Ed.) *Advances in Experimental Social Psychology,* Vol. 7, Academic Press, 1974.

____. *The development of prosocial behavior in children.* Morristown, N.J.: General Learning Press, 1975.(a)

____. To rear a prosocial child: reasoning, learning by doing, and learning by teaching others. In D. DePalma & J. Folley (Eds.), *Moral development: Current theory and research*. Hillsdale, N.J.: Lawrence Erlbaum Associates, 1975.(b)

____. *The development of prosocial behavior: Directions for future research and applications to education.* Paper presented at Moral Citizenship/Education Conference, Philadelphia, Pennsylvania, June, 1976.

____. *Positive social behavior and morality: Volume 1, Personal and social influences.* New York: Academic Press, 1978.

____. *Postive social behavior and morality: Volume 2, Socialization and development.* New York: Academic Press, 1979.

____, **& Baer, R. S., Jr.** Stimulus characteristics of a sufferer and difficulty of escape as determinants of helping. *Journal of Personality and Social Psychology,* 1974, *30,* 279-285.

____, **& Feinberg, H.** Positive and negative peer interaction and some of their personality correlates. Unpublished manuscript, University of Massachusetts, Amherst, 1977.

____. Personality, socialization, and the development of prosocial behavior in children. In D. H. Smith & J. Macauley (Eds.), *Informal social participation: The determinants of socio-political action, leisure activity, and altruistic behavior.* San Francisco: Jossey-Bass, Inc., 1980.

____, **& Kellett, D. S.** Increasing pain tolerance by information about aversive stimuli. *Journal of Personality and Social Psychology,* 1972, *21,* 203.

____, **& Sherk, L.** Need approval, children's sharing behavior, and recriprocity in sharing. *Child Development,* 1970, *41,* 243-253.

____, **Tursky, B., & Schwartz, G.** Self-control and predictability: Their effects on reactions to aversive stimulation. *Journal of Personality and Social Psychology,* 1971, *18,* 157-163.

Stotland, E. Exploratory studies of empathy. In L. Berkowitz (Ed.), *Advances in experimental social psychology,* Vol. 4. New York: Academic Press, 1969.

Strong, E. K. *Vocational interests 18 years after college.* Minneapolis: University of Minnesota Press, 1955.

Thibaut, J. W., & Kelley, H. H. *The social psychology of groups.* New York: Wiley, 1959.

Toda, M., Shinotsuka, H., McClintock, C. G., & Stech, F. J. Development of competitive behavior as a function of culture, age, and social comparison. *Journal of Personality and Social Psychology,* 1978, *36,* 825-839.

Turnbull, C. M. *The mountain people.* New York: Simon & Schuster, 1972.

Wilson, J. P. Motivation, modeling and altruism: A person X situation analysis. *Journal of Personality and Social Psychology,* 1976, *34,* 1078-1086.

Wrightsman, L. S. Personality and attitudinal correlates of trusting and trustworthy behaviors in a two-person game. *Journal of Personality and Social Psychology,* 1966, *4,* 328-332.

Yakimovich. D., & Saltz, E. Helping behavior: the cry for help. *Psychonomic Science,* 1971, *23,* 427-428.

Zeigarnik, B. Uber das Behalten von erledigten und unerlediglen Handlungen. *Psychol. forsch.,* 1927, *9,* 1-85.

DONALD MEICHENBAUM

Stability of Personality Change and Psychotherapy

7

Two individuals who are thirty years of age have a chance love affair. They live at opposite ends of the country; but each year, for twenty years, they arrange to meet in the same hotel room in order to spend a weekend together. Once every five years, you have the opportunity to peek in on their relationship. This basic scenario is employed by the Canadian playwright Bernard Slade in his popular play *Same time, next year.* As we watch this couple interacting, one may wonder, How much have they changed? What personality and behavioral consistencies are evident?

Imagine someone peeking in on you over the next twenty years (hopefully not in hotel rooms). What aspects of your behavior will likely remain consistent and what aspects will undergo change? Consider a list of your behaviors, from the more directly observable, such as handwriting, eating habits, or dressing style, to the less obvious, such as beliefs, values, and interpersonal and thinking styles. In twenty years you may be recognizable to your friends from your walk or accent, but where will the differences (if any) emerge? For example, the styles of clothes you wear may differ, but your desire to be fashionable may remain the same. Will you ever overcome your tardiness (or commitment to punctuality)? Moreover, can we predict, with any degree of accuracy, which of you will undergo change?

Obviously, the answer to these questions will be influenced not only by the specific behaviors we choose to observe, but also by the particular circumstances in which we choose to measure them. Some situations and stimuli (such as in hotel rooms) may foster spontaneous responses, while others may impose constraints. Had we observed Slade's peripatetic couple with their respective mates, instead of with each other, our conclusions about consistency and change might have been quite different.

Concern with the issue of change and stability in personality has been a major theme in literature. Whether we consider Eliza Doolittle in Shaw's *Pygmalion* or Crichton in Barre's *The Admirable Crichton,* the attempt to identify the mechanisms of change has represented a persistent conundrum that is the focus of the present chapter.

If fictional characters do not suffice in framing the question, then consider the autobiography of Malcolm X or the notoriety surrounding the Patricia Hearst case.[1] Or consider the nature of personality change that occurs in such diverse contexts as religious conversions, in the onset of neuroses and psychoses, in the course of psychotherapeutic treatment, in experiences induced by various drugs, and so on. In each of these situations there are many ways of describing and conceptualizing the transformations that occur. In each of these situations we can ask how much change has really occurred. The classic illustration that highlights the issue is the case of the adolescent girl who was an honor student, a member of various religious and civic clubs, never a so-called problem, who joined the Charlie Manson gang and who became subservient to the leader's will. Phenotypically, her behavior in the two situations of the home and gang seem diametrically opposed. How can we reconcile these discrepancies? Do they represent discrepancies? Exactly how will you differ in twenty years?

A useful framework to help conceptualize these issues was offered by Richard Coan (1972). Coan describes the nature of change that may occur under five headings; namely, expansion, restriction, replacement, integration, and disintegration. These headings should not be viewed as mutually exclusive categories; instead, they provide a framework for exploring the nature of personality change.

Expansion refers to changes that are described in terms of acquisition, accumulation, enlargement, diversification, or simply increase. The developmental changes that are reflected in the acquisition of new skills, ideas, interests, and attitudes illustrate changes that are subsumed under this category.

Under *restriction* Coan is referring to those behaviors that undergo change due to a reduction in the intensity and pervasiveness of various responses. An example of change falling under the heading of restriction is the development of performance from diffuse action to fine motor skills, or the process of selective inattention. As the developing child becomes socialized he learns to "inhibit" certain responses, and his behavior becomes more refined—a reflection of reduction.

Replacement describes the situation in which a given set of behaviors displaces elements of behavior that were heretofore present. Various interests and roles may be replaced, and new ways of dealing with the same circumstances may emerge.

The remaining types of change, integration and disintegration, involve changes in organization. *Integration* entails an increase in organization and systematization, with the consequences of greater stability of behavior across situations and

[1]Malcolm X changed from a criminal and drug addict into a minister and inspiring black leader; Patricia Hearst, kidnapped and under great duress, joined her kidnappers in criminal acts.

increased consistency between various modes of behavior, such as action, beliefs, and feelings. For example, a new self-concept or goal-objective may result in the reorganization of beliefs and behaviors. In contrast, *disintegration* results in a decrease in organization, consistency, and coordination. In some cases of psychopathology (e.g., psychoses), the process of disintegration leads to unstable and/or unpredictable patterns of behavior.

In reconsidering Slade's couple, we can consider the question of which behaviors have undergone change in terms of (a) expansion–what new skills, interests have these two characters acquired; (b) reduction–what excesses in their behavior have been reduced, what refinements have become evident; (c) replacement–what new patterns of behavior, or thought have displaced comparable patterns that previously existed; and finally (d) in terms of some hierarchical structure, what behaviors have undergone integration and disintegration.

My objective in posing these questions is not to "ruin" a highly entertaining evening at the theatre, but instead to have you wonder about the dimensions that can be employed to understand the transformation of personality and behavior. To answer these questions you will have to see the play.

The focus thus far has been limited to changes that occur in individuals. However, any attempt to explain personality change is short-sighted if it is only focused on the individual. We must recognize that the likelihood that a particular characteristic will appear constant over time is influenced by the environment, which also undergoes change. Our changing individuals are functioning in a changing world. In Slade's play, the couple live through the period of the Vietnam war, Kent State, Watergate, women's liberation, and so on. Any attempt to explain the changes we observe in the couple must take into consideration the specific circumstances. The changes and stabilities of personality are a reflection of *both* the inherent characteristics of the individual (e.g., temperament, intelligence) and the particular environment, and of the interaction of these individual characteristics with a changing environment.

THE ASSESSMENTS OF STABILITY AND CHANGE

The study of personality stability and change is an attempt to assess the degree of correspondence between samples of behavior over time. If we sample your behavior now, can we predict to another sample of your behavior at some future period of time? The more instances of your behavior sampled at the two respective points in time, the higher the likelihood of correspondence. If we only choose one instance of your current behavior and one instance of your behavior twenty years hence, the likelihood of achieving much accuracy is quite low. But insofar as we can obtain multiple samples at the two age periods, we can enhance predictability. Thus, in the same way that we can improve the reliability of a test by increasing the number of items on the test, we can increase predictability of personality by increasing the number of repeated behavioral samples.

Another important point is that the characteristics of items on a test differentially contribute to the reliability and the discriminability of a test. Similarly, the kinds of behavioral samples employed will influence the accuracy of future predictions. On a test, the value of items that are too easy and everyone passes, or that are too difficult and everyone fails, is quite limited. In the same way, in the prediction of your future behavior, the selection of situations that permit little behavioral variation will limit discriminability and predictability. In other words, stability of personality and behavior can be viewed as a problem in reliability.

Besides the number and type of sampled observations, another factor that determines the stability of behavior is the question of the timing of the respective assessments. The closer in time we sample your behaviors, the higher the likelihood of correspondence; and, conversely, the longer the intervening interval of assessments, the lower the likelihood of correspondence.

As we discuss the factors that influence the kind of stability coefficients we will obtain, it is important to keep in mind that personality stability reflects the relative agreement between two measurements of a person's position in relation to a group of individuals. If we assess Slade's couple over time on some set of measures–for example, those indices that we think reflect assertiveness–then whether or not we will obtain evidence for such stability will be influenced, not only by the couple's behavior, but also by the performance of the comparison group. The meaning of the couple's sampled behavior is influenced by both the comparison group's averages and variation on that measure. In order to tell whether our couple is high, medium, or low on some index, we must have some idea of the distribution of that particular behavior in a comparison population. Thus, the degree of correlation of samples of behavior over time will vary somewhat with the range or variation within the comparison group. The more homogeneous the comparison group of other couples, the smaller the degree of correlation between sample one and sample two. In other words, one of the factors that will influence any conclusions we draw about the stability of behavior will be the nature of the comparison groups.

The role of comparison groups in influencing our conclusions about stability of personality can be illustrated by the following example. Once again using Slade's play as a vehicle to highlight the issues in personality change, consider that we have followed this couple for twenty years, from age thirty to age fifty. What would have happened if Slade had also included two additional couples who were respectively twenty and forty at the beginning of the play, and we followed each of these couples for twenty years until they were forty and sixty? Technically, we now have three *cohorts,* or groups, and we are following each of them for twenty years as they go through their respective love affairs (sort of a three-dimensional soap opera).

Consider the following data on each of these couples. The couples were born in 1916, 1926, and 1936, respectively; when we begin our observations on them in 1956, they are twenty, thirty, and forty years old. When we conclude our twenty years of observation in 1976, they are ages forty, fifty, and sixty. Table 7-1 summarizes this data by including age and year of birth for the three couples (*A*, *B*, *C*).

Table 7-1. Model for Studying Personality Change

		Age				
		20	*30*	*40*	*50*	*60*
Cohort	1916			C_1	C_2	C_3
	1926		B_1	B_2	B_3	
	1936	A_1	A_2	A_3		

Each subscript next to the letter indicates a repeated ten-year assessment. Thus A_1, A_2, A_3 means that we have reassessed couple *A* on three occasions, when they were twenty, thirty, and forty. Couple *B* was born in 1926 and measured on three occasions, when they were thirty, forty, and fifty. Finally, couple *C* was born in 1916 and was assessed at ages forty, fifty, and sixty.

Table 7-1 illustrates the variety of different research strategies available to determine the stability of behavior. Our conclusions about stability of personality will in part be influenced by which groups we choose to employ in our comparison. Moreover, if we include groups of couples at each age, then how the particular sampled behavior is distributed in those respective groups of couples will also influence our conclusions about stability.

If we first consider the repeated assessment of any particular couple (e.g., A_1 A_2 A_3, or B_1 B_2 B_3), then we are following a *longitudinal* research strategy. This is a sensitive but expensive method for noting the degree of consistency over time. Hopefully, you can anticipate one of the problems with this approach. It is a problem of generalization. Since each of the respective couples has lived through a different period of time in a changing environment, any conclusions we draw from one population (e.g., couple *B*—whom Slade used) could not be readily extended to the other couples. The validity of each generalization and the comparability of each cohort has to be carefully demonstrated. In a moment, we will note a way in Table 7-1 of providing this check. But let us first examine a second research strategy that has been employed to study the stability of behavior. This strategy, which is known as a *cross-sectional* approach, is much more expedient, for it entails assessing the three couples at one time. Given the high incidence of marital separation and divorce, this efficiency is often quite attractive. For example, the researcher (or playwright) may select three couples (*A*, *B*, *C*) and assess them at one time, noting similarities and differences. In terms of Slade's play, it would have meant three one-act plays of different couples in the same hotel room (Neil Simon's play *Plaza Suite* is an example of this strategy). The cross-sectional strategy is designed to reflect the differences expected as a function of age. By taking a "slice of life" out of the twenty-, thirty-, forty-year-old couples, we should be able to discern any robust changes that may be evident. The problem–or perhaps you can anticipate it–is that the cross-sectional approach confounds cohort and age factors. The differences obtained among A_1, B_1, C_1 may be generational in nature, the result of the different couples growing up in different time periods that inculcated different habits, values, and customs, and not a reflection of an underlying developmental process of variation in age and experience. Surely, being born in 1916 versus 1936 will influence the nature of the couple's interaction. The conclusions drawn about the stability of personality and behavior will be affected by the confound between cohort and age.

Thus we are caught on the horns of a dilemma: on the one hand, the problem of generalization is inherent to the longitudinal approach; on the other hand, the confound of age by cohort limits the usefulness of the cross-sectional approach. Table 7-1 provides some solution by combining some of the elements of the two research approaches in the form of a *mixed-sectional* approach. This approach permits the investigator to obtain repeated assessments on several different cohorts over a shorter period of time than the longitudinal approach, and it also provides an assessment of the degree of comparability between cohorts. Put simply, by comparing B_1 and A_2; C_1, B_2, and A_3; and C_2 and B_3, we can determine if the respective couples, although born at different times, demonstrate comparability, thus permitting generalization across cohorts.

To test your understanding of the mixed-sectional approach, consider yourself a playwright. How many couples will you have? How many repeated assessments? How will you determine comparability across couples (or cohorts)? This is starting to sound like a soap opera such as "As the World Turns." Perhaps it is time to leave the world of theatre and look at some data on personality stability change.

My objective, up to this point, has been to convey the complexity of the issues in discussing personality stability and change. The conclusions drawn about stability will be influenced by a host of factors, including the following:

1. what behaviors we choose to sample, and the size and representativeness of the sample;
2. the setting in which we assess the behaviors;
3. the time interval between samples;
4. the comparison group; and
5. the particular research strategy employed.

See works by Block (1971), Bowers (1973), Fiske (1971), Nesselroade and Baltes (1974), and Schaie (1965) for a more detailed discussion of these factors.

EVIDENCE FOR STABILITY IN PERSONALITY AND BEHAVIOR

The psychological literature offers several examples of stability in behavior over time, and consistency across situations. Two prominent examples will be offered, and then we will note occasions when such stability and consistency may be absent. The first example comes from the literature on child psychopathology, especially the case of predicting adult psychiatric problems from child behavior problems.

To illustrate that such questions are not idle concerns of academicians, consider the following recommendation that was made in 1970 by President Nixon to the Department of Health, Education, and Welfare (HEW). President Nixon asked HEW to study the proposals of Arnold Hutschnecker, a psychiatric consultant to the National Commission on the Causes and Prevention of Violence. Hutschnecker had suggested that psychological tests such as the Rorschach should be administered to all six-year-olds in the United States to determine their potential for future criminal behavior. Such identified children would then be given psychiatric and psychological treatment. Teenage boys later found to persist in incorrigible behavior would be remanded to camps.

A similar proposal was offered by Bellak (1971):

> A psychiatric examination of children at school entrance time should be required, like vaccination. If a child is found to be in a markedly disturbed environment, school attendance should be denied unless parents are willing to have the child or themselves treated or advised. . . . In those who are already dangerously disturbed, enforced treatment might prevent many future Oswalds (whose mother was able to remove him from treatment) (p. 120).

My intent in citing Hutschnecker and Bellak is not to argue about the pros and cons (and dangers) of such assessments, but rather to highlight the critical role that the issue of personality and behavior stability and change will play in our future lives. Is aggressiveness in childhood predictive of later adult aggressiveness and psychiatric problems? How much stability has been found? The answers to these questions will have far-reaching implications for social policy and civil liberties. As Monahan and Cummings (1975) ask, "How many normal children would we label and stigmatize as 'dangerously disturbed' in order to isolate a future assassin?" (p. 161).

Some evidence concerning the consistency of aggressive behavior comes from a formidable study by Lee Robins. In her 1966 book, *Deviant Children Grown Up,* Robins reports on a 30-year follow-up study into adulthood of children who had been seen earlier in a St. Louis child-guidance clinic. These clinic children (referred primarily for antisocial behavior) were matched with a control group who had exhibited no psychiatric childhood disturbance. When interviewed

30 years later, Robins reports that the adult adaptation of these antisocial children is one of marked incompetence. Robins writes:

> We had expected that children referred for antisocial behavior would provide a high rate of antisocial adults, but we had not anticipated finding differences invading so many areas of their lives. Not only were antisocial children more often arrested and imprisoned as adults, as expected, but they were more mobile geographically, had more marital difficulties, poorer occupational and economic histories, impoverished social and organizational relationships, poor Armed Service records, excessive use of alcohol and, to some extent, even poorer physical health. The control subjects consistently had the most favorable outcomes, and those referred for reasons other than antisocial behavior tended to fall between the two (p. 68).

Before we conclude from Robins's data that we should endorse Hutschnecker's and Bellak's wholesale testing approach, it is worth noting that a host of childhood problems–including temper tantrums, learning problems, sleep and eating disturbance, special difficulties, and all problems other than antisocial behavior–did not seem to predict adult maladjustment. Only antisocial behavior in childhood predicted adult adjustment problems. Indeed, the more severe the child's antisocial behavior, whether measured by number of symptoms, by number of episodes, or by arrestibility of the behavior, the more disturbed was the adult adjustment.

The Robins data is provocative and bears careful replication and consideration, because the prediction and malleability of such antisocial behavioral patterns is a matter of grave concern. From the viewpoint of consistency of behavior over time, the Robins data, which employed a longitudinal approach, illustrates stability in one behavioral sphere (antisocial behavior), but not in others (childhood neurotic-like problems).

In terms of child-adult relationships, we could consider innumerable examples coming from the work on consistency of temperament differences (e.g., Chess, Thomas & Birch, 1968), intelligence (Honzik, MacFarlane, & Allen, 1948), and cognitive style (e.g., Witkin, Goodenough, & Karp, 1967).

Perhaps one further example from the child psychopathology literature will serve to illustrate the stable relationship between childhood and adult patterns of adjustment. In this instance we can consider the long-term effects of a childhood pattern of peer unpopularity. Unpopular children are more likely to be disproportionately represented later in life in a community-wide psychiatric register (Cowen, Pederson, Babigan, Izzo, & Trost, 1973); they are also more likely to receive bad-conduct discharges from the armed forces (Roff, 1961). Roff, Sells and Golden (1972) recently studied a sample of 40,000 children in 21 cities. Except for the lowest socioeconomic class, the relationship was highly positive between percentage delinquent and low peer-acceptance scores taken four years earlier. Thus the level of social competence evident in children seems to have long-term predictive value for adult psychopathology. These data provide further evidence for stability in personality and behavior over time.

At this point we might ask what mediates such behavioral consistency and stability. Some suggestions come from studies by Rausch, Dittman, and Taylor (1959) and Gil (1970).

Rausch and his colleagues observed the behavior of six institutionalized hyperaggressive boys in six settings. The children were observed upon awakening, at breakfast, at structured game activities, at unstructured social situations, meal time, and at informal snack time prior to going to bed. The observers dictated their observations into a tape recorder, and these were later coded into 16 categories of interpersonal behaviors, noting the patterns of behaviors separately for behavior toward adults and that toward other boys in the institution.

The results indicated that disturbed, hyperaggressive boys showed a steady and rather precipitous decline in friendly acts toward peers, as compared to normal children (Rausch 1965). The data corroborate the clinical observation that aggressive children have an "aptitude . . . for moving rapidly from an atmosphere of friendliness to one of wildly chaotic aggression" (Rausch, 1965, p. 497). Normal children, by contrast, seem to be better able to sense the incipient deterioration of a friendly sequence, and behave in ways that save the situation from running a downhill course. Thus, aggressive children can be characterized by the fact that they foster aggression-engendering situations to which they in turn respond aggressively.

Patterson and Reid (1970) have provided a similar analysis of aggressive children's maladaptive behavior. It appears that such children have the aptitude to coerce people in the environment to respond, and the mode of response by peers and adults is reciprocal. If the child yells, it is likely the adult will yell. If the child hits, the parent is likely to respond in a similar fashion, and vice versa. An observation of the dyadic relationships of such aggressive children with both peers and adults indicates the reciprocal nature of their interactions. In this way, the children are active in creating environments that help to maintain the consistency of their behavior across situations and its stability over time.

The interactional or transactional nature of children's behavior on significant others in their environment was also noted by Gil (1970). This investigator cited a clinical report on battered children that indicated that at least some such children are characterized by constant fussing and by a particularly grating cry. Such a pattern of behavior may thus provoke a "normal" parent to abuse his or her child. The possibility that some battered children may provoke parental attacks is supported by the observations that (1) frequently only one child in a family is abused; and (2) some of these battered children, as they move from one foster home to another, are subjected to repeated abuse, even though the foster parents had a "clean" record up to the time they received the child in question. Thus, in some cases of child abuse "deviance in the child was at least as substantial a factor in explaining the incidents as was deviance in the parent" (Bell, 1974, p. 6).

The studies on hyperaggressive children and battered children indicate that, through temperament and behaviors, the child shaped and defined situations, as well as being shaped and defined by them. Children not only respond to environments, but also create the environments to which they in turn respond.

An illustration of the way in which an adult individual engenders a stability-maintaining response from the environment is provided by a clinical example. The client's complaint was seemingly rather straightforward. She complained that every male she met would only respond to her as a "sex-object, trying to make me at every turn." The way in which she fostered such reactions, in terms of her appearance, walk, speech patterns, and so on, became part of the focus of therapy. She elicited reactions that confirmed her beliefs about males. The dyadic transactional nature of her interactions seemed evident to all but herself. Instead, she felt like the "helpless" victim of male onslaughts. The client was active in maintaining consistency of behavior and personality.

Bowers (1975) has noted that much of the evidence for the transactional nature and consistency of behavior has been offered in clinical examinations. Indeed, each of the examples for behavioral stability offered thus far was derived from clinical studies. To appreciate this observation, let us briefly note that the way that experimentalists have studied personality has been to present a standard situation to all persons in a treatment group and then to note the subjects' reactions. Such a commitment to standardization and the notion of an independent-variable-dependent-variable model has made it almost impossible to see, let alone investigate, those kinds of situations that a person ordinarily generates for himself (Bowers, 1976; Wachtel, 1973). Instead of viewing the relationship between two individuals (whether experimenter-subject, therapist-client, or our couples) as instances of an independent-dependent variable relationship, an alternative way to consider such a relationship is to view it as a dyadic relationship of two ongoing streams of behavior. The observer can set up a coding system to classify the behaviors of the respective participants, and this will yield a matrix of interactions. For example, in Slade's play we can code the interactional sequence between the participants and then note how these interactions change with time. Within such a model, one speaks of antecedent-consequent relationship rather than of independent and dependent variables per se.

In sum, the developmental psychopathology studies indicate the stability of personality and behavior (see Robins, 1972, for more details). Before examining the question of stability of personality in adults, a caveat concerning the child psychopathology data is in order. The warning is that one must proceed with caution in making predictions and social-policy decisions on the basis of childhood variables. Perhaps this is most clearly indicated by MacFarlane (1964), in summarizing her longitudinal study:

> Many of the most outstandingly mature adults in our entire group, many who are well integrated, highly competent, and/or creative, who are clear about their values, who are understanding and accepting of self and others,

> are recruited from those who were confronted with very difficult situations and whose characteristic responses during childhood and adolescence seemed to us to compound their problems. Among these were chronic rebels who were expelled from school, bright academic failures, one socially inept girl with blood pressure 4+ sigmas above the mean (now one sigma below), hostile dependents, unhappy, withdrawn schizoids. They include one full-blown adolescent schizophrenic, who without benefit of psychotherapy, now functions perceptively, creatively, and competently as a wife, mother, home builder, gardener, and community participant (p. 123).

Hutschnecker and Bellak take note!

The data thus far presented concerning stability of personality and behavioral patterns has focused on a small, selected percentage of the population. It may be easier to predict behavior for such an extreme group than for the whole population; although the MacFarlane quote indicated limitations in predictive accuracy for even such a selected population. What is the evidence for stability of personality when considering the entire population? A number of longitudinal studies of personality have attempted to answer this question, but each of the studies suffers from methodological limitations (see Block, 1971, for a review). However, one study by Block (1971) has overcome most of these problems, and provides clear evidence for the stability of personality over time. Block's subjects were 150 individuals who had participated in the Oakland growth and Berkeley guidance studies. The subjects were assessed at three points in their lives, namely, junior high school, senior high school, and in their middle thirties. A vast array of diverse data was available for the subjects at each of these time periods, including interview data, performance on standardized tests, news clippings, and more. Different types of data were available for each age period. In order to impose some consistency to the analysis, Block used trained judges to independently assess the subjects at each of the three data points. One group of raters would rate all subjects at the junior-high-school level on a *Q*-sort (i.e., a set of descriptive statements that the rater is asked to employ to describe each subject). A different set of raters would rate the same subjects, using the same *Q*-sort rating procedure, for senior-high-school data; and still a third set of raters would score all subjects at the adult level, also using the same *Q*-sort items. For example, the *Q*-sort items included such items as (a) behaves in a dependable and responsible way; (b) is a talkative individual; and (c) has a rapid personal tempo; behaves and acts quickly. In this way the clinical rater must determine the appropriateness of a broad range of behavioral patterns for a particular individual. The degree of correspondence of the *Q*-sort data across time periods reflects the degree of personality stability. Put another way, imagine yourself attending your junior-high-school reunion twenty years after graduation. Could you guess what your classmates are like? Why else do we attend such reunions? Perhaps we are all personologists at heart! As Block (1971) stated in describing such a hypothetical reunion:

> In the passage of almost a generation, the capriciousness of adolescence has been left and lives have taken their essential form and direction. There are the usual indicators of the passage and action of time—the formerly lissome and lithe may now be pudgy and stiff; the great adolescent dreams of glamour and omnipotence largely have been deflated by reality; for most, money, comfort, and status have become the order of the day. But such observations taken alone are too simple, too gross, and too established to be sufficiently true (p. 1).

As indicated, Block's data provided evidence for personality consistency over time. First the inter-judge agreement for pairs of raters was .75—a respectable level of reliability for such data. In terms of stability over time, the correlation of *Q*-sort composites for junior high school and senior high school was .75; the average correlation between senior high school and adult years (close to twenty years) was .55. These correlations indicate an impressive degree of stability, given the time span and the varying sources of data. Perhaps most interestingly, the average correlations of .75 and .55 disguise the fact that some subjects were much more consistent over time, while some more inconsistent. Indeed, the degree of consistency over time and situations becomes an interesting individual-difference dimension to examine in its own light.

MODELS TO EXPLAIN CONSISTENCY

In understanding the apparent consistency and stability of behavior across situations and over time, a number of different psychological models have been employed. Endler and Magnusson (1976) described four major models to explain the nature of personality stability and change: trait psychology, psychodynamics, situationism, and interactionism.

The *trait* model assumes that some hypothetical processes are the prime determinants of behavior, and these processes serve as a predispositional basis underlying behavioral constancies. The model assumes that there are stable individual differences for each of a number of trait dimensions (e.g., achievement, dependency, honesty). A review of the extensive criticisms of the trait approach for studying personality is beyond the scope of the present chapter. For such discussions, see Endler (1976), Mischel (1968), and Peterson (1968). Instead, the intent is briefly to describe the alternative models used to explain personality stability.

A second model employed to explain personality follows a *psychodynamic* conceptualization. This model postulates a basic personality core (e.g., id, ego, superego), and this core serves as a predispositional basis for behavior in differing situations. Quite often, a distinction is drawn between phenotypic and genotypic aspects of behavior. This model assumes a set of genotypic personality dispositions that endure, although their overt response forms may change. Both the trait model and the psychodynamic models subscribe to such a dispositionally based approach. The example given earlier about the honors student who joined the Manson gang illustrates such a genotypic-phenotypic model. Although the behavioral manifestation changed across settings, the psychodynamic model would argue that a common core conflict accounts for both sets of behavior. The outward form of behavior (phenotype) is guided by an inner core problem (genotype). The psychodynamic approach, as with the trait approach, has been criticized for assuming that seemingly diverse behaviors constitute symptoms of an "underlying" generalized core problem, rather than viewing those diverse behaviors as relatively discrete problems, often under the control of different causes and maintenance conditions.

Situationism, contrary to the trait and psychodynamic models, stresses the importance of situational factors as important determinants of behavior. The stimuli in the environment, the antecedents and consequents of the behavior, are seen as causal agents in explaining consistency of behavior across situations and over time. In fact, one could attempt to characterize the personality of situations in the same way that attempts have been made to characterize the personality of individuals.

Situationism argues that behavior is less stable than we ordinarily think it is. Rather, it is much more under the influence of varying situational variables. We tend, however, to perceive others and ourselves as being quite consistent (see Staub's Chapter 6 in this volume).

Investigators who highlight the role of situational variables usually point to an upper limit to the accuracy of prediction that can be obtained when using individual-difference variables. For example, Arthur (1971) reviewed personnel-prediction studies in military organizations and concluded that there is currently a sort of "sound barrier" effect since "no matter how much information about the individual one adds to the predictive equation, one cannot bring the correlation coefficient between individual characteristics and prediction criteria much above about .40" (p. 544). Similar conclusions have been derived in other areas, such as in the prediction of violent behavior and the prediction of runaway behavior from correctional institutions. (Monahan & Cummings, 1976; Megargee, 1970). Moos (1973, 1976) has summarized a number of instances in which the determining factor in affecting an individual's behavior and personality is the nature of the environment. The settings in which people function critically affect their behavior. Moos illustrates the effect of human environments on personality development with several literary examples. For example, Jonathon Kozol, in his book *Death at an Early Age,* describes the destructive impact on black children of the social and physical environments in the Boston public schools. Similarly, Thomas Mann, in *The Magic Mountain,* demonstrates how the social environment of a tuberculosis sanatorium affects a patient. As a result of these observations, Moos has developed systematic methods for measuring human environments. Thus, in any explanation of personality stability and change, predictive equations will include both information about the individual and about the nature of the human environment.

The *interactionism* model of personality emphasizes the role of person by situation interactions in personality, or the fit between the personality of the situation and the personality of the individual. As Endler (1976) stated, "behavior is a function of an inextricable, indispensable and continuous multidirectional interaction between persons and the situations they encounter" (p. 175). The examples offered earlier of the research by Rausch and Gil illustrate such an interactionist model of personality (this model is extensively discussed in Staub's Chapter 6 in this volume).

PROCESSES OF PERSONALITY CHANGE

The brief description of the four models of personality serves as a prelude for a discussion of how personality changes. The answer to two basic questions, "What entity or process is changing? and What makes it change?" will be influenced by which personality model is employed. Each model will determine the behaviors selected for observation, and each will offer different explanations. Getting back to Slade's couple, any attempt at explaining the personality and behavior changes that are evident will be influenced by the orientation of the particular personologist. How you observe and describe the behavioral changes and constancies in your fellow classmates at that 20-year junior-high-school reunion will be influenced by the implicit theory of personality you hold.

For purposes of illustration, we will examine the psychological mechanisms involved in explaining personality change that derive from an interactional model of personality. Let us look at the hypothetical case of a scientist who studies personality change (e.g., see Kelley, 1955). The scientist holds a set of beliefs and values, some of which are implicit (some people would consider them "unconscious"), while other beliefs are quite explicit. The beliefs about the phenomena under investigation give rise to conscious thoughts of which the scientist is aware. Let us call these conscious thoughts "*internal dialogue*," for it represents one of four basic summary constructs that can be employed to describe the change process. The internal dialogue in the form of hypotheses and hunches guides and influences what the scientist will attend to and how he or she will appraise phenomena. Following from such an internal dialogue, the scientist behaves (i.e., *behavioral acts*) by performing experiments that yield data. The data will be consistent or anomalous with the scientist's belief system. What the scientist says to himself or herself about the behavioral outcomes will determine whether the results of the experiment will be considered as evidence or merely discarded, and how he or she proceeds from there.

Thus, involved in the scientist's behavior are his or her (1) beliefs, or what I would more comprehensively term *cognitive structures*, (2) internal dialogue,

(3) overt experimental behaviors, and (4) evaluations of the consequences of his or her behavior. In the same way that these four constructs can be used to explain the behavior of the scientist, they can also be employed to explain personality and behavior change. Change can result from alterations in any one of the four. Note that change in any of the variables (viz., cognitive structures, internal dialogue, behavioral acts, and evaluation of behavioral consequences) will have reverberating effects on the others, since they are interdependent—a point to be elaborated below.

This process analysis of how the scientist operates is hypothetical in nature. As we learn more about how scientists actually function (e.g., see Brush, 1974; Hebb, 1975; Mahoney, 1976; Polanyi, 1958) we come to recognize the role of passion, emotion, and commitment in the scientific process. Scientists often create, distort, and selectively attend to the results of their experiments, in order not to alter their beliefs.

How can the four summary constructs used to describe our "hypothetical" scientist be employed to explain changes in Slade's couple? Let us briefly examine each of them and note how alteration of each may contribute to change.

The construct of "cognitive structures" is difficult to grasp and define. The term *cognitive structures* was made familiar by Edwin Tolman (1932) and Kurt Lewin (1935). Since that time the concept seems to have acted as a Rorschach inkblot card or "Linus' blanket" for cognitively oriented psychologists—one can see anything one wants in it, and it gives one a sense of security. Under the banner of "cognitive structures" fall such concepts as Miller, Galanter, and Pribram's (1960) *images and plans*, Piaget's (1954) *schema*, Sarbin's *roles* (Sarbin & Coe, 1972) and Hilgard's (1976) *control systems.*

By "cognitive structure" psychologists are referring to the organizing aspect of thinking that seems to monitor and direct the strategy, route, and choice of thoughts. It is an "executive processor" that holds the "blueprints" of thinking and that determines when to interrupt, change, or continue thought. Neisser (1962), following Piaget's notion of assimilation and accommodation, described the structural changes that may come about: *absorption*, in which new structures are developed that effectively contain old structures; *displacement*, in which the old and new structures continue to exist side by side; and *integration*, in which new structures at a more comprehensive level still contain parts of the old structures. Which process (i.e., absorption, displacement, or integration) will take place will depend upon the history and evaluation of the old structure and the development and value of the new structure.

Put simply, in Slade's play, the couple's cognitive structures undergo change. Their beliefs, values, and attitudes change, become restructured and reorganized, in part as a reaction to changes in environmental circumstances. Such events as the death of the male character's son in Vietnam, or the introduction of the women's-liberation movement have substantial impact on the couple's cognitive structures, which in turn affect their internal dialogue and overt behavior.

Note that there are a number of ways available to alter cognitive structures. One could directly challenge an individual's beliefs by inducing him or her to adopt different beliefs or to restructure old beliefs. *Or* one could provide the individual with cognitive and behavioral skills so that he or she behaves in a way that is incompatible with his or her prior beliefs. By providing the individual with anomalous data, this may also contribute to a change in cognitive structures. *Or* one could manipulate environmental consequences in such a way as to provide evidence that encourages the alteration of cognitive structures. In explaining the change process, personologists have usually differentially focused on only one of the processes that contribute to change. For example, in their work on belief systems and attitudes, some social psychologists have focused on the alteration of cognitive structures. A whole field has evolved, designed to explicate the parameters involved in explaining these changes. They have identified parameters that deal with the source of the message, the content of the message, and the characteristics of the recipient. In the case of the hypothetical scientist, the nature of the experiments (who conducted them, where, when, and under what circumstances, as well as the actual results) will influence the likelihood that the scientists's beliefs will be altered. Similar factors are involved in the alteration of the belief systems of Slade's couple.

A second summary construct that helps to explain the change process is *internal dialogue*[2]. This construct refers to conscious thoughts that one is aware of–or, put colloquially, what you tell yourself. Part of the task of psychology is to try to make sense of (i.e., develop a conceptualization system for) "what goes on in one's head." Some theorists have suggested that the most important aspect of one's internal dialogue, in terms of explaining and predicting behavior, is one's own expectations. Others argue that the best way to conceptualize internal dialogue is in terms of how one "appraises" events, while still others have focused on the self-monitoring and self-evaluation aspects of one's internal dialogue. Each group of personologists has identified some aspect of the internal dialogue and has sought to explain and predict behavior in terms of a particular concept. Indeed, some theorists have argued that what one says to oneself is unimportant in explaining behavior (Unfortunately, for some people this seems true!). Instead, they argue, one can best explain behavior change on the basis of the nature of the environmental events that precede and follow behavior. These theorists, who employ a Skinnerian, or operant, framework, go so far as to eschew the concept of personality as well as such mediational concepts as "cognitive structures" in explaining behavior change.

But getting back to Slade's couple, we can recognize many changes in their "internal dialogue." How they appraise events and each other, the expectations they hold, the style and content of their inner speech and images, all seem to

[2] Beck (1976) has noted that for a good part of their working life, people monitor their thoughts, wishes, feelings, and actions. Sometimes there is an internal debate as the individual weighs alternatives and courses of action and makes decisions. Plato referred to this phenomenon as an "internal dialogue."

undergo change. One of the major reasons for these changes is the acquisition of new behavioral skills. The female protagonist goes to college while the male protagonist, who was initially the hard-driving businessman, takes up yoga and joins Esalen. Personality change follows from the acquisition of new skills or the disinhibition of behavioral acts that are already in the repertoire. An example of the disinhibiting process is the situation in which the female character becomes more interpersonally assertive. There is some suggestion that the interpersonal skills required to be assertive were already in her repertoire, and that it was the content of her internal dialogue (i.e., the expectation that negative consequences would follow any assertive act) that inhibited her behavior. As a result of her experiences in college, the content of her internal dialogue, as well as her cognitive structures, undergo change. This results in changes in how she evaluates the consequences of her behavioral acts.

In summary, it is being suggested that the characters in Slade's play operate in a similar fashion as the scientist, with their own implicit personality theories, beliefs, (cognitive structures), their own hypotheses and expectations (internal dialogue). They perform their own personal experiments in terms of their "behavioral acts." These personal experiments elicit consequences from significant others in the environment. How these consequences are appraised will determine the nature and persistence of the change that will occur. Thus, when we consider the question of personality change, there are different levels of behavior that are involved in the process. Each personality theorist will substitute his or her own operating concepts for each of the four processes–of cognitive structures, internal dialogue, behavioral acts, and evaluation of outcomes. As you appraise each theory of personality change it will be useful to note how the theorist deals with each process. Each theorist will provide an explanation of the mechanisms involved in accounting for the kind of personality changes that are exemplified in Slade's couple. You will just have to see the play, and judge for yourself which explanation of change is most adequate.

PERSONALITY CHANGE THROUGH PSYCHOTHERAPY

Thus far, the discussion of the nature of change has been quite general. Perhaps some examples taken from the field of psychotherapy will further illustrate the way in which the four processes (cognitive structures, internal dialogue, behavioral acts, and evaluation of behavioral consequences) interact in contributing to change. But before providing specific examples, let us first consider the broader issue of the nature of psycotherapy.

The nature, and the related issue of the effectiveness, of psychotherapy represent immense topics upon which tomes of material have been written. The present objective is to provide an introductory overview before we consider a specific example of the mechanisms of change in operation.

A good number of authors have attempted to specify the prototypic characteristics of psychotherapy. That this attempt has led on occasion to confusion is illustrated by Raimy, who in 1950 defined psychotherapy as "an unidentified technique applied to unspecified problems with unpredictable outcomes. For this technique we recommend rigorous training." In the last quarter of a century the field of psychotherapy has made significant strides, so we can now begin to answer the more specific questions, "What treatment, by whom, is most effective for this individual with that specific problem, under which set of circumstances?" Let us briefly examine what has transpired during the last 25 years in order to understand the nature of change in the field of psychotherapy.

In 1952 Hans Eysenck wrote an epic paper that called into question the efficacy of psychotherapy. His paper initiated a debate that is still with us. This debate has not infrequently been marked by extremist views and professional rancor. What Eysenck asked in his article was whether psychotherapy is superior to no therapy, and secondly, whether some forms of therapy are superior to others. The field is full of various adversaries claiming the merits of their particular therapy approach, be it psychoanalysis, behavior therapy, or some other variant. Peruse the shelves of your local bookstore to appreciate the range of available claims; "how-to" books abound, often with little accompanying supportive data.

Two recent literature reviews by Luborsky, Singer, and Luborsky (1975) and Smith and Glass (1977), as well as a recent major empirical study by Sloane, Staples, Cristol, Yorkston, and Whipple (1975) have rekindled interest in the entire question of treatment efficacy. These three groups of investigators arrived at similar conclusions in their evaluations of comparative treatment outcome research: therapy is more effective than no treatment, and different treatment approaches are equally effective.

A searching evaluation of these conclusions has been offered by Kazdin and Wilson (1978). They critically question the strategy of comparing various treatment approaches in a type of box-score analysis whereby different therapy techniques are collapsed and compared with supposedly other different treatment procedures. Such an approach is subject to what Kiesler (1966) calls "unformity myths." One of these myths is the assumption that psychotherapy refers to a uniform homogeneous treatment. Thus when psychotherapy is compared to behavior therapy, one must quickly recognize that there are many different forms of psychotherapy and that the term *behavior therapy* represents a summary rubric subsuming several different techniques. Thus, claims to the contrary that some global procedure such as behavior therapy is effective or ineffective relative to some other therapy must be qualified. For example, the behavioral-therapy procedures differ in their respective efficacy with performance-based methods, such as participant modeling being superior to behavioral techniques that rely upon imaginal (e.g., systematic desensitization) or vicarious (e.g., symbolic modeling) sources of behavior change.

Kiesler also indicates that the "uniformity myth" should not be imposed on other aspects of therapy, such as the treatment routines, or the various indices of outcome effectiveness. Moreover, it is necessary to distinguish between what therapists actually do and how they describe what they do, or the psychological litany or theorizing that accompanies each therapeutic approach.

What has happened in the last 25 years is that the field of psychotherapy has become much more sophisticated and critical in specifying the treatment goals and presenting problems in specific measurable terms. This objectification has begun to provide some initial data that specific treatment techniques are indeed indicated for certain problems and on which techniques are effective for what problems (see Kazdin & Wilson, 1978 for a list of these pairings).

While some investigators have been mainly preoccupied with the issue of relative efficacy, other investigators have speculated about the mechanisms that underlie change, not only in psychotherapy, but in any situation in which change may occur—such as in primitive medicine, religious healing, or thought reform.

The most articulate of this group is Jerome Frank (1974), who in his fine book *Persuasion and Healing* explored the possible common factors that underlie change in these many areas. He indicates the following common features: (1) First, the authority attempting to induce change is given a certain degree of authority which helps him (usually male, but not always) inspire "faith" in the client. The healer, whether it be a psychotherapist, a shaman, or a religious healer, is viewed as a potent figure in his own right, capable of producing important influences and changes. This authority is created through elaborate symbolic paraphernalia, special systems of training, social expectations, the use of special treatment settings, payment of fees, and the like. (2) A second major element is the practitioner's wish to help the person who has sought him out. The treatment process is not routine or perfunctory, but implies a definite personal commitment to aide the client. Frank indicates that even in such change regimens as Chinese thought reform, these processes operate. (3) The practitioner acts as a mediator between the suffering individual and the larger society. In part, the healer protects the client from the effects of society by creating a situation in which greater freedom without punishment is possible. The therapist, in some sense, becomes society's representative and attempts to lead the client in emotional and behavioral difficulty back to a mode of expected behavior. The change agent (healer) is charged by society to normalize behavior of the deviant. (4) Usually, there is a confession by the client of past errors, and the healer usually accepts whatever the person has done in the past. (5) The healer offers some theoretical system that helps explain why the patient is suffering. Frank indicates that the validity of the particular theoretical system is less important than its impressiveness, consistency, and ability to engender belief on the part of both the client and healer. The theory usually represents the articles of faith that help to make sense of the client's presenting problems and the processes of change.

(6) Finally, a central feature is the active involvement of both the modifier and the subject in the change process over a number of sessions.

Compare these features that have been proposed by Frank as characterizing the conditions that contribute to change with the following list of therapist behaviors stated as ingredients of psychotherapy, offered by Gottman and Markman (1978):

1. The therapist conveys his expectation that change is possible and likely to occur.
2. The therapist conveys a faith that every problem has a solution.
3. The therapist helps the client elaborate and specify the problems presented.
4. The therapist provides a new language system for organizing behavior and events. This may include a *relabeling* of what is "pathological," what is "healthy," (problems and goals), and perhaps etiology.
5. The therapist gives client normative data for client's experiences in therapy (e.g., "It is common to feel panicky at this point. We *expect* people to feel that way.").
6. The therapist provides ground rules (e.g., about fees, coming to sessions, number of sessions, calling if unable to come, homework, practice).
7. The therapist describes goals and methods for attaining goals.
8. The therapist structures situations that require approach instead of avoidance; therapist may also restructure situations so that it is more likely that approach behaviors will be rewarded naturally.
9. The therapist conveys the belief that positive consequences follow approach and negative consequences follow avoidance.
10. The therapist conveys an "experimental" norm:
    a. First *try* it
    b. *Then* evaluate it
    c. Then modify it
    d. Then try it again.
11. The therapist conveys the message that he cares about the client (he is listening, empathetic, supportive).
12. The therapist teaches alternative ways of behaving and thinking with consideration of step size (small enough to maximize likelihood of success), pacing (mostly at client's own pace), and feedback (specific).
13. The therapist restructures norms of social interaction in behavior setting of importance (e.g., changes consequences of specific behavior exchanges, and changes eliciting stimuli).
14. The therapist reinforces client for trying new behaviors, for sticking to programmed interventions, and for personalizing change within client's own style.
15. The therapist fades self out and insures that the client attributes change to self, not to therapist, and provides for transfer of training.

The Gottman and Markman list conveys the variety of specific behaviors that often characterize the therapeutic encounter. Let us take an example of one therapy procedure and note how these procedures are employed to bring about change.

A SAMPLER: THE TREATMENT OF ANGER

Many different examples could be offered, but since the illustrations offered earlier in the personality stability section focused on anger and aggression, the therapy example will similarly deal with the treatment of aggression. The study to be described was conducted by Novaco (1974). He treated 34 volunteer clients (18 male, 16 female), ranging in age from 17 to 42. Prior to treatment, the clients' problems in controlling anger were quite intense, as illustrated by the fact that several clients had physically assaulted others, including their marital partners and children; one had had a fist fight in the public library, while several others had destroyed property and possessions.

Treatment began with the clients being brought together in small groups to discuss the duration and extent of their anger problems. The therapist conducted a situational analysis in order to have the clients ascertain the particular aspects of provocations that triggered anger, and more specifically, to explore the thoughts and feelings that clients emitted in provocation encounters. This self-exploration was facilitated by having clients vicariously relive recent anger experiences by closing their eyes and "running a movie" of the provocations, reporting the sequence of their feelings and thoughts.

During this initial phase the focus of treatment was on a cognitive reappraisal of the clients' angry feelings and aggressive behaviors. The clients were taught to differentiate various types of provocations such as annoyances, frustrations, ego-threats, assaults, and inequities. For example, in the case of a policeman who had a problem in controlling anger, a variety of provocations were noted. These included (1) annoyances, such as a drunk getting sick in the back seat of the cruiser; (2) frustrations, such as citizens refusing to give assistance; (3) ego-threats, such as the policeman walking into a bar when someone says, "Here comes super-pig"; (4) assaults, such as a suspect spitting at the policeman; and (5) inequities, such as the policeman's getting a suspension for an unavoidable occurrence.

The discussion of the nature of provocations naturally led to a discussion of additional factors that contributed to anger and aggression. Using our policeman as an illustration, these factors included the role of *setting events*—prior circumstances that influenced how the policeman would behave, such as statements by the watch commander or trouble with the police car. Such events elicited arousal that adversely influenced thinking processes. Another contributing factor could be labeled *cognitive determinants*—recollections, expectancies that preceded and accompanied the response to provocations, such as the officer's ruminations about criticism from his supervisor or attitudes towards particular groups. Situational cues, or aspects of the behavior setting, also acted as an elicitor of the policeman's anger, such as an individual's long hair.

Thus, as a result of the initial educational phase of training, Novaco's clients no longer conceptualized aggression as a unitary event, but rather came to view their reactions as complex and composed of a sequence of cognitive, behavioral, and physiological components that were differentially elicited by distinguishable provocations. Indeed, Novaco provided a reconceptualization of anger and aggression that noted that the feeling of anger the clients experienced was influenced by the clients' thoughts, that is, by the self-statements and images they produced. As Novaco told his clients, "A basic premise is that anger is fomented, maintained, and influenced by the self-statements and images that are made in provocation situations" (p. 33). In short, what the client perceived as a provocation, what he said to himself and imagined when provoked, and the content of his self-statements, influenced the anger reactions. For example, prior to treatment, when provoked, the client's thoughts tended to include beliefs about the necessity for success, intolerance of mistakes, unreasonable expectation of others, necessity for retaliation, perceived threat to self-worth, and need to be in control. Thus, provocation-related self-statements–such as "Who the hell does he think he is; he can't do that to me." "He wants to play it that way; I'll show him." "He thinks I'm a pushover; I'll get even"–in combination with emotional arousal, defined the anger reaction.

Following the initial educational phase of therapy that focused on cognitive reappraisal, the next step in Novaco's treatment involved the provision of a set of methods for the self-regulation of anger. More specifically, the clients had been given the rationale that one's anger reactions consisted of two components, namely, emotional arousal and cognitive activity (i.e., client's appraisals, attributions, self-statements, and images). During the second skills-acquisition and rehearsal phase of treatment, the clients would learn to control each of the components. The clients were taught to use relaxation to enable them to reduce arousal, and they were taught cognitive controls in order to control their attentional processes and thoughts, images, and feelings. The cognitive training would make clients aware of the negative anger–instigating self-statements and images they emitted when provoked, and would replace this with coping stratagems.

In order to achieve the cognitive self-control skills, the clients were asked to conduct homework assignments of (1) listening to their anger-related self-statements; (2) performing situational analyses of anger-provoking situations, and (3) ordering these situations into an hierarchal fashion on index cards. These homework assignments revealed that the anger situation could be viewed as consisting of a sequence of stages: (1) when possible, preparing for the provocation, (2) the impact and confrontation, (3) coping with arousal, and (4) a reflective period, allowing self-reward for dealing with the conflict. Thus, the anger and subsequent aggression was not seen as a single spontaneous event; but instead, the homework assignments were designed to have the clients view their aggression as going through a sequence, a sequence that could be interrupted and redirected into a more socially acceptable form of expression. In order to aid the clients to rechannel their feelings in a more constructive fashion, a number of cognitive stratagems or self-statements were offered that the clients could employ at each of the respective stages of the anger-aggression sequence. Table 7-2 provides an illustrative list of the coping self-statements that clients could employ. Note that the goal of treatment was *not* to have the clients deny their feelings of anger, but rather to teach the clients to express such feelings in a more socially acceptable fashion.

Common to each of the packages of self-statements listed in Table 7-2 is the notion that it is not events per se that provoke anger, but rather the clients' constructions and beliefs about those events. Secondly, clients need not be victims of their thoughts and beliefs, but can actively control and change them, thus manifesting self-control. Finally, the clients' maladaptive feelings, thoughts, and behaviors are now to be viewed as signals, cues to use the coping procedures that they will rehearse in therapy. Whereas prior to treatment such maladaptive

Table 7-2. Examples of Anger Management Self-Statements Rehearsed in Stress Inoculation Training

Preparing for a Provocation

This could be a rough situation, but I know how to deal with it.
I can work out a plan to handle this. Easy does it.
Remember, stick to the issues and don't take it personally.
There won't be any need for an argument. I know what to do.

Impact and Confrontation

As long as I keep my cool, *I'm* in control of the situation.
You don't need to prove yourself. Don't make more out of this than you have to.
There is no point in getting mad. Think of what you have to do.
Look for the positives and don't jump to conclusions.

Coping with Arousal

Muscles are getting tight. Relax and slow things down.
Time to take a deep breath. Let's take the issue point by point.
My anger is a signal of what I need to do. Time for problem-solving.
He probably wants me to get angry, but I'm going to deal with it constructively.

Subsequent Reflection

a. Conflict unresolved

Forget about the aggravation. Thinking about it only makes you upset.
Try to shake it off. Don't let it interfere with your job.
Remember relaxation. It's a lot better than anger.
Don't take it personally. It's probably not so serious.

b. Conflict resolved

I handled that one pretty well. That's doing a good job!
I could have gotten more upset than it was worth.
My pride can get me into trouble, but I'm doing better at this all the time.
I actually got through that without getting angry.

Reprinted by permission of Dr. Ray Novaco, University of California, Irvine.

feelings and behaviors would act as harbingers of behavioral and emotional distress, as a result of treatment these cues would become reminders to engage in different internal dialogues and to emit different adaptive behaviors.

During the course of treatment the clients cognitively and behaviorally rehearsed—by means of imagery rehearsal and role-playing—how to cope with provocations, beginning with the least provoking situation and progressing to the most provoking. For example, in the treatment of the policeman, the skills training focused on the officer's role as an interventionist in a conflict between disputing parties. The policeman was given (a) strategies in how to defuse provocations, such as tactics for physical separation of disputants and interviewing skills; (b) conflict resolution techniques, such as methods for improving communication; and (c) ways of insuring personal safety, such as defensive skills. Novaco indicates that the role playing with the policeman included scenes which "directly challenge the officer's manhood, question his maternal ancestry, or remark on his wife's occupation."

In summary, the Novaco treatment for clients with problems in anger control included: (1) an educational phase in which clients were given a conceptualization of how to view their anger reactions in terms of a sequence of stages that involved cognitive and arousal processes; (2) relaxation and cognitive skills training, the latter in the form of self-instructional rehearsal; and (3) an application phase, in which clients were asked to use imagery and behavioral rehearsal techniques.

Novaco found that the cognitive-behavior modification treatment relative to a variety of control groups was highly effective in reducing anger as assessed by laboratory-based provocations—which included imaginal, role-playing, and direct-experience modes using both self-report and physiological indices—and by anger diary ratings. As Novaco states:

> The control skills that were taught to persons having chronic anger problems involved their becoming educated about their anger patterns, learning to monitor and assess their anger, learning how to alternatively construe provocations, to mitigate the sense of personal threat, and instructing themselves to attend to the task dimensions of a provocative situation (p. 106).

It is interesting to note that the clients in Novaco's study reported that an important aspect of the treatment was the idea of being "task-oriented" when presented with a provocation, thus defining the situation as a problem that calls for a solution rather than a threat that calls for attack. In this way, the client is encouraged to focus his attention on the issues involved and to avoid responding in ways that escalate the provocation sequence. Meichenbaum (1977) has summarized how such cognitive-behavior-modification treatment procedures have been employed with other clinical populations.

WHAT CHANGES IN THERAPY, AND HOW DOES CHANGE COME ABOUT?

An analysis of the treatment regimen developed by Novaco for anger-control clients will elucidate the mechanisms involved in behavior and personality change. It should be noted, however, that there is much debate about what are the necessary and sufficient conditions required to foster change, and moreover, what are the mechanisms involved. (For example, see Bandura, 1977; Frank, 1974; Meichenbaum, 1977; Rogers, 1975; Worschel & Byrne 1964, for a discussion of these issues.)

Another way to frame the concern about the nature of the mechanisms involved in behavior and personality change is to recognize that the student of psychotherapy is faced with a conundrum. Many therapists, espousing a wide variety of theories and techniques, claim to be therapeutically effective. In some instances their claims are empirically supported. Moreover, behavioral change results from nonprofessional contacts with persons encountered during the course of day-to-day life. The conundrum, then, is attempting to understand and explain the behavioral change process as it occurs in so many different contexts. What are the underlying mechanisms of change that are common to the various procedures and contexts in which change occurs? What accounted for the improvement of Novaco's anger-control clients? Perhaps a clinical example, taken from a somewhat different therapeutic context, will be helpful in answering these questions.

In describing the successful treatment of psychoanalysis, Jerome Singer explains the change in a client as follows:

> A patient experiences a sudden sense of unrest or annoyance upon entering a room. Under some past conditions he might have hastily left the room or perhaps talked rudely in response to questions raised. His analytic experience now alerts him to the fact that this sudden unease is occasioned by an irrational anticipation or transference in the situation. He replays in his mind the thoughts just previous to entering the room or what he was thinking about immediately prior to this situation. On this mental screen, he "instant replays" the thoughts and perceptions that occurred and suddenly is aware that he had been thinking about some obligation to one of his parents and that on entering the room he noticed across the way an elderly gentleman who rather resembled his father. He now perceives that his distress is a combination of anticipatory image plus the scene occurring in the room and generally is freed of his anxiety and certainly is less likely to engage in an irrational and self-defeating bit of behavior in this new situation (1974, p. 64).

The Singer quote nicely illustrates several points concerning the change process. First, in order to bring about change, the client must recognize some "behavior" in which he engages (be it a set of thoughts, images, physiological or behavioral responses) *or*, in some instances, the interpersonal responses of someone else. Thus, Singer's patient became "aware of", "sensitive to" his sudden sense of unease and his preceding thoughts. The client's "recognition" is a necessary, but not sufficient, condition to bring about change. This recognition or self-awareness acts as a cue for producing a certain internal dialogue. The content of the client's internal dialogue, and indeed what the client will attend to, is guided by the orientation of the therapist and the nature of the conceptualization that evolves between the client and the therapist. The client's internal dialogue may be in terms of psychoanalytic interpretations as in the Singer example, or arousal and accompanying cognitive evaluation as in the Novaco example. Indeed, clients seem to have sufficient life experiences to provide data consistent with a variety of therapy conceptualizations, thus being able to maintain the employment of a host of therapists of widely different persuasions.

Prior to therapy, when a client notices some maladaptive behavior, this is usually the occasion for him to produce an internal dialogue comprised of negative self-statements and images which have a deleterious effect on performance. The recognition of anger-engendering thoughts, feelings, physiological reactions, interpersonal behaviors–triggers inner speech that often fosters a sense of "helplessness" and "hopelessness," a fear of "losing one's mind," a sense of demoralization, all of which have been described by Frank (1974), Raimy (1975), and Strupp (1970). For example, upon entry into therapy, an anger-control client may claim that he is a "victim" of his feelings and thoughts; he may believe that external events are causing his malady. He may simply feel unable to control his anger. Rarely does the client consider the role of his own thinking processes and/or the interpersonal meaning of his behavior as sources of disturbance.

However, as a result of therapy a *translation* process takes place. The translation is from the internal dialogue that the client engages in prior to therapy to a new language system that emerges over the course of treatment. Whereas, prior to therapy the anger-control client may view his aggression as a sign of "losing his wits," during therapy he may come to view the anger-aggression reaction in terms of a "communication" problem, or as a manifestation of a deep-seated conflict about guilt, or as a behavioral repertoire that is maintained by secondary gains. Which reconceptualization or translation predominates will be influenced by whom the client sees in therapy. This view is consistent with Jerome Frank's notion, mentioned earlier, about the important role of the healer's theoretical system.

The translation process is the result of what occurs both in and outside of therapy. In therapy, the therapist uses a host of clinical tools, such as reflection, explanation, interpretation, information-giving, and cognitive modeling, to provide the conditions whereby the client will change what he says to himself. Outside of therapy, the client engages in coping behaviors that have been discussed and rehearsed in therapy. The coping behaviors lead to new behavioral outcomes and different reactions from significant others in the client's life.

These behavioral outcomes and reactions elicit an internal dialogue in the client that affects both his cognitive structures (e.g., belief about himself, beliefs about his ability to cope, etc.) and his ongoing behaviors.

The scenario is thus set for explaining the behavior-change process. The basic processes of change have been introduced in the form of: the client's behaviors and the reactions they elicit in the environment; the client's internal dialogue, or what he says to himself before, accompanying, and following his behavior; and the client's cognitive structures that give rise to the specific internal dialogue. In short, behavior change occurs through a sequence of mediating processes involving the interaction of inner-speech, cognitive structures, behavior and their resultant outcomes. If an individual (whether a client, scientist, or whatever) is going to change his pattern of responding, he must introduce an intentional mediational process. The mediational process involves the recognition of maladaptive behavior (either external or internal), and this recognition must come to elicit inner speech that is different in content from that engaged in prior to therapy. The altered private speech must then trigger coping behaviors. Some clients require explicit teaching of such coping responses, and this is where the technology of behavior therapy is of particular value.

Let us examine this change process more microscopically by viewing it as consisting of three phases. These phases should not be seen as a lock-step progression. Rather, they form a flexible sequence, during which cognitive structures, inner speech, and behaviors, with their resultant outcomes, interweave in contributing to behavior and personality change.

Phase 1: Self-Observation

The first step in the change process is the client's becoming an observer of his own behavior. Through heightened awareness and deliberate attention, the client monitors, with increased sensitivity, his thoughts, feelings, physiological reactions, and/or interpersonal behaviors. As a result of the translation process that evolves in therapy, the client develops new cognitive structures (concepts) which permit him to view his symptoms differently. For example, in Novaco's treatment the anger-control clients learned to recognize and attend to the chain of events that contributed to the anger-aggression reaction sequence. The clients were taught to attend to low-intensity incipient elements of their aggressive behavior. The anger-control patients were taught to reconceptualize their aggressive behavior into a more differentiated concept involving various components, stages, and various setting events. In short, over the course of treatment, Novaco was able to foster a translation process; a process that helped to alter what the client said to himself about his maladaptive aggressive behavior. Thus, attending to one's maladaptive behaviors takes on a different meaning–a meaning that contributes to a heightened vigilance or, to use the colloquial expression, a "raised consciousness."

As a result of therapy, the client must come to view his thoughts and behavior differently. The anger-control client must come to see that he is no longer a "victim" of such thoughts and feelings, but an active contributor to his own experience. The recognition of the prodromal signs of the maladaptive behaviors must trigger a different internal dialogue. An internal dialogue that notes the opportunities for engaging in adaptive behaviors, behaviors that will be discussed and rehearsed in therapy. The process of self-observation is a necessary, but not a sufficient, condition for change.

The exact behaviors upon which the client will focus depends upon the conceptualization process that evolves during therapy. The important role of this conceptualization process in therapy needs to be further underscored. Whereas the client usually enters therapy with some conceptualization of his problems (as well as expectations concerning therapy and the role of the therapist), the client's conceptualization of his problems must undergo change if he is to alter his behavior. One goal of the (re)conceptualization process is for the client to redefine his problems in terms that will give him a sense of understanding and, with it, the feelings of control and hope which are necessary for acts of change. One of the byproducts of the increased self-awareness and the translation process is that the client gains a sense of control of his emotional state, thoughts, and behaviors. In short, the client is changing what he is saying to himself about his maladaptive behaviors.

Many observers of the therapy process, such as Frank (1972) and Marmor (1975), have also pointed to the importance of this *translation* process in the therapy enterprise. This has been most explicitly stated by Lewis:

> A look at various schools of psychotherapy reveals that many of the operations involved consist of translations, supplying new verbal categories for old ones. Therapists speak of "differentiating fine shades of feeling from one another," and "improving communications." A patient's initial statement, "I'm afraid of heights," may become translated in the course of therapy into various other statements depending upon which conceptual framework the therapist holds and transmits to the patient. If the therapist is a psychoanalyst, the patient might say much later, "I'm not really afraid of physical heights–I know this now–it is rather that as a child I feared another type of physical fall–that is, sexual surrender. I was afraid of a symbol–being on a cliff no longer seems so scary." If the therapist is a behaviorist, the translation proceeds along a different path: The patient may say, "I now realize that I am lumping all heights together, and that I can train myself to relax in a situation of slight elevation, so that I am finding that I feel more and more relaxed in higher and yet higher ones." An existential translation might be "I realize that I have been deceiving myself with this symptom–that I never before could tolerate the idea of nothingness–of nonexistence. But, sharing this basic fear with my therapist has diminished my misguided fear of heights" (1972, p. 81).

It is unlikely that clients engage in the formal internal dialogue that Lewis has described. Rather, their thoughts more likely approximate a series of automatic reactions. As Goldfried, Decenteceo and Weinberg (1974) have indicated, because of the habitual nature of one's expectations or beliefs, it is likely that such thinking processes and images become automatic and seemingly involuntary, like most overlearned acts. The Lewis quote, however, underscores the translation process that contributes to change. A similar observation has been offered by two psychoanalysts, Ezekiel and Mendel. Ezekiel (1965) suggested that the essence of the psychoanalytic method is that it gives meaning to apparently meaningless sequences of thoughts and actions, and thus provides a rational explanation for apparently irrational behavior. Mendel (1968) suggested that the assignment of meaning is part of every therapist-patient interaction, a process that is independent of the theories or techniques of the therapist. Mendel states, "All schools [of psychotherapy] help their patients to assign meaning to behavior, thoughts, fantasies, dreams, delusions, and hallucinations."

A number of observations are important concerning this initial self-observation phase and about the translation process. First, it is not being suggested that each and every therapy conceptualization will prove to be equally effective in facilitating change. One of the more essential variables that determines therapy outcome is the degree to which a given conceptualization leads to specific behavioral changes that can be transferred to the real-life situation. Does a particular conceptualization that evolves over the course of therapy help the client to engage in behavioral acts in the environment; encourage the client to conduct "personal experiments" that will provide constructive feedback?

Secondly, we must be concerned with how the therapist prepares the client to accept (implicitly) a particular conceptualization or therapy rationale, with its accompanying treatment intervention. Some therapists are very directive and didactic, and seem to force upon the client a particular conceptualization by power of their personalities, jargon, or positions. In some cases such a "hard-sell" approach clearly does prove successful. But the therapist must be concerned not only with the client's self-statements and attributions concerning his presenting problems, but also with those concerning the therapy process and dependence on the therapist. An alternative way to proceed is to have the client and therapist evolve a common conceptualization so that the client feels he is an active participant and contributor.

The manner in which the therapist queries the client about his presenting problems, the type of assessment procedures the therapist employs, the kinds of homework assignments he gives, and the type of therapy rationale he offers, all influence the conceptualization process. Thus, the therapist tries to understand the client's description and definition of his problem, but does not merely accept uncritically the client's view. Instead, the therapist and client attempt to redefine the problem in terms that are meaningful to both of them. Note that a client's acceptance of a particular conceptualization of his problem is not usually a formal, explicit agreement, but rather an implicit byproduct of the interaction between client and therapist. With skill, the therapist has the client come to view his problem from a different perspective, to fabricate a new meaning or explanation for the etiology and maintenance of his maladaptive behavior.

The initial phase of the cognitive theory of behavior change is concerned with the increased awareness that evolves from the translation process; but more must occur if change is to take place.

Phase 2: Incompatible Thoughts and Behaviors

Intrinsic to all therapies is the client's reconceptualization of his problems. The initial stages of therapist-client interaction foster this "translation" process. Furthermore, an implicit premise that guides the initial contacts of therapy is that the client must learn to attend to his maladaptive behaviors and thus begin to notice opportunities for adaptive behavioral alternatives. As the client's self-observations become attuned to incipient low-intensity aspects of his maladaptive behavior, the client learns to initiate cognitions and behaviors that interfere with the maladaptive ones. The self-observation signals the opportunity for producing the adaptive thoughts and behaviors. This point was illustrated before, with Singer's quote; the recognition of the maladaptive behavior triggered an internal dialogue. The content of what the client learns to say to himself will vary with the conceptualization that emerges in therapy. If the client's behavior is to change, then what he says to himself, and/or imagines, must initiate a new behavioral chain, one that is incompatible with his maladaptive behaviors.

One task of therapy is to have clients become aware of the role their thoughts and images play in the behavioral sequence, as illustrated in Novaco's treatment. In this way, clients can interrupt the maladaptive-response chain by controlling automatic thoughts and by producing incompatible thoughts and behaviors. For example, in Novaco's treatment, the clients' anger reactions that appeared habitual in nature (i.e., not premeditated) would be "deautomatized," so that the maladaptive behavior came to be preceded by cognitive activity occurring within the client's awareness. Such "forced mediation" increases the separation between stimuli and responses, and thereby provides an additional opportunity for interrupting the behavioral sequence and producing incompatible thoughts, images, and behavior.

Along with the self-recognition of the maladaptive acts, feelings, and thoughts come accompanying thoughts (inner speech), the content of which is guided by the translation that has evolved in therapy. Not only does the inner speech have functional properties with regard to other ongoing streams of behavior, such as affecting attentional and appraisal systems and physiological responses; it also has an impact on the client's cognitive structures. The client learns that he can organize his experiences around the new conceptualization and can do so in a way that enables him to cope more effectively. This "reinforcement" of the therapist's conceptualization helps to consolidate the client's newly emerging cognitive structures.

In summary, the refocusing of the client's attention, the alteration in appraisal and physiological reactions, will help change the internal dialogue that the client brought into therapy. In turn, the internal dialogue comes to guide new behavior, the results of which have an impact on the individual's cognitive structures. This leads us to the third phase of the change process, which has to do with the client's emitting coping behaviors *in vivo*, and what he says to himself about the outcomes of these "personal experiments."

Phase 3: Cognitions Concerning Change

In Novaco's treatment, the clients practiced the coping behaviors they had learned in therapy *in vivo* with significant others. These "personal experiments" by the clients in their everyday experiences led to interpersonal consequences. How the clients viewed these consequences, what they said to themselves about the reactions to their changed behavior, are important determinants of the nature of behavior change that will be evidenced. Whether the client views these outcomes and reactions as consistent with or discrepant with his cognitive structures (e.g., beliefs) will influence the nature of the change. How the client appraises and conceptualizes the reactions or nonreactions of significant others will influence what he says to himself, which in turn will influence the behavioral acts, and so on.

The third phase of this explanation of behavior change is concerned with the process of the client's producing new behaviors in his everyday world and how he assesses the behavioral outcomes.

Note that some clients require specific training in the coping-behavior skills (e.g., assertive training), while other clients have the skills within their repertoire, but negative expectations interfere with the clients expressing the desirable coping behaviors. In either case, just focusing on such skills training is not sufficient to explain the change process. For, what the client says to himself about his newly acquired behaviors and their resultant consequences will influence whether the behavioral change process will be maintained and will generalize. A person can behave in a variety of new ways because these ways pay off; and yet, he may not be willing to assume that he is a changed person or that he has in any sense gotten anything out of the therapy process. To the extent that the client changes both his behavior and his internal dialogue—to that extent, therapy becomes a success.

Another way to consider this question is to ask what will the client be willing to consider as *evidence* to alter his cognitive structures? Like the scientist, our client has a host of "defensive" rationalizations and cognitive techniques to discount or accept the importance of data derived from behavioral outcomes. The issue of what constitutes evidence becomes critical for both the scientist and the client. Why? Because if the change process is to be lasting, then one must not only teach new behavioral skills, alter internal dialogue, but one also must influence cognitive structures.

The reader may now view each of the many therapy procedures as differentially focusing on any one or more of the three basic processes, cognitive structures, inner speech, and behavioral acts. Some therapies, such as Albert Ellis's rational-emotive therapy, primarily focus on cognitive structures, challenging premises and beliefs. Aaron Beck's approach to therapy focuses more on getting clients (especially depressed clients) to engage in new behavioral acts so they can examine the inner speech which follows from behavioral outcomes. Once the client's inner speech is examined, the implications this has for the underlying cognitive structures is examined. In Novaco's cognitive-behavioral treatment of anger control, the focus was on altering the clients' inner speech by reappraising their anger, which encouraged the production of new behaviors and an examination of the resultant behavioral outcomes, which permitted a further exploration of the clients' cognitive structures. The behavior-therapy approaches (namely those taking an operant orientation) limit their focus to the acquisition of new behaviors, and insure that the resultant behavioral outcomes will be favorable by means of manipulating graded task assignments and environmental consequences (reinforcements).

If this explanation of behavior change is "valid" and heuristically useful, then therapists should be concerned with all three basic processes: cognitive structures, inner speech, and behaviors and the interpretation of their impact. Focusing on only one will likely prove insufficient.

Where should therapists begin? Should they focus most on cognitive structures, *or* try to alter inner speech, *or* teach new behaviors and manipulate environmental consequences? These are important research questions. Beck's depressives might require therapists to focus on behavioral events and work towards inner speech and cognitive structures. Ellis's neurotics may be most responsive to "frontal" attacks on their cognitive structures. Anger-control clients may need cognitive-skills training that focuses on inner speech. Although each therapy approach focuses primarily on only one of the three mechanisms (cognitive structures, inner speech, and behavioral acts) it is suggested that the other two processes are also involved in change.

In summary, it is proposed that a three-stage process can explain behavior and personality change resulting from both therapeutic and non-therapeutic interventions. The change comes about by means of a sequential mediating process. First, the client becomes aware of some element of his behavior, either intra- or interpersonal. That is, he must first become an observer of his thoughts, feelings and/or behaviors by means of heightened awareness. This process is facilitated by means of a conceptualization process, or translation of how the client views his problem. The language system of the conceptualization process will be influenced by the therapist's orientation.

Secondly, the process of self-observation contributes to the "deautomaticity" of the behavioral act, and acts as a stimulus for the client to emit incompatible thoughts and behaviors. The third stage, which determines the persistence and generalization of treatment effects, involves the nature and content of the client's internal dialogue and images about behavior change.

The model of change that has been proposed indicates that cognitions influence behaviors, which influence environments, which in turn influence cognitions, and so on. A causal interactive circularity, or what Bandura (1978) characterizes as a reciprocal determinism, is established. Within such a social-learning model, functioning and change involves a continuous interdependence among behavior, mediational processes, and external events.

There is not an inevitable prime mover of behavior, although the relative influence of these separate interactive influences will vary across individuals and situations. From the viewpoint of change, intervention at one phase (either behavior, mediational processes, or external events) may result in change. Although various theorists differentially emphasize one particular phase as being central, the present position is that all aspects of the cycle come into play. Theories and procedures that delimit their focus to only one element are unlikely to prove satisfactory. It is hoped that the present discussion conveys some of the complexities that must be considered in understanding the change process.

Now that you have a conceptual framework to describe the mechanisms involved in change, are you ready to attend Slade's play? How about that class reunion?

REFERENCES

Arthur, R. Success is predictable. *Military Medicine,* 1971, *136,* 539-545.

Bandura, A. Self-efficacy: Toward a unifying theory of behavior change. *Psychological Review,* 1977, *84,* 191-215.

____. The self-system in reciprocal determinism. *American Psychologist,* 1978, *33,* 344-358.

Beck, A. *Cognitive therapy and emotional disorders.* New York: International Universities Press, 1976.

Bellak, L. The need for public health laws for psychiatric illness. *American Journal of Public Health,* 1971, *61,* 119-121.

Block, J. *Lives through time.* Berkeley, Calif.: Bancroft Books, 1971.

____. *Recognizing the coherence of personality.* Paper presented at the Symposium on Interactional Psychology, Stockholm, June, 1975.

Bowers, K. Situationism in psychology: An analysis and critique. *Psychological Review,* 1973, *80,* 307-336.

___. *There is more to Iago than meets the eye: A clinical account of personal consistency.* A paper presented at the Symposium on Interactional Psychology, Stockholm, June, 1975.

Brush, S. Should the history of science be rated X? *Science,* 1974, *183,* 1164-1172.

Chase, M. The impact of correctional programs: Absconding. In R. Moos (Ed.), *Evaluating correctional and community settings.* New York: Wiley, 1975.

Chess, S., Thomas, A., & Birch, H. Behavioral problems revisited. In S. Chess and H. Birch (Eds.), *Annual progress in child psychiatry and child development.* New York: Brunner/Mazel, 1968.

Coan, R. The changing personality. In R. Dreger (Ed.), *Multivariate personality research.* Baton Rouge, La.: Claitors Publishing Division, 1972.

Cowen, E., Pederson, A., Bakigan, H., Izzo, L., & Trost, M. Long term follow-up of early detected vulnerable children. *Journal of Consulting and Clinical Psychology,* 1973, *41,* 438-446.

Endler, N., & Magnusson, D. Personality and person by situation interactions. In N. Endler and D. Magnusson (Eds.), *Interactional psychology and personality.* Washington, D.C.: Hemisphere Publishing Corp., 1976.

Eysenck, H. The effects of psychotherapy: An evaluation. *Journal of Consulting Psychology,* 1952, *16,* 319-324.

Ezkiel, H. Experimentation within the psychoanalytic session. *British Journal of Philosophy and Science,* 1965, 7, *25.*

Fiske, D. *Measuring the concepts of personality.* Chicago: Aldine Publishing Co., 1971.

Frank, J. The bewildering world of psychotherapy. *Journal of Social Issues,* 1972, *28,* 27-43.

___. *Persuasion and healing.* New York: Schocken Books, 1974.

Gil, D. *Violence against children.* Cambridge, Mass.: Harvard University Press, 1970.

Goldfried, M., Decenteceo, E., & Weinberg, L. Systematic rational restructuring as a self-control technique. *Behavior Therapy,* 1974, *5,* 247-254.

Gottman, J., & Markman, H. Experimental designs in psychotherapy research. In S. Garfield & A. Bergin (Eds.), *Handbook of psychotherapy and behavior change.* New York: John Wiley & Sons, 1978.

Hebb, D. Science and the world of imagination. *Canadian Psychological Review,* 1975, *16,* 4-12.

Hilgard, E. Neodissociation theory of multiple cognitive control systems. In G. Schwartz & D. Shapiro (Eds.), *Consciousness and self-regulation,* Volume 1. New York: Plenum Press, 1976.

Honzik, M., MacFarlane, J., & Allen, L. The stability of mental test performance between two and eighteen years. *Journal of Experimental Education,* 1948, *17,* 309-324.

Kazdin, A., & Wilson, T. *Evaluation of behavior therapy.* Cambridge, Mass.: Ballinger, 1978.

Kelley, G. *The psychology of personal constructs.* New York: Norton, 1955.

Kieslar, D. Some myths of psychotherapy research and the search for a paradigm. *Psychological Bulletin,* 1966, *65,* 110-136.

Lewin, V. *A dynamic theory of personality.* New York: McGraw-Hill, 1935.

Lewis, W. *Why people change: The psychology of influence.* New York: Holt, Rinehart, & Winston, 1972.

Luborsky, L., Singer, B., & Luborsky, L. Comparative studies of psychotherapies: Is it true that everyone has won and all must have prizes? *Archives of General Psychiatry,* 1975, *32,* 995-1008.

MacFarlane, J. W. Perspectives of personality consistency and change from the guidance study. *Vita Humana,* 1964, *7,* 115-126 (Karge, Basel 1964).

Mahoney, M. *The scientist: Anatomy of the truth merchant.* Cambridge, Mass., 1976.

Marmor, J. The nature of the psychotherapeutic process revisited. *Canadian Psychiatric Association Journal,* 1975, *20,* 557-565.

Megargee, E. The prediction of violence with psychological tests. In C. Spielberger (Ed.), *Current topics in clinical and community psychology.* New York: Academic Press, 1970.

Meichenbaum, D. *Cognitive-behavior modification: An integrative approach.* New York: Plenum Press, 1977.

Mendel, W. The non-specifics of psychotherapy. *International Journal of Psychiatry,* 1978, *5,* 400-402.

Miller, G., Galanter, E., & Pribram, K. *Plans and structure of behavior.* New York: Holt, Rinehart & Winston, 1960.

Mischel, W. *Personality and assessment.* New York: Wiley, 1968.

Monahan, J., & Cummings, L. Social policy implications of the inability to predict violence. *Journal of Social Issues,* 1975, *31,* 153-164.

Moos, R. Conceptualizations of human environments. *American Psychologist,* 1973, *28,* 652-665.

____. *The human context: Environmental determinants of behavior.* New York: Wiley, 1976.

Neisser, U. Cultural and cognitive discontinuity. In T. E. Gladwin & W. Sturtevant (Eds.), *Anthropology and human behavior.* Washington, D.C.: Anthropological Society of Washington, 1962.

Nesselroade, J., & Baltes, P. Adolescent personality development and historical change: 1970-1972. *Monograph of the Society for Research in Child Development,* 1974, *39,* No. 1, 1-80.

Novaco, R. *Anger control: The development and evaluation of an experimental treatment.* Lexington, Mass.: Heath & Co., 1975.

Patterson, G., & Reid, J. Reciprocity and coercion: Two facets of social systems. In C. Neuringer & J. Michael (Eds.), *Behavior modification in clinical psychology.* New York: Appleton-Century-Crofts, 1970.

Peterson, D. *The clinical study of social behavior.* New York: Appleton-Century-Crofts, 1968.

Piaget, J. *The language and thought of the child.* New York: New American Library, 1955.

Polanyi, M. *Personal knowledge: Towards a post-critical philosophy.* Chicago: University of Chicago Press, 1958.

Raimy, V. *Training in clinical psychology.* New York: Prentice-Hall, 1950.

____. *Misunderstanding of the self; Cognitive psychotherapy and the misconception hypothesis.* San Francisco: Josey-Bass, 1975.

Rausch, H. Interaction sequences. *Journal of Personality and Social Psychology,* 1965, *2,* 487-499.

____, **Dittman, A., & Taylor, T.** Person, Setting and change in social interaction. *Human Relations,* 1959, *12,* 361-378.

Robins, L. *Deviant children grow up.* Baltimore: Williams & Wilkins, 1966.

____. Followup studies of behavior disorders in children. In H. Quay & J. Werry (Eds.), *Psychopathological disorders in childhood.* New York: John Wiley & Sons, 1972.

Roff, M. Childhood social interactions and young adult bad conduct. *Journal of Abnormal and Social Psychology,* 1961, *63,* 333-337.

____, **Sells, B., & Golden, M.** *Social adjustment and personality development in children.* Minneapolis: University of Minnesota Press, 1972.

Rogers, C. The necessary and sufficient conditions of therapeutic personality change. *Journal of Consulting Psychology,* 1975, *21,* 459-461.

Sarbin, T., & Coe, W. *Hypnosis: A social-psychological analysis of influence communication.* New York: Holt, Rinehart, & Winston, 1972.

Schaie, K. A general model for the study of developmental problems. *Psychological Bulletin,* 1965, *64,* 92-107.

Singer, J. *Imagery and daydream methods in psychotherapy.* New York: Academic Press, 1974.

Sloane, R., Staples, F., Cristol, A., Yorkston, N., & Whipple, K. *Psychotherapy versus behavior therapy.* Cambridge, Mass.: Harvard University Press, 1975.

Smith, M., & Glass, G. Meta-analysis of psychotherapy outcome studies. *American Psychologist,* 1977, *32,* 752-760.

Tolman, E. *Purposive behavior in animals and men.* New York: Century, 1932.

Wachtel, P. Psychodynamics, behavior therapy, and the implacable experimenter: An inquiry into consistency of personality. *Journal of Abnormal Psychology,* 1973, *82,* 324-334.

Witkin, H., Goodenough, D., & Karp, S. Stability of cognitive style from childhood to young adulthood. *Journal of Personality and Social Psychology,* 1967, *7,* 291-300.

Worchel, P., & Byrne, D. *Personality change.* New York: Wiley, 1964.

SALVATORE R. MADDI

The Uses of Theorizing in Personality

8

Arguments for the importance of theorizing about human behavior have been made by many psychologists and philosophers. However persuasive, these arguments can be discounted as mere speculation by psychologists steeped in detailed observation, experimentation, and helping attempts. In contrast, this chapter attempts to strengthen the case for theorizing by arguing in a particularly psychological fashion. Instead of starting with rules of logic or metaphysics, let us consider the psychological activities involved in the theorizing process. Through a close examination of the workings and consequences of this process, we will see how theorizing deepens understanding in concrete, practical ways.

Theorizing involves the interplay of symbolization, imagination, and judgment. Typically, the beginning is the observation of some phenomenon that stimulates curiosity but eludes understanding. Important in the attempt to understand better is the descriptive step of classifying the observed phenomenon into some category of meaning. This step is primarily symbolization, as the classification inevitably highlights some aspects of the phenomenon, thereby elevating them to the status of the essential features. But considerable imagination is also involved, as it is virtually impossible for the classification reached to be the only one that can fit the phenomenon. Even more imagination comes into play when further theoretical steps are taken. These steps involve conceptualizing for the classified phenomenon its antecedents (the factors which bring it about) and consequences (the effects which it has). More imagination is involved in these steps because they are guided even less than is classification by empirical constraints, being further removed from the original observations. As theorizing concerns itself progressively more with postulating antecedents and consequences, the phenomenon under consideration is juxtaposed with other phenomena having similar or opposite antecedents and consequences. Before long, the theorizing effort becomes more comprehensive than what began as the observation of one intriguing phenomenon.

My colleague, Suzanne C. Kobasa, has my gratitude and admiration for the help she provided at all stages in the development of this chapter.

The farther the theorizing effort goes toward developing such an overall system of understanding, the more are symbolization and imagination supplemented by judgment. This is because many decisions must be made for which there is initially little direct empirical guidance, and hence the theorist is thrown on to his common sense and general wisdom. Because common sense and wisdom represent the kind of accumulation of experience in an area that constitutes expert status, the more they are employed in conceptual decision-making, the greater the likelihood of validity to the theorizing.

The theorizing process just outlined can be engaged in with regard to any sort of phenomenon—animal, vegetable, or mineral. But when the phenomenon is human behavior, theorizing effort may very likely be personological. Personology is the systematic study of whole persons, with the emphasis upon describing the interrelated behaviors occurring in a person that persist over time and situations, and explaining them as expressions of personality. An example of theorizing in personology might involve the initial observation that persons differ in the degree to which they dominate conversations and engage in disputatious interchanges. These observed activities might be classified or described as competitive behaviors (recognize that they could also have been classified as gregariousness). Then it might be theorized that competitive behavior expresses an underlying personality disposition called need for achievement (recognize that the disposition of insecurity could have been used instead). Additional theorizing effort might concern the antecedents of various levels of need for achievement—for example, the degree of independence training instituted by parents during a crucial period in the subject's late childhood. It might also be theorized that the consequences of various levels of need for achievement include not only competitive behavior, but also (1) values justifying hard work and the assumption of personal responsibility for task outcomes, (2) a preference for risky rather than routine tasks where the outcome can be influenced by one's own skills, and (3) an inability to trust others completely. Recognize that although this scheme would be initially speculative, it would yield several hypotheses concerning antecedents and consequences of need for achievement that could be tested empirically in order that the validity of the theorizing be determined. Finally, an even more elaborate level of theorizing would involve construing a relationship between the need for achievement and other needs, such as for affiliation, power, and sex.

Within personology there are currently many different personality theories and many gradations of involvement in the theorizing endeavor. Although substantive differences among theories will be discussed at various points in this chapter, the main emphasis will be upon the process of theorizing itself. Of course, theorizing leads to substantive theories, and sometimes the use of substantive theories provides a stimulus for renewed emphasis upon the theorizing process. But it is the effects of attempting to interpret and understand behavior that will be emphasized here, regardless of the content of these attempts. Needless to say, all personologists—and all persons, for that matter—engage in theorizing in their work and everyday life. But theorizing can be constant or intermittent, intense or meager, innovative or conventional. It is along these dimensions that it is fruitful to consider gradations of involvement in the theorizing process.

Theorizing should be regarded as vigorous when it is engaged in continually, intensely, and in a manner that leads to innovations in theory content. Thus, fresh observations, classifications, and conceptualizations of antecedents and consequences are continually being made. The content of these theoretical efforts shifts frequently as a function of continuing attempts to improve understanding. Some of the concrete advantages for personology that could result from widespread vigorous theorizing are detailed in the assertions that follow.

In order to dramatize the value of vigorous theorizing, in what follows there will also be discussion of the disadvantages resulting from widespread practice of two less intense commitments to the theorizing process. One of these should be called passive theorizing, because the commitment is to a theory already formulated. In this approach, effort is spent trying to fit observations into time-honored theoretical formulations. Hence, theorizing is intermittent rather than continual, moderate rather than intense, and concerned with preserving the content of existing theories rather than introducing innovations.

The other approach might be called minimal theorizing. Persons engaged in this approach usually regard themselves as against theorizing altogether and as avoiding it in their attempts to gain knowledge. They view their observations, classifications, and concepts as somehow objective and uninterpretive renditions of reality.

ADVANTAGES OF VIGOROUS THEORIZING

Assertion 1: Through vigorous theorizing, one can come to appreciate the main aims of personality study

There is no way of symbolizing, imaging, and judging vigorously in the process of observing and explaining phenomena without sooner or later considering what the whole point is of the inquiry. This is at least in part because the theorizing effort involves so many choices which could be made in one direction or another that it becomes difficult to believe that one is engaged in a wholly objective activity. As this awareness dawns, the theorizer turns more and more toward questions of the nature of his explanatory efforts that differentiates it from others. Such consideration is less a sign of unfortunate existential turmoil than of scientific maturity, for in the process of making explicit what was implicit about the inquiry, its major aims emerge. Then these aims can be employed as guides, rendering future theorizing more precise and consistently directional.

Considerations of what makes personology the particular kind of inquiry it is have generally resulted in an emphasis upon the behavioral differences among persons existing in what appears to be the same situation. Attempts to explain this phenomenon in terms of stable differences in personality has led to an emphasis upon individual differences that persist not only across situations but also over time.

Thus personology emerges as an inquiry aiming to understand what makes each person distinct from other persons. Once appreciated, this emphasis upon individuality can serve as a guide. For example, the study of one dimension of individual differences (e.g., the competitive behavior mentioned earlier) no longer seems quite enough. One wants to supplement it by the study of several other individual differences (e.g., persistence, cooperativeness, commitment) in order to more closely approximate the overall pattern of a person's behavior wherein lies true individuality. Hence, an aspect of the individuality aim of personology becomes the aim of studying wholistic patterns of behavior.

In turn, vigorous theorizing concerning individualistic patterns of behavior provoked consideration of the questions of development, intentionality, and human nature. It is the theorizer's position on human nature that will determine how he explains individuality. For example, if one assumes that all persons start at birth being alike, as do most personality theorists (Maddi, 1976), then individuality at maturity will have to be explained as the result of developmental learning. But if one assumes important genetic differences as birth, as do Sheldon and Stephens (1942), then one need not emphasize developmental learning at all. When one emphasizes development, it becomes important to consider just what goes on in this process. Genetically determined differences among persons may manifest themselves gradually, through a maturational process requiring little actual learning. Or individual differences at maturity may result from differences in socialization experiences, with emphasis put on the learning process. Whenever emphasis is put on learning, questions arise concerning intentionality. Does the person's experience result in an intention, a willful pursuit of a goal; or is learning more a matter of mechanical conditioning without the operation of consciousness? Such an unavoidable part of personality study is working out a clear position concerning human nature, development, and intentionality, that adopting this endeavor as an aim would seem quite useful.

Current Personological Practice. Now let us consider to what degree the personality field does indeed hold the aims presented above. It is certainly true that if individual differences and their organization into wholistic patterns expressing individuality are considered anywhere in psychology, it is in the personality area. It is also true that considerations of human nature and intentionality receive more attention from personologists than from other kinds of psychologists. Further, development is certainly emphasized as much in the personality area as anywhere. It would appear that, in an overall sense, personology has the aims one would expect to have derived from attempts at understanding its subject matter through vigorous theorizing. These aims seem to have developed during the period from the late nineteenth through early twentieth century, when the major personality theories (e.g., Freudian, Jungian, Adlerian) were being formulated.

Since that time, the pace of theorizing has slowed, with few new theories being introduced. Most personologists regard themselves as part of an already established theoretical tradition, applying and seeking confirmation of existing formulations rather than breaking new ground. In this, they tend toward passive rather than vigorous theorizing. Further, quite a number of psychologists who still regard themselves as being in personality study in some sense, appear to be disenchanted with the theorizing endeavor and uninclined to consider what the special role of their area might be. Though still publishing in personality journals, many of them seem to be searching for general laws with concepts and methods that disregard and even mask individual differences (Bowers, 1973). In general, there seems such an absence of attention to wholistic patterns of functioning that Carlson (1971) was provoked to write an indictment entitled, "Where is the person in personality research?" Concomitant with this tapering off of vigorous theorizing in favor of passive and sometimes minimal theorizing, there seems to be a deepening loss of purpose, direction, and organization in the personality field. This is what would be expected, if it is vigorous theorizing that stimulates concern with the basic aims of an area of inquiry.

Especially intriguing is the case of radical behaviorists (e.g., Skinner), who appear to have a clear sense of purpose and direction, despite an ideological commitment to avoid theorizing. Although they do not regard themselves as personologist, they do seek to understand human behavior, and practice so-called behavior-modification therapy. They contend that human and animal behavior can and should be explained without recourse to theory, thereby denying the importance of such considerations as organismic nature and intentionality (e.g., Skinner, 1953).

For a full appreciation of the extent to which radical behaviorists theorize minimally, it is instructive to read their journals. In animal experiments, it is customary to deprive the subjects of food or water until they lose a specified amount of weight before the study begins. It is also customary to use food or water as the reinforcement. When the subject performs in order to obtain the food or water, it is said that learning has taken place. But the use of deprivation and substances that ease the deprivation are described and justified only as conventions, discovered empirically, are employed merely because they "work." Nor is the subject regarded as having intended to perform as it did. This minimal theorizing carries over to the human level as well. The behavior-modification therapist (1) believes humans learn in the same way as to animals, (2) is disinterested in and obtains little information about the needs, drives, instincts or motivations defining the human being, and (3) believes that his clients have very little insight into their difficulties. Having decided with his client what the goals of the therapy should be, the behaviorist proceeds to construct a reinforcement schedule that should produce the desired effect.

The popularity of behavior-modification theory is based in part on its apparent simplicity. But recent findings are suggesting that this simplicity may be more apparent than real. Unexpected side effects of reinforcement schedules, peculiar "misbehaviors" resulting from an insufficient recognition of species-specific behaviors, and the emergence of self-control as a vexingly important factor in learning and performing are all forcing recognition that some additional conceptualization must be done (Hunt, 1977). In the opinion of Hernstein (1977), an influential radical behaviorist, greater theorizing effort should be spent specifically concerning what constitutes organismic nature (witness species-specific behaviors and the apparent link between certain deprivation procedures and certain reinforcements) and the role of intentionality (witness the importance of self-control). Thus, radical behaviorists may be forced into vigorous theorizing by the complexity of behavior, despite their ideology of minimal theorizing.

Recommendations. Personologists need to become more aware of the nature of the enterprise they are engaged in. This is true with regard to not only the observations but also the explanations that are of special relevance in personology. Inevitably, this will involve attention to what makes personality study different from other kinds of inquiry both inside and outside of psychology.

One way in which greater awareness of the personological enterprise can come about is through the self-scrutiny of persons in that area. Everyone engaged in personality study should list the reasons why he is doing that rather than something else. Then these reasons should be scrutinized both individually and collectively. Indeed, such scrutiny might well be the subject of systematic research. A step in this direction has been taken by Henry (1971) in his study of the helping professions. But his emphasis was largely on demographic and early-experience factors. More to the present point would be studies classifying the interests and values of personologists regarding their actual work.

Also of use are metatheoretical analyses of the personological enterprise. For example, Maddi (1976) has suggested the necessary parts of a personality theory, and indicated something of their respective functions. He argues that personality theories need (1) a core statement, which covers the overall directionality and structural entities that are unlearned and inherent (human nature); (2) a peripheral statement, which organizes the recognized learned characteristics (e.g., disposition, traits, motives) into a typology delineating the various life-styles persons can come to show through experience; and (3) a developmental statement, which links the core to the periphery through detailing the learning which takes place as the result of various kinds of interaction the person can have with his parents, others, and social institutions. It is the periphery which is the proximal cause of observed behaviors, with the core and the developmental process serving as the causes of the periphery. Inherent in this model for personality theorizing is the identification of one or more personality types as ideal (full developmental maturity) and the others as one form or another of maladjustment. This evaluative stance determines what is regarded as ideal and deviant development. Psychopathology occurs when maladjusted personality types encounter sufficient stress to breakdown (Maddi, 1970). Therapy is called for when breakdown has occurred, and has the functions of (1) returning the person to the maladjusted state (in which he is at least suffering less), and (2) creating a microcosm of ideal development so that growth in the direction of the ideal personality type is stimulated.

Metatheoretical analyses of the sort mentioned above can lend order and coherence to the personological enterprise. Perhaps we can take contemporary social psychology as a model. In that field, there is considerable inquiry into the nature and aims of the enterprise (e.g., Gergen, 1973, 1976; Gottlieb, 1977).

Assertion 2: Through vigorous theorizing, one can learn from history

Part of a vigorous commitment to theorizing is curiosity about the theorizing efforts of others. This curiosity is not restricted to one's contemporaries alone. In the difficult task of understanding human behavior, the theorizer will tend to perceive himself as part of a tradition, attempting to profit from the insights of the past. Even if the theorizer is insistent upon an ego-gratifying orginality, he will regard his attempts enhanced by a sufficient understanding of the past to know how best to break with it.

Current Personological Practice. Most personologists are quite ahistorical. They are primarily research-oriented and, perceiving themselves as empiricists, feel there is little to learn from history. The most recent research is to be trusted most, due to methodological advances in the measurement of variables and the analysis of data. Also, they regard personality study as a new area of inquiry, and therefore find little of use in the emphases of the ancients. There are a few personologists steeped in the comprehensive theories of personality who have more interest in history; but they are in the minority at present, and tend to be regarded as soft-headed by their research-oriented counterparts.

Although it is difficult to see one's own times in perspective, it would appear that recent emphases in personology have recapitulated the past in a manner wasteful of time and effort. A notable example is the recent person-situation controversy. Begun from within personology (Mischel, 1968), the controversy hinged on the contention that the individual-differences approach had proven a failure, and that the best understanding of human behavior emphasizes its control by situational forces. Before long, social psychologists (e.g., Bem, 1972) had taken up the cause of situationism. What followed was a flurry of articles on one side or another of the issue, with the controversy raging over seven years or more. Near the end of the controversy, some situationists were claiming that their original intent and statements were exaggerated (e.g., Mischel, 1973), while some person advocates insisted that they never meant their formulations to exclude the importance of situations (e.g., Adelson, 1969). Predictably, this led to an interactionist accord, in which both sides agreed that a full understanding of human behavior requires attention to both person and situation variables as they interact (e.g., Ekehammer, 1974). The final step in the ending of the controversy involved setting it in proper perspective, first by referring the matter to the purview of history (e.g., Bowers, 1973), and then by discerning that only a pseudo-issue was involved (Carlson, 1975).

As several personologists have by now pointed out (e.g., Bowers, 1973; Cronbach, 1975), the interactionist accord outlined above was called for in the past as recent as 1957. In his presidential address to the American Psychological Association, Cronbach (1957), a figure of considerable influence and wisdom, contrasted the experimental (roughly emphasizing situations) and correlational (roughly emphasizing persons) traditions, advocating a combination of both in an interactional inquiry. Cronbach's recommendations were of an order of sophistication which would have obviated much of the recent controversy. Had his views been properly appreciated, they could have been built upon with profit, and the wheel would not have had to be reinvented. But in order for this to have taken place, the psychologists most intimately involved in the recent controversy would have needed more of an interest in history.

I may be accused of an excessively rational view of how science develops. Progress is not a straight line, the rejoinder goes. This rejoinder is only as convincing as the evidence that new knowledge resulted from a controversy, however it might have been unnecessary in some completely rational world. Let us look, therefore, at what has been learned as the result of the recent person-situation controversy. Endler and Magnusson (1976) have recently promoted an interactionist approach, building upon accords deriving from the controversy. One assumption they make is that the best way of defining units of personality is as interactions between person and situation. This is precisely the usage advocated by Sullivan (1953) some time ago. Also, in their exposition, Endler and Magnusson (1976) indicate how common it has been to overlook the importance of interactions. This fails to recognize that Murray and Cattell, to mention just two very different and yet influential personologists, long ago included among the concepts of their formal theories person, situation, and interaction variables. Murray (1938) referred to both objective stimulus forces (*alpha press*) and subjective perceptions of these (*beta press*), and called for study of the interactive effects of both on behavior. Cattell (1965) inserted into his behavioral equations a factor representing *modulating states*, or deviations in the effects of situations produced by individual perceptions of them. Indeed, Endler and

Magnusson seem to measure situations only subjectively—situations as perceived by individuals—and hence have an incomplete interactional approach. Oddly, Murray and Cattell, for all their identification as excessively person-oriented theorists, believed more than Endler and Magnusson seem to that situations should be measured objectively or at least consensually, and that this measurement should be the baseline against which individual perceptions of situations should be scrutinized. In some ways, the work of Endler and Magnusson is neither as original nor as sophisticated as that which preceded it. It may well be that Endler and Magnusson, and the research-oriented personologists they speak to, will do more interaction research than have Murray or Cattell, and this is certainly valuable. But perhaps such research could have been done already if earlier interactional approaches had been properly appreciated. Once again, a greater interest in history would have been helpful.

Mischel's (1973) recent formulations of personality have also been heralded as an advance arising from the recent person-situation controversy. In this article, Mischel seeks to correct what he regards as misinterpretations of his position. He does not want to be associated with the view that personality does not exist. It is not fruitful, he contends, to debate whether it is persons or situations that really control behavior. What is apparent to him is that behavior is a function of the interaction between persons and situations, and that this interaction should be studied rather than debated. Whether some psychologists are right in insisting that Mischel has abandoned his former position, he is currently espousing a viewpoint not exactly unheard of in personology.

In considering what available studies on person-situation interactions show, Mischel (1973) contends that they "highlight the idiosyncratic organization of behavior within individuals, and hence the uniqueness of stimulus equivalences and response equivalences for each person." As do Endler and Magnusson, Mischel refers to a person's perceptions of situations and responses to these perceptions as person-situation interactions. This version of person-situation interactions is surely the most consistent with traditional personological usage.

Mischel also contends that for each person, various perceived stimuli and various responses achieve functional equivalence, despite how differently they may be organized in others. It is these functionally equivalent stimuli and responses that lend consistency and individuality to the person's functioning. This, of course, is precisely Allport's (1937) position, in which the personal disposition or trait is defined as "a generalized neuropsychic structure (peculiar to the individual), with the capacity to render many stimuli functionally equivalent, and to initiate and guide consistent (equivalent) forms of adaptive and stylistic behavior." In his discussion of adaptive and stylistic behavior, Allport made abundantly clear his belief that what are now being called person-situation interactions are the important units of inquiry, and that persons not only perceive and behave very differently from each other in any given situation, but also shift in behavior from situation to situation. Personal dispositions are far removed from actual behavior; and while they influence it, that influence is complex enough so that the personologist should not expect simple response repetition from situation to situation. To his credit, Mischel (1973) attributes to Allport the position they both espouse in the statement, "Such data provide encouragement for idiographic study (Allport, 1937) but not for the predictive utility of 'common' (nomothetic) personality traits."

What is especially mystifying is how Allport could have been regarded as the culprit, in the critiques made by Mischel (1968) and others (e.g., Endler and Magnusson, 1976) regarding trait theory. Trait theory is supposed to emphasize response repetition across situations, and is therefore at variance with the evidence concerning the importance of person-situation interactions. But no one could have disagreed with this rendition of trait theory more than Allport. The personal traits or dispositions Allport emphasized as the true units of personality were highly specific to individuals, lending only a modicum of consistency to behavior, which consistency could only be discerned through careful, long study of the learning histories of particular persons. In an attempt at magnanimity, Allport (1937) did suggest that common or average traits might have some limited utility in understanding group trends in behavior, but he never assumed such units to have any real status as personality characteristics. Agreeing, Mischel (1973) concludes

> Obviously people have characteristics and overall 'average' differences in behavior between individuals can be abstracted on many dimensions and used to discriminate among persons for many purposes. . . . The available data . . . *do* imply that the particular classes of conditions must be taken into account far more carefully than in the past, tend to be much narrower than traditional trait theories have assumed, and for purposes of important individual decision making, require highly individualized assessments of stimulus meanings.

From the views of at least one eminent figure in the recent person-situation controversy, it appears that the resulting interactionist accord has not broken new ground so much as reaffirmed the Allportian position that it originally misconstrued. Presumably this misconstrual would have been less likely had those participating in the controversy been more avid students of history.

Lest it seem that I have neglected important aspects of Mischel's (1973) recent position, it must be recognized that he advocates what he regards as a reconceptualization of personality. In this, he emphasizes cognitive styles or strategies rather than what he regards as the static units of trait theory. These include encoding strategies and personal constructs, behavior and stimulus-outcome expectancies, subjective-stimulus values, and self-regulatory systems and plans. However useful and exciting his pronouncement may be, it should be recognized that these variables derive very closely from the personality theorizing of Rotter (1964) and Kelly (1955), both of whom were teachers of Mischel—

whose theorizing predates the person-situation controversy. But to know the work of one's teachers does not really testify to an appreciation of history. Indeed, Allport's (1955) propriate functions and stylistic traits include much that is similar to Mischel's emphasis. To a lesser degree, so does the theorizing of Murray (1938), Cattell (1965), Binswanger (1963), Boss (1963), and Frankl (1960). Actually, if there is any validity to the claim of "reconceptualization," it is in the break with psychoanalytic theories. But surely any vigorous appreciation of history would recognize the myriad of personality theories which have been available that are not psychoanalytic.

Recommendations. I do not mean to criticize particular psychologists. Certainly, Mischel, Endler, Magnusson and the others who have participated in the recent person-situation controversy are spirited, talented, productive members of their profession. I have merely tried to show, through the extended example of a recent and exciting spurt of research and writing, how time and effort might have been saved by a greater involvement in history.

Personologists will be encouraged to learn from the past if they develop the kind of appreciation of the aims of their inquiry that was mentioned in the last assertion. Once we are sure of what we should be studying and why, it will seem more natural to learn from others having attempted similar study. The value of studying seminal works of the past is that in this fashion personologists can (1) become more alert to the dimensions and thrusts of traditions they may be working in but not quite appreciating, (2) find a stimulating source of congenial insights, and (3) pinpoint exactly what they cannot agree with in traditions, what feels alien. In this manner, the personologist will be aided in his own attempts to understand, and experience himself as part of a community of scholarship that has a past as well as a present.

Assertion 3: Through vigorous theorizing, one can appreciate the relevance of work in other fields

As indicated above, vigorous theorizing will stimulate an interest in the work of others, either as a source of insight or as a springboard for innovativeness. This interest will be expressed not only historically but also with regard to one's contemporaries. Nor will this interest, whether historical or contemporary, be restricted only to those defined as being within one's own field. The person theorizing vigorously will quickly come to appreciate the special sense in which work outside of one's own field can be stimulating and illuminating. Those in neighboring fields make intellectual assumptions and apply methods of inquiry that are sufficiently at variance with those of one's own field, such that their work is likely to be a source of what William James called "the electric sense of analogy." But it is also quite possible for work in neighboring fields to bear very directly on the validity of formulations in one's own area.

When the commitment to theorizing is passive or minimal, there is little interest in work in neighboring fields. Perhaps one clings faithfully to a particular theory and is therefore little motivated to become familiar with anything else. Or perhaps one regards all knowledge of real value to reside in the data of one's own field, and on that ground has little motivation to look elsewhere for insights. Whichever the reason, work in other fields is likely to appear as irrelevant or distracting unless one is engaged in vigorous theorizing.

Current Personological Practice. As a group, personologists are less interested in work going on in other fields than one would hope. In several other fields, questions very similar to those raised by personologists are being considered. Still other fields concern themselves with aspects of the human organism having importance for personality functioning, even though they make little attempt to actually demonstrate the relevance for personology.

It is certainly true that most personologists have been influenced by work in other fields at some time during their development. Thus, Maslow's early training in animal laboratories remained important to him later. Freud's education as a physician colored his theorizing and influenced his approach to treatment. Certainly, personologists who rely upon experimental designs in their research have been influenced by other fields of psychology and physics in which such approaches are conceived of as the major source of reliable knowledge. It is also true that some personologists regularly monitor ongoing work in other fields. For example, McClelland (1961) remains conversant with economic theory and practice regarding developing nations. Some personologists remain abreast of developments in areas such as medicine and social psychology.

Commonly, however, personologists are content to read their own journals and converse among themselves. Personology is such an integrative field that one would at least expect its psychologists to keep up with other fields of psychology, and its psychiatrists with other fields of medicine. As a general rule, such monitoring occurs little. One could also expect personologists to be conversant with relevant developments in philosophy, physiology, cultural anthropology, and sociology, among the fields at a bit more of a distance from everyday personality study. Very little cross-fertilization from such fields seems to occur.

Recommendations. In order to break up insularity, it will have to be demonstrated that work in other fields is actually relevant to personological concerns, and can help settle issues and deepen insights. One possibility is for the annual conventions of the American Psychological Association, American Psychiatric Association, and similar regional organizations to include on the program persons and work from neighboring fields in some format that will put them in interaction with the personologists in attendance. The guiding themes for such programs could include such questions as: How does the emphasis upon decision-making in the contemporary study of cognition and social interaction articulate with personality theory? How does contemporary philosophical analysis of Freud's writings illuminate psychoanalysis? How does research presently being done on brain function bear on the recent person-situation controversy? To give just a flavor of how such questions might be answered, let me mention some relevant work from neighboring fields.

The eminent philosopher, Ricoeur (1977), has recently engaged in a detailed and sympathetic analysis of Freudian theory and practice. He poses the questions, "Is psychoanalysis an empirical science?" and "Is psychoanalysis a phenomenological approach?" The occasion for the first question is the charge by another philosopher, Nagel (1959), that psychoanalysis utilizes concepts that are incapable of yielding up definite empirical predictions by the process of deductive elaboration so relied upon in science. Rapaport (1958) attempted to reply to that criticism by translating key psychoanalytic concepts into operational statements, and many psychoanalysts felt the scientific status of their discipline preserved. Ricoeur contends that psychoanalysis does not deal in observations but rather interpretations, and hence, that Rapaport's efforts are misguided. Psychoanalysts do not follow their patients around observing what they do and say; they receive their patient's reports of the past (interpretations) and respond to these messages (interpretations again). Not dealing in observations, psychoanalysis should not style itself a science in the ordinary sense. It is more like history. This striking conclusion might seem threatening, but that is far from Ricoeur's intent. For his broad, sophisticated mind, science is only one of several useful methods of inquiry that can help in the betterment of life.

In determining whether psychoanalysis amounts to a phenomenological approach, Ricoeur finds many points of agreement between the two methods. Both assume that initial awareness will not necessarily coincide with final awareness, for the process of reflection stands between the two states. Both make the process of communication and dialogue important. But the two approaches part company on two grounds. First, where the phenomenological method is rather open-ended about what the result of self-reflection shall be, psychoanalysis is committed to the use of self-reflection to investigate hidden desires of a libidinous or aggressive nature. Secondly, the importance of *transference* (the imposition of the therapist of the patient's sexual or aggressive feelings unconsciously appartaining to his parents) in psychoanalysis has no counterpart in phenomenology. Freud (1925a, b) is very clear that the therapist should use the energy of transference love or hate to motivate the patient to go further into self-awareness. In order to do this, the therapist must never give in to the patient's desire, even when it is expressed as a demand. Here psychoanalytic theory and practice come together in a result that is quite unique. Once again, in distinguishing psychoanalysis from an accepted approach to which it bears some similarity, Ricoeur attributes to it important and worthwhile originality. He would not understand why psychoanalysts might wish to be considered phenomenologists.

In concluding that psychoanalysis stands alone as a method of interpretation which is neither observational nor phenomenological, Ricoeur is an appreciative evaluator. He finds strength and vitality in its uniqueness. He regards the question of its validity not at all jeopardized by his conclusions. Validity is a pragmatic matter concerning whether psychoanalysis helps persons. In critiques like this one, done by persons skilled in the evaluation of theories, there is much for personologists to learn.

Shifting from philosophy to biology, we find the general belief in psychology that its viewpoints should make sense in the light of physiological facts. It is all the more surprising, therefore, that work in physiology bearing on the recent person-situation controversy has been almost completely overlooked by those engaged in the debate. Fortunately, Stagner (1976) has organized this work in a manner which illuminates its significance.

The prevailing opinion among neurophysiologists construes the evidence to be against the situationist implication that there are specific responses to specific stimuli. The cortical response evoked by even a highly constant input, such as a flash of monochromatic light, is extremely variable. It appears that repetition of what is objectively the same physical stimulus produces a variety of central nervous system responses. Responses may vary not only as a function of collateral inhibition (effects of simultaneous stimulation in the same or other sensory modalities) but also by ongoing changes in facilitative or inhibitory inputs from other parts of the central nervous system itself (e.g., John & Morgades, 1969).

Further difficulty for extreme situationism is caused by findings (e.g., Pribram, Spinelli, & Kambach, 1967; Spinelli, 1970) to the effect that the cortical response produced by a new stimulus is a function not only of its physical properties but also of the physical properties of stimuli which preceded it. The organism seems to construct neural representations not of single external events but of composites of many events organized along functional lines (Stagner, 1976). Commenting on such findings, Pribram (1969) concludes:

> Somewhere between the retina and the visual cortex the inflowing signals are modified to provide information that is already linked to a learned response, for example, the monkey's intention to press one panel or another. Evidently what reaches the visual cortex is evoked by the external world but is hardly a direct or simple replica of it.

And if this be true of monkeys, how much more do central nervous system processes affect perception in the human?

As if all this were not problem enough for situationism, there are findings (Begleiter, Projesz, Yerra, & Kissin, 1973) indicating the influence of contextual cues upon cortical response to external events. The subject's task was to press one button in response to bright light flashes, and another in response to dim. Bright and dim flashes were also accompanied by distinctive auditory cues. After the training series, subjects received light flashes half way between the original bright and dim flashes. Half of these were accompanied by the auditory cue for bright, and half by the cue for dim. In over 90 percent of trials, not only did the button pressed correspond to the auditory cue, but also–and crucially–the cortical response corresponded to the subjectively reported brightness associated with that cue (rather than to the "actual" brightness of the flash). It would seem that contextual cues are used to convert an ambiguous stimulus into a member of a familiar category not only at the level of motor response but even neural response. Further, there is conscious "misperception" of the stimulus consistent with the motor and neural response.

Accumulating neurophysiological evidence leads away from the notion of specific responses to specific stimuli, and toward an emphasis on generalized patterns of perceiving and responding (Stagner, 1976). This direction is much more consistent with trait theory and interactionist positions than it is with situationism. The neurophysiological evidence was being reported all during the time of the recent person-situation controversy, and is historically linked to the previous work on "gating" (e.g., Bruner, 1957). Why didn't these findings play a role in obviating a controversy found only later to be a pseudo-issue?–presumably, either because participants in the controversy did not know about the findings or because they did not deem it important to integrate work from another area of psychology into their formulations. In either case, there is a failing of vigorous theorizing at the root.

Assertion 4: Through vigorous theorizing, one comes to appreciate the underlying meaning of what is observed

How is the decision reached that enough observational and explanatory effort has occurred for completeness? The standard answer–that one observes and explains until full understanding and predictability has been achieved–is not wholly convincing. This answer only raises the question of how much understanding and predictability is enough to be satisfying? In the final analysis, the end point of inquiry is as much a function of the limits of curiosity of the inquirer as of anything else.

If there is anything certain about vigorous theorizing, it is the associated insatiable curiosity and questioning attitude about observed phenomena. The curiosity takes one form in what may be called descriptive questions, such as "What is this?"; "How is it organized?"; "Can it be changed?"; and "How is it similar to and different than other things?" But, not stopping at the descriptive level, the questions soon shade over into underlying meanings. Common in vigorous theorizing are such questions as, "What is it good for?"; "How did it come about?"; "What are its implications and effects?"; and "Into what overall frame of reference does it fit?" The more vigorous the theorizing effort, the longer and more remote from the obvious specifics of observation is the list of questions generated and answers pursued.

Concomitant with the insatiable questioning inherent in vigorous theorizing is recognition of the underlying implications of assumptions made in the attempt to explain observations. This appreciation of underlying implications is not very common, and is quite striking when encountered. For example, the sociologist Homans (1967) argues that the mere existence of social norms is an insufficient explanation of behavior that conforms to them. Somewhere along the line, the person who conforms to the norms *decides* to do so. A more complete explanation would include recognition that norms are effective only insofar as persons accept them as authoritative and find conforming to them rewarding. Even if most persons do so, the act of acceptance (which is a kind of decision) is an underlying implication of the formulation. Homans even argues that apparently sacrosanct economic formulations, such as the laws of supply and demand, imply decision-making as an underlying process. It is only because persons have decided to value something that its price can increase without a decrease in sales resulting.

Homans is, of course, assuming that at least some persons can make decisions which would invalidate the laws of supply and demand. Lest this appear too naive, it should be recognized that something similar is argued by a distinguished economist, Scitovsky (1976), in his recent extolling of the nonmaterialistic aspects of human nature. But whether or not this particular argument is compelling is not of chief importance here. These examples are raised only to show that even well-accepted formulations that seem complete to many can be questioned further and their underlying assumptions exposed. It is a characteristic of vigorous theorizing to do just this.

These examples are also useful for illuminating an additional feature of vigorous theorizing. Through searching for underlying implications of formulations, vigorous theorizing will usually travel the path of comprehensive, unifying thought rather than so-called middle-level theory. Homans starts with conventional sociological and economic formulations, adds to them psychological implications (e.g., decision-making), and arrives at biological considerations (e.g., organismic bases for positive and negative reinforcements) as well. The end result is a comprehensive view which combines the typical approaches of several social sciences, and which amounts to a statement on human nature and its expressions in the affairs of persons. Homans is not unusual in this. The completeness of middle-level theorizing is illusory. Once the underlying implications of formulations are scrutinized, the movement is rather inexorably toward comprehensive, unifying views.

Another relevant characteristic of vigorous theorizing is the recognition that the act of observation itself involves theorizing. One cannot theorize vigorously without becoming aware that, at the data level, one must classify the phenomena observed if those observations are to have any discernable meaning. As indicated at the outset of this chapter, the classification achieved is simply never the only one possible. Hence, reflection upon one's own actions as an observer alerts one to the theorizing inherent in making data statements. It is impossible to observe uninterpretively and thereby discern objective reality. The most that can be hoped for is consensus among observers, which amounts to agreement that the interpretations involved in defining data are plausible and repeatable. As it is quite valuable (indeed indispensable) to have consensus in observations, vigorous theorizing will lead in the direction of the formulation of rules for describing what is observed (a data language, if you will).

Current Personological Practice. In general, personology, more than other fields of psychology, is characterized by recognition and appreciation of underlying meanings. It is, after all, the field which studies individual differences and individuality, thereby recognizing that persons perceive, respond, value, and decide complexly and idiosyncratically. To the extent that comprehensive, unifying theories exist in psychology, they do so in the personality area. The content of these theories indicates an appreciation of the "overdetermined" character of events and behavior, and concerns such expressions of interest in underlying implications as assumptions regarding human nature. The reliance on such measurement techniques as projective tests, in which the investigator has considerable leeway in defining the subject's responses, indicates the willingness of personologists to regard the act of observation as a creative rather than objective activity.

This is not to say, however, that all personological practice bespeaks the concern with underlying implications characteristic of vigorous theorizing. The comprehensive, unifying theories certainly exist, but they are currently quite unpopular. Academically based personologists in particular regard them as seductive overgeneralizations, and advocate middle-level theorizing as the way of science. Some personologists will do considerable research concerning such variables as internal versus external locus of control and need for achievement without feeling any pressure to theorize generally about human decision-making and its role in reaching overall life-goals. Radical behaviorists define a reinforcement as that which alters the rate of an operant response, without any concern about the content of that reinforcement. Even when it becomes apparent that the class of positive reinforcements involves nutrients and the class of negative reinforcements involves pain and danger, the radical behaviorists will deny any biological or functional definition of reinforcements, insisting that they are discovered empirically and retained because they "work."

Current personological practice is not only moving away from comprehensive, unifying theorizing, but also appears somewhat attracted once again by the notion that one can observe objectively if sufficient care is taken. For example, Fiske (1974) is not only concerned by disagreements in concept formulation, but also by lack of inter-observer agreement in the measurement of behavior. According to him, this disagreement occurs because personality theories define behavior too macroscopically and inaccurately, thereby providing unreliable guides to observation. He advocates dispensing with personality theories, and observing the smallest units of behavior possible in the least interpretive way

In this fashion, he believes personology can chart behavior objectively, and he implicates inter-observer agreement as the appropriate measure of this supposed objectivity.

Fiske points to the work of Duncan (1972) as paradigmatic of the right approach to observation. Utilizing videotapes, Duncan has observed persons interacting together and has abstracted from these data the nonverbal cues or rules whereby signals are given that someone is starting or ending speech. The study does not consider individual differences. It is true that high levels of inter-observer agreement are reported. But a surprisingly great deal of training is necessary for scorers to agree in applying Duncan's rules for observation. If he had somehow arrived at bedrock objectivity, should not agreement among observers be more spontaneous, or at least less arduous to obtain? A rejoinder might be that observers have been so twisted by the personality theories we all have assimilated that they must be "debriefed" in order to observe objectively. Clearly, there is no way of disentangling this interpretational possibility from the one that there is no such thing as objective observation. From the purview of vigorous theorizing, it would appear that a scrutiny of Duncan's data and findings should disclose, in his choice to observe just certain cues for initiating and ending speech, his own subjective construction (theory) of the environment. Similarly, Fiske's proposed direction for personology expresses a behavioristic preference on his part rather than a necessary conclusion for anyone else. One might as easily contend that, with a similarly rigorous regimen for training observers, many of the observational variables currently reporting low inter-observer agreement might emerge as comparable in consensual validity to those of Duncan.

Recommendations. Although personology has traditionally invested in the scrutiny of underlying meanings that leads to comprehensive formulations, it is at present in danger of altering this and adopting a position somewhere between accepting the modest aspirations of middle-level theorizing and embracing the illusion of theory-free objectivity. In order to stop this trend from accelerating, steps must be taken to stimulate realization that observation is an act involving decisions deriving from theoretical considerations, and that comprehensive theories represent a worthy aspiration for personologists.

Greater observational sophistication (and, for that matter, precision) may be gained through a campaign to build a bona fide data language subscribed to by all personologists. At the moment, what passes for a data language is essentially the usage of ordinary parlance (Mandler & Kessen, 1959). Perhaps the only personologist who attempted to devise a data language is Murray (1938), who proposed *proceedings* and *serials* as the important data units. A proceeding is a functionally significant event occupying time and having a definite beginning and end (e.g., a conversation, a daydream). A serial is a functionally organized set of proceedings (e.g., a love affair, a summer vacation). Rudimentary though this attempt at a data language is, there is little else to turn to in contemporary personality study. Occasionally, concepts are confused with observations (e.g., to think that one has observed a superego in a person's decrying of irresponsibility) in a manner that demonstrates by its looseness the crying need for a data language. Concepts are interpretations specific to a particular theory; and when they are confused with a data language, the investigator is acting as if his interpretation of an observation is the only possible one. All one needs is another investigator with another concept confused for data, and one can easily conclude that the data are so unreliable that one should give up the study of personality. All that has occurred, of course, is a confusion of concepts with data.

The campaign to build a data language might begin by instituting a policy whereby all manuscripts submitted for publication must include, in the procedure section, a clear description of the rules that governed observation. These rules should cover not only what was observed, and how, but what was not observed, and why. Once an accumulation of attempts of this sort at a data language has occurred, the next step might be a series of workshops in which participants would consider the pros and cons of their various rules for observation. The aim of all this would be to develop reasonably broad agreement among personologists on a set of data terms and rules for observation. Devised by consensus, this data language would not jeopardize any particular explanatory theory held by one group of personologists or another. Rather, it would formulate data in terms that are agreeable to all major explanatory theories. Indeed, the employment of such a consistent data language would then permit greater clarity in comparison of the explanatory capabilities of various theories, through such principles as parsimony and relevance.

The task of convincing personologists of the dignity in aspiring to comprehensive theories is more difficult because it is less concrete than developing a data language. One thing that will help is to provoke consideration of the aims of personology, as discussed under Assertion 1. In this regard, it should become apparent that personology is, among the various fields of psychology, the one most suited to integrating knowledge from the others into a coherent picture of the whole human being. After all, is there a more important task in psychology?

Convincing personologists of the value of comprehensive theorizing will be aided by demonstration that it can be scientific in the sense of being precise and having implications for research. This will be a difficult task, especially because existing personality theories (which certainly show tendencies in the direction of being comprehensive) are widely believed to be imprecise and limited as stimulants to research. Recently, Maddi (1976) has provided a basis for reconsidering the scientific utility of personality theories. He suggests, among other things, that the typological statements of these theories are rife with empirical implications. For example, Adler (1964) organizes persons into four types: *active-constructive* (which is the ideal), *active-destructive, passive constructive,* and *passive destructive* (which is the most maladjusted). Jung (1933b) favors the typology of *introverted-rational, extroverted-rational, introverted irrational,* and *extroverted irrational.* Rogers (1959) details many stylistic characteristics of the *fully functioning person* as opposed to the *maladjusted person.* Each of these formulations (and many others that could have been selected as examples) has many definite implications for how observed behavior is to be understood. These implications take the form of predictions regarding the co-variation of organization of aspects of behavior both at a given moment in time and over time. Armed with a consensually validated data language with which to describe behavior, researchers could actually test the peripheral statements of personality theories against each other, and in that fashion gain in knowledge concerning the empirical promise of theories. A combination of this kind of research and that to be discussed under the next assertion should, once it begins to accumulate, convince even the most wary that comprehensive theorizing can be scientific.

Assertion 5: Through vigorous theorizing, one can pose issues the resolution of which will advance knowledge

When the emphasis upon theorizing is vigorous, differences of opinion are regarded not only as common but as important as well. Such differences, honestly faced and properly articulated, represent occasions for clarifying debate and incisive research. The emphasis in these endeavors becomes the resolution of issues as the goal of inquiry. When issues are resolved, those committed to vigorous theorizing will embrace the knowledge gained, surrendering or modifying former beliefs so as to assimilate the new insight. Elsewhere (Maddi, 1976), I have referred to this general orientation as comparative analysis.

In extolling comparative analysis, I do not mean to give the impression that it is easy to organize disagreements into sharp issues. Nor is it easy to participate in debate and issue-resolving research. Hardest of all is changing one's views when the knowledge gained through debate and research require that. But vigorous theorizing rapidly convinces one that there is no real alternative to comparative analysis. At that point, one begins to derive from comparative analytic activity the same sort of satisfaction involved in the mastery of any complex behavior requiring concentration and skill. The secondary gain is the rapid advance in the field that will take place once comparative analysis becomes a major mode of inquiry.

A widespread, comparative analytic orientation stimulates development of a field by joining the efforts of persons, rather than permitting the dissipation of their energies in competitive, partisan disputes. This conjoining of efforts toward the end of determining which are the really worthwhile theories in the area spurs development of sophistication as to the essential nature of the field, and determining the best way to express this essence in further theory and practice. The field emerges into a fully mature stage of development when, armed with really trustworthy and effective theories, it applies its knowledge in some way that significantly changes (hopefully improves) the process of living.

Current Personological Practice. It is my impression that personology is in an unnecessarily prolonged infancy (Maddi, 1976). To be sure, there is now and then a controversy in the empirical literature (eg., the person-situation studies). So too are there a few celebrated cases of sharp theoretical disputes (eg., Freud and Jung on whether artistic productivity is a sign of neuroticism or extraordinary fulfillment of human potentiality). By and large, however, personology has not defined itself in terms of issue resolutions. We have had a reasonably coherent set of theories for some time now. Even the occasional theory added to the store already available turns out, on second glance, to be more a rephrasing or elaboration of an earlier one than a new departure. More and more personality research gets done each year, and yet we do not progress at all rapidly toward a time when we will be able to abandon some theories as empirically unviable. This is at least in part because the great preponderance of research is partisan from beginning to end. There are virtually no studies appearing in journals which are conceived explicitly as attempts to resolve issues.

This prolonged infancy of personology has probably been brought about by the de-emphasis on theorizing that began shortly after the major personality theories were first promulgated. The largest factor in this de-emphasis seems to have been radical behaviorism, in which theorizing of any sort is regarded as a wasteful, if not actually dangerous, activity for anyone interested in being scientific. Many academically based personologists were undoubtedly swayed by this view to the belief that personality theories are too broad and abstract to ever permit precise predictions and empirical tests. This abandonment of comprehensive theories seemed more advantageous than expending effort toward their further development. Without commitment to and practice of vigorous theorizing, there is little chance that comparative analytic activity will develop.

The delayed appearance of a comparative analytic orientation has had deleterious effects. The many disagreements inevitably contained in a field with as many different theories as personology have remained unresolved long enough to fester. By now, these disagreements are beginning to seem to some as signs of confusion and failure. For example, Fiske (1974) argues that the disagreements among personality theorists concerning the definition and usage of what should be semantically similar concepts is a major basis for invalidating the concepts themselves. If there is so much confusion as to what a concept is, then the behavioral consistency that the concept purports to describe probably does not exist, and the concept itself is an obstacle to clear observation. In a recent review article, Sechrest (1976) takes a similar view in an extremely pessimistic portrayal of the field. For these and no doubt other personologists, disagreements provide yet another basis for deciding that personality does not exist and is futile to study.

Recommendations. Steps need to be taken to hasten a comparative analytic orientation in as many personologists as possible. With so many disagreements existing, an appropriate and practical way of redefining the personality field is in terms of major issues separating theories. In this fashion, the posing and resolving of issues in debate and research will become a much more central activity of personologists than has been true. For the existing generation of personologists, this shift in emphasis toward issues can be encouraged through conferences and workshops organized carefully to place disagreements in an overall intellectual frame of reference. Personality courses should also be taught from a comparative analytic viewpoint, so that new generations of personologists will be well equipped for posing and resolving issues. The necessary research designs and rules of debate are already available for issue resolution. What is needed is a recognition of its importance as a mode of inquiry.

Maddi (1976) has employed the comparative analytic approach on a large number of personality theories. They seemed classifiable into three models, each with two versions. Issues based on disagreements among these models were pinpointed.

The conflict model proposes that human behavior is best understood as expressive of two constant and inevitably opposed forces, in the face of which compromise is necessary and adaptive. The psychosocial version of this model, best exemplified by Freud (1925c, 1952) sees one great force as originating in the individual (the id) and the other as originating in society (the common good as defined by taboos and sanctions). Psychosocial conflict theories see an antagonism between the individual (regarded as basically antisocial) and society (regarded as necessarily repressive), and conclude that the individual must be socialized to conform with social norms and values if a satisfying and effective life is to be achieved. It is this kind of thinking that led Freud to regard some personality types (e.g., oral, anal, phallic) as immature because insufficiently socialized (pregenital), and one type (the genital) as ideal in the sense of having overcome infantile (antisocial) expressions of the instincts. On balance, the theories of Murray (1938) and most ego psychologists (e.g., Erikson, 1951) are still more expressive of the psychosocial conflict model than other forms of thought.

The intrapsychic version of the conflict model, notably exemplified by Jung (1933a, 1953), locates both great forces within the person. The human being emerges from such formulations as a house divided, in the sense that each great force clamors for maximum expression and is incompatible with expression of the other. Effective life entails not only accepting the fact of one's contradictory nature, but also arranging a compromise whereby each force is expressed only to the degree that is consistent with expressing the other as well. The basic expression of the intrapsychic conflict model in Jung's theory is the assumption that the conscious mind (which he defines as the *ego*) is inevitably opposed to the *collective unconscious* (defined as essences or primordial images, which have never been and can never be conscious, and through their presence in all persons represent universal but uncontrollable sources of energy and strength). Styles of life favoring expression of the ego or the collective unconscious to the detriment of expression of the other are ineffective and immature because onesided. Selfhood, the Jungian ideal, involves accepting the existence of both ego and collective unconscious, and attempting expression of both in a life that will be characterized by rational mastery along with uncontrolled intuitive functioning. Other intrapsychic conflict theorists are Rank (1945), Angyal (1951), and Bakan (1966).

In contrast to the conflict model, the fulfillment model assumes only one great force, and explains human functioning as the progressively greater expression of that force (Maddi, 1976). Compromise is never ideal according to this model, and occurs when society has interposed obstacles to individual development. Such obstacles need not occur, however; and if they do not, then complete fulfillment of the person will ensue. Fulfillment theorists are natural social critics, and extoll individuality, whereas conflict theorists tend to regard social restrictions as necessary in order to curb anti- (or at least a-) social tendencies present in the individual.

The actualization version of the fulfillment model, best exemplified by Rogers (1956, 1961), defines the great force as the tendency to actualize the potentialities contained in a sort of genetic blueprint. If the person receives unconditional positive regard from the significant others (such as parents) with whom he interacts, he will become an ideal (fully functioning) person (trusting himself, living spontaneously, changing continuously). But if the person is misfortunate enough to experience conditional positive regard from significant others, he will become maladjusted (distrusting himself, living in a stereotyped way, never changing). Another theorist who is more in the actualization camp than anywhere else is Maslow (1955).

The perfection version of the fulfillment model, notably exemplified by existential psychology (May, 1958; Binswanger, 1963; Boss, 1963; Kobasa & Maddi, 1977), defines the great force as the attempt to reach a developmental pinnacle through strenuous striving. Whereas the emphasis in the actualization version is on surrendering undefensively to an organismically conditioned fleshing-out of a genetic blueprint, the emphasis in the perfection version is on overcoming human frailties through decision-making and striving in order to reach a consciously appreciated sense of the good life. Through making decisions oriented toward the future, a person becomes increasingly authentic, according to existential psychologists, showing individuality, subtlety, differentiation, and relating intimately with others and actively with social institutions. When decisions are made so that the status quo is maintained, the person eventually becomes inauthentic, showing conventionality, grossness, stereotypy, and relating contractually with others and conformingly with social institutions.

Other theorists expressing the perfection version of the fulfillment model are Adler (1964), White (1960), Allport (1955) and Fromm (1947).

Finally, the consistency model is quite different from the other two (Maddi, 1976). No great, unchanging force is postulated. Rather, the basic assumption is that of negative feedback. There is some sort of norm resulting from experience, and the events of any given moment may be consistent or inconsistent with it. Consistency brings quiescence, the inconsistency triggers attempts to reestablish consistency. In this fashion, all human behavior is to be understood as a kind of rational trial-and-error.

The cognitive-dissonance version of the consistency model, best exemplified by Kelly (1955), hinges on the adequacy of personal constructs as bases for predicting events. Inaccuracies of prediction bring anxiety and attempts to alter the constructs, such that prediction will be improved in the future. This dynamic principle, plus various characteristics of personal constructs (e.g., permeability, generality), give individual personalities their particular quality. The activation version of the consistency model, best exemplified by Fiske and Maddi (1961), refers to the customary (or characteristic) level of activation as the norm, and to the actual (or momentary) level of activation as that which contrasts with the norm. Through learning, persons come to differ in the magnitude of customary level of activation. Those who are relatively high, spend most of their time attempting to correct for actual levels of activation that are too low; and those who are relatively low do the opposite. This distinction, and several others, permit the statement of a number of personality types.

In considering the three models, each with two versions, it is possible to discern several issues. Those discussed by Maddi (1976) are: Is all behavior defensive?; Is the highest form of living adaptive or transcendent?; Is cognitive dissonance invariably unpleasant and avoided?; Is all behavior in the service of tension reduction?; Does personality show radical change after the childhood years have been passed? Various personality theories are on one side or another of most of these issues. For example, Freud would regard all behavior as defensive and in the service of tension reduction. Further, he would regard radical change after childhood as rare (especially outside of psychotherapy), and would emphasize adaptiveness as the mark of ideal development. In contrast, Rogers would consider only some behavior to be defensive and in the service of tension reduction. The highest form of behavior for him would be transcendent, and continually changing even after the childhood years. Existential psychologists would agree with Rogers, but also regard cognitive dissonance as not invariably unpleasant and avoided. Many further examples could be given.

Of major significance is the possibility that such issues could be the subject of carefully planned research. The accumulated results of studies aimed at issue resolution could, in a short period of time, provide personologists with a basis for deciding which of the available theories are the most fruitful. Then energies could be directed toward further development of these theories, and those less fruitful could be discarded. Maddi (1976) claims that even existing research can provide some basis for evaluation of theories. But such evaluations are not conclusive, because the relevance of existing research to the issues is sometimes a matter of considerable interpretation. Conclusive evaluation remains for a time when there is a corpus of findings deriving from research aimed squarely at issue resolution. Although Maddi has formulated issues that appear relevant, they are not the only ones imaginable. Nor are the models he proposes the only way in which existing personality theories can be classified. There is room for and need of considerably more emphasis upon comparative analytic functioning.

Assertion 6: Through vigorous theorizing, one can appreciate what measurement operations and research designs are central to personality study

It is often said that the history of science is a chronology of methodological advances. Though containing much truth, this view must be understood in perspective. The scientists and philosophers of science taking this view accept that major theoretical directions and issues exist and are appreciated by many if not all investigators. Therefore, the stumbling block to the knowledge with which to solve problems and resolve issues becomes methodological. It is precisely because the methodological tail does not wag the theoretical dog that investigators can concentrate on problems of measurement, research design, and data analysis, considering their solution to be breakthroughs. It is with the direction lent by theory that investigators can gracefully face the months and sometimes years of arduous work in search of appropriate, workable methods.

To the vigorous theorizer, measurement operations and research designs are not limited in number or given in a manual, but rather are as numerous as can be invented so as to be relevant to some theoretically defined problem. According to this view, theoretical concepts have a meaning determined by linguistic usage (Mandler & Kessen, 1959) that is definite and unalterable. Measurement operations must be selected so as to be appropriate to the meaning of concepts. Take, for example, Rogers's (1959) concept of *organismic trusting,* which refers to a predisposition to make decisions and take actions on the basis of emotional reactions to events. This concept must be appreciated in the entire context of Rogers's personality theory, which emphasizes actualized functioning (of which organismic trusting is a sign) as involving a conscious understanding of self. In measuring organismic trusting, it would make little sense to employ projective tests. Because organismic trusting by definition involves a keen appreciation of the importance of using emotional reactions as guides to decision-making and action, the indirectness involved in asking subjects to compose stories about other persons is actually a potential source of measurement error. Projective tests are presumably best for providing information about aspects of personality that are either rendered unconscious through the action of defenses, or at least rendered beyond the subject's conscious appreciation by virtue of an unsophisticated outlook on life and self. It would be much more consistent with Rogers's emphasis to measure organismic trusting in direct self-description.

Among available techniques of direct self-description, questionnaires would seem less relevant than autobiographical statements. This is because Rogers (1961) insists that the subject knows himself better than any investigator can, and hence, it is too distorting to force subjects to twist their experience into a form permitting the answer of questions formulated by investigators. Any psychometrician will wax eloquent about the measurement vagaries of autobiographical statements. But, as they are theoretically relevant, engaging in vigorous theorizing would increase the likelihood of spending time and effort improving their precision and reliability, rather than substituting something less appropriate because it is initially sounder methodologically. It is in this context that one might understand the history of science as intimately associated with methodological advance.

Theorizing vigorously encourages a similar attitude toward research design. He would appreciate the strong and weak points of various designs for particular theoretically defined tasks. If an appropriate design does not exist for testing a theoretical formulation, he would try to invent one. What would be avoided at any cost is the reliance upon an inappropriate design because it has proven valuable in another area or has the trappings of scientific respectibility. For example, experimental designs are especially valuable for determining the effects of one or a very small number of external events on behavior. A treatment might be applied to one group of subjects, and their subsequent behavior compared to that of another group comparable in all ways except not receiving the treatment. Pure experimental designs are not useful for studying (1) individual differences in the perception of and reaction to external events, (2) the organization of various aspects of behavior into personal styles, or (3) the influence of persons on external events (Bowers, 1973). The weakness of experimental designs is precisely in the areas of most importance for personality study. Correlational designs are much more useful in studying the organization of aspects of behavior into styles (Cronbach, 1957). For studying individual differences and the influence of persons on external events, either correlational designs or modified experimental designs, in which both external events and individual differences variables are included, should be valuable (Bowers, 1973). To give an example of the latter, groups of persons high and low in the personality variable, need for achievement, could be selected for study. One half of each group could receive the experimental treatment of being subjected to a competitive examination, while the other half does not receive this treatment. The behavior of interest might be number of examination problems worked on per unit of time. Such a modified experimental design permits one to determine the effect of the external situation of competitive examinations, the personality variable of need for achievement, and the interaction between the two.

Current Personological Practice. There exist side-by-side in personology both attempts to extend methodology to fit theoretical requirements and attempts to fit theoretical concerns into existing, accepted methodology. This situation is not new, having apparently characterized much of the history of the field as to selection of both measurement operations and research designs.

Concerning measurement operations, Freud and other early psychoanalysts showed methodological ingenuity in assuming that the most valid information about personality comes through free associations in the context of psychotherapy. This assumption is a direct expression of the theoretical view that only in extremely private, secure situations where critical faculties are relaxed will the defensive, image-maintaining tendencies of humans be circumvented enough to expose the underlying (and presumably more real) aspects of personality. That this approach has not been taken too seriously by researchers stems in part from the jeopardy to accurate measurement constituted by (1) the therapist's typical use of his own memory as a recording device, and (2) the possibility that the therapist influences the verbalizations of his patient. Nonetheless, the use of psychotherapy sessions is theoretically relevant. It is to the credit of Rogerians that, agreeing on this relevance, they have been conscientious about accuracy of recording through such techniques as videotaping. But the problem of therapist influences on clients is still thorny.

For some personality theories, psychotherapy sessions are not the most valid sources of information, because the mental difficulties (e.g., neurosis, psychosis) dealt with in psychotherapy are not regarded as expressive of human nature. The need of a basis for getting behind image-maintenance tendencies without resorting to the psychotherapy session was one factor leading to the development of projective tests. Murray (1943) displayed considerable ingenuity in devising the Thematic Apperception Test, a projective technique whereby subjects express their inner needs by composing stories about persons depicted on cards. Projective techniques have continued to be popular in clinical practice, but have been assaulted by psychometricians as unreliable and subject to inter-scorer disagreement. This concern with the imprecision of projective tests is one factor in the gradual ascendancy of questionnaires in personality research. Questionnaires seemed to be worth depending upon to many because of their accepted use in intelligence and attitude measurement. The ascendancy of questionnaire methodology has persisted despite accumulating evidence that response biases, such as acquiescence and socially desirable responding, may severely jeopardize the validity of such approaches to personality measurement (e.g., Jackson & Messick, 1958). The general (though by no means proven) belief that questionnaires are the best and easiest way to measure personality has led to their use in areas of dubious relevance. For example, their use to measure defenses must surely be a more indirect, inferential, and problematical approach than is involved in projective tests. Although it is admittedly easier to construct reliable questionnaires than projective measures, the latter have greater theoretical relevance with regard to many personality constructs. The blanket reliance upon questionnaire methodology would clearly seem strange indeed to a vigorous theorizer.

In the process of presenting a modern-day justification of projective methodology, McClelland (1958) has also made valuable suggestions concerning the theoretically relevant use of various measurement approaches. He argued that the motive construct has the following important characteristics that should guide measurement decisions: (1) that the measure refer to striving toward a goal, (2) that it reflect at least momentary satiation when the goal is reached, and (3) that it concern personal rather than societal goals. He organizes available findings persuasively to indicate that projective measures of motives are the only ones that meet all three theoretical criteria. Questionnaire measures typically show little or no correlation with projective measures of the needs for achievement, and such measure has a different set of correlates in behavior (McClelland, 1958). Scrutiny of these results suggests that projective measures tap personal goals whereas questionnaire measures tap societal (image-maintenance) goals. In this openness to whatever measurement conclusions seem warranted from the interplay of theory and findings, McClelland exemplifies vigorous theorizing. Happily, several measurement authorities (e.g., Fiske, 1971; Wiggins, 1973) have attempted to generalize McClelland's position in the direction of a classification of the characteristics (including strengths and weaknesses) of various measurement approaches.

There have been a number of other innovative attempts to develop theoretically relevant methodology in the personality area. In an era of nomothetic (average) measurement, Allport (1937) was often the lone champion of morphogenic (individualistic) attempts, though he seems to have been joined of late by Mischel (1973). More recently, Allport (1962) could at least summarize a few approaches that seemed relevant to pinpointing individuality. Also, productive use has occasionally been made of the subject's actions in performance situations (e.g., Allport & Vernon, 1933). Measurement of action in personology is somewhat unusual, but particularly relevant to behavioristic theories.

Despite occasional signs of innovativeness in measurement, there is a disturbing tendency on the part of conservative methodologists to throw the baby out with the bath water. The most notable instance of this in recent years results from the contention that the reliability of personality measures is generally too low (Mischel, 1968; Fiske, 1974). This has led Fiske (1974) to conclude that personality constructs are by their nature too broad in definition to refer to any actually occurring, consistent behaviors. He advocates giving up personality theorizing in favor of supposedly uninterpretive observation of small behavioral units.

The conclusion that unreliability of measures demonstrates the unavoidable flaws of personality theorizing is serious and should be scrutinized carefully. Clearly, it is not the only conclusion possible. If measures are too unreliable, the fault could as easily lie with the measurement operations as with the personality theorizing. After all, personality theorizing is done by experts who generally base their statements on extensive observation and reflection. To scoff at this is to assume that we know all there is to know about adequate measurement, a position no vigorous theorizer would want to endorse.

In evaluating Fiske's conclusion, careful consideration should be given to how low the reliability of a measure can be before it must be regarded as insufficient. The answer to this question should not be looked for anywhere but within the personality theories that have defined the constructs being measured. Would a measure with perfect reliability be desirable? What would be measured in such a case is something that by definition does not change. Most, if not all, personality theories consider personality characteristics to develop, result from, interact with, and influence social and environmental events. A definite implication of this is that personality characteristics change at least to some degree. For example, if one asked a subject his opinion on something, one would expect that opinion to change more from first testing to second than would his response to a query regarding his name. So a personality measure with perfect reliability would clearly not be the goal.

In order to determine the level of reliability that is too low for comfort, one must still turn to the personality theory instigating the measurement attempt. A careful reading of the theorizing concerning certain types of personality variables indicates that a surprisingly large amount of unreliability can be tolerated. The motive concept, for example, is defined as waxing and waning, depending upon levels of satisfaction or frustration (e.g., Murray, 1938; McClelland, 1958), and therefore carries within it considerable expectation of change from testing time to testing time. Indeed, as mentioned before, McClelland (1958) considers motive measurement to be inappropriate if it does not take into account the satiability built into the concept. On this basis, he argues that the rather low reliability of projective measures of need for achievement is desirable—if it can be shown to stem from the momentary satiation that comes about through the act of fantasizing about relevant behaviors and successes. Atkinson (1958) correlated the need for achievement scores obtained on each story of the projective measure with that of each other story. The results indicate a kind of saw-toothed effect, in which writing a story high in the need for achievement seems to satiate one momentarily, leading to the immediately following story being low in the need; the story immediately following this is high again, and so forth. This effect occurs in most persons, regardless of their overall score on need for achievement. In this case, the modest reliability of fantasy-measures of the need is desirable because it stems from a theoretically expected waxing and waning.

This is not to say that all personality constructs are defined in terms of such substantial levels of moment-to-moment change. Certainly, traits, for example, denote reasonable (though by no means complete) stability over time. But it is not a simple repetition of responses that is denoted in most trait definitions. As mentioned earlier, trait theorists tend to take the interaction between persons and situations into account much more than one would realize from the literature framing the recent person-situation controversy. Allport (1962), for example, considered personal dispositions to be underlying characteristics that render many stimuli and responses (that need not have any obvious connection) functionally equivalent. A personal disposition is also fairly unique to an individual. In order to develop a theoretically adequate measure of a personal disposition, the investigator must observe a person for a period of time before making measurement decisions, and must then plan a measure recognizing that the disposition under consideration will manifest itself in different ways in different situations. According to Allport (1962), the typical measures of traits are quite inadequate for anything but average measurements. For him, the average describes no one very well, and hence he would not have been surprised in the slightest by the general unreliability of available trait measures. But in contrast to Fiske and Mischel, Allport would have laid the fault at the feet of those investigators who did not take theorizing seriously enough to attempt relevant measurement. It is probably true that some trait theorists emphasize response repetition more and individuality less than Allport; but even they have regarded the manifestation of traits to be more complex than has been admitted by most investigators. In this context, the general unreliability of measures is either irrelevant, in that the measures are inappropriate to the theories and are therefore of little interest, or is understandable, stemming from erroneous attempts to translate theory into measurement. In either case, there is little justification for deciding that personality does not exist and should not be the subject of theorizing and measurement efforts.

In turning to personological practice in the area of research design, we find the same mixed picture as in measurement approach. Among psychologists, personologists have been rather ingenious in tailoring research designs to theoretical directives. Correlational designs, with their emphasis on determining which perceptions, feelings, and actions go together, have been used more in personology than anywhere else; so too for the case-study approach, with its utility in pinpointing individuality by studying one person over a significant period of time. But the traditional experimental design has also been firmly entrenched in personality study, despite its inadequacy for disclosing individual differences, interactions between person and situation, and frank person influences on situations. As indicated earlier, much of the recent contention that person variables are unimportant stems from reliance upon an experimental approach which prejudges the issue and is therefore inappropriate. Fortunately, there seems to be a gathering interest in that modified form of the experiment which includes both treatments (situational effects) and person variables (in the form of groups differing in motives, traits or other personality characteristics) as they effect behavior. The modified experiment is certainly more relevant to personological concerns, being especially useful in studying the interaction between persons and situations.

Recommendations. More personologists should realize that there is nothing magical about measurement approaches and research designs. They should be utilized, modified, or invented to fulfill the directives from personality theorizing. Certainly, care should be taken to determine and ensure the effectiveness of measurement approaches and research designs, but the criteria of effectiveness should derive from theoretical needs.

Personologists will be aided in taking this attitude by recommendations made earlier that involve increasing reliance upon theorizing itself. But they will also be aided with regard to measurement approaches by generally accepted knowledge concerning the strengths and weaknesses of the various existing procedures from the point of view of personological aims. In this regard, insights of the sort available in McClelland (1958) and Fiske (1971) should be emphasized in teaching and by journal editors. Something similar is feasible regarding research design. Emphasis in teaching and editing should be on an appreciation of the strengths and weakness of designs for the personological job at hand. This attitude will be furthered by highlighting unusual uses of designs, such as correlations over a time period so that causal inferences are possible (e.g., McClelland, 1961), and modified experiments permitting study of the interaction between person and situation (e.g., Moos, 1969). The insights in such unusual measurement and design approaches, coupled with an increased reliance on theorizing in general, should stimulate ingenuity.

Assertion 7: Through vigorous theorizing, one can recognize and fulfill an ethical task

In discussion of other assertions, it has become clear that vigorous theorizing in the personality area will sooner or later lead to concern with the goals of inquiry. Substantively, this will involve interest in individual differences and the underlying meanings of observed behavior. With such concerns, it is inevitable that vigorous theorizing will lead to evaluation of the strengths and weaknesses of different life styles encountered. Whether the criteria of evaluation appear initially biological (e.g., that is best which leads to physical survival) or social (e.g., that is best which leads to adjustment to norms), the enterprise is finally ethical. To recognize this, one need only appreciate the possibility of deciding against physical survival (e.g., martyrdom) or adjustment (e.g., confrontation politics). To turn away from such criteria as survival or adjustment is essentially an ethical matter.

It is understandable in this context that the comprehensive theories of personality delineate, from among the styles of life they recognize, one that is considered a developmental ideal (e.g., genital character for Freud, selfhood for Jung, fully functioning person for Rogers, active-constructive type for Adler, the productive orientation for Fromm, authenticity for existentialism). The respective ideals represent the kind of life valued by the theorist and his followers.

Hardly to be avoided, such ethical judgments are part of what it means to theorize vigorously about the human condition. The search for life's meaning has always arisen from and been guided by the wish to live well.

Nor would the vigorous theorizer be faint hearted about the practical application of personological evaluations in everyday life. Having been as conscientious as possible in the decision about which way of functioning is ideal, he would endorse efforts to educate persons toward that way. Therapy and assessment, those two principal applications of personology, would seem worthwhile activities to the vigorous theorizer. It would be important for the therapy or assessment to apply well a carefully arrived-at personality theory, for which there is sufficient empirical support to warrant a provisional conclusion that it is promising. To refrain from doing therapy and assessment until some glorious future in which the empirical validity of personological formulations will be apparent beyond any doubt is, in the context of vigorous theorizing, to shirk one's responsibility as a supposed expert in human affairs. As long as persons suffer and fear that they are not living well, the personologist has a moral obligation by virtue of the work he has taken on to minister as best he can to these needs. In the face of such responsibility, he does not have the leisure to sit back and wait for the gradual accumulation of evidence which may someday leave no doubt regarding theoretical formulations.

This is not to say that the personologist need have no qualms whatsoever about the provisional status of the formulations he applies. It would be best if practice were restricted to only the therapies and assessments of theoretical formulations that have achieved considerable empirical validation. Though some time away, that goal will seem valuable to a vigorous theorizer. In the meanwhile, practice can only be justified on the basis of the sincere efforts of the personologist to gain as much relevant knowledge as possible, and the associated belief that he will therefore be able to do some good. The practitioner must present himself this way to his client in order for the vigorous theorizer to conclude that the final moral responsibility has been met. What the practitioner will have accomplished in this way is to admit publically the provisional nature of his formulations and to encourage the client to decide whether he wants to proceed with the therapy or assessment.

Current Personological Practice. Academically based personologists currently tend to avoid theorizing evaluatively about the ideal life, and certainly do not recognize any public obligation in this area. The comprehensive personality theories, of course, all include reference to a personality type that is ideal. But these theories play a less central role in personality study than they did previously. At the present time, personology is typified by middle-level theorizing and research conducted on particular behavioral correlates of particular personality characteristics (e.g., internal versus external locus-of-control work). Although it is possible to derive implications from this work for evaluations of life styles, most personologists do not engage actively in such endeavors.

When evaluations of life style do get made, it is usually in the guise of the notion of mental health and illness. Although this notion is still used by practitioners, it is under a cloud conceptually, following years of serious criticism from the "anti-psychiatry" (e.g., Szasz, 1961; Rosenhan, 1973) and "anti-labeling" (e.g., Goffman, 1958; Scheff, 1963) movements. These movements have been very useful in alerting personologists to the fact that their judgments of mental health or illness emanate from values (masquerading as objective conclusions) concerning the good life rather than from biological (medical) or social (conventional) necessities of living. In other words, the essentially ethical status of evaluations of life styles has been laid bare. This expression of vigorous theorizing can only be regarded as beneficial to the field, however painful it may be in the short run.

But for some personologists, the recognition that evaluations of life styles are value laden has resulted in an unwillingness to evaluate at all. If personological evaluations amount to victimization either by the power elite (as claimed by the "anti-psychiatry" movement) or by the masses (as claimed by the "anti-labeling" movement), then it is better to accept persons appreciatively in their triumphs and tragedies. But this extreme reaction essentially denies any value to theorizing about personality and its development. Carried too far, it obviates all analysis of underlying meanings of behavior. There is finally no point to identifying individual differences if no investigation of their relative strengths and weaknesses is permissible. Such excessive reactions are inconsistent with vigorous theorizing because they stifle curiosity by regarding some possible conclusions to be inappropriately hurtful. The dilemma of how to theorize about the good life, without victimizing persons, badly needs solution.

Turning to attitudes concerning the importance of practicing therapy and assessment, we find personologists divided. Those engaged in practice obviously approve of what they are doing, and they are a goodly number. Many influential, academically based personologists, however, regard practice skeptically, and are wary of involving themselves in the training of practitioners. The academically based personologists fear that practitioners give up thinking, that their methods do not work and go unevaluated, and that to practice is to engage in the victimization discussed above. On their part, practitioners regard their work as all that is of real value in personology, and see their struggle to find effective methods as on a higher moral plane than the "ivory-tower" play of their academically based colleagues. It is not so terrible that this difference of opinion exists. What is unfortunate is that the issues separating the two camps are never really joined in constructive fashion. Each camp keeps more or less to itself, not being willing to risk a confrontation. The existence of disagreement is hardly inconsistent with vigorous theorizing; but the failure to structure it as an issue and work toward its resolution is.

The final consideration of ethical importance concerns the practice of therapy and assessment. Very few practitioners care to recognize that they influence their clients toward a particular view of the good life, and that this view is held more on the basis of expert opinion than demonstrated fact. Most practitioners feel that their views of what will lead the client to fulfillment have been demonstrated resoundingly either in systematic research or in clinical experience. The truth of the matter is that outcome research finds virtually all psychotherapies studied to show a modest, equivalent amount of ability to alleviate symptoms (e.g., Eysenck, 1952, 1966). Also, it seems very easy for persons in authority to influence the behavior of those who are not (e.g., Frank, 1961; Truax, 1966).

Protestations to the contrary, currently practiced psychotherapy probably does influence clients, and cannot be justified on the basis of unequivocal facts. Academically based personologists respond to this by detaching themselves from the practice of therapy. This reaction is as unrealistic as that of the practitioner who merely insists that his therapy is bolstered by fact and that his only role is catalyst to the client's self-determined direction (Maddi, 1973). There is currently little attempt on the part of therapists to systematically disclose their particular view of the good life to clients as a sincere, expert opinion but not an unequivocal, demonstrated fact. This state should be difficult for a vigorous theorizer to accept.

Recommendations. It is important that more personologists theorize deeply and systematically about what constitutes the good life, and that the resulting views be debated and researched. Helpful in the initial theorizing will be knowledge of work in such relevant fields as philosophy (see Assertion 3), where considerable attention has been given to questions of human fulfillment. Then the recommendations made under Assertion 5 for organizing theoretical disagreements into issues for resolution can be applied. Of particular value in resolving issues regarding which personality types are ideal is research that starts with behavior regarded by many relevant theories to be noteworthy. Then the predominant personality type(s) expressing this noteworthy behavior can be determined as a way of resolving issues. For example, persons showing the noteworthy behavior called creativity can be studied in order to determine their personality type. Freudian, Rogerian, existential, and other theories would differ as to what the results of each investigation should show. What personology has to gain through such research is greater understanding of the strengths and weaknesses of various life styles.

One attitude retarding the development of sophisticated views on the good life conceptualizes personality study as an investigation of that which exists rather than that which is possible. Science, it is said, can only determine the way things are—everything else is speculation better left to philosophers and novelists. The trouble is that personology is so deeply involved with practice, with the attempt to help persons live better, that this attitude about what is scientific often leads to advocating the statistically average life as the only worthwhile way to be. What started out being an unnecessarily conservative view of the nature of scientific inquiry becomes a value put upon conformity. None of this is necessary. Personologists could easily enact a psychology of possibility (Maddi, 1976), in which rare and admirable persons are selected for study, with the results serving as a model for the rest of us. Maslow (1955) used such an approach in his study of self-actualized persons. The difficulty is that his procedure for selecting subjects and studying them was very informal and vague. Such studies convince no one and strengthen the view that possibility is not a fit subject for scientific effort. But there is no reason why rare persons could not be carefully selected and rigorously studied. The answers to questions such as "What constitutes their rarity?"; "How did they get to be the way they are?"; and "What are the differences between them and more usual persons?" can provide empirical guidance for the personologist in his heavy but important responsibility to point the way to persons struggling to live in the best possible manner.

It is also important that the ideally unitary nature of theory, research, and practice be better implemented. Education for theoretical and research activities should not occur separately from education for practice. A similar viewpoint prevailed some years ago as the Boulder Model (to commemorate the place where the planning conference met). This approach was subsequently judged to have been a failure, though I think this conclusion to have been premature. It is, probably, much more difficult to conduct education for theory, research, and practice in an integrated fashion than separately. Also, integrative educational attempts will probably only have maximum effect on students predisposed to regard all three functions as important. None of this should be a deterrent to integrative education. It may well be that if attempts at integrative education are combined with education for vigorous theorizing, more frequent success will result. In any event, the contemporary move toward segregating theory and research training in Ph.D. programs and practical training in D.Psy. programs seems unwise. It is only if the values and institutional arrangements exist whereby there can be easy interplay among theorizing, research, and practice that personology will grow vigorously and fulfill its obligation to help needy persons.

Finally, it is necessary that those doing therapy and assessment make a more complete disclosure to their prospective clients than is common these days. Recognizing that when therapy is successful, clients change, the disclosure should include (1) admission that there are many forms of therapy and assessment and that they differ in their views of the good life; (2) presentation of the intellectual and personal reasons whereby the practitioner deems the procedures he will employ worthwhile and effective; (3) admission that at the present time no one therapy or assessment technique emerges from the research literature as definitely better than the others; and (4) the necessity for the prospective client to decide whether the form of therapy or assessment being offered is consistent with his values and goals in life (Maddi, 1973). Through such a disclosure and informed consent, the practitioner will have to clarify for himself and others just what he does and why he does it, and the client will have to make a meaningful commitment that endorses certain proposed changes in his life style. This procedure gives recognition to the essentially ethical nature of not only the personological enterprise, but of life decisions in a more general sense.

The frank disclosure recommended may be distasteful to some therapists because their faith is so deep in their position. Others may deem the procedure unwise, recognizing that a definite asset in convincing the client to lead a new way of life is to make it seem as if he discovered it himself. These reactions are not serious obstacles to what I am proposing. One can overcome distaste and forego craftiness if one recognizes clearly that to not do so is to be unethical.

Many therapists should be able to manage making a disclosure and obtaining informed consent, because they do not seriously disagree with the conclusion that what they do is teach their own views of the good life to their clients. But there are some therapeutic approaches that specifically deny this conclusion, and their practitioners will be sorely pained by what I am saying.

One such approach is the overly eclectic, pragmatic attitude in which the therapist contends that he does "whatever is needed" to help his client recover, and justifies what has been done in terms of its having "worked." Such a practitioner would have difficulty communicating his view of the good life at the outset of therapy; he does not have a consistent one, but borrows something from a theory here and a technique there, as he reacts rather mindlessly to concrete problems. Is the client in a mental hospital? Then do what gets him out. Is he having trouble with his boss? Then help him ease the difficulty fast. Is he depressed? Then do whatever removes that mood. There is no grand design, and so there is nothing to communicate. But like all excessively practical approaches, this one borders on immorality, in the light of evidence that therapists remake clients in their own image. Such practitioners should scrutinize and juxtapose all of their various reactions to clients' problems, and hope through such analysis to discover the various fragments of views on the good life that they rely upon. Then they can concern themselves with resolving possible incompatibilities among the fragments by serious thought, discussion, reading, and research. Only in this fashion will they have a chance of emerging with some consistent sense of what life is all about, so this can be communicated to clients. It is no defense of the excessively practical approach to cite the enormous social needs that make abstract inquiry seem a luxury. This is no more than a restatement of the excessively practical orientation that is the difficulty in the first place. Very few of the insights and theories that have produced significant advances in the history of human beings would have been possible had not some persons engaged in vigorous theorizing despite everyday pressures.

Other approaches having special difficulty with a procedure of disclosure and informed consent are those which insist that the therapist does nothing more than implement the goals of his client. Rogerians, for example, insist that the client knows himself best, and that the therapist's role is restricted to creating the conditions for relaxation of defenses by appreciating, truly hearing, and approving of the client. As clients recover, it is presumed that they will not only develop individualistically, but will also all share the characteristics of "fully functioningness," such as openness to experience, existential living, organismic trusting, and spontaneity. The therapist never imagines that these characteristics are there because he has subtly conditioned his client. They are believed to emerge because they express human nature. Aggressiveness, planfulness, and principled behavior are presumably not expressive of human nature.

It is hard to escape the conclusion that although Rogerians have been in the forefront of the movement to dispense with the concept of mental health, they have adopted a concept of human nature that underlies a quite similar intellectual cop-out. Rogers has not even bothered to specify the content of the "inherent potentialities" that he assumes point the actualization tendency in a particular direction. Perhaps Rogerian therapists shape the client toward the characteristics of fully functioningness because they believe in them—but instead of admitting this, insist that what is being carried out are the client's wishes which express his true nature. If this is so, then the Rogerians are skirting immorality in their justification of therapy.

The clearest example of an approach which regards the therapist to be handmaiden to the client's goals is behavior-modification therapy. Skinnerians assert that theirs is a technology for behavior modification which is all the more scientific for carrying no value judgment in it. They can be persuasive when discussing stuttering or autism or some other grossly disruptive behavior, the correction of which is such an undisputed good that no value judgment seems to be involved.

When pressed further on just what changes should and should not be made, the behavior-modification therapist is likely to say that he brings about specifically those changes wished by the client. But suppose a client asked for aid in becoming courageous enough to assassinate the President. What would the therapist say or do? He might turn the patient away, indicating disinterest or even opposition to such an aim. If he did this, he would be admitting that his behavior-modification technology is in the service of his assumptions as to what is good and bad. Alternatively, he might engage the patient in conversation, on the expressed or private presumption that the stated aim was not the real one. Perhaps the client just wants to feel more effective or to change his life substantially. In choosing this alternative, the therapist would be showing the subjugation of technology to a theory of the good life no less than if he were to turn the client away. It is only by aiding the client to gain courage to murder that the therapist would be true to his non-evaluative stance. And yet we all know he would not do that. The upshot of all this is that when the behavior-modification therapist insists that he is catalyst rather than manipulator, he is acting irresponsibly. Instead, he should scrutinize the implicit, intuitive theorizing which guides his decisions, so that it can be explicitly stated, and its strengths and weaknesses judged by colleagues and prospective clients.

In this struggle to the explicit, the behaviorist might assert that he is interested in efficiency, in restoring his client to smooth functioning. If no answer is offered to the obvious next question, "Smooth functioning for what?", the behaviorist is very likely–though perhaps unwittingly–endorsing an adjustment view in which the mark of the good life is playing the social roles assigned to you well and effortlessly. The assumption here is that society, as currently constituted, is the best that can be wrought. If this is what behavior modification therapists believe, then let them admit it and try to argue for it.

CONCLUDING REMARKS

Vigorous theorizing is very practical. Through it, the personologist can become fully involved in the intellectual and practical aspects of his subject matter, enter into a scholarly relationship with persons in related disciplines, and recognize the traditions into which his work fits. In addition, he can carry his inquiries further, gain deeper and more comprehensive knowledge, devise appropriate methodology as needed, and shoulder better his social and ethical responsibilities. He will be interested in and able to evaluate the relative strengths and weaknesses of substantive theoretical formulations concerning personality development and the ideal life style.

In all this, the personologist engaging in vigorous theorizing will have a clear sense not only of what he is studying, but also of why its study is worthwhile. The more the field is populated by vigorous rather than passive or minimal theorizers, the greater will be the corporate sense of common purpose and direction. There will be sharp disagreements expressed in debate and research, but the climate will be a constructive one based on a mutual sense of the importance of issue resolution. Gone will be the present doldrums concerning disarray in the personality field, and doubts as to whether personality exists at all. And if personologists can manage vigorous theorizing without worrying too much about their scientific status, neither will anyone else. Scientific activity is broader and more robust than we have been imagining of late.

REFERENCES

Adelson, J. Personality. *Annual Review of Psychology,* 1969, *20,* 217-252.

Adler, A. *Problems of neurosis.* New York: Harper Torchbooks, 1964.

Allport, G. W. *Personality: A psychological integration.* New York: Holt, 1937.

____. *Becoming: Basic considerations for a psychology of personality.* New Haven, Conn.: Yale University Press, 1955.

____. The general and the unique in psychological science. *Journal of Personality,* 1962, *30,* 405-422.

____, & **Vernon, P. E.** *Studies in expressive movement.* New York: Macmillan, 1933.

Angyal, A. A theoretical model for personality study. *Journal of Personality,* 1951, *20,* 131-142.

Atkinson, J. W. (Ed.) *Motives in fantasy, action and society.* Princeton, N.J.: Van Nostrand, 1958.

Bakan, D. *The duality of human existence.* Chicago: Rand McNally, 1966.

Begleiter, H., Porjesz, B., Yerre, C., & Kissin, B. Evoked potential correlates of expected stimulus intensity. *Science,* 1973, *179,* 814-816.

Bem, D. J. Constructing cross-situational consistencies in behavior: Some thoughts on Alker's critique of Mischel. *Journal of Personality,* 1972, *40,* 17-26.

Binswanger, L. *Being-in-the-world: Selected papers of Ludwig Binswanger.* New York: Basic Books, 1963.

Boss, M. *Psychoanalysis and daseinanalysis.* New York: Basic Books, 1963.

Bowers, K. S. Situationism in psychology: An analysis and a critique. *Psychological Review,* 1973, *80,* 307-336.

Bruner, J. S. Mechanism riding high. *Contemporary Psychology,* 1957, *2,* 155-157.

____. Neural mechanisms in perception. *Psychological Review,* 1957, *64,* 340-358.

Carlson, R. Where is the person in personality research? *Psychological Bulletin,* 1971, *75,* 203-219.

____. Personality. *Annual Review of Psychology,* 1975.

Cronbach, L. J. The two disciplines of scientific psychology. *American Psychologist,* 1957, *12,* 671-684.

____. Beyond the two disciplines of scientific psychology. *American Psychologist,* 1975, *30,* 116-127.

Cattell, R. B. *The scientific analysis of personality.* Chicago: Aldine, 1965.

Duncan, S. D., Jr. Some signals and rules for taking speaking turns in conversations. *Journal of Personality and Social Psychology,* 1972, *23,* 283-292.

Ekehammer, B. Interactionism in personality from a historical perspective. *Psychological Bulletin,* 1974, *81,* 1026-1048.

Endler, N. S., & Magnusson, D. Toward an interactional psychology of personality. *Psychological Bulletin,* 1976, *83,* 956-974.

Erikson, E. H. *Childhood and society.* New York: Norton, 1951.

Eysenck, H. The effects of psychotherapy: An evaluation. *Journal of Consulting Psychology,* 1952, *16,* 319-324.

____. *The effects of psychotherapy.* New York: International Scientific Press, 1966.

Fiske, D. W. The limits for the conventional science of personality. *Journal of Personality,* 1974, *42,* 1-11.

____. *Measuring concepts of personality.* Chicago: Aldine, 1971.

___, & **Maddi, S. R.** *Functions of varied experience.* Homewood, Ill.: Dorsey Press, 1961.

Frank, J. *Persuasion and healing: A comparative study of psychotherapy.* Baltimore: Johns Hopkins University Press, 1961.

Frankl, V. *The doctor and the soul.* New York: Knopf, 1960.

Freud, S. The dynamics of transference. In S. Freud, *Collected Papers.* London: Institute for Psychoanalysis and Hogarth Press, 1925. (a)

___. Observations on transference love. In S. Freud, *Collected Papers.* London: Institute for Psychoanalysis and Hogarth Press, 1925. (b)

___. Instincts and their vicissitudes. In S. Freud, *Collected Papers.* London: Institute for Psychoanalysis and Hogarth Press, 1925. (c)

___. *Totem and Taboo.* New York: Norton, 1952.

Fromm, E. *Man for himself.* New York: Harcourt, Brace & World, 1947.

Gergen, K. J. Social psychology as history. *Journal of Personality and Social Psychology,* 1973, *26,* 309-320.

___. Social psychology, science and history. *Personality and Social Psychology Bulletin,* 1976, *2,* 373-383.

Goffman, E. Characteristics of total institutions: Introduction. *Symposium on prevention and social psychiatry.* U.S. Government Printing Office, 1958, pp. 43-49.

Gottlieb, A. Social psychology as history or science: An addendum. *Personality and Social Psychology Bulletin,* 1977, *3,* 207-210.

Hall, C. S., & **Lindzey, G.** *Theories of personality.* New York: Wiley, 1970.

Henry, W. F., Sims, J., & **Spray, S. L.** *The fifth profession.* San Francisco: Jossey-Bass, 1971.

Herrnstein, R. J. The evolution of behaviorism. *American Psychologist,* 1977, *32,* 593-603.

Homans, C. G. *The nature of social science.* New York: Harcourt, Brace & World, 1967.

Hunt, H. F. Behavior therapy for adults. In S. Arieti (Ed.), *American handbook of psychiatry.* New York: Basic Books, 1977.

Hull, C. L. *Principles of behavior.* New York: Appleton-Century-Crofts, 1943.

Jackson, D. N., & **Messick, S.** Content and style in personality assessment. *Psychological Bulletin,* 1958, *55,* 243-252.

John, E. R., & **Morgades, P. P.** The pattern and anatomical distribution of evoked potentials and multiple unit activity elicited by conditioned stimuli in trained cats. *Communications in behavioral biology,* Part A. Vol. 3, No. 4. New York: Academic Press, 1969.

Jung, C. G. *Modern man in search of a soul.* New York: Harcourt, Brace & World, 1933. (a)

___. *Psychological types.* New York: Harcourt, Brace & World, 1933. (b)

____. The relations between the ego and the unconscious. In H. Read, M. Fordham, and G. Adler (Eds.), *Collected works.* Princeton, N.J.: Princeton University Press, 1953.

Kelly, G. A. *The psychology of personal constructs.* New York: Norton, 1955.

Kobasa, S. C., & Maddi, S. R. Existential personality theory. In R. Corsini (Ed.), *Current personality theories.* Itasca, Ill.: Peacock, 1977.

Lundin, R. W. *Personality: A behavioral analysis* (2nd ed.). New York: Macmillan, 1974.

Maddi, S. R. The search for meaning. In M. Page (Ed.), *Nebraska symposium on motivation.* Lincoln, Neb.: University of Nebraska Press, 1970.

____. Ethics and psychotherapy: Remarks stimulated by White's paper. *Counseling Psychologist,* 1973, *4,* 26-28.

____. *Personality theories: A comparative analysis* (3rd ed.). Homewood, Ill.: Dorsey Press, 1976.

Mandler, G., & Kessen, W. *The language of psychology.* New York: Wiley, 1959.

Maslow, A. H. Deficiency motivation and growth motivation. In M. R. Jones (Ed.), *Nebraska symposium on motivation.* Lincoln, Neb.: University of Nebraska Press, 1955.

May, R. Contributions of existential psychotherapy. In R. May, E. Angel, & H. F. Ellenberger (Eds.), *Existence: A new dimension in psychiatry and psychology.* New York: Basic Books, 1958.

McClelland, D. C. Measuring motivation. In J. W. Atkinson (Ed.), *Motives in fantasy, action and society.* Princeton, N.J.: Van Nostrand, 1958.

____. *The achieving society.* Princeton, N.J.: Van Nostrand, 1961.

____, **Atkinson, J. W., Clark, R. A., & Lowell, E. L.** *The achievement motive.* New York: Appleton-Century-Crofts, 1953.

Mischel, W. *Personality and assessment.* New York: Wiley, 1968.

____. Toward a cognitive social learning reconceptualization of personality. *Psychological Review,* 1973, *80,* 252-283.

Moos, R. H. Sources of variance in responses to questionnaires and in behavior. *Journal of Abnormal Psychology,* 1969, *74,* 405-412.

Murray, H. A. *Explorations in personality: A clinical and experimental study of fifty men of college age.* New York: Oxford, 1938.

____. *Thematic apperception test.* Cambridge, Mass.: Harvard University Press, 1943.

Nagel, E. Methodological issues in psychoanalytic theory. In S. Hook (Ed.), *Psychoanalysis, scientific method and philosophy.* New York: New York University Press, 1959.

Pribram, K. H. The neurophysiology of remembering. *Scientific American,* January, 1969, 73-86.

____, **Spinelli, D. N., & Kamback, M. C.** Electrocortical correlates of stimulus, response, and reinforcement. *Science,* 1967, *157,* 94-96.

Rank, O. *Will therapy and truth and reality.* New York: Knopf, 1945.

Rapaport, D. The structure of psychoanalytic theory: A systematizing attempt. In S. Koch (Ed.), *Psychology: A study of a science.* New York: McGraw-Hill, 1958.

Ricoeur, P. *Freud and philosophy: An essay on interpretation* (tr. Denis Savage). New Haven, Conn.: Yale University Press, 1970.

Rogers, C. R. A theory of therapy, personality and interpersonal relationships, as developed in the client-centered framework. In S. Koch (Ed.), *Psychology: A study of a science.* New York: McGraw-Hill, 1959.

____. *On becoming a person.* Boston: Houghton Mifflin, 1961.

Rosenhan, D. On being sane in insane places. *Science,* 1973, *179,* 250-258.

Rotter, J. B. *Clinical psychology* (2nd ed.). Englewood Cliffs, N.J.: Prentice-Hall, 1964.

Sarnoff, I. *Personality: Dynamics and development.* New York: Wiley, 1962.

Scheff, T. J. The role of the mentally ill and the dynamics of mental disorder. *Sociometry,* 1963, *26,* 436-453.

Sechrest, L. Personality. *Annual Review of Psychology,* 1976.

Scitovsky, T. *The joyless economy.* New York: Oxford, 1976.

Sheldon, W. H., & Stephens, S. S. *The varieties of temperament.* New York: Harper, 1942.

Skinner, B. F. *Science and human behavior.* New York: Macmillan, 1953.

Spence, K. W. The postulates and methods of "behaviorism." *Psychological Review,* 1948, *55,* 67-78.

Spinelli, D. N. OCCAM: A content addressable memory model for the brain. In K. H. Pribram & D. E. Broadbent (Eds.), *The biology of memory.* New York: Academic Press, 1970.

Stagner, R. Traits are relevant: Theoretical analysis and empirical evidence. In N. S. Endler & D. Magnusson (Eds.), *Interactional psychology and personality.* New York: Hemisphere, 1976.

Sullivan, H. S. *The interpersonal theory of psychiatry.* New York: Norton, 1953.

Szasz, T. S. *The myth of mental illness: Foundations of a theory of personal conduct.* New York: Harper, 1961.

White, R. W. Competence and the psychosexual stages of development. In M. R. Jones (Ed.), *Nebraska symposium on motivation.* Lincoln, Neb.: University of Nebraska Press, 1960.

Wiggins, J. S. *Personality and prediction.* Reading, Mass.: Addison-Wesley, 1973.

Author Index

Subject Index